Progressive States' Rights

CONSTITUTIONAL THINKING

Sanford Levinson
Jeffrey K. Tulis
Emily Zackin
Mariah Zeisberg
Editors

PROGRESSIVE STATES' RIGHTS

The Forgotten History of Federalism

Sean Beienburg

University Press of Kansas

Published by the University Press of Kansas
(Lawrence, Kansas 66045), which was
organized by the Kansas Board of Regents
and is operated and funded by Emporia State
University, Fort Hays State University, Kansas
State University, Pittsburg State University,
the University of Kansas, and Wichita State
University.

This book will be made open access within three
years of publication thanks to Path to Open,
a program developed in partnership between
JSTOR, the American Council of Learned
Societies (ACLS), University of Michigan
Press, and The University of North Carolina
Press to bring about equitable access and impact
for the entire scholarly community, including
authors, researchers, libraries, and university
presses around the world. Learn more at https://
about.jstor.org/path-to-open/.

Library of Congress Cataloging-in-
Publication Data

Names: Beienburg, Sean, author.
Title: Progressive states' rights : the forgotten
    history of federalism / Sean Beienburg.
Description: Lawrence: University Press of
    Kansas, 2024. | Series: Constitutional
    thinking | Includes bibliographical references
    and index.
Identifiers: LCCN 2023014172 (print) |
    LCCN 2023014173 (ebook)
    ISBN 9780700636198 (cloth)
    ISBN 9780700636204 (ebook)
Subjects: LCSH: States' rights (American
    politics)—History—20th century. | Federal
    government—United States—History—
    20th century. | Progressivism (United
    States politics)—History—20th century.
    | Constitutional law—United States—
    History—20th century.
Classification: LCC JK325 .B39 2024 (print) |
    LCC JK325 (ebook) | DDC 324.2732/7—
    dc23/eng/20230520
LC record available at https://lccn.loc
    .gov/2023014172.
LC ebook record available at https://lccn.loc
    .gov/2023014173.
British Library Cataloguing-in-Publication Data
    is available.

CONTENTS

FOREWORD

Emily Zackin

It is an honor to offer this foreword to Sean Beienburg's fascinating *Progressive States' Rights*. I do so in my capacity as a new editor, along with Mariah Zeisberg, of the Constitutional Thinking series that Sanford Levinson and Jeffrey Tulis developed and continue to edit. Since its inception, this series has published books that question received wisdoms about our constitutional system, encouraging readers to think afresh about its development, pitfalls, and promises. I am hard-pressed to think of a book more in keeping with this spirit of unorthodox and earnest inquiry than the one you now hold in your hands. Its explorations are richly rewarded, exposing an unexpected and provocative vein of constitutional thought.

I suspect the first thing that comes to mind for many readers when they think about Progressive-Era federalism may be the idea that states serve as laboratories of democracy. Indeed, the phrase "laboratories of democracy" is generally attributed to the progressive jurist and Supreme Court justice Louis Brandeis. In his dissenting opinion in *New State Ice Co. v. Liebmann* (1932), Brandeis wrote, "It is one of the happy incidents of the federal system that a single courageous state may, if its citizens choose, serve as a laboratory; and try novel social and economic experiments without risk to the rest of the country."[1] In this dissent, Brandeis was arguing that nothing in the Constitution barred a state government from requiring ice distributors to secure state licenses. As Alan Tarr has noted, Brandeis was focused on the virtues of experimentation.[2] The preceding lines of the dissent make that clear:

The discoveries in physical science, the triumphs in invention, attest the value of the process of trial and error. In large measure, these advances have been due to experimentation. In those fields experimentation has, for two centuries been not only free but encouraged. Some people assert that our present plight is due, in part, to the limitations set by courts upon experimentation in the fields of social and economic science.

This is one well-known idea of how states might be progressive—by developing new public policies that, if successful, other states or the federal government can then adopt. Importantly, though, that is not the progressive federalism at the center of this book.

The version of federalism that this book takes up is not a system of decentralized experimentation or administration that enables the larger polity to pursue a common good. It is, instead, an institutional arrangement that presumes the subnational polities disagree on a common good, or, at least, that there are many goals they may not hold in common. These subnational polities have accepted the irreconcilable differences between them and have managed to unite by limiting the choices over which the central government has control.[3] This federalism, the one at the heart of this book, is defined by the boundaries it places around the authority of the national government and by the states' rights against that government.

Across US history, this form of federalism has been most closely associated with white supremacy, most recently as a southern defense of Jim Crow systems of segregation, disenfranchisement, and exploitation and, before that, of slavery. Beienburg acknowledges that one of the major uses of states' rights has been to fortify racial oppression against the federal government's efforts to secure equal rights for Black citizens. He demonstrates, however, that this was only one invocation of states' rights while others have been notably reformist. The early decades of the twentieth century witnessed many of these campaigns to use states' rights for progressive (and Progressive) purposes. This book excavates these startling claims about the constitutional limitations on federal power over the states.

Immersed in the federalism debates of the early twentieth century, we encounter a commitment to progressive causes that did not automatically bring with it a belief in expansive federal power. Many prominent Progressives certainly sought to enlist the national government in addressing social and economic problems, but others voiced the kinds of federalism claims that we now associate with the political right. These Progressive arguments against federal authority were sometimes motivated by a desire to shield state-level labor law from federal courts. However, Beienburg takes pains to demonstrate that not all Progressive arguments in favor of federalism served Progressive policy ends. Through his look at the debates on federal spending to prevent maternal and infant mortality (the Sheppard-Towner Act of 1921), he demonstrates that some Progressives opposed the federal enactment of this quintessentially Progressive program, not because they opposed its aims or methods but because they believed that only the states were constitutionally empowered to carry them out.

It is certainly surprising to find that those on the Left once opposed congressional authority to enact welfare-oriented public policies, but it may be even more striking to encounter an argument for active state-level government from avowed conservatives. Beienburg describes a school of thought that constitutional checks on national authority could only be preserved if states were allowed to engage in energetic regulation. Those who held this position consequently coupled their commitment to limited federal authority with a capacious view of state powers to enact welfare-state policies. The surprise in both cases is that people seem to have distinguished their positions on the desirability of welfare-oriented governance from their views on the Constitution. The New Deal and the political developments that followed have made it harder to imagine that one could make these distinctions.

To some originalists, the history described in these pages will read as evidence that the true meaning of the Constitution, the one we ought to reinstitute, requires tight constraints on federal power. The fact that even some Progressives argued for states' rights might, for such readers, confirm the illegitimacy of the New Deal and all that's come after. A set piece in such discussions of federalism is that the Constitution, as ratified in 1787, clearly delineated separate spheres of authority for the federal and state governments. This system, generally labeled "dual federalism," is often invoked to critique the present, offered as evidence that the original constitutional system, as it was meant to operate, has been distorted, if not entirely discarded.

As I read this book, however, it is engaged in a different kind of project.

The aim of this book, it seems to me, is not to argue for a return to an idealized dual federalism but to describe a type of thinking about federalism that has been largely lost to history. In fact, I think this book is speaking not only to originalists but also to modern-day progressives who endorse the New Deal's reshaping of our constitutional order. For such readers (and I count myself among them), one reason to recover these Progressive-Era federalism debates is to illuminate the nature of the New Deal transformation. After all, to appreciate a transformation, it is not sufficient to know how its object looked afterward; it is also essential to understand what came before.

In this respect, this work joins the wave of scholarship on the Progressive Era that has sought to revise simplistic accounts of the US Supreme Court in this period. Traditional narratives portrayed the Lochner Court as a runaway institution, bent on substituting its own policy preferences for those of elected legislatures. Newer scholarship has revised this account by reconstructing the Fourteenth Amendment doctrine that the Supreme Court was trying to interpret and apply. Howard Gillman has demonstrated that the Court understood the Fourteenth Amendment to prohibit class legislation, and that it was attempting to interpret and apply that prohibition in a rapidly changing economic landscape. This old understanding of neutrality and equality collided with the new realities of twentieth-century industrial capitalism and inequality, making it nearly impossible to apply in ways that appeared consistent or impartial. This understanding of the Lochner era implies that the New Deal Court neither caved to political pressure (as its critics would have it) nor returned to reason (as its champions claimed), but that it abandoned doctrine that had become unworkable.[4] This revisionist, forward-looking work on the Lochner Court was instructive because so much of the previous scholarship had looked at the early twentieth century through the lens of all that came after. That backward look had made it hard to see all that was really there or to understand the nature of its transformation.

Progressive federalism is another strand of constitutional thought from this period that has been hard to see from our vantage point in the twenty-first century. We are accustomed to thinking of laissez-faire policies and states' rights arguments as naturally paired, two features inherent in US conservatism. With its careful look at ideas about federalism that predated the New Deal, this work denaturalizes that pairing. In so doing, it helps us better understand the political developments that followed. In particular, it prompts us to ask how the tight and enduring link between laissez-faire governance and states' rights developed.

Part of the answer surely lies in the way white southerners were integrated into the national party system after the New Deal. Poor southern whites, who had long identified as Democrats, might have formed an alliance with the northern working class. Instead, they became a bulwark of the Republican party, aligned with Northern business in their opposition to redistribution and regulation. Republicans forged this alliance by fusing a commitment to laissez faire principles with a defense of states' rights.[5] By the late twentieth century, the argument that some sphere of regulation belonged to the states had become largely indistinguishable from the claim that the regulation was, itself, illegitimate.

One legacy of that politics is that, for more than half a century, the Left has not simply been wary of claims about constitutional limitations on federal authority but has defined itself in opposition to them. To be an advocate of racial and gendered equality and redistributive, regulatory governance was to be in favor of national power and required the forceful rejection of the idea that states should be left alone to govern themselves. But there was a time before those links were quite as strong. As this book demonstrates, there was a time when at least some left-leaning reformers thought of states, and even of states' rights, as helpful to their cause.

There are, to be sure, many reasons to think that progressive goals are inherently better served by federal, rather than state- or local-level, policymaking. Centralized economic regulation may be necessary to prevent states from engaging in a race to the bottom, competitively reducing protections for workers and vulnerable citizens in an effort to attract capital from neighboring states. In addition, subnational regulation of a global economy may be woefully ineffective. Finally, if we conceive of rights as universal, possessed by all on equal terms, it makes little sense to allow states to decide whether to guarantee and protect them. States' important role in administering elections, coupled with their long history of intentionally disenfranchising their citizens, makes this concern about decentralizing rights enforcement even more pressing. Given a choice between federal and state policymaking, progressives have good reasons to choose the former. However, a separate question is what they ought to do when deprived of that choice.

Since control of Congress and the presidency are uncertain and the federal courts increasingly inhospitable, proponents of progressive politics may well wonder what role states might play in their campaigns. This work demonstrates that state-level actors can think seriously about their role in the larger constitutional system, and that federalism can be more than a smoke screen for opposition to racial equality or economic regulation. It suggests that progressive political projects might use states—not just to erect progressive rights above a federal floor but perhaps even as a resource to resist federal policies. Of course, if they mobilize this resource, today's progressives will almost certainly want to do it without subverting the federal government's constitutional authority to serve progressive ends. In the conclusion to this work, Beienburg offers concrete suggestions about how one might chart this treacherous course. Regardless of whether anyone follows this particular path, it seems clear that those on the political left have new reasons to reconsider the potential of state-level politics and the desirability of checking federal power. As a new generation of scholars and political actors work out the future of US federalism, this remarkable book will help them make sense of its past.

ACKNOWLEDGMENTS

"Human beings are not born free, but indebted; their identities are more defined by what they owe than by what they own."[1] With that in mind, I begin by acknowledging some of those to whom I am so indebted, both professionally and personally. I won't repeat in full my acknowledgments from my previously published but concurrently researched book. Consult that for more detailed whys—but in terms of the who:

I received generous financial support from Princeton University and its American studies program and the Miller Center at the University of Virginia. I also want to thank the staff at Princeton's Firestone Library as well as the Wisconsin Historical Society in Madison, Wisconsin.

I have received, both on this project and in my academic career more broadly, generous feedback and mentoring. From the public law and American political history community at Princeton University: especially Paul Frymer, Keith Whittington, and Dirk Hartog, but also Chris Achen, Robby George, Ben Johnson, Herschel Nachlis, James Oakes, Geoff Sigalet, Phil Wallach, Omar Wasow, Sean Wilentz, and Brad Wilson. From my earlier time at the Claremont Colleges: Phillip Argento, Justin Crowe, Gary Kates, Charles Lofgren, George Thomas, Robert Woods, and especially Susan McWilliams.

In addition to those folks from my places of study, I have received much helpful feedback on and conversations about various parts of this project from Matthew Brogdon, John Dinan, Mark Graber, Paul Herron, Ken Kersch, Helen Knowles, Emily Pears, Alan Tarr, Michael Zuckert, and the anonymous reviewers of this manuscript.

I thank the Jack Miller Center and *American Political Thought* for allowing me to incorporate material from my essay titled "Progressivism and States' Rights: Constitutional Dialogue between the States and Federal Courts on Minimum Wages and Liberty of Contract" *American Political Thought* 8 (2019): 25–53, https://doi.org/10.1086/701530, © 2019, by the Jack Miller Center.

This book's publication history started with Chuck Myers, whose encouragement in the book's early stages I remain grateful for, but with his retirement the project moved to David Congdon and the University Press of Kansas, as well as the editors of the Constitutional Thinking series: Jeffrey Tulis, Sanford Levinson, Mariah Zeisberg, and especially Emily Zackin. David, Erica

Nicholson, Jenn Bennett-Genthner (for terrific copyediting), and the Kansas team have helped make this book much stronger, and I'm very grateful for all the time and effort they have invested in this project.

As I moved to the later phases of this book's writing, my colleagues in the School of Civic and Economic Thought and Leadership at Arizona State University under the directorship of Paul Carrese provided a home to work on this, creating a community devoted to the study and appreciation of American constitutionalism and American political thought.

A few family and friends are owed thanks for their especially generous support of and interest in my academic career. Of my extended family, Bruce and Joanne McCallum, Cara McCallum, Stephanie Sullivan, and Brad Grandy warrant special thanks, as do Pam and DeMont Grandy, who let me stay at their home to work on these projects during summers (and whom I accidentally omitted last time, so consider this a correction to those acknowledgments). Of my friends, listed in order from having known me the longest: Trevor Lagers, Jordan Perry, Joe Wachtel, Steven Hurtado, Alexander Haines (who also read much of this manuscript), Richard Jordan, and Ross Williford.

Although I mostly just listed the who instead of the why this time, there are two acknowledgments I will largely reproduce from before.

My brother, Matt: I consider myself very fortunate indeed that our paths could cross twice more after Phoenix, first in Claremont and then Princeton, before now reconvening back in Arizona. In addition to being a reader for both of these books, he has always been, and I hope will continue to be, my most treasured conversationalist and my closest adviser, with perhaps one exception.

Matt and I were raised by our grandparents and, after the death of my grandfather, Steve Beienburg, by my grandmother, Helen. Raising two boys alone was not exactly the plan for a quiet retirement she anticipated, which makes her many sacrifices on our behalf all the more appreciated. Years ago, in conversation a few weeks before we both finished graduate school, Matt and I both acknowledged that any successes we have are due to her and our failures in spite of her, and I have since wanted to put that in writing that she and others might see it. That both Matt and I ended up working in the realms of politics and education is a result of her teaching us to cherish the value of civic knowledge in preserving a well-functioning constitutional republic. I hope she will find this project a fitting tribute.

Ditat Deus.

Introduction: States' Rights Returns

Whereas, the national government of the United States has during the past several years assumed the exercise of powers ... [that are] destroying the rights of the people of the several states and striking at the foundation of the fundamental principles on which the republic was established. ... The underlying principles on which the republic was founded are being cast aside, and the flag of national domination has been raised as a standard, in the place of the self-reliant flag of home rule. ... Federal officials are found in every quarter of the land whose duties have heretofore been unheard of. ... The day of awakening has arrived and the growing power of the national government must be further curtailed.

Resolved by the Senate, the Assembly Concurring, that [the] Legislature ... call upon the legislatures of the several states ... to call a convention ... [with] the purpose of the preservation of the self-governing right of the states ... and to restore to the states and to the people certain rights now exercised by the national government ... contrary to the intent of the federal constitution.

Those sound like the words of John C. Calhoun's South Carolina legislature and its veiled defense of slavery in the tariff crisis of 1832, or the Mississippi government's protest of federal orders to admit James Meredith and desegregate Ole Miss in 1962. They are neither. Nor are they the product of hardline twenty-first-century Arizonans or Texans protesting against the Affordable Care Act.

That resolution cleared both houses in Wisconsin in February 1921—the same Wisconsin that boasted Senator Robert La Follette as its great progressive champion against corporate power.[1] The statement condemned nationalizing abuses committed by politicians across the spectrum: from the Left, the progressive Woodrow Wilson's efforts to block states from imposing tough regulations on railroads, while bristling, from the Right, against the kind of financially redistributive bills as one endorsed by the conservative Warren Harding. The newly inaugurated governor John Blaine, a progressive Republican ally of La Follette, had blasted both of these policies as outrageous federal overreach in his staunchly states' rights inaugural address the month before. The legislature obliged him in making clear the state's displeasure at this consolidation of power in Washington.[2]

Wisconsin's pushback against federal development with a strong sense of states' rights was not typical. After all, it had been the notorious liberal outlier in defying proslavery court orders in *Ableman v. Booth* before the Civil War, and it remained a widely acknowledged innovator in labor law through the 1920s.[3] Nonetheless, while Wisconsin is perhaps the most striking example, it illustrates a broader pattern: states' deployment and development of states' rights rhetoric, and the implementation of policies and protests opposing federal constitutionalism, were both far broader, and lasted longer, than conventionally assumed. Contrary to accounts that suggest that states rights' has primarily served as a cover for southern racism,[4] in the years before the New Deal states outside the South, especially in New England, were as or more likely to invoke decentralist claims, for progressive as well as conservative ends.

Today, we often assume, and the Supreme Court demands, a regime not merely of judicial review but federal judicial supremacy, with the courts as the exclusive guardians of the Constitution.[5] American constitutional history is filled with debates over the proper agents and locations of constitutional interpretation: the Marshall Court's decisions in cases such as *Marbury v. Madison*, Andrew Jackson's assertion of independent presidential analysis in his famous Bank and Maysville Road vetoes, Lincoln's insistence in following *Dred Scott* for the parties but refusing to accept the Taney Court's constitutionally faithless holding, and Franklin Roosevelt's criticisms of the New Deal Court's conservative "Four Horsemen" bloc (and his intention to openly defy the Court's decision in the Gold Clause Cases not on constitutional but on policy grounds).[6]

Political science and legal scholarship have recently helped bring Congress, the president, and other nonjudicial actors back into our understanding of the process of constitutional development.[7] But, with the clear exception of research into state constitution-making and amending, and a handful of other recent works, states and state officials have been largely left behind.[8]

This book aims to correct both these historical and theoretical omissions by looking to the states as competing sites of constitutional discourse. In so doing, it follows the logic of the *Federalist*, in which both James Madison and Alexander Hamilton repeatedly envision the states as interpreters and enforcers of the Constitution.[9]

If, as constitutional historian Donald Lutz contends, "federalism lies at the heart of the United States Constitution," Gary Gerstle is equally right in observing that "we have long known, even if we had trouble remembering," this central role of states in American political development.[10] Among those who had forgotten were the many law professors stunned by the close call in *NFIB v. Sebelius* (2012), when five justices on the US Supreme Court voted to overturn the Affordable Care Act, arguably the most important legislation in years, on federalism grounds (though a last-minute switch by Chief Justice John Roberts, who had initially voted with his colleagues to strike the mandate, saved it with an alternative construction of the tax power).[11]

Among those who have remembered federalism's central role in the legal and political order, however, are state governors, legislators, and attorneys general constitutionally mobilizing against the federal government (or, in some cases, forcing it to do their bidding).[12]

Long-serving Texas governor Rick Perry's *Fed Up!* encapsulated the conservative variant of this impulse with a manifesto designed to "push back on Washington" and elevate (or return) the role of the states as the primary agent of American government. Perry (or his ghostwriter Chip Roy, subsequently the chief of staff to Texas Senator Ted Cruz and then a member of Congress himself) hailed resolutions asserting claims of state sovereignty and affirming the Tenth Amendment and has particular praise for such efforts to resist federal efforts to regulate marijuana and firearms.[13] Elsewhere Perry/Roy cite *Printz v. United States*,[14] reminding state officials of the noncommandeering doctrine that means states can refuse to enforce federal legislation, used here as a public declaration against that federal power.[15] *Fed Up!* concludes with an explicit call for popular constitutionalism, with citizens engaged in dialogue and voting behaviors aimed to punish legislators who do not enforce and abide by the Constitution.[16]

Progressives, too, have begun to sound such tones.[17] For understandable historical reasons, progressives have long hesitated to use the language of states' rights, but one need not search too hard for parallels during the presidency of Donald Trump.[18] During the early parts of the Trump presidency, California, under Governor Jerry Brown, was approvingly spoken of as the head of state of a quasi-independent political entity resisting a conservative national government—strikingly similar rhetoric to that used by progressives in the early part of the twentieth century.[19] The California government, upset with the Trump administration's aggressive immigration enforcement, invoked that same Tenth Amendment noncommandeering doctrine in resisting efforts to punish the Golden State and its municipalities for adopting sanctuary city policies refusing to cooperate with federal immigration officials.[20] After federal efforts to ensure national rather than state-based emissions standards, the Sierra Club titled a disapproving piece "Donald Trump Doesn't Care About States' Rights."[21] A July 2019 op-ed in the *New York Times* proposed that progressive "reformers should take an unexpected route: states' rights" in defeating gerrymandering.[22] In August 2022, advisors to Gavin Newsom and Barack Obama called for a new "progressive federalism," particularly their form of "resistant federalism." In response to progressive dismay at *Dobbs v. Jackson Women's Health* (2022) and a filibuster-crippled Congress, they counseled fellow progressives to turn to the Tenth Amendment in a variety of spheres, most notably in the noncommandeering domain and by proposing state constitutional amendments codifying *Roe v. Wade*-like rights into their own constitutions.[23] (Within six months of *Dobbs*, three states—California, Vermont, and Michigan—had done just that.) This, in addition to states acting as laboratories of democracy in raising minimum wages, expanding the categories eligible for antidiscrimination law, and the like, as the progressive federalist justice Louis Brandeis called for long ago.[24]

Sebelius thus was less an outlier than a wake-up call; federalism and vertical constitutionalism play a central role in contemporary politics, from Tea Party Republicans on the right to Colorado's defiance of federal marijuana laws and talk of "Calexit" and the Second Vermont Republic on the left.[25]

Perhaps even more surprisingly, states seem committed to invoking constitutional claims to resist federal politics *outside the courts*, not only through symbolic resolutions but amendments to state constitutions and, in some rare cases, nullification bills threatening arrest of federal officials.[26]

At the turn of the twentieth century, Martha Derthick suggested that states appeared to be strengthening policy dialogues with national legislators but noted that this was less pronounced in the constitutional sphere: "For the states, it is one thing to talk back to Congress, quite another and much harder thing to talk back to the federal courts."[27] Today, it appears they are doing that. State officials, echoing the messages of presidential candidates, issue resolutions, obstructive legislation, and even constitutional amendments designed to protest federal law-making. From abortion law to gun rights to campaign finance to welfare, and even interstate commerce authority, state actors increasingly engage the federal government on decidedly constitutional grounds.[28] Members of state government are insisting they have a role in constitutional interpretation and enforcement. Whether with the Affordable Care Act, DACA, or firearms on the right, or efforts to litigate environmental policy or resist Donald Trump's restrictive immigration politics on the left, states are again important actors in *federal constitutional debates*.

The role of state intervention in antebellum constitutional politics has been widely studied, but we know far less about state clashes with the federal government afterward.[29] This relative inattention to postbellum state constitutional politics has produced a distorted understanding of constitutional dialogue in American history. For example, by confining state constitutional resistance largely to the crucial but unrepresentative case of southern racial conservatism, it has downplayed other expressions, such as the nation's strong progressive decentralist tradition. This now forgotten tradition reached its peak in the years before the New Deal constitutional revolution largely—but not totally— pushed that door closed and temporarily pushed states, like federalism more broadly, to the margins of national politics.

This book recounts how states intervened in national constitutional politics through nonjudicial means in the years leading up to the New Deal. This inquiry, combining political science, political history, constitutional law, and American political thought, attempts to understand the important contemporary phenomenon of state constitutional interpretation by reconstructing a political history of state constitutionalism. This history reveals several features—and simultaneously complicates, if not refutes, several myths—about federalism's role in the American tradition, each of which will be elaborated afterward.

1. Federalism—or "states' rights"—is not primarily a doctrine left to the South to wield as a cudgel against the North. In fact, one could make a plausible case that except for the singular, though crucial, exception of race, state legislatures and governors in the North were as or more likely than southerners to invoke states' rights claims before the New Deal, particularly on economic issues, and indeed that its legacy was heavily or even primarily a progressive one.

2. Constitutional theories that privilege nonjudicial actors—so-called extrajudicial or popular constitutionalism—ought to take seriously state constitutional politics.
3. States provide a venue to keep political conflicts alive, and this is no less true of the constitutional sphere than in more conventional policy debates.

I now elaborate on each of these themes.

1. Federalism—or "states' rights"—is not primarily a doctrine left to the South to wield as a cudgel against the North.

Anyone proposing a serious treatment of federalism as a part of nonjudicial constitutionalism must contend with the sordid legacy of states' rights and racism, with many holding the former to be little more than a veiled cover for the latter.

The racial order of southern Democrats indeed led to the most intense and consequential invocations of states' rights, as we might expect from a southern political system organized around the maintenance of white supremacy.[30]

But, contrary to claims that states' rights arguments have served primarily as a cover for southern racism, nonsouthern states freely invoked constitutional federalism, for progressive as well as conservative ends, whereas southern states almost exclusively confined federalist objections to racialized issues, otherwise tending toward tolerance or enthusiasm in support of federal power. In short, white supremacy may have been the most *substantively important* use of federalism, but it was arguably an *unrepresentative* case— which tells us more about the importance of race than about federalism itself. The claim in this book is not that racism and federalism have not been deeply connected in American history; of course they have. It is instead to show that, contrary to those who have reduced federalism to little more than a technique to advance racism, there is nothing inherent in a connection between race and federalism, and many claims for "states' rights" in American history either had nothing to do with race (or even, in some cases, served anti–white supremacist ends). The rearguard invocations of "states' rights" by opponents of integration in the 1950s loom large in historical memory and helped discredit federalism for generations of progressives, but, as the cases in this book will bear out, they were not necessarily the most representative.

More broadly, the political history of the Progressive Era reveals that there was no perceived contradiction between progressive policy preferences and what we would today see as a form of originalism, a constitutional methodology that tended to be widely shared until the New Deal judicial revolution.[31] Thus, while what we would now describe as conservative legal thought has long been interested in federalism, the connection between decentralization and conservative politics is a more recent historical development.[32] In other words, "conservative" legal thought was often joined to *progressive politics* — and could be again.

In recent years, some scholars and thinkers—most notably Heather Gerken—have defended a form of progressive federalism, but this has generally been in the form either of cooperative federalism, in which federal and state power grows together to implement progressive aims, or of policy experimentation before making a national settlement.[33] The traditional, more decentralized zero-sum form of "dual federalism," which joined a robust state police power to a limited federal power (and, in turn, limited financial assistance to the states) has seen few devotees on the contemporary left.[34]

As this book argues, this is a sharp change from much of American history, where progressives—even *radical progressives*—viewed America's decentralized constitutional order with an enthusiasm that matched or, perhaps, at times, exceeded its support among conservatives. For them, states' rights and a robust conception of states' police powers were inseparable. Thus, while we might not find it interesting to hear that a governor of Arizona would declare "I am, first of all, a believer in states' rights," it perhaps is more surprising to realize the year was 1923 and the speaker was George Hunt, the longtime progressive governor of what was then one of the most progressive states of the Union, who saw no tension between that and a traditional Democratic commitment to constitutional federalism.[35] Similarly, it would likely not surprise readers to witness a conservative journalist begin an analysis of a recent Supreme Court case with a preface defending states' sovereignty: "The dissenting opinion . . . is actuated . . . by a strong conviction that the Federal power should not be used to interfere with the sovereignty of the States. . . . With this conviction [we] would on almost any other issue agree. Nothing is more important constitutionally than to preserve against Federal aggrandizement the authority of the States."[36] Yet this example, too, comes not from a contemporary conservative commentator but rather from a leading progressive journalist of his day—Walter Lippmann, a founder, alongside Herbert Croly, of the *New Republic*, the opinion journal initially associated with Theodore Roosevelt but which soon became the predominant progressive publication in the country more generally.

It was northerners, Republican and Democrats alike, who were more willing to have states assert independent constitutional authority across a variety of issues. Progressives—who were, it should be remembered, distributed between both the Republican and Democratic Parties—not only viewed the states as laboratories of democracy in which to test new social and protective labor policies but also as political entities resisting centrally imposed market nationalism. Rightly or wrongly, from the beginning of first the populist movement and then the progressive movement that partly developed from it, these progressives identified federalism and localism as key parts of their ideology, believing that they would ultimately help them control powerful social forces, especially powerful corporations. Federalism was both a sword upholding the sovereignty of the states to be robust and active local governments experimenting with new policies and a shield in preventing federal intervention, especially by federal courts, in ways that would either constrain or displace such efforts.

Some of the most important progressive thinkers—such as Theodore Roosevelt and Herbert Croly—as well as most or almost all post–New Deal progressives, were ardent nationalists, and thus we tend to associate the progressive movement with antipathy to federalism.[37] Yet even Woodrow Wilson's New Freedom, much like the thought of Wilson's progressive federalist Court nominee Louis Brandeis, initially cited states' rights and decentralist themes as avenues to achieve Progressive goals, as Wilson occasionally did through his presidency, even as his progressivism is generally acknowledged as functionally turned toward a more Rooseveltian, nationalist perspective. Yet the nationalist views of these individuals, important as they were, were not shared by all or perhaps even most progressives prior to the New Deal. For example, Roosevelt's key political allies William Howard Taft and Elihu Root (as well as the conservative member of the triumvirate Henry Cabot Lodge) all cared deeply about federalism, as did many of the then-important but now lesser-known, especially western, populists and progressives of the late nineteenth and early twentieth century.[38] So, too, did Herbert Hoover and leading Democratic progressives like Al Smith and, perhaps most surprisingly, a pre-presidential Franklin Roosevelt.

Thus, accounts that understand federalism to be primarily within southern racial conservatism are incomplete at best, as northerners, including northern Republicans, were equally eager to invoke federalism before the New Deal realignment.[39] While John C. Calhoun became something of a bogeyman among legal thinkers, with nullification and a compact theory understanding of state sovereignty reviled after the Civil War, what Keith Whittington calls a "centrist federalism" survived to represent a broad consensus.[40] Building on a political tradition represented by Andrew Jackson, this "states' rights" position chartered a course between Calhoun's state sovereignty, on the one hand, and a centralizing nationalism on the other, and remained the core of American constitutional thought even through and after Reconstruction, including among most of the Radical Republicans.[41] This extended not merely to states' rights, but to states' enforcement of those rights through their own political processes, rather than merely through petitioning national institutions in Washington via judicial filings.

In arguing progressives had a commitment to that era's mainstream understanding of federalism, this also means they excluded arguments such as nullification, which were considered illegitimate by almost all defenders of states' rights. Repudiation of nullification was a central hallmark of mainstream constitutional thought and thus something progressive defenders of federalism, like defenders of federalism more broadly, undertook as part of the maintenance of a balanced and constitutional federalism.[42]

Today, we generally collapse constitutional and policy views into the same axis: for example, if one is conservative on regulatory policy, one is also conservative on constitutional theory (meaning they lean toward originalism and a more decentralized federalism), with progressives mirroring those in the opposite direction. Yet, as this work shows, not only is there no necessary connection between these two axes, but this history of the years before the New Deal demonstrates that among the most committed to what we would today think of as constitutional conservatism were those most interested in progressive policy views.

An important corollary of the argument that progressives were within the mainstream understanding of limited federal power is that many of the era's leading conservatives sided with progressives on questions of state police power (and, in some cases, on the merits of the policies, even if they recoiled at equivalent federal activity). Most readers will be surprised to find Calvin Coolidge, generally regarded as a paragon of laissez-faire conservatism, siding with progressives in defending and advocating robust use of the states' regulatory powers (or the federal government where a federal enumerated power clearly existed) on issues like minimum wages or maternal health. They had both a principled reason to do this, in consistently applying their legal principles, but they also alluded to a tactical reason: they understood that for limited federal power to survive, it would have to be coupled with robust uses of state police power. In other words, unlike today, where conservatives tend to sharply conflate regulation from either the states or the federal government as an interchangeable "Big Government," many—again, not all—conservatives of the Progressive Era had little trouble reconciling their constitutional conservatism limiting federal power with strong regulatory action by the states.

2. Elaborating on an argument I previously proposed,[43] **constitutional theories that privilege nonjudicial actors—so-called extrajudicial or popular constitutionalism—ought to take seriously state constitutional politics**.

These intellectual traditions have pushed back against judicial supremacy—the idea that the courts are the exclusive and appropriate interpreter of the Constitution—and, building on Jefferson's notion of departmentalism, have looked to presidents, members of Congress, and, in the case of popular constitutionalism, citizens themselves as duty-bound deliberative participants in the American constitutional project.[44] But curiously, even as the states have provided useful examples, "popular constitutionalists" have generally hesitated in incorporating states into their projects looking to nonjudicial interpretation.[45] As a point of clarification, before proceeding: this book uses the terms *popular constitutionalism* and *extrajudicial constitutionalism* interchangeably, as many scholars do, but the focus in this book is not on citizen behavior or "the people" but on how nonjudicial *institutions* participate in constitutional politics.[46]

Governors, state legislators, and social movements have offered constitutional discourse as sophisticated as any in Congress, and state officials can take seriously their oaths and obligations to participate in constitutional enforcement, especially when they perceive abdication by national institutions traditionally entrusted with that task.[47] Stated more bluntly, legal belief about the Constitution can constrain the political behavior of state elected officials, even when doing so is electorally unwise.[48]

The argument is not that invocations of federalism are always principled, but neither is it that invocations of federalism are always opportunistic.[49] Federalism arguments, like constitutional arguments in general, can obviously be opportunistic, insincere, or mere pretexts for higher-order substantive values, or reduced to cliches and mottos rather than good-faith analysis. This study does not dispute that. The claim here is instead a humbler one, that a commitment to federalism, like constitutionalism in general, can and does actually motivate political behavior, and that these cases illustrate numerous instances of political figures at the state level taking positions that are sometimes electorally unwise in order to follow those commitments. The aim of the study is not to say precisely how much constitutional discourse is principled or opportunistic—though it is clear that the legal culture of the 1920s included a far more widespread commitment to federalism and constitutional discourse than exists today. It is simply to push back on notions of legal realism reducing constitutional debate to shallow pretext rather than substantive grappling with serious issues that can indeed drive political decision-making.

For example, state-level debates on the Sheppard-Towner maternity bill — never previously studied—offered an impressive level of political discourse as rich and thoughtful as the congressional debate that preceded it in the US Capitol. Thus, this research serves as a friendly amendment to theories of "popular constitutionalism" often criticized for ignoring states and a general lack of institutional grounding.

Fairly prominent political actors are increasingly counseling evasion, noncompliance, and even outright defiance of federal constitutional development. This book aims to help us better understand these increasingly relevant questions of federalism and state constitutional resistance and interpretation by reconstructing the history of state reaction to federal constitutionalism during the early twentieth century.

Recovering the role of states in shaping and enforcing constitutional meaning, as they did in asserting the centrality of progressive federalism, thus offers some support to so-called extrajudicial or popular constitutionalism.

This book shows that, if not quite going so far, as Mark Tushnet has called for, in "tak[ing] the Constitution back from the courts," in the early twentieth century state officials at least refused to wholly cede it to judges.

3. Third, **states provide a venue to keep political conflicts alive, and this is no less true of the constitutional sphere than in more conventional policy debates**.

Much of the initial impetus of American political development (APD) research derived from a desire to come to terms with the absence of socialism in America. Thus, in light of that ostensible American exceptionalism, such scholarship sought to understand alternate paths toward centralized government.[50] Reintegrating states into this line of research shows that we may have neglected the endurance of decentralizing, centrifugal forces that operate in the other direction.[51]

As we know from classic political science works from the likes of E. E. Schattschneider, losers in a political conflict will expand the scope of that conflict; in effect, they will move the dispute from the forum in which they lost to a new one where they can try again.[52] In constitutional issues, we usually think this conflict expansion means going to the federal courts, after one loses at the legislative level, to try again. However, state *politics* serve this function by providing an institutionally legitimate venue of political pushback to national institutions. By protesting or resisting a national policy, a state can avert the settlement of an issue until the party that initially lost regains control of the national levers of power to undo or reverse that policy. Understanding states as footholds of political resistance also helps answer one of the critiques of popular constitutionalism as wispy and ephemeral, rather than anchored in clear institutions.

Federalism also has the related advantage, as Heather Gerken has noted, of ensuring political losers can remain a part of the "loyal opposition," maintaining not merely the possibility of retaking power at the national level but also a toehold at the subnational; defeat is thus neither final nor total, incentivizing further participation in the system (rather than violence, withdrawal, secession, or the like).[53]

Outline of the Book

This book tells the story of the states' efforts to shape constitutional discourse to ensure that a protective welfare and regulatory governmental regime would be built in the states, rather than the national government, in the years before the New Deal. These state-level actors not only aggressively participated in constitutional politics and interpretation, but they specifically sought to create an alternative model of state-building that would pair a robust state power on behalf of the public good with a traditionally limited national government.

The project is organized as a series of case studies of the major conflicts from the Progressive Era through the New Deal in which multiple states engaged in constitutional dialogue in opposition to congressional or judicial actions on the Constitution.[54]

The first chapter will reconstruct the understanding of federalism that developed after Reconstruction, which structured the debate of this era—both in terms of how the powers of the states and federal government were divided as well as the role that states were understood to play in enforcing that division of powers. It will use Elihu Root, a central political figure of his time, to lay out the vision of progressive federalism—of robust state power to act on the public good coupled with a more limited understanding of federal power—a vision that subsequent chapters will show was deeply held by many of the era's most important and prominent politicians, such as William Howard Taft, Charles Evans Hughes, William Borah, Al Smith, and, initially, Franklin Roosevelt. For such figures, states' rights and a robust conception of their police powers was a central feature, perhaps even the central feature, of American constitutionalism.

The remaining chapters will recreate the political histories of these cases— beginning with the national sphere (either the judicial decision or congressional enactment) before detailing how the states responded.

Chapters 2 and 3 will turn to the Promotion of the Welfare and Hygiene of Maternity and Infancy Act, known as the Sheppard-Towner Act—arguably the first federal welfare program and one which modeled the grant-in-aid programs that define much of federal policy today. Indeed, structurally speaking, Sheppard-Towner was quite similar to the exchanges established by the Affordable Care Act. Just as the exchanges depend on states opting into federal subsidies to make a national policy work, so did the Sheppard-Towner Act, inducing states with a small subsidy if they agreed to assist in the federal goal. And yet, even though the goal—healthy mothers and children in light of the experiences of the war—was one that was all but universally approved, and required minimal expenditure, the bill foundered, as state officials—including many progressives—ferociously assailed the program by charging that the expansion of the federal government into positive rights protections exceeded its constitutionally enumerated powers.

This is an especially striking and perhaps even counterintuitive finding insofar as it is one in which progressives sided with more political conservatives in attacking what many saw as a progressive policy goal, in some cases offering equivalent in-state proposals to avoid a precedent endorsing federal intervention in this domain. Many progressives so invoked federalism, both out of the deep-seated and principled commitment to what they understood their constitutional obligations to be, and others as a way to preserve state autonomy for their own welfare states. Whatever the reason, Sheppard-Towner was one of the most sustained instances of constitutional dialogue between the states and federal government in the period, and these chapters will recover the political history of those debates.

Chapters 4 and 5 will recreate the constitutional pushback to the so-called "liberty of contract," in which states tried to reassert their police powers over economic regulations, specifically the power to regulate minimum wages and protect union workers in contract negotiations, against federal courts, citing "liberty of contract." It will show how those seeking to use the states' regulatory powers to tame corporate excess prized federalism as a constitutional justification to do so, and that this commitment was part of the movement's founding, dating back to the populist movement that helped give rise to progressivism itself.

Chapter 6 will explore the fall of progressive federalism, with both the New Deal revolution and the efforts to resist it, from both the Left, with Huey Long deploying nullification, and arguably the Right, as Mainers flirted with radical resistance. The fundamental result of this period is that progressives' commitment to federalism, dating back to the beginning of the movement and continuing through the decades of the Progressive Era, went into eclipse in the wake of the 1936 election and changes in jurisprudence shortly thereafter.

Finally, chapter 7 will conclude by discussing the slow resurgence of federalism in the twentieth century, discussing the implications of state politics for constitutional interpretation, and briefly consider the possibilities of and conditions necessary for a return to progressive federalism as a solution to our polarized political climate and the resulting gridlock in Washington.

The cases highlighted in this book include three of the ways that federal activity can displace the states' use of their police powers — some more directly, and some less, but all of which can, as Felix Frankfurter observed, result in the same outcome, with the states sapped of the discretion and then ultimately the expectation of using their police powers without federal direction or permission, as the case may be.[55]

First, and most obviously: federal judicial action, wherein judges striking down state laws creates a clear prohibition of a state's use of its police powers. (This is the subject of chapters 4 and 5 on liberty of contract).

Second, federal legislation can have a direct effect: the supremacy clause makes any federal law authorized by an enumerated power or other part of the Constitution supreme over state laws, so, assuming such an authorization exists, the federal government, too, can trump state laws. (This comes up, in passing, in chapters 5 and 6 but is more directly covered in a previous treatment of Prohibition.)[56]

Third, federal legislation can interact more subtly, not simply trumping states' discretion in their use of the police powers but, especially when keyed to an expansive understanding of the spending clause, instead can crowd it out or effectively induce the states to do the federal government's bidding. The stronger the inducement, the more likely to drift from "cooperative" to "coercive" federalism. (The legal line, of course, is harder to draw, as the courts have found.)[57] This is the subject of chapters 2 and 3, in which the states feared even a clear and easily refused example of "cooperative federalism"— Sheppard-Towner—could inevitably lead to the latter.

Before moving on, it is worth clarifying and reiterating what is meant by the concept of progressive federalism: it is simply a commitment of those with progressive policy views to decentralized federalism and a robust use of the states' police powers. As this book will show, during the Progressive Era and through the first parts of the New Deal, progressives—not all of them, by any means, but many of them, including some of the movement's central figures—shared essentially the same constitutional understanding of decentralized federal-state relations as did the era's moderates and conservatives. (In establishing that understanding, the book covers, how, within the Progressive Era, federalism was also more broadly understood and practiced by nonprogressives in cases where the states disputed the fidelity of the federal government to the US Constitution.)

What this study will show is that contrary to our popular understanding, among those most committed to what we would today think of as constitutional conservatism, many of those were also interested in progressive policy views. That includes applying the doctrine both when it was politically expedient to advancing progressive policy goals (as in the liberty of contract cases discussed in chapters 4 and 5) and sometimes when it was not so obviously so (as in Sheppard-Towner, covered in chapters 2 and 3). In short, during the Progressive Era, progressives not only had a broad instrumental reason to support federalism—because the police powers were an appealing tool to check corporate power—but also because many had the same principled reasons to defend and be bound by this mainstream understanding of constitutional obligations.

CHAPTER ONE

State Constitutional Interpretation in American Political Thought before the New Deal

Those who would pronounce [decentralized federalism] impossible, offer no alternative to their country but schism, or consolidation; both of them bad, but the latter the worst.

—James Madison, editorial in *National Gazette*

The true and only way to preserve state authority is to be found in the awakened conscience of the states ... and in the vigorous exercise for the general public good of that State authority which is to be preserved.

—Elihu Root, "How to Preserve the Local Government of the States"

Resistance to centralizing politics and a concurrent commitment to local government has deep ideological undercurrents dating back to the old court-and-country debates in England, which then translated to the American context. Colonial Americans understood the 1688 Glorious Revolution to be not merely about limiting arbitrary government through law and legislative supremacy, as the British Parliament came to interpret it, but also to be about what we would now call federalism. After all, the American theater of that revolution had been overthrowing James II's efforts to consolidate many of the colonies into a singular Dominion of New England, destroying the local government they had come to interpret as part of their English inheritance and colonial practice.[1] Indeed, the 1774 Declaration and Resolves of the First

Continental Congress—less well-known than the nearly identical Declaration of Independence of its successors in the second Congress—shows the revolutionaries' core critique was that the British had abandoned their traditional principle of local self-government.[2]

Not all the members or contributors to the Constitutional Convention favored this tradition. Alexander Hamilton hopefully speculated that good administration by a newly created central government would enable it to "triumph altogether over the state governments and reduce them to an intire [*sic*] subordination, dividing the larger states into smaller districts."[3] John Jay, though not a participant, had written George Washington before the Convention, similarly proposing subordination of states to the federal government except where useful otherwise.[4] Madison discussed the feasibility of similar efforts but remained more guarded in his normative views of doing so (other than firmly endorsing the national veto he would champion at the Convention as part of his more centralizing Virginia Plan, but which was blocked in favor of the more limited judicial enforcement of constitutional rights against the states via the supremacy clause).[5] James Wilson, although later the originator of the argument that the federal government did not need a Bill of Rights since the federal government was carefully limited in its powers, clearly had nationalist leanings at the Convention, though he distanced himself from Hamilton's contempt for the states.[6]

But regardless of the ambitions of the more nationalist members who sought consolidation in reaction to the failed Articles of Confederation, the final Constitution more closely reflected Connecticut's Roger Sherman; Sherman's success in implementing his states' rights commitments arguably made him the father of the finished Constitution as much or more than Madison.[7]

As Pauline Maier's history of the constitutional ratifying conventions explains, the major sticking point in securing ratification of the Constitution was in winning over pivotal skeptics who, like Sherman, supported a stronger government than the troubled Articles of Confederation provided but who nonetheless insisted on seeing that primacy would remain with the states before they would sign on. In short, they wanted a *stronger* central government but not a *strong* one.[8] Most of the authority to act for the public good would remain with the states; the federal government would receive only those powers enumerated to it in the text of the US Constitution and, under the Supremacy Clause, only these would be supreme. As Elihu Root observed, "Under this provision an enactment by Congress not made in pursuance of the Constitution, or an enactment of a State contrary to the Constitution, is not a law. Such an enactment should strictly have no more legal effect than the resolution of any private debating society"[9]

It is worth pausing to emphasize here that, unlike notorious provisions such as the Three-Fifths or Fugitive Slave Clauses, the basic structure of federalism and a limited government were hardly a grudging concession made to accommodate southern slavery. It was, instead, a common and extensive belief of both southern *and* northern delegations to both the Constitutional Convention and the subsequent ratifying conventions—the price of achieving the latter, in fact. Northerners had normatively appealing reasons such as local control, representativeness, or diversity to support federalism—hence Connecticut's Sherman or Massachusetts's Elbridge Gerry, or many others, insisting on it at the Convention against the Virginian Madison's more nationalizing plan. A more radical example: New York's non-Hamilton delegates John Lansing and Robert Yates left in protest at what they viewed as the excessive centralization developing (while Gerry ultimately declined to sign). Skeptical states' rights anti-federalist majorities had to be persuaded to agree in Massachusetts' ratifying convention.[10] Southerners shared many of those more appealing reasons to defend federalism as well as an additional incentive—the maintenance of slavery—to be for states' rights.

Indeed, if one looks to the state constitutions and Declarations of Rights in existence at the time of the creation and ratification of the Constitution and Bill of Rights, it seems that, if anything, northerners celebrated federalism more. If one also includes Vermont, which joined the Union in 1791, for a total of fourteen states, twelve had state constitutions at the time. (Rhode Island and Connecticut still used their colonial charters [the 1663 charter and 1639 Fundamental Orders of Connecticut, respectively]). Of these twelve states, seven had language praising federalism and states' rights. But not, perhaps, the seven states we might expect.

Every New England state with a constitution had a proto–Tenth Amendment in it. As John Adams's 1780 Massachusetts Constitution observes, "The people of this Commonwealth have the sole and exclusive right of governing themselves as a free, sovereign, and independent state; and do, and forever hereafter shall, exercise and enjoy every power, jurisdiction, and right, which is not, or may not hereafter, be by them expressly delegated to the United States of America, in Congress assembled." Perhaps most strikingly, more concise but substantively identical language similarly appears in the 1793 constitution of the new state of Vermont—four clauses after an explicit ban on slavery within the state's boundaries. Of the mid-Atlantic states, Pennsylvania—the most antislavery of them—had an explicit states' rights clause, New York had a somewhat oblique but still clearly federalist provision, while New Jersey—where abolitionism was weakest—did not.[11]

Of the six southern states, only North Carolina and Maryland had federalism provisions in their constitution, each including nearly identical language as the northern states. Notably, no such provision appears in the South Carolina or Georgia Constitutions—the two slavery hardliners at the Constitutional Convention.[12] In other words, the state constitutions suggest an almost inverse relationship between celebrating federalism and slavery: the more abolitionist areas in New England and Pennsylvania valorized federalism the most and the most doggedly proslavery Deep South the least.[13]

The fact that southern states could and later would make an appeal to a widely revered principle (federalism) to advance a specific issue (slavery) is hardly an indictment of federalism itself or those delegates of North and South who appealed to it on a range of issues more broadly (and who, even had they wanted to eliminate it, had little actual ability to successfully do so). In sum, then, at the time of the Founding, North and South had their own independent reasons for endorsing states' rights with sentiment, if anything, stronger in the North—and that is part of why federalism remained such a ubiquitous framework into the period this text covers.

Thus, even though Hamilton clearly loathed the states and looked forward to their total disappearance, Jay had little more use for them, and Madison did not hold the firm commitment to states' rights that he did after the Constitution's enactment. Their *Federalist Papers*' alter ego *Publius* recognized that most Americans remained committed to their states and decentralized governance and conceded to that fact.[14]

Contrast Hamilton's private hopes of consolidation with his *Federalist* 32: "An entire consolidation of the States into one complete national sovereignty would imply an entire subordination of the parts. . . . . But as the plan of the convention aims only at a partial union or consolidation, the State governments would clearly retain all the rights of sovereignty which they before had, and which were not, by that act, EXCLUSIVELY delegated to the United States." In effect, the three Publii had to sell the Constitution as Sherman's vision, not their own.

And thus, as part of that effort, the *Federalist* repeatedly insists not only that the powers of the central government are limited in a fundamentally federal polity but also that states will have a role to play in enforcement of the constitutional bargain limiting national power.[15]

While a useful reassurance to the pivotal skeptics of national power, the Framers embedded several institutional features to guarantee that the states' policing role would occur. As Madison observed in a 1792 *National Gazette* entry, expanding on his reasoning in the more famous *Federalist* 10 and 51, the balance of national and state power struck by the Constitution should and would be preserved by politically arming both sovereignties to compete on behalf of constitutional liberty, as he believed they had done: "So, it is to be hoped, do the two governments possess each the means of preventing or correcting unconstitutional encroachments of the other." Should this system of decentralized federalism work, he concluded, it "may prove the best legacy ever left by lawgivers to their country":

> Those who would pronounce it impossible, offer no alternative to their country but schism, or consolidation; both of them bad, but the latter the worst, since it is the high road to monarchy, than which nothing worse, in the eye of republicans, could result from the anarchy implied in the former. Those who love their country, its repose, and its republicanism, will therefore study to avoid the alternative, by elucidating and guarding the limits which define the two governments.[16]

And, indeed, that is what he proposed in the 1798 Virginia Resolution, in which he encouraged states to signal one another to use all "necessary and proper measures" to "interpose" against illegal federal expansion (in the form of the Alien and Sedition Acts, against which Madison's primary objection was not the First Amendment but the Tenth). Or, in the words of John Taylor of Caroline, the zealously Jeffersonian Virginia politician who sponsored the 1798 Virginia Resolution, the states would serve as "sentinels" of federalism.[17] As many historians have later shown, Madison intended these "necessary and proper measures" to be the regular politics built into the constitutional order: memorials from state legislatures, instructions to senators, and the like. Moreover, as Jonathan Gienapp argues, this state legislative signaling was designed to mobilize the ultimate backstop, the citizenry who would block any efforts to deviate from the original public meaning to which they had agreed.[18]

John C. Calhoun notoriously concluded that those checks were insufficient to protect slavery and thus augmented lawsuits and electoral politics with a new technique of state enforcement of constitutional federalism: nullification.[19] Although both James Madison and most later commenters, even secessionists like Jefferson Davis, recoiled at any effort to connect Calhoun's extratextual remedy with Madisonian thought and the so-called "Spirit of

1798," Calhoun's destabilizing theory helped weaken states as sovereign constitutional interpreters after the Civil War.[20]

Discrediting Calhoun's corollary of states as unilateral nullifiers need not and did not discredit Madison's initial structures of state enforcement, but some state checks against the federal government nonetheless decayed in the decades after the Civil War. This reduction in the states' enforcement of constitutional meaning took place even as states' rights and federalism, passed from the Founding through the Jacksonian era, remained central to the mainstream constitutional thought of both parties in the nineteenth century.

Most (but by no means all) Whigs did have a more capacious view of the enumerated powers than did the Jacksonian Democrats, and often a nationalist theory of the Union's origins. But it is worth pausing here to note that even the more centralizing National Republicans and Whigs endorsed the basic contours of this federalist ideology, as did John Marshall, whose Commerce Clause opinions siding with the federal government were careful to acknowledge the federal government was one of limited and enumerated powers.[21]

As Emily Pears has shown, the Whigs, like the National Republicans and Federalists, identified strongly with the national government as an object of veneration and sought to use infrastructure to help cultivate loyalty to it—in this they shared the Virginians' somewhat greater tolerance of federal power and concessions to some of Hamilton's arguments as compared to more hardline Old Republicans and Jacksonians.[22] But, the National-Republicans-turned-Whigs were still political descendants of and intellectual heirs to the fundamentally states' rights party of Jefferson and Madison. Thus the National Republicans and Whigs argued that they remained committed to federalism and, at least rhetorically, praised American federalism's balance of powers limiting the federal government; constitutional federalism, for them, just gave sufficient authority to do what they wanted, but not much more. (It's also worth reiterating that attachment to the Union fit perfectly within the thought of Andrew Jackson, despite the latter's narrower views of several of these federal powers.)[23]

The Whigs' primary differences with the era's Democrats were a belief in a more expansive interstate commerce power that could be used for internal improvements and infrastructure (including with the Bank) to create a stronger interstate commercial market and in the legitimacy of the tax power to be used for protective tariffs; these could also generate goodwill for the Union. All of this, they thought, could be reconciled with a good-faith reading of the limited powers granted to the federal government. As House Speaker and future senator Henry Clay (KY) explained, they sought to "promote so-cial intercourse, to facilitate commerce between the states, to strengthen the bonds of our union, to make us really and truly one family." While these ini-tiatives strengthened attachment to the Union, it was still within a plausible, not strained, interpretation of the enumerated powers.[24]

This mattered to Clay because he still professed a commitment to states' rights and to the "great principles of 1798" as he built off the political pro-gram of the Jeffersonian Albert Gallatin and pushed for the National Sys-tem.[25] As he observed in his 1818 speech on infrastructure (and reiterated later with the Maysville Road debate), Congress was limited to enumerated pow-ers and could not act outside them, nor would he abet the improper form of consolidation adding powers not given by the text.[26] But, he argued at some length, an authority to build roads comes from three enumerated powers: the post-road, interstate commerce, and, anticipating President Eisenhower's ar-guments about the Interstate Highway System, defense, insofar as military power needed to be quickly moved and deployed.[27] The result: "No legitimate power of the state governments is intrenched upon, no attribute usurped—for to them is still left every municipal power, and every power essential to their sovereign character as federate states."[28] Indeed, as David Currie noted, Clay actually criticized Monroe's Cumberland Road tollgate memorandum because it decoupled the spending power from the enumerated powers and, thus, in Clay's words, "sets up a power boundless in its extent, unrestrained to the ob-ject of internal improvements, and comprehending the whole scope of human affairs."[29]

While Daniel Webster embraced a very robust interstate commerce power—an exclusive one that would be wielded, as the Dormant Commerce Clause, against the states—Webster similarly praised American federalism for ensuring "local institutions for local purposes, and general institutions for general purposes"; after all, he noted, states should not pass laws for each other, considering the geographic and cultural diversity of the states across the vast Union. The system and its "limits of constitutional power" in the federal government resulted in a system that was very well balanced and one already "kept from too much leaning toward consolidation by a strong tendency in the several States to support each its own power and consideration."[30]

Thus, like both James Madison and Clay, Webster distinguished between what he regarded as a good form of consolidation and an un-American one, the conversion of the Union to a unitary state with effectively plenary powers over the citizens. According to all three of them, consolidation, in the sense

George Washington had used it in proposing the US Constitution, had meant to strengthen the intellectual and political ties of the Union and create a respectable, well-defended, and enduring nation. It did not mean, in the words of Clay, "the alarming sense of the phrase," or what Webster reiterated was "consolidation" in the "obnoxious" or "odious sense, in which it means an accumulation in the Federal Government, of the powers properly belonging to the States."[31]

In short, the National Republicans, and then Whigs, took the doctrine of limited federal power seriously and carefully invoked and justified support from enumerated powers in the debates over whether the federal government could subsidize multistate roads via the interstate commerce and post-roads powers, or the taxing power, or neither, and they came to somewhat different answers with not just each other but also the Jacksonians.[32] It is, of course, possible that this was pretextual, and as the Jacksonians charged, the National-Republicans-turned-Whigs were, in their private preferences, consolidationists of the kind the New Dealers would become. But whether honestly held convictions or necessary pretexts, even the relatively "nationalist" Whigs professed a commitment to a limited and federal government and claimed to be following in the Jeffersonian states' rights tradition; their relative tolerance for federal power compared to stricter Jacksonians should not be overstated to fashion them as forerunners of the unitary thought first of either the Progressive or post–New Deal Democratic Parties.

Abolitionists of both Democratic and Whig ancestry could thus, without any shame, cite federalism in passing antislavery personal liberty laws in the 1850s—that was part of why South Carolina's secession manifesto decried northern uses of federalism as some of its opening counts in justifying secession.[33] It was also part of why not just Lincoln and mainstream Republicans but even many of the Radical Republicans remembered and preserved federalism in discussing their vision of a post–Civil War America. They may have been less likely to explicitly cite states' rights in their platforms than the Democrats (though they did occasionally), but they still honored the principle. Hence, the Reconstruction Constitution was one which chastened the states by raising the floor of core rights they had to follow—adding the Bill of Rights, due process, and legal equality or equal protection to the preexisting limits on the states previously found in Article I, Section 10—but it was a Constitution that still preserved the fundamentally federal structure of America and the core limits on federal power.[34] Charles Sumner may have perceived a new fount of plenary federal power springing from Appomattox, but both his Senate colleagues and then eventually the US Supreme Court held that it did not (except as written into the text of those Reconstruction amendments.)[35]

As was soon demonstrated by the justices in striking down Sumner's 1875 Civil Rights Act, the Supreme Court remained fundamentally committed to states' rights and policing federal expansion beyond constitutional boundaries.[36] It exercised that power relatively sparsely in early America—more often than those who contend it never occurred except for *Marbury v. Madison* and *Dred Scott*, but still relatively infrequently.[37] During the decades of Republican dominance between the Civil War and the New Deal, however, federal courts policed federalism zealously, at least until after the construction of the Roosevelt Court almost ceded the field.[38] Even before the Roosevelt Court, however, the justices acted in relatively few federalism cases.

It is worth pausing to emphasize *why* the Court could take a relatively hands-off role with relatively few cases testing exercises of congressional power in the nineteenth and early twentieth centuries: national parties and legislators served as gatekeepers, preventing most federal legislation from even reaching the justices' desks. As Robert Post notes, there was not merely a legal but moral component to this period's belief in the propriety of ensuring powers were divided and the federal government limited, a phenomenon he dubs "normative dualism" (as in a normative commitment to a dual federalism in which the spheres of the states and federal government were clearly divided).[39]

There was little need for stern judicial expositions of, say, the Commerce Clause or the spending power with John Tyler vetoing the reauthorization of a Third Bank of the United States or Grover Cleveland blocking funding of the distribution of seeds in a drought.[40] What generally mattered—and what citizens generally saw covered in, for example, the newspapers—was state politics.[41] Though disagreeing about applications in particular controversies, most actors shared and remained guided by a fairly consistent, broadly decentralist constitutional vision, disagreeing more narrowly on application.

The decentralized structure of parties—heavily dependent on local and state organizations skeptical of losing influence to a federal government—added an institutional incentive to enforce this localist ideology. In this conceptualization, the party system largely structured constitutional debate both before and after the Civil War; the parties might have differed precisely on which elements of government needed to be most carefully limited, but the two parties broadly competed on delivering the good of "limited government," at least through the New Deal. With something close to a broad bipartisan consensus delivering a largely hands-off federal government, and before Supreme Court incorporation of the Bills of Rights against the states even after the passage of the Fourteenth Amendment, states could remain fairly detached from federal activity, which mostly left them alone.[42] This vindicated Martin Van Buren's defense of political parties as the most important constitutional guarantors, helping bridge the people of the states on behalf of what was perceived as the proper constitutional vision of limited government. As Sidney Milkis explains, Van Buren learned from the coordination problems Jefferson and Madison had experienced in opposing the Alien and Sedition Acts with the Virginia and (and Jefferson's companion) Kentucky Resolutions, and Van Buren therefore set out to build a more enduring political organization on behalf of the Constitution and its states' rights orientation. The broad contours of Van Buren's system lasted, as the subsequent chapters will show, until the New Deal.[43]

But federalism was not merely a negative doctrine checking federal power but also, at its core, included a positive component, drawn from English common law and authorizing the states to act on behalf of the people's welfare and for the good of their communities, with policies and goals tailored to the unique needs and preferences of the many people in a country as diverse as the United States.[44] It is easy to forget that, strictly speaking, the Tenth Amendment—codifying the implicit logic of the enumerated powers in Article I, Section 8—reserves *powers*, not rights, to the states.[45] Or, stated in the terms of constitutional doctrine, the states were left with what Madison's *Federalist* 39 had called "the residuary sovereignty of the states" or what constitutional law subsequently dubbed "the police powers": the presumptive authority to regulate on behalf of the health, welfare, safety, and morals of the people, except where prohibited by constitutional text (either by the United States or their own state constitution).[46]

Alexis de Tocqueville summarized the breadth of the police powers: "Americans believe that in each state the social power ought to emanate directly from the people; but once that power is constituted, they imagine so to speak no limits to it; they willingly recognize that it has the right to do everything"—meaning states' rights brought with it a robust conception of their police powers.[47]

As Justice John Harlan (I) observed for seven justices in upholding state vaccinations in the 1905 case of *Jacobson v. Massachusetts*, perhaps the canonical case explaining the states' police powers on behalf of health, welfare, safety, and morals:

The mode or manner in which those results are to be accomplished is within the discretion of the State, subject, of course, so far as Federal power is concerned, only to the condition that no rule prescribed by a State, nor any regulation adopted by a local governmental agency acting under the sanction of state legislation, shall contravene the Constitution of the United States or infringe any right granted or secured by that instrument.[48]

Harlan allowed, as he had in the earlier case of *Mugler v. Kansas* (1887) upholding the authority of states to ban alcohol, that the courts would also potentially strike at laws which were purely pretextual and thus arbitrary and not really legislative power: "If a statute purporting to have been enacted to protect the public health, the public morals, or the public safety has no real or substantial relation to those objects, or is, beyond all question, a plain, palpable invasion of rights secured by the fundamental law, it is the duty of the courts to so adjudge, and thereby give effect to the Constitution."[49] But these would be rare events: "[The federal courts] should not invade the domain of local authority except when it is plainly necessary to do so in order to enforce that law"; they were not to simply institute their policy judgement on the states, as doing so would violate both separation of powers and federalism.[50]

As a bitter Oliver Wendell Holmes—the paradigmatic progressive justice of the first part of the nineteenth century—observed later, citing his famously acidic dissent discussed in chapter 5:

As I intimated in *Adkins* . . . police power often is used in a wide sense to cover and . . . to apologize for the general power of the Legislature to make a part of the community uncomfortable by a change. I do not believe in such apologies. I think the proper course is to recognize that a state Legislature can do whatever it sees fit to do unless it is restrained by some express prohibition in the Constitution of the United States or of the State.[51]

In these and other contemporary cases at the turn of the twentieth century, Harlan, Holmes, and their fellow justices had to assess new kinds of regulations appearing throughout the different levels of government. The increasingly centralized power of the industrializing economy in the 1890s and early 1900s generated demands for a stronger government to check business—by the federal government in the limited spheres where it was empowered to do so and by the states everywhere else within their authority. Thus, for example, the states began to engage in more aggressive forms of regulation by setting rates for those companies that were "clothed with the public interest," or what we might think of as utilities or quasiutilities.[52]

Part of their additional incentive is that the Supreme Court had effectively held that the power to regulate commerce among the states could not be used to regulate manufacturing in such a way as to stop states from generating comparative advantages against one another. The earlier case of *United States v. E.C. Knight* (1895) curtailed federal regulation of manufacturing—in this case, to block the creation of a massive multistate sugar conglomerate—even if the resulting consolidation by definition, according to Justice Harlan in dissent, operated in multiple states and had significant effects on the nation's markets. (Harlan, a devout defender of federalism, in fact, argued that failing to check multistate spillovers actually harmed states' rights, since states would be subjected to other states' economic policies.)[53]

Even more controversially, and over the protest even of the Court's progressive federalists (and some subsequent originalist conservatives), in the 1918 case of *Hammer v. Dagenhart* the Court extended *E. C. Knight* to conclude that even regulations merely on *shipping* such goods across state lines could actually be regulations on manufacturing themselves.[54] Justice Holmes (joined by Brandeis, McKenna, and Clarke) objected that Congress merely regulated the interstate shipment, not the intrastate manufacturing itself—and thus was consistent with federalism—and all of them but Clarke agreed that direct regulation of manufacturing exceeded Congress's authority.[55] Holmes and others argued it was also inconsistent with other cases of the time, in which even a deeply federalist Court approved federal prohibitions on the interstate shipment of alcohol under the 1913 Webb-Kenyon Act, for example, to prevent spillover effects.[56]

Especially in such situations where the effects of one state spilled over into others (but the Court had concluded were not covered by federal authority), far-sighted observers argued that it was especially important for states to robustly exercise their police powers in ways that would disincentivize broader national interventions. They were trying to square the circle of creating effectively national solutions through state-based means—and, indeed, they found at least a partial solution: state compacts to pass protective uniform economic legislation proved immensely popular to political elites for precisely this reason.[57]

In short, as perceptive political actors acknowledged that changes in the industrializing economy required more interventionist and uniform substantive policies, policy entrepreneurs tried to reconcile progressive ends with a deeply federalist constitutional conservatism, believing they could do so within the logic of the Constitution. Moreover, as even many of the conservatives of the era agreed, they had to defend active state governments in order to maintain popular support for constitutional limits on the federal government.

This vision, reiterating that states' rights in the sense of limiting federal power should be and must be linked to robust state police powers, was perhaps most fervently stated by Elihu Root, a lawyer who served as Roosevelt's secretary of war (and then state), senator, and a Republican elder statesman (Root was also seriously considered for Roosevelt's blessing as his presidential successor—Roosevelt thought him the best suited but questionably electable—but Root apparently declined consideration).[58] But, as the subsequent chapters will show, Root's vision was far from that of a marginal figure or obscure theorist. It was also shared by many of the era's leading and centrally placed political figures: William Howard Taft (president and chief justice), Charles Evans Hughes (justice, 1916 Republican presidential nominee, secretary of state, and then chief justice), Al Smith (the progressive Democratic governor of New York and de facto leader of the Democratic Party throughout the 1920s), and, at least before his presidency, Franklin Roosevelt, who succeeded Smith as governor of the nation's most populous state.

The question they had was fairly straightforward: In the face of the modern economy, and modern life more generally, "in what way," Root asked, "can the power of the States be preserved?"[59]

For Root, there was "but one way in which the States of the Union can maintain their power and authority under the conditions which are now before us, and that way is by an awakening on the part of the States to a realization of their own duties to the country at large."[60]

Root obviously did not object to differences in either mores or policies between the states, or seek a bland homogenization, but he did recognize that there were realistic limits to the variety that could exist within a federal polity without stress to the system and a resulting backlash: "If any state is maintaining laws which afford opportunity and authority for practices condemned by the public sense of the whole country, or laws which, through the operation of our modern system of communications and business, are injurious to the interests of the whole country, that state is violating the conditions upon which alone can its power be preserved."[61]

Thus, outliers who either created spillover effects damaging other states, especially in the economic realm, or engaged in policies that grossly offended the shared morals of the rest of the country should not be surprised to find themselves facing pressure from the rest of the Union, even potentially pressure that violated the Constitution.

While Root was himself a lawyer, and one deeply committed to the forms and structures of constitutional decentralization, he recognized, even if lamenting the fact, that many Americans were more result-oriented than he and would not long tolerate the possibility that *no* institution could regulate on behalf of the public good:

> It is useless for the advocates of states' rights to inveigh against the supremacy of the constitutional laws of the United States or against the extension of national authority in the fields of necessary control where the states themselves fail in the performance of their duty. The instinct for self-government among the people of the United States is too strong to permit them long to respect anyone's right to exercise a power which he fails to exercise. The governmental control which they deem just and necessary they will have.[62]

What Root ultimately feared was that these policy anomalies would result in the destruction of the constitutional order altogether, displaced by dubious legal interpretations that would disregard the structural limits on the Constitution. In the end, he sighed, "the people will have the control they need either from the States or from the national government, and if the states fail to furnish it in due measure, sooner or later construction of the Constitution will be found to vest the power where it will be exercised—in the national government."[63]

As a result, he firmly pleaded with state legislatures and governors to fulfill the logic of constitutional federalism: they must use the states' Tenth Amendment police powers not merely as a shield defending them from federal intervention but also as a sword acting on behalf of the public good and people's welfare: "The true and only way to preserve state authority is to be found in the awakened conscience of the states . . . and in the vigorous exercise for the general public good of that State authority which is to be preserved."[64]

Root believed that a conservative understanding of the constitutional structure was perfectly compatible with progressive policy views. In 1933 he explained that "constitutional government rests upon two bases, national strength and local self-government . . . both essential to the continuance of our free democracy."[65] The challenge, then, was to ensure that each part of the government acted within its own sphere—seeking not only to reflect the wishes of their citizens but, in a very Madisonian logic, to ensure that they fought for, rather than ceded, their own institutional power. That is not to say Root necessarily drew the line correctly in all cases in deciding what went in each sphere—his antipathy to allowing federal control to prevent economic spillover effects, as fellow Roosevelt ally Holmes believed was necessary to maintain a meaningful federalism, arguably fits uneasily with making Root's overall theory sustainable, but Root at least offered both an analytical framework and a realistic assessment of how to preserve federalism.[66]

Since Root was instrumental in the 1912 election, serving as an ally to William Howard Taft's self-styled battle on behalf of constitutional fidelity, and that election was a major intellectual battle over the relationship of progressive thought to federalism, it is worth a brief detour into that campaign, including its fallout and the ideas therein.[67] Although it was about ideas, it still involved people: Roosevelt's inner circle of Root, Lodge, and Taft all found themselves painfully turned against their former compatriot in order to do their perceived duty to the Constitution. At one time, Taft returned from "a day of such speeches, all of them attacks on his challenger[.] Taft cried in private as he told a reporter, 'Roosevelt was my closest friend.'"[68]

The incumbent president Taft, for his part, had a respectable progressive record to point to in seeking reelection.[69] He had been a more aggressive trust-buster than Roosevelt and objected to Roosevelt distinguishing between good and bad consolidations of business power rather than more consistent enforcement of the Sherman Act. He had shepherded through the Mann-Elkins Act of 1910 (expanding on the 1906 Hepburn Act, passed during Roosevelt's presidency and which had expanded on the Interstate Commerce Commission's initial forays into federal railroad regulation). As the election developed, Taft's primary motivation in continuing his campaign was less to secure his own term in the White House than to block Roosevelt's election and the legitimation of Roosevelt's growing antipathy to constitutional government housed in his Progressive Party. While most of the fears of Taft, Root, and Lodge—Roosevelt's inner-circle-turned-opponents—concerned Roosevelt's rethinking of the separation of powers and relationship of the president to popular opinion, federalism, too, played a part. Taft's one campaign speech in September 1912 observed Roosevelt's party seemed most invested in issues "having no national jurisdiction of policy" under the Constitution.[70]

The 1912 Progressive Party platform called for much more governmental activity, especially federal activity, against corporate power, as well as a recognition that "the union of States [had] in all essential respects become one people." This contrasted with the Democrats' stock platform pledge, which the Progressives' condemned as an "extreme insistence on states rights." (The latter plank continued Democrats' decades-long and rote invocation of states' rights in their platform.) More specifically in developing their anti-corporate platform, the Progressives called for various regulations where the states had power, and various regulations where the federal government had power, while alluding to possible constitutional amendments to realign the distribution of authority and empower the government as necessary (as presumably they would be).[71]

Roosevelt himself was not even that constrained (and would, first in an October 30 preelection rally and again in his 1913 autobiography, go even further in decrying states' rights as a "fetish," on top of his repeated calls for massively reimagined unilateral executive power in an almost plebiscitary presidency). Roosevelt's New Nationalism, building off the work of political theorist Herbert Croly, sought to use federal and specifically executive power in sweeping ways to control what Roosevelt increasingly believed was corporate control over America and American workers.[72]

Woodrow Wilson positioned the Democrats as a reasonably safe alternative that drew on traditional understandings of constitutional power—and thus could draw on traditional Republican elites and voters as well, many of whom tactically defected to the New Jersey governor to stop Roosevelt.[73] Against Roosevelt's centralizing New Nationalism, Wilson, aided by his ally Louis Brandeis (a former Taft supporter), posited a "New Freedom." This sought to achieve many of the same ends—taming excessive combinations of economic power—shared by Roosevelt as well as Taft. But, similar to Taft and unlike Roosevelt, Wilson did not propose to tame corporate power by massively raising up federal power but by narrower interventions cutting down consolidated economic power. Thus, in the spirit of Jeffersonian or Jacksonian democracy, which would decentralize economic power (rather than, as under Roosevelt, use federal power to channel it for good), Wilson's vision proposed a variety of tools that would implement less direct federal management of the economy. Chief among these New Freedom initiatives were tariff reform, banking reform, and reinvigorated antitrust and anti-monopoly efforts.[74]

Wilson had a long record as a critic of constitutional government and broadly favored the replacement of the more complicated Madisonian system of checks and balances with something more like the British system (although Wilson also favored some direct democratic elements such as the initiative and referendum—but not a recall of judges or judicial decisions).[75] But, in the years before the 1912 election, Wilson had carefully pivoted between conservatism and progressivism in order to remain broadly acceptable to the American electorate. Part of that, of course, meant matching the Democratic Party's traditional invocation of states' rights (which its 1912 platform would cite, as it had for decades). Perhaps surprisingly, in light of his views critical of the separation of powers, Wilson defended a strikingly orthodox view of American federalism—one which led Roosevelt to deride Wilson as armed with the "old flintlock muzzle-loaded doctrine of states rights."[76]

Then Professor Wilson's major constitutional law treatise, written a few years earlier in 1908 and based on lectures delivered the year before, is very respectful of America's decentralized federalism and sounds communitarian at times.[77] Its treatment of state versus federal power is far more traditional than its theory of flexible-living constitutionalism and its sharp critiques of the Madisonian system of the separation of powers (and, arguably, constitutionalism itself), which have helped generate Wilson's reputation as perhaps the leading progressive intellectual.[78] *Constitutional Government in the United States* recognized not just the distinct natures of America's communities but the serious costs to self-government that came from elevating "moral and social questions" to federal concerns. This was especially true, he worried, if done by "deliberate adding to the powers of the federal government by sheer judicial authority . . . [which] saps the legal morality upon which a sound constitutional system must rest."[79]

In his 1907 lectures soon reprinted as *Constitutional Government*, Wilson's take on federalism sounded very much like 1906 Root: "The remedy for ill-considered legislation by the states, the remedy alike for neglect and mistakes on the part of their several governments, lies, not outside the States, but within them. . . . In no case will their failure . . . prove that the federal government might have forced wisdom upon them." It only proved, Wilson contended, that states may be poorly structured internally, especially in terms of representation, but it would be "fatal to our political vitality really to strip the states of their powers and transfer them to the federal government."[80]

Thus, it would be unsurprising that Wilson's political program was heavily influenced by one of the primary figures of this book: Louis Brandeis, who blended progressive politics with a commitment to federalism.[81] At least as announced, Wilson's New Freedom was compatible with—indeed, arguably, equivalent to—major strains of progressive federalism. In the words of Sidney Milkis, "Wilson's progressivism was carefully calibrated to conform to the

Jeffersonian traditions of the Democratic Party," and his New Freedom "deliberately, if uneasily, joined to individualism, support of the two-party system, and limited constitutional government," especially states' rights.[82] The *London Times* aptly dubbed the party's 1912 platform "constitutionally conservative, and socially and economically progressive," a sentiment later echoed by the *New York Times*.[83]

Wilson would crow, in late 1914, about his success in achieving his New Freedom trio via the Underwood Tariff, Federal Reserve Act, and the Clayton Act and Federal Trade Commission Acts.[84] Drawing on Jacksonian thought, Wilson's antitrust policy sought to reinvigorate the original Sherman Antitrust Act and break up monopolies (as had Taft), whereas Roosevelt distinguished between good and bad monopolies.[85] Further illustrating the compatibility of Wilson's progressivism and states' rights, the tariff's sponsor and namesake was Oscar Underwood—whose commitment to federalism would lead him to be tagged a "conservative" a decade later.[86]

Of course, as critics have noted—such as the quotation beginning this book—Wilson's governance, especially after 1914, moved left and came to more closely resemble New Nationalism, ironically leading Herbert Croly, among others, to embrace Wilson as a champion of progressive thought and especially national power. Croly, for his part, considered only the Underwood Tariff part of New Freedom, with the rest having taken a more New Nationalism turn. (Others, especially latter conservative critics of Wilson, argue he simply reverted and had been purely posturing, perhaps even serving as a sort of Trojan horse to get Democrats into the progressive movement.) Thus, at least some of the Republicans' campaign in 1916 had been against what they argued was Wilson's excessive use of federal power, with President Wilson having adopted much of what New Nationalism had called for and which Professor and Governor Wilson had criticized.[87]

To what extent Wilson himself was privately a nationalist favoring consolidating power and only positioned himself as a states' rights defender for instrumental electoral reasons, or viewed New Freedom as an intermediary stopgap on the way to a national community reflecting genuine popular opinion, or was a then true believer in limited federal government before changing is beyond the scope of this study. What matters is that he recognized the broad appeal of a progressive federalism that sought to use the robust but divided powers of the constitutional system to check corporate power and act, within the appropriate spheres, for the public good. Such a position could garner the support of, for example, a Louis Brandeis, a James McReynolds, and

George Hunt, to note three very different figures who supported his effort to bridge "conservative" constitutionalism with progressive policy views, with states and the federal government each active within their appropriate spheres.

There was another part of the federalism puzzle that also interested Root: if, as noted previously, he believed state legislatures were obligated to indirectly fight for their own authority (by demonstrating prudent use of the police powers), were state legislatures *also* authorized to fight for their own power against federal usurpation? If so, how?

While states' rights and a robust conception of their police powers remained a centerpiece of constitutional thought, there was an additional question: Were national institutions—courts and parties—the only legitimate way to enforce the balance of power? Did states still have a role to play beyond judicial filings, or had the Civil War settlement modified Publius's system as the price necessary to prevent another conflict?

Some scholars (and the occasional populist political figure) have argued that passage of the Seventeenth Amendment helped to lock states out of constitutional politics in the second decade of the twentieth century, since their legislatures lost the ability to select senators sympathetic to the prerogative of states. Indeed, Woodrow Wilson condemned the original Senate selection process precisely because of his fears that it enabled the possibility of states checking federal action.[88]

At the time of its passage, then Senator Root (R-NY)—who had moved to Congress's upper chamber after service in Roosevelt's cabinet—was a lonely voice fearing that the Seventeenth Amendment would quickly enable the growth of national power. Whether Root was right or not about the implications of removing state legislatures' role in shaping constitutional development, it is not obvious that the Seventeenth Amendment meaningfully disempowered state legislatures: the Seventeenth Amendment arguably confirmed a development that had already functionally taken effect with de facto popular "advisory" voting.[89]

The end of state control of the Senate, whether via the Seventeenth Amendment itself or the forces that created it, might indicate that the states had to hope that the best defense was a good offense. Root feared that with the proposed Seventeenth Amendment, the most—perhaps only—effective way to prevent federal consolidation would be through aggressive state action preempting federal efforts in the first place. Any subsequent efforts to block federal overreach would have to come merely from the judiciary.[90]

But this was not so. As the subsequent chapters will demonstrate, while states—with one peculiar exception—continued to revile Calhoun's nullification during the Progressive and New Deal Eras, they nonetheless retained a role in constitutional dialogue through speeches, memorials, and even bills. And state legislators used those to defend the mainstream constitutional understanding upholding the prerogative of the states to robustly use their police powers free of unconstitutional federal intervention.

CHAPTER TWO

Against Motherhood and Apple Pie:
The Sheppard-Towner Maternity
and Infancy Protection Act of 1921

> More and more the federal government is taking over the powers of the states, and
> our nation is in a headlong rush to centralize all government at Washington [by] a
> species of bribery.
>
> —John J. Blaine, governor of Wisconsin to the legislature

President Warren Harding came to office with a well-established general aversion to government experimentation and a stated fiscal conservatism. Nonetheless, in 1921 he backed a bill through Congress which observers have sometimes regarded as the beginning of the federal welfare state: the Sheppard-Towner Maternity and Infancy Protection Act of 1921.[1]

Sheppard-Towner was, as critics noted at the time, another early example of the regime of grant-in-aid programs by which states receive federal subsidy in exchange for agreeing to spend their own money on federally approved purposes—often called "cooperative federalism." Such grants-in-aid, which have grown to become a sizeable portion of federal outlays (and federal influence),[2] were becoming more popular with Washington policy-makers in the early part of the twentieth century, especially after ratification of the Sixteenth Amendment's creation of a federal income tax in 1913. They were not only increasing in frequency but changing in kind: whereas federal contributions to states had historically been land grants—most notably, the 1862 Morrill Act supporting the establishment of colleges—with the end of federal land distributions Congress increasingly packaged aid as direct financial expenditures to the states. Even when administered in the form of the federal government using its power as a property owner to provide land grants, these had been contested by critics who charged that the funded aims were beyond the powers of the federal government.[3] Such challenges became even more pronounced after the turn from land grants to taxation as the revenue source, but especially as the subject of such grants expanded during the Progressive Era.

The debate over the constitutionality of these grants, especially those more tenuously tied to an enumerated federal power, broke out in earnest with Sheppard-Towner, as the states contested what they feared would be an entering wedge, initially a minimalist form of cooperative federalism that would eventually displace the states' police powers in the domain of health. But the strange part is *where* this discussion broke out: constitutional debate in Congress was relatively minimal, and the Supreme Court, for its part, effectively refused to decide the case on standing grounds. Thus, it was in state capitols—not Washington, DC—where Americans first seriously considered the constitutionality of a federal positive-rights regime, and they did so in what became one of the most sustained examples of constitutional debate between state governments and the federal government between Reconstruction and the New Deal. And that debate—a well-publicized, reasonably sophisticated disagreement without resort to Calhounian assertions of nullification or outright defiance—offers a compelling example of the sort of constitutional dialogue hoped for by scholars who argue nonjudicial actors have an obligation to enforce the Constitution.[4] Those resisting Sheppard-Towner did so with scrupulous constitutional logic, by declining to accept funding, trying to repeal it legislatively, and pursuing test cases in the Supreme Court. As one would expect from those committed to the mainstream constitutional understanding of federalism, nullification was not among the tactics employed to vindicate states' rights.

Opposition was nonpartisan, nonregional, principled, and procedurally sound. While pushback was strongest in New England, opposition appeared across the country—in the Midwest, Northwest, and a handful of southern states. Despite being passed by Republicans in Washington, for instance, many of the bill's most committed opponents in state capitols were members of the GOP, who themselves were joined by many Democrats. Nor was this opposition a question of policy views disguised within more noble-sounding constitutional claims—some of the states that held out the longest actually spent more on their own equivalent programs.[5]

Indeed, as the detailed case treatments and legislative histories will make clear, Sheppard-Towner shows that many state legislators and governors were willing to both oppose their own policies and pay a political price by opposing Sheppard-Towner on constitutional grounds.

Moreover, although much of the opposition to Sheppard-Towner came from conservatives and libertarians, and, therefore, in many ways it might appear at first glance to be a standard case of conservative federalism—that is, conservatives invoking states' rights claims to defeat federal passage of a progressive policy goal—the fact that so many prominent progressives joined with conservatives makes clear that something larger was at work. In fact, these progressives, who came especially—though not exclusively—from the Northeast, mobilized resistance to the bill by refusing to have their states participate in Sheppard-Towner's grant-in-aid formulation and its regime of cooperative federalism. In doing so, these progressive opponents used almost-identical arguments in favor of decentralized federalism commonly associated with constitutional conservatism today.

This is doubly striking because it arguably undercut an immediate progressive policy goal. Many progressive skeptics of Sheppard-Towner explicitly noted the policy itself was sound and desirable, yet nonetheless they opposed its enactment at the federal level, fearing that it would set an undesirable precedent that would allow federal meddling in the states' police powers—in this case, specifically health—as they had come to fear in other realms. In their view, a principled commitment to federalism, which involved not only protecting their own states' sovereignty but also their constitutional oaths, required opposition both to their own policy preferences and even their own electoral viability in opposing a popular bill.

As with most invocations of constitutionalism, there were also opportunistic reasons to either make or, alternatively, reject federalist arguments concerning Sheppard-Towner. On the one hand, progressives had especially good reason to fear that a more consolidated government would suppress their experiments in protective labor legislation (which will be covered in more detail in chapters 4 and 5); conversely, many conservative critics who usually invoked federalism were strikingly meek in silently acquiescing (due to fear of newly empowered women voters) to a bill that they would normally object to on constitutional grounds.

Yet even as some progressives opposed Sheppard-Towner on opportunistic grounds, it is clear that many of their most prominent peers did so out of a principled commitment to states' rights. Indeed, such progressives joined in

making effectively identical constitutional arguments as conservatives, sometimes to their electoral peril, because they believed they were obligated to follow the Constitution.

The next two chapters will recreate this dialogue: this chapter will briefly
lay out the politics of federal passage before turning to state consideration
of Sheppard-Towner in the South, West, and Midwest, while the subsequent
chapter will turn to the Northeast, where opposition was stiffest, before finally
turning to federal repeal. As grants-in-aid are, arguably, one of the primary and
heavily contested sources of federal power today, and the Sheppard-Towner
debate perhaps most thoroughly illustrates the constitutional features of these
issues, it offers an especially important case study of the contours of American federalism.

Clearing Congress

The Sheppard-Towner Act was the brainchild of longtime social reformer Julia Lathrop, the head of the federal Children's Bureau, which had itself been
recently authorized within the Department of Commerce and Labor as a sort
of data repository to collect information on, among other things, child mortality. Although most of the bureau's subsequent energy would be directed at improving rural conditions, the maternity and infancy health initiative that gave
rise to it had grown out of progressive concerns for the health of urban children.[6] Moreover, while the impetus for the Bureau's authorization came from
women's groups organized by Florence Kelley and support from progressives
like Theodore Roosevelt, constitutional conservatives like William Howard
Taft and the congressional delegation from Massachusetts had also provided
key assistance for its passage in 1912.[7]

In drawing up a subsequent bill to combat some of the evils her bureau had
encountered, Lathrop looked to the Smith-Lever Act, a 1914 grant-in-aid program that had offered matching federal funds to states that made grants to agricultural education.[8] The bill would offer similar, though fairly limited, funds
to those states that chose to create (and partially fund) a maternity and children's bureau providing health information to mothers aimed at reducing infant mortality and illness.[9]

Representative Jeanette Rankin (R-MT), the first woman to hold that office, brought the specific plan for Sheppard-Towner to Congress in 1918. Although Rankin was unable to guide the bill to passage, as Theda Skocpol

observed, Rankin's initial failure probably proved to be a blessing since the bill—thus branded as progressive wartime legislation—likely would have been repealed as part of the general reaction against that era's policies.[10]

After various Children's Bureau policy proposals bounced around in the Democratic Congress for a few years, the GOP landslide of 1920 opened a new policy window, into which stepped Republican Horace Mann Towner from Iowa and Morris Sheppard, a Texas Democrat. Towner, a former judge and law professor, was a reformist member of Congress who would later sponsor the first proposal to have a federal cabinet-level Department of Education (Smith-Towner in 1920 and Sterling-Towner in 1923), which would have administered grants-in-aids to the states funding education. Towner, however, was appointed as governor of Puerto Rico, on account of his service on the committee overseeing that territory, and his education bill was later taken up (unsuccessfully) by a different cosponsor (as Sterling-Reed), where it again inspired controversy over federal overreach into education.[11] The Yale-educated, Shakespeare-quoting, labor-friendly Sheppard was marked by both progressive leanings and a friendliness to national power, which most famously combined in his stewardship of the Eighteenth Amendment—Prohibition—which was once widely referred to as "the Sheppard Amendment." (He was also one of the few Senate prohibitionists to actually abstain from alcohol.)[12]

That the bill's policy impact was minimal—incentivizing states to establish offices and programs with consultations and information related to maternal and infant health—was irrelevant. For critics, even those who did not fear the lurid tales of government snoopers circulated by the bill's critics, Sheppard-Towner marked a dangerous expansion of the federal government into a domain they believed traditionally, and constitutionally, belonged to the states.

The shift from land grants to direct expenditures from tax-derived revenue more clearly exposed the long-standing constitutional question of whether the federal government could subsidize ends not connected to its constitutionally enumerated powers. The distribution of land for such purposes had itself been challenged in the nineteenth century, but Congress seemed to be on at least relatively firmer footing in distributing its own property as it saw fit.[13] Direct expenditure from tax-derived revenue, however, more clearly implicated debates about whether the government could tax and spend for any purpose or merely in pursuance of the enumerated powers—in other words, whether Alexander Hamilton or James Madison and Thomas Jefferson had been right in 1791 and 1792.

Most notably in his "Report on Manufactures" released on December 5, 1791, then Treasury Secretary Hamilton had argued that the power to tax and spend "for the general welfare" was a freestanding power "left to the discretion of the National Legislature," and thus could be used to subsidize desirable manufacturing.[14]

This was, suffice to say, a controversial position. Then Secretary of State Jefferson argued that, as bad as it had been to so loosely treat the enumerated powers and thus authorize a national bank, as Hamilton had convinced Washington to do over the Virginians' pleading the year before, treating "general welfare" as an independent grant of power, as Hamilton now proposed, negated the very purpose of enumerated powers and the core logic of the Constitution—anything could be said to advance the general welfare.[15] Now serving as the de facto floor leader of Congress, Madison noted in a debate in 1792 that the power to tax and spend for "the general welfare" had been lifted almost verbatim from the Article of Confederation and yet no one had ever assumed it to be a freestanding power. Moreover, many of those who voted to ratify the Constitution had been specifically promised that such an interpretation had been illegitimate, a fact which Madison found especially compelling.[16]

As Madison observed, neither the Constitution nor the even more decentralist Articles could ever have been passed had Hamilton's interpretation been the understanding of that power. Instead, Madison argued, reiterating almost verbatim arguments he had made in *Federalist* 41, it was "always considered as clear and certain, that the old Congress was limited to the enumerated powers; and that the enumeration limited and explained the general terms" because anything else would "convert the government from one limited as hitherto supposed, to the enumerated powers, into a government without any limits at all."[17] In Jefferson's even blunter formulation: "To consider [general welfare] as giving a distinct and independent power to do any act they please, which might be for the good of the Union, would render all the preceding and subsequent enumerations of power completely useless."[18]

Though Madison and Jefferson had defeated Hamilton on the specific issue of the bounties (but not the bank),[19] and the Jeffersonians and subsequent Democrats had leaned toward that understanding of the tax-and-spending power in the early nineteenth century, the issue had never been truly settled. The turn toward land distribution, favored by post–Civil War Republicans and combined with tenuous connections to enumerated powers, had enabled its postponement, but the growing regime of grants-in-aid threatened to reopen it.

In the decade before taking up Sheppard-Towner, Congress had passed the

Weeks Act (helping states fight forest fires), the Smith-Lever Act of 1914 (for establishment of and instruction by agricultural colleges), the Federal Roads Act of 1916, the Chamberlain-Kahn Act of 1918 (a wartime measure to control venereal disease), and a pair of vocational rehabilitation initiatives: the Smith-Hughes Vocational Education Act of 1917 and the Smith-Fess Industrial Rehabilitation Act of 1920. It had also considered Towner's controversial proposal for an increased federal role in education.[20]

As Kimberley Johnson has shown, the development of these grants-in-aid and other forms of so-called cooperative federalism had many causes in the preceding fifty years and were the product of years of canny efforts to build up a political infrastructure supporting that vision of cooperative federalism. Although Republicans were often more hostile to passing federal legislation in the era, when they passed such legislation they tended to want it federally administered (rather than having its administration filtered through the South's racial orders). Conversely, Democrats tended to favor such local administration, both for that reason and because they were more likely to be out of national power. It is no accident, therefore, that many such grant-in-aid initiatives passed under Woodrow Wilson's presidency, as he believed they were a way to bridge the traditional states' rights perspective of the Democratic Party with the more nationalist ambitions of other Democrats in his coalition.[21]

While many progressives were interested in the decentralized federalism created by the Constitution, others, of course, were not, viewing it as an obsolete relic of an older preindustrial society.[22] More nationalist progressives like the political theorist Herbert Croly, for instance, who were ultimately less interested in or even openly hostile to federalism, saw grants-in-aid and similar programs as a stepping stone to ultimately nationalizing more politics, gradually steering states toward following the federal will and building up a cadre of policy experts and connections that could be expanded on later. This wing of progressive activists were ultimately not as committed, as an abstract principle, to constitutional decentralization, instead making temporary allegiance with the state police powers as a step toward a much more expansive and protective central government.[23]

It is significant, though, that such progressives who were uninterested in federalism still had to work within it because its basic assumptions were so widely accepted—including by so many of their fellow progressives. Certainly, as Wilson recognized, grants-in-aid could be more easily justified within the American constitutional order than direct federal regulations of those subjects; thus, grants-in-aid offered a sort of opportunistic federalism for the nationalists. Those of the Jeffersonian or Madisonian constitutional persuasion might and did still object on the grounds that topics like maternal care were not enumerated among federal responsibilities in the Constitution (though some grants, such as support for veterans or roads, could be derived from such powers, akin to Henry Clay's distinction between federal involvement in roads under the commerce and post-road powers and horror at the prospect of the federal government spending money independent of an enumerated power, as discussed in chapter 1). Conversely, those who saw the spending power as a more freestanding one, as Hamilton did, would have no difficulty justifying the states exercising the option of accepting a federal expenditure.

The Republican platform of 1920 had not formally endorsed Sheppard-Towner (as had the Democrats, Socialists, and Farmer-Labor Parties), but then-candidate Warren Harding strongly embraced the proposed bill nonetheless. While the campaigning Harding had savagely condemned "paternalistic social welfare program[s]," he had explicitly exempted Sheppard-Towner from his diatribes.[24] Once inaugurated, the new president reminded Congress that he meant what he told the American people and he expected action. In an April 1921 message to Congress, Harding stated that he "assume[d] the maternity bill, already strongly approved, will be enacted promptly, thus adding to our manifestation of human interest." Nor was this simply cheap talk; Harding and Republican National Convention vice chair Harriet Taylor Upton broke a legislative stalemate by leaning on the arch-conservative, anti-suffragist Samuel Winslow, who had bottled the bill in his House Committee on Interstate and Foreign Commerce.[25]

Debate in the Senate was vicious but the result preordained. The July 22, 1921, vote was 63–7, with two additional absent senators opposing the bill but using paired voting. Senators James Reed of Missouri and William King of Utah, both Democrats, led the opposition, joined by William Borah (R-ID), Edwin Broussard (D-LA), George Moses (R-NH), Francis Warren (R-WY), and Thomas Watson (D-GA). Two northeastern Republicans, William Dillingham of Vermont and James Wadsworth of New York, paired with absent supporters; thus, nine senators, from across the ideological spectrum, from among the most progressive to the most conservative, went on record in opposition. (The bill's opponents had a progressive tilt, with five of the nine on the progressive side, including Georgia's Watson, one of the handful of most progressive members of Congress.)[26] The misanthropic Reed, apparently H. L. Mencken's favorite politician, was particularly quotable in his caustic attacks on its supporters.[27] While the states' rights-committed Reed, an able lawyer himself, made substantive constitutional arguments against the bill, he mostly left these to the constitutional lawyer King and instead focused on rhetorical barbs. Reed seemed to especially enjoy needling Children's Bureau chief Julia Lathrop, her lieutenant and successor Grace Abbott, and the other predominantly female staffers, as when he insinuated that the bureau was dominated by old maids who consequently could not understand kids.[28] Indeed, the Missourian so hated the bill that, when informed that a critical vote was taking place, he dashed out of the barber's chair without coat or collar, dressing himself on the way, to make sure to block it. As such, he proposed renaming Sheppard-Towner "A Bill to Organize a Board of Spinsters to Teach Mothers How to Raise Babies," which "was rejected without a roll call, amid broad smiles."[29]

Reed's rank misogyny aside, two other lines of inquiry were widely pursued in the bill's congressional debate: states' rights and creeping socialism. King and Wadsworth, Tenth Amendment hardliners both, despite the former being progressive and the latter an ultraconservative, took the lead in railing against the slow but pronounced expansion of the federal government in the preceding decade. Of particular interest is the opposition of William Borah, the great progressive, leading prohibitionist, and independent Republican from Idaho, who attacked Sheppard-Towner on states' rights grounds. Borah would later explain his vote to a constituent as resulting from his hatred of the "centralization of power."[30] Nor was this mere rhetorical opportunism on a specific policy Borah disliked: he opposed others whose policies results he was sympathetic to; for example, offering a nearly identical argument against the proposed child labor amendment, which he decried as the "most pronounced invasion of local self-government that has ever been proposed."[31] He would also cheer, on states' rights grounds, the court's decision to overturn Franklin Roosevelt's National Recovery Act, which had allowed the federal government to regulate the local sale of chicken, in *Schecter Poultry v. U.S.* (1935).[32] The opposition of this contrarian progressive icon, a "son of the wild jackass" as he was known, suggested that the impulse of many progressives against centralizing national tendencies still survived.[33]

Interestingly, even many of the bill's supporters acknowledged this fact with some trepidation; for example, William Thomas, a Colorado Democrat, did not join the nine holdouts but voiced worries about the nationalizing precedent; other supporters expressed similar reservations.[34] Considering the widely acknowledged gulf between senators' private views and the votes they cast in light of intense lobbying (to be discussed later in this chapter), these very probably expressed the senators' true beliefs. However, in addition to the alternative, broad neo-Hamiltonian construction of the general welfare clause of the spending power voiced by supporters, Democrat Key Pittman of Nevada offered a view akin to Elihu Root's extolling the need for dynamic state government preventing federal expansion.[35] Pittman agreed that states *should* be the actors, but, he insisted, this was a case where they had neglected their duties and the situation required federal nudging.[36]

The bill's architect Julia Lathrop, a cagey political actor, tried to assuage these federalist concerns, all but promising that her agency would simply rubber-stamp state decisions. She insisted that the Children's Bureau would not meddle with state affairs and instead would act mostly as a clearing house for information.[37] Lathrop could credibly claim a hands-off position due to Representative Towner's early drafting, as he had modified the bill to make federal control minimal.[38] He had experience in trying to draft legislation creating weak conditions for grants-in-aid to try to assuage federalist concerns: Towner's other controversial bill (Smith-Towner/Sterling-Towner), attaching grants-in-aid to states as part of creating a Department of Education to administer said grants, scrupulously avoided setting curriculum or school policy, beyond setting as conditions of receiving the grant that the schools had to be open for six months, have compulsory education, and be taught in English.[39]

Unfortunately for Lathrop and Towner, what Joseph Chepaitis characterized as a "lunatic fringe" fixated on claims that a communist bureaucracy would use the Sheppard-Towner bill as a Trojan horse to forcibly invade the sanctity of the home, destroy the traditional social fabric, and encourage abortion and other forms of moral decay.[40] And, as with Smith-Towner's possible creation of a Department of Education, the concern was often less with the bill itself and more that it would be the first step in ever more aggressive federal control.[41] For a time, the discussion turned away from what Chepaitis describes as "more rational arguments based on the principles of economy and states' rights" and was displaced by concerns about the home, which sometimes extended to paranoid red-baiting. As the bill allotted only relatively small sums and the operation was fairly straightforward, economy and inefficiency, the usual watchwords of the day, were only occasionally raised in Congress and the legislatures; the arguments were predominantly either constitutional or about the sanctity of the home against the power of the government.[42]

Many states would later insist on provisions guaranteeing that sanctity of the home by explicitly banning uninvited government agents from entering in their Sheppard-Towner acceptance bills; for example, in Arizona, "no official, or agent, or representative of the Child Hygiene Division . . . shall enter any home or take charge of any child over the objection of the parents, or either of them, or such person standing in loco parentis, or having custody of such child." But this was overly cautious: Sections 8 and 9 of the federal bill already forbade federal officials from such activity.[43] Moreover, the bill would sunset after five years—presumably enough time to nudge the states into action. In other words, passage of the bill, at both the federal and state level, depended on convincing skeptics that the states' sovereignty remained basically unchanged and that the states were effectively receiving a blank check.

The final Senate vote was 63–7; after Harding broke a logjam in Winslow's committee, it cleared the House by a similar 279–39 margin, with 113 abstentions. If one adds the paired and late voting, the final tally was 321 in favor, 80 against, and 30 whose position was unclear. Opposition was particularly intense in New York and Massachusetts: seven of sixteen Massachusetts congressmen, including both Democrats, opposed the bill while roughly one in four Texans and delegates from Illinois rejected it.[44]

In an ironic turn of events, among the no votes was Alice Robertson (R-OK), who, after the electoral defeat of initial sponsor Jeanette Rankin, was the lone woman remaining in Congress. Robertson mocked what she found to be inflated claims of women's political clout. Sheppard-Towner, she sniffed, was the product of women who "get a thrill over teacups by passing resolutions to bring about a new order in governmental affairs" or were pushed by activist Florence Kelley's "sob stuff."[45] Robertson would return home to Muskogee, Oklahoma, to gloat that she had stood firm when her male peers got "cold feet."[46] But Robertson had lost this vote: the "entering wedge for socialism" had passed.[47]

As Robertson had alluded to, the extremely effective lobbying by the Women's Joint Congressional Committee (WJCC) and allies such as the National Consumers League helps explain the wide margins for the bill. The WJCC, an umbrella group and information clearinghouse for legislative policies of special concern to women, offered a particularly effective ground campaign. Congressmen and other Washington observers described the lobby as powerful; perhaps the most powerful ever to reach Washington, DC—high praise at a time in which the feared Anti-Saloon League operated. Senator William Kenyon of Iowa, one of the architects of the bill along with his fellow Iowan Towner (as well as an old prohibitionist and progressive ally of Sheppard), observed it, laughed that Sheppard-Towner would have been crushed in a cloakroom vote if the private grumblings of his peers were accurate.[48] Kenyon was probably right, as his political acumen was widely recognized: Harding named him a federal judge as a way to rid himself of a political rival in 1924, only for those same instincts to mean Coolidge considered the progressive Kenyon to balance the ticket in 1924—Kenyon instead favored the states' rights progressive Borah—before finally serving on the Wickersham Commission assessing Prohibition, warning Hoover support for it had collapsed.[49]

This extremely effective mobilization that so amused Kenyon, one critical newspaper observed, was causing legislators to forget the bill was not only "paternalistic" and a subsidy to the backward South but "very objectionable from the constitutional standpoint."[50] A wire report agreed that the so-called "baby bill battle" had generated a historic firestorm of activity.[51]

Anecdotal and statistical evidence both suggest that much of the congressional support for Sheppard-Towner resulted from uncertainty about and fear of a consolidated "woman's vote," fears which the WJCC was happy to play up.[52] Debate on the bill took place within a perfect policy window: *after* the ratification of the Nineteenth Amendment but *before* widespread national women's suffrage. (The amendment was ratified in August 1920 but, for a variety of reasons, female turnout in that fall's election had been low.) Thus, elected officials had little information with which to gauge its popular support; few wanted to determine if the WJCC was bluffing or if its claims of Sheppard-Towner as a litmus test for newly enfranchised women were in fact true. Moreover, as part of its lobbying effort, the WJCC took out innumerable ads in magazines and other print media targeted to women.[53] Therefore, as Alf Landon supporters would do in 1936, vastly inflating electoral opposition to FDR based on the *Literary Digest* in the absence of better polling, lawmakers appear to have overstated the support for and the salience of Sheppard-Towner based on the media climate.[54]

Anticipated countermobilization by the American Medical Association (AMA) also proved fairly weak in 1921. Some of its members opposed the bill during passage but did not mobilize anything close to the clout of the WJCC. Indeed, the AMA's governing body only officially condemned the bill in May 1922, long after passage, when it denounced the bill as a "socialistic scheme unsuited to our form of government." (The pediatrics wing dissented and endorsed the bill, as it would in the future.)[55]

This muted opposition was the product of a different AMA than the one that would, ironically, be partly constructed by Sheppard-Towner itself. The bill's sponsors accurately assumed that members of the AMA and the professional medical establishment left the preventative health field mostly untouched—seeing it as women's work, unlike treatment, which it reserved for itself. By this logic, an organization predominantly made of female bureaucrats and staffers would claim different ground than the turf occupied by the medical old guard. However, the fighting about Sheppard-Towner made that old guard aware of the growing importance of preventative care—as well as the increasing willingness of the federal government to enter fields previously left to the states, including medicine.[56] As a result, as its members had done decades earlier in medicalizing abortion and assimilating a field previously seen as women's (midwife) work,[57] the post-1921 AMA emerged with both an expanded sense of its own jurisdiction and a concomitant fear that the federal government would continue to expand its reach. When the next Sheppard-Towner fight began, a new, far more politically active AMA would stand ready—but not yet.

The trajectory of the Roman Catholic Church would follow a similar path. It was divided in its opinions during the early stages of Sheppard-Towner's political development but increasingly hostile as the years went on. (Protestant institutions seemed to take little to no notice in the bill's early or late stages.) While much of the rest of the Catholic leadership was neutral or even mildly supportive, American Jesuits (who then held a strong devotion to states' rights) were implacable foes from the start.[58] Their magazine warned that failure to guard states' rights would result in a monstrous totalitarian state: "Out of the Federalized clinic, along a Federalized Road comes the Federalized child to the Federalized School. . . . If we do not awake to the danger at our doors, we shall have a Sovietized United States within another generation."[59] While the ordained Catholic leadership did not formally oppose the bill, however, many of the rank-and-file, or at least lay Catholic leaders, seemed to take their lead from the Jesuits: of the states which either never accepted Sheppard-Towner or did so late and grudgingly, nearly all—Louisiana, Maine, New York, Rhode Island, and Vermont—had significant Catholic populations.[60]

While the AMA and Catholic Church wavered, consistent opposition arose from the loosely aligned consortium behind the Woman Patriots, the Sentinels of the Republic, and the National Association of Manufacturers. Cooperation among them was easy, as all argued on largely similar grounds: for a sort of constitutional originalism, against centralization's pernicious effects on state sovereignty, and most certainly against anything smacking of Soviet-style collectivism—which was an easily met standard in their minds. The Woman Patriots, led by Harriet Frothingham (who would give her name to one of the two Supreme Court cases challenging Sheppard-Towner), developed out of the anti-suffrage movement and remained strict in their constitutional interpretation —demanding, for example, a specific constitutional amendment to authorize Sheppard-Towner. A group of Massachusetts businessmen led by Louis Coolidge and others concerned about the growth of federal power formed the Sentinels of the Republic, which operated as a clearinghouse for information about federal power and specifically grants-in-aid. Thus, organizationally speaking, the Sentinels were the mirror of the WJCC.[61]

The third major player in opposition was the National Association of Manufacturers (NAM), a business group founded in 1890 and largely dedicated to warding off federal economic legislation. Like the rest, NAM was constitutionally conservative, but it was particularly savvy strategically; for example, in seeking to avoid the precedent of national regulation at all costs, it actually lobbied for *stronger* state child labor laws to reduce the demand for federal legislation, perfectly fulfilling Root's logic. Its members exercised similar prudence here: of the three umbrella groups against Sheppard-Towner, NAM was the least visible due to its bad optics, consciously allowing the Sentinels and Woman Patriots to take the lead on the issue. Although these groups often provided much of the intellectual ammunition against Sheppard-Towner, working with several senators, in 1921 they were clearly outnumbered by the WJCC. Like the AMA, however, their voices would grow louder and help overwhelm the federal renewal efforts.[62]

Finally, as with many other progressive reforms, Sheppard-Towner resulted in part from mobilization for the European conflict, as childhood diseases hampered the war effort. Military officers made clear that draft boards, scrambling to assemble an expeditionary force, had to turn back many potential soldiers and sailors due to lingering effects from preventable childhood diseases. (Such concerns, after all, had justified the Chamberlain-Kahn Act's effort to combat venereal disease.) Thus, military leaders implicitly argued, improving the health of mothers and infants today would help the generals fight the wars of tomorrow.[63] Similar demographic data appeared in congressional hearings (which suggested that eighteen thousand mothers and two hundred thousand infants died annually from preventable causes); private data from Metropolitan Life Insurance corroborated claims that childbirth killed more women than anything except tuberculosis.[64]

Lobbying took place on both sides, then, but with the disorganized AMA and the uninterested Catholic leadership leaving the field to the Woman Patriots and their allied groups, the WJCC could leverage the support of the military and a uniquely favorable lobbying window in such a way that few legislators dared to cross it. Congress had passed its first (admittedly very minor) federal welfare program, but the Women Patriots and other critics soon took their belief that Sheppard-Towner violated states' rights outside Washington—to the states themselves.

Sheppard-Towner Moves to the States

By the terms of the federal law, state legislatures had to pass enabling acts as well as independent appropriations in order to participate in Sheppard-Towner, though. Governors could agree to temporary participation, akin to a recess appointment, since many state legislatures would not meet again until early 1923. Legislatures of five states—Delaware, Minnesota, New Mexico, New Hampshire, and Oregon—had preemptively accepted the terms before Harding had even signed the bill. But elsewhere throughout the country, state officials decided to use the enabling vote as an opportunity to passively register their protest against the unconstitutionality of the bill: they would not obstruct the federal government, but they would refuse to participate.

For most of the next decade, various states would hold out or protest—with conservatives and progressives, Republicans and Democrats, objecting to what in the end was, at least on its own terms, a relatively insignificant bill, but one they feared would be used to help destroy decentralized federalism. Perhaps most strikingly, one sees progressives pushing back against a conservative federal government (the Harding administration)—but using federalist arguments against a substantively progressive bill.

At the end of 1923, forty of the forty-eight states had agreed to join the program, with most of the holdout states from the Northeast, in addition to others where coalitions of progressives and conservatives threatened passage (see map 2.1). The forty participating by 1923 includes New York, which had to replace a hostile governor, as well as New Jersey and Washington, whose legislatures approved over gubernatorial vetoes. Louisiana joined in 1924, Vermont and Rhode Island in 1925, and Maine and Kansas in 1927. The legislatures of Connecticut, Illinois, and Massachusetts would never accept funds, although governors of the first two had initially agreed to participate.[65] And other states, though not naming Sheppard-Towner—much less refusing it—passed generic resolutions disapproving of grants-in-aid.

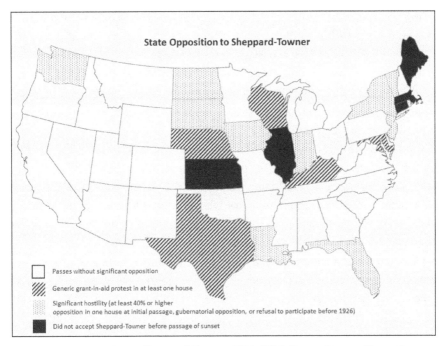

Map 1. State opposition to Sheppard-Towner, 1921–1929. *Source*: Prepared by author.

The South

Despite the South's reputation for aggressively asserting states' rights, the response of southern states to Sheppard-Towner suggests that Americans' allegiance to federalism was perhaps actually less rooted in the South than elsewhere. Indeed, in contrast to the more *northern* states described in the subsequent sections, in the solidly Democratic states of the lower South, most votes to accept Sheppard-Towner appear to have been quick and decisive in its favor: a handful would sometimes vote against the bill if they did not have to put their name to a roll call and their anonymity could be preserved, but roll call votes were usually unanimous or near-unanimous—though, consistent with Congress, the region was marked by fairly high abstention rates, presumably from those who thought the bill unconstitutional but did not want to risk putting their name to a vote that would enrage their newly enfranchised constituents.[66]

Among the first legislatures to support the bill after passage were, curiously, a pair of states from the upper South with strong states' rights traditions. With a vote in February 1922, Virginia became the first test of Sheppard-Towner in a stronghold of the Democracy. The vote in the conservative Old Dominion—though not yet in the hands of Harry Byrd and his ultraconservative states' rights–committed machine—was quick and decisive.[67]

Signs of resistance were more pronounced in Virginia's neighbor to the north, however. Although the final vote makes passage in Maryland appear somewhat inevitable, a closer look at its tangled legislative history reveals a bitter constitutional struggle.

As had occurred with prohibition, Maryland had become the site of a very public constitutional fight whose specifics were well covered in the media, as legislators seriously debated whether Sheppard-Towner was constitutionally equivalent to previous grants-in-aid or whether it was a new and illegal intervention into domestic state affairs and thus a violation of the states' rights so cherished by the state's political class.[68]

Women's organizations rallied on both sides. An assortment of groups followed the example of their national WJCC compatriots in support.[69] Against them, however, was the Women's Constitutional League of Maryland, which engaged in a massive lobbying effort of in-person meetings and a sustained letter-writing campaign both to local and national papers. Their manifestoes were wide-ranging, with praise for New York governor Nathan Miller's stand against the bill, constitutional discussions of the general welfare clause of the tax-and-spend power and federalism, anxieties about contraception, red-baiting, and concerns for precedents that would redistribute spending to poorer states. Finally, foreshadowing Phyllis Schlafly's movement and its warning about the drafting of women for military combat, they seized the platform to decry most women's legislation and especially the possibility of jury service through a state Equal Rights Amendment.[70]

The Women's Constitutional League took the lead in answering one of the major counterarguments advanced by the bill's supporters: Why oppose federal aid to maternity programs but not the other grant-in-aid programs? The league itself was initially less than precise in articulating a bright line, largely relying on policy critiques, but gradually sharpened their intellectual case. They argued that efforts to act on individuals opened a different, and potentially far wider, sphere of federal interference and permanent bureaucracy than funding agricultural efforts. Moreover, aid directed toward private individuals, according to the league, induced a sort of lethargy and government dependence, adding even more reason to oppose the bill.[71]

Later, in a back-and-forth letter campaign conducted in the pages of the *New York Tribune*, the league offered a clearer distinction. Cordelia Gibbs, the league's secretary, argued that maintaining the health of the market and protecting the food supply were implicitly derived from the constitutionally enumerated power to regulate commerce, with no equivalent authorization creating federal bureaucracy for a welfare state. Failing to see that distinction, Gibbs warned, meant one failed to appreciate that "local self-government is the cornerstone on which our democracy rests."[72] In her response to the *Tribune*, Florence Kelley replied that she could not understand how one could have a fear of federal aid for mothers but not for armories or agricultural colleges. "Why is it reasonable," she asked, "to take Federal money to educate boys for the national good after they have grown up, but dangerous to take it for keeping them alive through infancy?"[73]

Gibbs offered a textualist response, arguing that defense and interstate commerce were explicit constitutional powers, whereas welfare was not. Moreover, negligent Congressmen may have ignored their duty to "support the Constitution in regard to maintaining those rights reserved to the States," Gibbs explained, but they would soon be reminded of that obligation by angry constituents. Kelley's parting observation that Virginia had signed onto Sheppard-Towner, and therefore Maryland ought to, gave Gibbs an easy opening to further defend state prerogative. "Since Maryland is a sovereign state," she patronizingly observed, acceptance by its southern neighbor "should not carry any weight" in Annapolis.[74]

The same questions of federal power over various grant programs reappeared in the Maryland House, along with the usual discussions of federal control (or safeguards against it), as well as the warnings of socialism. As in Washington, DC, delegates acknowledged, sometimes grudgingly, sometimes enthusiastically, the strong lobbying presence of women. Nonetheless, approximately a third of the house revolted against the bill, with a final vote of 63–35 on March 29, 1922, following similar tabling votes. (Foreshadowing a nasty legislative process in the senate, a revote was nonetheless demanded). Initial forecasts predicted a much closer, maybe even losing, result in the senate.[75]

The final 18–3 vote in the upper house might suggest those predictions had been wildly off base, but a closer look at the bill's preliminary 18–8 vote (during its earlier "second reading") reveals that five senators had moved from "no" votes to abstention out of protest against the leadership's procedures to ram the bill through.[76]

These senators had been very clear, in fact, about their hostility to the bill. Senator Robert Biggs (D-Baltimore), one of the eventual abstainers, had given a publicized speech decrying Sheppard-Towner (and federal regulation of coffin sales) as eroding states' rights and converting citizens to wards of the national government.[77] If the positions of the other four were not well-known before, they were by the time the bill came up for a vote: they had staged a widely covered filibuster to run out the clock on the senate session. When the leadership kept the body open beyond its formal closure, the five stormed out, with one (Senator George Frick, D-Baltimore) speaking for them and declaring "that the State Senate is not now a legal body, the constitutional limit to its session having been reached."[78] Governor Albert Ritchie—a states-rights fanatic and well-known critic of grant-in-aid programs—nonetheless refused to intervene and block the bill, instead suggesting, like New York's similarly states' rights–committed Al Smith would, that there was no reason to penalize Maryland once Congress passed the legislation.[79]

Ritchie's extremely uncharacteristic decision to tolerate what he almost certainly believed was an unconstitutional exercise of federal power offers circumstantial evidence for the powerful lobbying movement operating in late 1921 and early 1922. Throughout the rest of his career, Ritchie zealously cultivated an image of himself as a paragon of traditionalist, Jeffersonian states' rights politics, including specifically his opposition to grants-in-aid—but not with Sheppard-Towner's initial fight, where his federalism appeared to buckle to opportunism.

Like many Marylanders, Ritchie took states' rights quite seriously, but he became especially associated with the doctrine as a result of his loud opposition to Prohibition, which he constantly denounced in appealing to the states' rights tradition of Grover Cleveland.[80] As a result of such efforts, by the late 1920s many observers considered him the leading states' rights Democrat in the nation, and Ritchie himself schemed to use prohibition as the starting point in remaking the American party system as one between federalist Democrats and consolidationist Republicans.[81] (And also, potentially, to make himself president, though he turned down Franklin Roosevelt's offer of the vice presidency in 1932.)[82]

In recommending his candidacy for the 1932 presidential race, the state's Democrats cited in particular the states' rights fanaticism that made him the ideal Marylander to guide the national party.[83] Only two years after he approved Sheppard-Towner, at a convention of the League of Women Voters—which had prominently endorsed the bill—Ritchie condemned grant-in-aid programs as violations of states' rights, explaining that doctrine to be "the arch on which the institutions of our country were founded."[84] And yet, when he had a clear opportunity to prop up that arch, Ritchie had passed.

Ritchie was not the only fainthearted states' rights advocate to momentarily back down for Sheppard-Towner, however, as he was joined by Millard Tydings, whose states' rights devotion would frequently challenge the New Deal from the United States Senate. Then-state Senator Tydings's final vote for the Sheppard-Towner resolution (and excused absence from voting for the companion bill) is in sharp contrast to the beliefs that would make him a target of the purge of disloyal Democrats in 1938.[85] However, before he could enrage FDR, state Senator (and former Maryland House Speaker) Tydings had to become US senator first. Thus a vote for Sheppard-Towner may have been the lesser evil for an ambitious politician who planned on rising through the ranks and would not want to cross the as-yet untested power of the WJCC lobby.[86] Tydings himself would join Democratic senators from Massachusetts and Utah in successfully filibustering a renewal plan in 1931.[87]

Sheppard-Towner joined Prohibition in actually mobilizing a resurgent states' rights rhetoric in Maryland's Senate. In 1924, the senate debated a bill to withdraw from Sheppard-Towner, which the committee on federal relations had endorsed. Senator Frick again led the forces decrying the bill on states' rights grounds. Senator McCulloch, the bill's author, added that he now opposed more than Sheppard-Towner but every grant-in-aid, including road work. Senator McIntosh, now senate president, handed over the chair so that he too could reiterate his opposition (he had been one of the walkouts two years before). The momentum had clearly turned—but not enough. McCulloch's repeal bill failed by one vote.[88] Frustrated senators brought several resolutions demanding the repeal of all federal aid to the states; the most extreme cleared the senate by an almost 3 to 1 margin.[89]

Maryland's upper house also cleared a resolution urging Congress to pass the so-called Wadsworth-Garrett amendment, which had been hatched by the same states' rights and business-oriented groups opposed to Sheppard-Towner as a way to block other centralized policies like child labor laws. Unsurprisingly, then the namesake and chief sponsor of the Wadsworth-Garrett amendment was New York senator James Wadsworth, an ardent foe of Sheppard-Towner.[90] The amendment had initially been kicking around since Prohibition; for example, in New Jersey, both the libertarian Democrat Edward Edwards and the former Republican governor William Runyon endorsed a Wadsworth-Garrett-like plan in 1920.[91]

Purportedly designed to increase popular participation in the amendment process, Wadsworth-Garrett was a sort of meta-amendment of Article V. Its various versions operated somewhat differently—some blocking legislative ratification until voters had a chance to vote for legislatures, some demanding popular convention approval—but the common aspiration was to slow amendments by forcing more popular input that would recoil against centralization. A de facto "embargo" on future amendments was the real hope of the amendment's proponents.[92]

These same elements again would try to block Sheppard-Towner in 1927, but the state legislative leadership squelched these challenges. Thus, an order to cease compliance with Sheppard-Towner died in a House committee,[93] and a senate protest against all federal aid met a similar end. Only an endorsement of Wadsworth-Garrett survived the 1927 session.[94]

The strength of opposition to Sheppard-Towner in Maryland proved atypical for the South, as others readily embraced the bill, especially in the Deep South (albeit with high numbers of abstentions). Despite opposition from Georgia progressive US Senator Tom Watson, when the Peach State's legislature considered the bill during the summer of 1922, it passed with little formal dissent, by spreads of 106–5 and 38–0–15.[95] West Virginia voted even more favorably than its parent state, with *zero* dissents from either roll call.[96] After the Arkansas house unanimously amended the bill to include a sanctity of home provision, the final floor vote was 65–8, with twenty-seven abstentions; the Senate vote was without dissent, twenty-four votes for to zero against, with eleven abstentions.[97] Alabama's chambers were slightly closer, but still 3–1 ratios in each.[98]

Mississippi also backed it, though the state also produced one of the most surprising illustrations of the unexpected alignments of federalism in the years before the New Deal. With its governor Earl Russell gushing about the bill's importance,[99] one Mississippi paper ironically sounded like Charles Sumner in dismissing states' rights claims in an almost incredulous tone, mocking New Englanders for what the editors even conceded were principled arguments for constitutional decentralization: "The state of Massachusetts is not fighting the law because the commonwealth disapproves of child and maternity welfare. Many activities within the state give proof to the contrary. The contention is that the act as it now exists is an invasion of STATES RIGHTS under the tenth amendment. . . . It is to be hoped that [the Supreme Court] will uphold the law."[100]

Both Tennessee and Florida, however, were somewhat less eager to sign on than most of the South. In Tennessee, seven of thirty senators, including one of its few Republicans, voted no. The house vote was fairly similar: sixty-one in favor to twenty-one opposed. Interestingly, one member in each house made the unusual request to explain his vote in the journal. In the senate, Democrat Lucius Hill grumbled about supervision from DC, adding that he regretted the precedent of federal cooperation in road building. Democratic Representative Sam Bratton had clearly felt the sting of WJCC pressure, as he explained his no as a protest against the ferocious lobbying effort he had received. Moreover, he added in a muted accusation against his overly ambitious colleagues that he could afford to vote his conscience as one not trying to gain higher office.[101] Florida nearly blocked the bill. Like the lower house of most states, its house vote was extremely lopsided: fifty-six in favor, two against, and thirty-two abstentions. The senate vote, however, was one of the closest of any state chamber, a fairly tight 17–12 after an initial failure.[102]

Only one southern stated blocked the bill—but even then, temporarily. Louisiana, still in the hands of relatively conservative officials before Huey Long's takeover,[103] was the lone southern state to even briefly opt out of Sheppard-Towner, passing on the bill during its 1922 session before easily approving it in 1924. In the interim, Governor Henry Fuqua had pledged support for the bill, but otherwise little seemed to have changed during the two years.[104] One senator requested time to make a statement, explaining that, though he had once feared the program's intervention in the home, he had decided that the state bill's drafting prevented government meddling in the home—even if the officers somehow procured a warrant.[105]

As recent political history shows us, many Texans happily remind the rest of the nation that it used to be its own country (and some allege it could be again). By one metric, that sense of Texan identity and a self-appointed duty to police federal powers is true: a perusal of the state's legislatures journals in the 1920s shows the Texas legislature produced a voluminous stack of states' rights protests on a variety of issues.

Yet for all these protests, the Texan legislative history for Sheppard-Towner is nearly identical to that of most other states: a little under half the state senate objecting, but an overwhelming majority of the house accepting aid from the federal government. The vote in Austin's lower chamber was 95–25, with an additional twenty-eight absent or abstaining. Floor debate managed to mix sexism and states' rights, with one opponent observing he would "be damned first" before he would "turn Texas affairs over to a board of old maids at Washington."[106] Among the dissenters, it is worth noting, was John H. Wessels, the lone Republican in either branch of the legislature.

A senate proposal to establish a protocol in which counties would opt-in to Sheppard-Towner by referendum was narrowly defeated on a 13–14 vote, while a sanctity of home provision passed easily. Unlike the (sadly unrecorded) frantic speechmaking during earlier consideration of the bill, newspaper observers explained that the final vote was low key—no crowds of women filled the galleries, and little discussion occurred.[107] Senate approval of the final vote was 19–11 (and 14–12 for appropriation); one dissenter demanded that the record print his explanation that the bill was paternalistic and yet another example of handing a state's rights to the federal government.[108]

That sentiment seemed to animate Senate Concurrent Resolution 11, a state sovereignty protest adopted from the state Democratic Party platform that passed almost concurrently with Sheppard-Towner. The resolution was what one might expect: assertions of state primacy, "strict construction," and the belief in autonomy except where "specifically delegated"—all of these said to be in opposition to "centralization as advocated by monarchists." However, the latter half is of more direct relevance: a pledge to "oppose to the extent of our ability every effort by Congress . . . to extend the powers of the federal government . . . and thereby weaken the sovereignty of the states," and a request, akin to the Virginia and Kentucky resolutions, to have other states join them in a "re-consecration to the principles of State Sovereignty and the plain mandates of the Constitution." The senate approved on a voice vote, but the house put it to a roll call. This generated a surprisingly high level of dissent, considering it was a symbolic resolution that did little more than reprint the platform adopted by the only real party in the state.[109]

So how did Texans fare on this pledge to uphold Jeffersonian principles? To be consistent, legislators arguably should have split those two votes: to vote yes on behalf of state sovereignty and no on Sheppard-Towner, suggesting a consistent decentralization, or no on sovereignty and yes on Sheppard-Towner, suggesting disinterest in states' rights.[110] However, it is harder to justify matched yes votes, proclaiming a belief in a strictly construed, Tenth Amendment–oriented, Jeffersonian "plain mandate" constitutional language, on the one hand, and Sheppard-Towner participation on the other.

Nonetheless, *even in states' rights Texas*, 55 percent of legislators did precisely that. Of the 102 members who cast either yea or nay votes on both issues, twenty-two suggested a consistent nationalism by voting no on sovereignty and yes on Sheppard-Towner. Fewer than 20 percent cast paired votes that were consistently states' rights oriented (with another five voting for federalism in practice but declining to endorse the platform).[111]

Pairing these two votes suggests that, even in Texas, strict construction and states' rights were slippery at best and shallow rhetoric at worst, and that perhaps Texans were well represented by their senior senator (and the bill's champion and namesake, Senator Morris Sheppard). Austin took the bait "with the avidity of a trout," the *St. Louis Post-Dispatch* mocked, drawing an unfavorable contrast between the tough-talking Texans and New Yorkers who actually remained true to the Constitution.[112]

Another paper would make the same observation during the child labor amendment debates. The editors of the *Port Arthur News* pointed out the silliness of Texan "ultra champions of states rights," vetoing an *amendment* to the Constitution on states' rights grounds when they had rolled over for the mere Sheppard-Towner bill—a bill not forced down their throat but sponsored, after all, by one of their own. The maternity bill and road aid demonstrated the functional obsolescence of states' rights, a doctrine already "shot to pieces first on many battlefields . . . and given final burial when southern legislatures ratified the 18th and 19th amendments."[113] The editors of the *Wichita* (TX) *Daily Times* had observed this hypocrisy the year before, laughing at a Texas Democratic Party platform that, in endorsing Sheppard-Towner, "by indirection . . . adopted an attack on states' rights." Unlike the suddenly retrograde Yankees of Massachusetts, the paper continued, Texan Democrats "in a lucid interval, thought [the saving of 'the lives of a good many babies'] worthy of more consideration than states' rights."[114]

The story gets even more interesting when one goes back to the very early days of that legislature's session, when a memorial to Congress pleading for an end to grants-in-aid had failed in the house after near unanimous (21–3) passage in the senate. Unfortunately, the house killed it on a voice vote, so one cannot compare the composition of those votes to the Sheppard-Towner acceptance or state sovereignty resolutions. The text of the memorial reads like a preemptive apology and justification for endorsing bills such as Sheppard-Towner:

> Even though the legislatures of the several states may not approve of, or endorse the purpose of the appropriation, said legislatures . . . are forced to make an appropriation to meet the conditions imposed by the national Congress, so that the people of the respective States may obtain and

receive a pro rata part of the funds going to other States out of moneys raised by taxation of all the people.[115]

A 1925 effort to repeal Sheppard Towner, pushed by Dallas state senator John Davis, generated an outpouring of hostility and counter-lobbying by women's groups. Notably, however, Davis cited a recommendation of the Board of Control of the Texas budget and framed this as a move toward greater "economy"—in an era when that word had an almost talismanic quality.[116]

In short, even Texas, which consistently raised federalism objections on nonracial issues, nonetheless bit its tongue at the prospect of federal money. On Sheppard-Towner, like Prohibition, Maryland's political class comes across as the clear outlier in being relatively consistent among southern states.[117] More broadly, as the contrast with other regions of the country makes clearer, and as several contemporaries observed at the time, Sheppard-Towner offers some justification for those who suggest southern invocations of federalism had a significant or even predominant strain of opportunism, covers for defenses of their racial order rather than a principled commitment to constitutional decentralization.

The West

If there was one part of the country that edged out the passive acceptance of Sheppard-Towner in the South—doing little to weigh in on the issue of constitutional federalism—it was the recently settled territories west of the Rockies. Washington was the only state in which acceptance was even minimally controversial, as its passage somewhat resembled New Jersey's brief interbranch squabble. Republican governor Louis Hart refused to give the provisional gubernatorial acceptance, explaining that he did not believe himself authorized to issue such a policy in the absence of legislative approval, but his message to the next meeting of the joint assembly encouraged them to do so. Both houses easily approved of the bill. Hart *did* line-item veto part of the bill involved in internal organization of Washington's bureaucracy but approved all parts having to do with the federal program itself.[118]

Otherwise, the West proved extremely eager to sign onto Sheppard-Towner.[119] Oregon and New Mexico had beaten Harding to approval in 1921 while legislators from Arizona and Wyoming signed on without dissent, even as the former had the devoutly states' rights progressive George Hunt as governor.[120] Arizona's leading newspaper, for example, did not even mention federalism in discussions of the bill.[121] Utah, despite sending to the US Senate implacable foe and ardent progressive William King (and eventually his ally, fellow Democrat Elbert Thomas who would filibuster a renewal bill in 1931), also unanimously accepted the bill, although as in much of the South there were a high number of abstentions perhaps indicating opposition that went unvoiced in light of lobbying pressures.[122]

Of the remaining western states, only Idaho offered more than nominal opposition—though even there the vote was far from close once a sanctity of home provision to prohibit the entry of officials into the home without permission had been added.[123] A combined total of three Republicans objected in California's legislature, with one futilely declaring, "Federal aid is a disease."[124] Colorado's senate unanimously approved a sanctity of home provision and then passed the final bill with Democratic senator S. W. Debusk offering a lone dissent; a handful registered opposition in the lower chamber.[125] With the newspapers watching, and keenly aware of pressure from organized labor and women's groups, Nevada's senate similarly insisted on a sanctity of home provision but passed the bill. The house quickly ratified the upper chamber's action; indeed, the final passage proved so bloodless as to shock the journalists assembled.[126] With the sanctity of the home guaranteed not only from federal officials (in the original bill) but reiterated for state officials (in the acceptance resolutions), the West resisted its often-surly progressive federalism and embraced Sheppard Towner more than any other region.

Why the opposition among the states' progressives in Congress (such as Borah and King) did not translate to state legislative opposition is perhaps a puzzling finding. Western acceptance of Sheppard-Towner cannot be ascribed to the shifting electorate after the Nineteenth Amendment: women had voted in the West before other regions of the country, so the threat of newly enfranchised, politically angry women could not be leveraged there as elsewhere. Perhaps the relatively poor western states viewed themselves as net beneficiaries of financial redistribution and were simply more sympathetic to grants-in-aid; in other words, their opportunistic federalism was in this case to ignore the doctrine, though as will be elaborated further, that self-interested financial explanation is not sufficient for the rural Midwest, Maine, or some of the other major opponents of Sheppard-Towner.

Regardless, of what made the West, like the South, so easily accept Sheppard-Towner, it is clear that our traditionally perceived strongholds of federalism—the West and especially the South—were not the ones invoking it here, as the popular account of that doctrine would hold. It was the Midwest and especially the Northeast—the regions where the memory of the Civil War should have, according to our popular accounts, made them hostile to invoking states' rights—that instead were the ones most vocally supporting the tradition of states' rights that had existed since the Founding.

The Midwest

Although the Midwest does not usually come to mind as a bastion of states' rights protest, and though most of its states would have been net beneficiaries of redistribution, state legislatures in that region offered a surprising amount of resistance to Sheppard-Towner. Irritated protests about grants-in-aid were not confined to the South, as the midwestern states' experience with Sheppard-Towner shows. While nearly all the states of the region opted into Sheppard-Towner by 1923, that final acceptance masks a significant level of regional hostility that first had to be overcome and the frequency with which state officials believed themselves qualified to participate in federal constitutionalism. In other words, they understood their role to include the policing of constitutional federalism, rather than merely ceding constitutional adjudication to the courts

Passage of Sheppard-Towner was not troubled in all midwestern states. The legislative history of the quasi–Southern Missouri more closely matched those of its fellow former slave states than its other neighbors. Despite the efforts of the *St. Louis Post-Dispatch* to appeal to the examples of holdouts Massachusetts and New York in "restor[ing] constitutional government," both of Missouri's houses agreed to the bill on a voice vote.[127] Minnesota legislators had a bloodless preemptive passage before the ink was even dry in Congress, with only one dissenter—a lawyer—opposing the bill in either house.[128] Michigan's Senate passed it on a 75–13 vote in the house and a 23–7 vote in the senate. A few legislators asked to make remarks, citing constituents' beliefs or lobbying, but none raised even oblique constitutional issues.[129] President Harding's home state of Ohio was even more firm in its support, with a particularly pliant senate giving a unanimous roll call vote and only nominal dissent raised in the house (two Republicans broke ranks to vote against it).[130]

Wisconsin offered an interesting test case, as perhaps the leading state that mixed progressive substantive policies with a strong commitment to Tenth Amendment decentralization. The state's progressive governor,[131] Republican

John Blaine, delivered blistering states' rights speeches in his addresses beginning the legislative sessions. Seething about the Esch-Cummins Act, in his first address in January 1921, Blaine protested against the federal government taking control of *intrastate* railroads, adding that he not only had filed a lawsuit in his previous capacity as attorney general but asking the legislature to warn Congress and the Interstate Commerce Commission off of violating "the indeafeasible [*sic*] constitutional right [of] the state of Wisconsin to conduct its own affairs . . . without interference from Washington."[132] Angry as he was about that, grants-in-aid were his particular target in 1921. Blaine warned: "More and more the federal government is taking over the powers of the states, and our nation is in a headlong rush to centralize all government at Washington . . . a dangerous tendency, and we should guard against such centralization." This was being accomplished, he continued, through one of two methods: the first, "under the pretense of regulating interstate commerce," and the second, "a species of bribery . . . [which] need not succeed unless the state gives its consent." This "species of bribery"—grants-in-aid—were, he conceded, often "desirable," "in the interests of humanity," and "sought . . . to coerce the less progressive states into adopting certain legislation." Be that as it may, he concluded, the states should generally undertake the same measures independently, and thus he urged the legislators to decline the federal nudge.[133] The legislature was at least somewhat receptive to their progressive governor's pleas against taking grants-in-aid like Sheppard-Towner, passing the states' rights resolution with which the book began.

Thus, a Wisconsin paper had reason for hope in approvingly noting Maine governor Percival Baxter's states' rights veto of his own state's participation and wish that other states would follow suit.[134] Perhaps Wisconsin, too, would balance progressivism and federalism. But the tension between those two commitments went slack: Madison's house initially approved the bill without opposition (though roughly one-third of the body was absent or did not vote) and then agreed to the senate's barely passed version, with only a handful of dissenters.[135]

Nebraska's 1923 session mirrored that of Madison, with legislators resentfully accepting the aid while backhandedly protesting it. When it came time to accept or reject the appropriation, Nebraska's legislators continued to participate in a practice they claimed to despise. A unanimous roll call vote approved it in the senate, while two Democrats and a Republican dissented in the house, explaining their votes on federalism grounds.[136] The year before, Nebraska's legislature had actually agreed to a protest resolution, grumbling that federal grants-in-aid generated excessive taxes on state citizens as well as inappropriate federal control over state institutions.[137] In 1923, the year they approved Sheppard-Towner, legislators apparently decided to be consistent: Senator Anderson had offered an even more explicitly states' rights protest, which the leadership bottled in committee. Another representative resurrected a similar bill calling for the repeal of all such aid laws in 1925, but this was killed—with Senator Anderson himself having repented and now backing such conditional grants. In an exceptionally strong instance of deference to Washington's constitutional politics, the Speaker of the House took the time to explain his vote on grounds that he did "not think [he was] competent to criticize the Federal Government."[138]

Throughout the rest of the Midwest, passage was dicey and often required external intervention, especially in upper houses or where efforts to expedite passage (requiring supermajorities) foundered. Although Iowa's federal legislators Horace Mann Towner and William Kenyon—whom Harding had since appointed as a federal judge—had been among the architects of the federal bill, its papers split and the Des Moines state house was less enthused.[139] Early newspaper coverage of the 1923 session discussed Representative Gallagher's protests against grants-in-aid, whether for the road bill or Sheppard-Towner, as violations of states' rights, though reports correctly predicted most of his allies would fall away when it came time to actually reject money.[140] Intense women's lobbying reversed a house appropriation committee vote, with only Gallagher willing to speak out against the bill in the end.[141] Although Iowa's house passed the acceptance resolution by comfortable margins in two votes, enough senators stayed firm to make the vote tight, with the vote even failing in February 1923.[142]

That was also what briefly happened in South Dakota, where legislators overcame a procedural bump to approve the bill.[143] Thus, South Dakota's legislature did not cross its Republican governor William H. McMaster, who had implored the legislature to pass the bill with a religious guilt trip: "Maternity and childhood," McMaster declared, "possess certain inalienable rights. . . . There are certain things in this world which are bigger and more important than the almighty dollar. Men of old followed the Star of the East and brought gifts. The glory of old still hallows the days of nativity."[144] Whether the legislators agreed with this theological imperative—and thus feared divine retribution—or were simply uneasy about political repercussion, they fulfilled the governor's request to pass the bill.

Opposition was even stiffer in their neighbor to the north, where it was uncharacteristically centered in the lower chamber. Although North Dakota's legislators had passed a resolution to Congress on behalf of Sheppard-Towner proposals in 1921, that support quickly faded.[145] After unanimous passage in North Dakota's senate—an ostensibly one-party Republican body riven between two bitterly opposed ideological factions—the bill narrowly failed in the house.[146] Minnie Craig, a first-term but influential Non-Partisan League–aligned Republican who would become state speaker in the early thirties, had to switch her vote from aye to nay to force a reconsideration. One member requested to make a statement likely designed to antagonize his foes in the left-leaning Non-Partisan League, characterizing Sheppard-Towner as "the most un-American, socialistic and iniquitous piece of legislation the Federal Government has ever put on its statute books."[147] Unfortunately for that representative, Mrs. Craig's effort to bring the bill back up succeeded, with decisive, almost 4–1 approval the following day.[148]

Indiana also followed the pattern of passage after a failed senate vote. Five Republicans joined with all fourteen of the body's Democrats to initially block passage by an expedited rule (twenty-one Republicans voted to accept Sheppard-Towner) before passing it by 30–12 a week later.[149]

In addition to the many near-misses, Kansas and Illinois actually rejected the appropriation and held out on Sheppard-Towner, though in later years Topeka eventually relented while Springfield's resistance outlasted the program. Illinois's senate passed the bill, but its house offered a terse acceptance of a negative committee report.[150] Resistance in Illinois is fairly easy to explain. Although the federal bill had caught the American Medical Association and its allied groups off-guard, by the time the bill reached Illinois, the base of the organization's lobbying arm, they had been able to mobilize.[151] The AMA received support, as the conservative *Chicago Tribune* joined the efforts of the medical community. Of those afflicted with "the tendency to crowd more and more improper functions upon the federal government," the editors were blunt: "They must be fought."[152] Moreover, Illinois behaved like other wealthy hold-out states, trying to put together an in-state equivalent to retain control, which the *Tribune* had urged in opposing the federal bill.[153] Kansas's legislative record is harder to understand, since it produced almost no paper trail of any kind—a senate voice vote and a house decision to simply ignore the bill altogether.[154] Four years later, the leadership in Kansas would successfully retry passage, with a handful of senators and roughly a quarter of the house dissenting. One member of the house took the floor to mock the program as a failure of excessive bureaucracy—which Congress had itself rec-

ognized in phasing out the bill—but no other protests were raised.[155] Kansas's
legislative leaders had the good sense, however, to kill a proposed resolution
against grants-in-aid, avoiding the embarrassment of the hollow protests from
the legislatures of Texas, Wisconsin, or Nebraska, all of which took money
anyway.[156] Moreover, Kansas, like Vermont and Connecticut, was the most
consistent in refusing federal grants in the 1920s, the only three states declining both Sheppard-Towner and the Industrial Rehabilitation Act of 1920, the
previous grant in aid program.[157]

In that sense, Kansas, heavily settled by New England abolitionists, merely
followed its long-ago cousins—for it was in the Northeast, not the supposedly
states' rights obsessive Dixie, where opposition to Sheppard-Towner proved
the stiffest. It was in those two nonsouthern regions of the country where
cross-ideological coalitions of conservatives and progressives, even those who
agreed with the narrow policy outcome of Sheppard-Towner, were defensive
of a robust sphere of state sovereignty in which the federal government could
not act. Progressives had an incentive to protect that sphere so they could
build their own regulatory states, and conservatives, especially those interested in limiting federal power, recognized, as Root had warned, that it would
have to be coupled with robust uses of the state police power. But they also,
as the next chapter will more clearly show, criticized or opposed, on principled grounds, even an immensely popular, and ideologically desirable, policy
on the principled grounds their constitutional oaths required them to oppose it.

CHAPTER THREE

Sheppard-Towner II:
Yankee States' Rights

The exercise of that power appears to pass with little or no effective challenge either within or without the Congress. The time has arrived ... to ask every patriotic citizen who loves our country and cherishes its institutions to take note.
—Nathan Miller, governor of New York, address to the New York bar

If the State of Maine refuses Federal Aid and sends forth a strong protest against the expansion of this dangerous and undermining doctrine, all lovers of liberty throughout the nation will take heart. The State of Maine then will be hailed as the leader in the movement to return to the fundamental doctrine of our forefathers, that a state is sovereign and will brook no interference in its own internal affairs.
—Percival Baxter, governor of Maine, Sheppard-Towner veto message

As the previous chapter demonstrated, most states embraced Sheppard-Towner fairly painlessly—certainly in the West, with the South having some minor pockets of resistance, and the Midwest more divided. But in the Northeast— whether the descendants of old Yankees in New England or immigrants in the mid-Atlantic, progressive or conservative, Republican or Democrat—states and state officials exercised their states' prerogative to interpret the Constitution and oppose what they viewed as a violation of it and an invasion of the federal government into the states' police powers—even though the direct financial cost was low but the political cost was often high.

Some still accepted the federal contribution, reasoning that the constitutional evil had already been accomplished with federal passage, so there was little reason to spitefully refuse the grant. But for other state officials, even those, progressive and conservative alike, who were sympathetic to welfare expenditures, the principle of allowing grants-in-aid to cover spheres clearly unconnected to the enumerated powers—and, therefore, federal intervention into the states' police powers—had to be arrested before it continued to grow. That opposing Sheppard-Towner, a low-cost maternity bill that almost literally embodies motherhood and apple pie, was widely believed to be politically unpopular indicates that for many such opponents, the opposition was principled.

As with the Affordable Care Act's exchanges, states raised their constitutional objections by simply refusing cooperation. By not accepting the subsidy and instead appropriating their own supplement, states could cripple the federal effort within their borders. But unlike the current day debates over the Affordable Care Act, which were fairly cleanly sorted ideologically, in the 1920s, progressives joined conservatives in raising states' rights objections to Sheppard-Towner. Conversely, and perhaps surprisingly, looking at Sheppard-Towner and similar health and labor measures through the lens not simply of policy but the constitutionalist framework of progressive federalism perhaps suggests the need for a more nuanced reassessment of the era's figures. By incorporating both state and federal politics, a supposedly reactionary figure like Calvin Coolidge instead looks much more like Al Smith—someone supporting progressive goals at the state level while opposing them at the federal one, someone for whom states' rights and a robust conception of their police powers were deeply linked.

The widespread refusal of states in the Northeast to simply opt into Sheppard-Towner helped keep the issue a live one for a half decade until the coalition in control of Washington changed. As this chapter will show, that widespread refusal also illustrated the sophistication with which state actors— not all, by any means, but many—took seriously constitutional debate, offering far more thorough analysis of the legal issues than either Congress had or the US Supreme Court would have in assessing the constitutionality of Sheppard-Towner in 1923. Finally, although present elsewhere, as the previous chapter showed, the political fights over Sheppard-Towner showed that many state officials took their constitutional obligations extremely seriously, opposing a policy some personally supported and which they had every reason to believe their voters did.

Thus, one consequence of the Seventeenth Amendment (and its antecedent Oregon Plan movement) became clear, as state legislators felt that the incentives of senators in Washington and the state governments had sharply diverged, and they consequently they felt the need to protest on behalf of state sovereignty.[1] And protest they did.

The Mid-Atlantic

New York was among the earliest opponents of Sheppard-Towner and remained focused on building a constitutional case against it. Its Republican governor Nathan Miller, a former appellate judge and president of the state bar, condemned the bill on states' rights grounds—which he raised on many other issues—and feared it would be a wedge for inserting unconstitutional federal expansion into a positive-rights welfare state.[2] Governor Miller had zealously defended the authority of New York against federal overreach before,—most notably in opposing federal efforts to displace state regulation of intrastate water-power production and health laws, as well as national Prohibition.

Unlike many of the other leading opponents of the grant-in-aid regime, and some of his own progressive allies in New York state politics who would work with him against Sheppard-Towner, Miller himself was quite clearly a conservative. He had both a past (and future) in corporate law (he was the primary legal counsel opposing the steel seizure in *Youngstown Sheet and Tube v. Sawyer*).[3] He wielded the governor's veto pen aggressively—said to be one of the two most zealous during his term in office—against bills he found unconstitutional.[4] Like many of his time, he argued strenuously against what he saw as class legislation—legislation aiming to specifically benefit only some groups of people rather than society as a whole, which was often that era's code for prolabor legislation.[5]

Even his views of class legislation were more relaxed than some, as he recognized "labor and agriculture, while not constituting distinct groups or classes, have one thing in common: they are and should be the objects of special care by government, as the individual farmer standing alone is utterly unable to cope with modern business conditions, and the individual working man standing alone is utterly unable to deal on terms of equality with his employer."[6] He argued that this was perfectly compatible with the worker's compensation law he shepherded through, and he also opposed efforts to suppress unions.[7] Though Miller believed inequality in bargaining power required a protective government to step in and ensure safe and healthy workplaces,

Miller opposed minimum wage and old-age pensions on policy grounds, arguing that they were a form of class legislation, and similarly criticized a general
statewide public health-insurance system as an improper uses of state power.
Nonetheless, he did believe the state was obligated to help combat child illness and hence supported the state equivalent of Sheppard-Towner as one of
the many other progressive social welfare policies he had passed.[8]

Miller was thus comfortable across the spectrum of the GOP, from its conservatives to its progressives. Miller himself had been an early ally of the progressive Republican Herbert Hoover, whom Miller had nominated at the 1920
GOP convention (after Hoover declined Franklin Roosevelt's overtures to run
as a progressive Democrat), and Hoover had in turn backed Miller in New
York.[9] Moreover, Miller's legislative right hand in the New York Senate was
Frederick Davenport, a Hamilton College political science professor and recent Progressive Party gubernatorial nominee who had only recently returned
to the GOP and who would rally the New York Republican Party's progressive
faction to join the opposition to Sheppard-Towner.

Miller and his legislative allies were not unthinking reactionaries, and they
repeatedly distinguished the Sheppard-Towner grant-in-aid from federal support for roads and other constitutionally enumerated powers. Moreover, Miller
supported the regulation of even *intrastate* commerce when necessary to
achieve regulation of goods moving across state lines.[10] Miller recognized that
an increasingly integrated economy would mean that much more commerce
crossed state lines and therefore the applicability of federal power to commerce would increase, even as Miller insisted the actual constitutional powers
as well as proper interpretation of those powers would remain the same. The
meaning of the federal commerce power, he insisted, was fixed; it was just that
the Framers had wisely built in a power that would scale up and capture more
economic activity as the nature of that activity became increasingly interstate.

But, in contrast, as Miller explained at a speech to the New York Bar Association, "A discovery appears to have been made by Congress of a new
and hitherto undreamed of power to legislate on any subject which it deems
to involve the general welfare, and under that interpretation it has recently
passed . . . [Sheppard-Towner]." Miller worried that Washington had forfeited
its responsibility to guard constitutional government; as such, he announced,
he would seek to arrest that trend:[11] "The exercise of that power appears to
pass with little or no effective challenge either within or without the Congress.
The time has arrived . . . to ask every patriotic citizen who loves our country
and cherishes its institutions to take note."[12]

The state legislature stood behind Miller, blocking the Duell bill that would have accepted Sheppard-Towner, and instead Albany advanced an alternative, in-house state equivalent drawn up by the progressive Frederick Davenport. The Davenport Bill spent $100,000 of state money; Sheppard-Towner would have matched a state expenditure of $75,000. Thus, in demonstrating their commitment to support the worthwhile aims of the project while rejecting federal intervention, the legislators' proposal actually spent *more* on equivalent maternity programs than the state's contribution to procure a matching federal allotment would have been.[13] As Miller explained late in life, "I refused to accept the state's allotment under the Sheppard Towner Act on the ground that that would inevitably lead to the usurpation of state power by the Federal Government, but we provided for visiting nurses with State Funds."[14]

The social activist and National Consumers League executive Florence Kelley, who considered Sheppard-Towner the crowning achievement of her career, found this display of constitutional nitpicking incredible: "If states' rights do not trouble the people of Virginia, once the home of Jefferson Davis and the headquarters of the Confederacy, what ails Governor Miller? Why does he remain, at this late day, still unreconstructed?"[15]

Kelley may not have been a fan, but the *New York Times* backed its governor, praising his Bar Association speech for its rousing defense of constitutional decentralization. Before approvingly excerpting Miller's specific textual arguments, the *Times* wistfully insisted that Americans of all regions had once guarded states' rights "and were jealous of federal ingestion in their affairs." Now, the people "have been blind or easy about it of late." The result was that in DC, "they have not merely a paternal, but a maternal government, as the Sheppard Towner law shows. . . . Sentimentalists, Socialists, cranks, and job hunters are busy. . . . Economy means the finding of new ways to bleed the taxpayers, new grants at the dictations of coteries of busybodies, new posts for the ever-lasting meddling, muddling federal supervisors and regulators of all things and persons."[16]

A very public, rather acrimonious fight gripped New York politics for the next year. Critics, especially women's organizations, attacked Miller for neglecting his self-professed claims to "economy"—the era's term for fiscal conservatism—by rejecting funds on behalf of a "theoretic prejudice."[17] At a public debate, the bewildered United Organization for the Sheppard-Towner Maternity Bill struggled to understand "why, aside from states rights . . . do you justify [refusing Sheppard-Towner?]"[18]

Miller, for his part, did not think he needed another answer: the Constitution was enough. Indeed, he seemed totally unmoved by such cavalier consti-tutionalism, brushing off reports that showed his position to be an electoral loser.[19] Instead, Miller rebuffed the idea that he was to mirror the public's day-to-day views expressed in polls. If voters did not like his job, they could re-place him in an election. Until then, he said, he would fight against the slow cession of state power that was both "unconstitutional" and "utterly contrary to our scheme of government."[20] Miller was not wholly without support: per-suaded by his arguments, the Women's Municipal League of New York re-voked their endorsement of Sheppard-Towner and decided that they too agreed such programs should be state, not federal, endeavors.[21]

As part of the 1922 campaign, Miller's ally Davenport, the progressive state senator who sponsored the in-house state maternity bill, published a lengthy piece in the *New York Times* defending Miller's record. The progres-sive Davenport highlighted two of Miller's great accomplishments in particu-lar: "economy" and state-level progressive legislation protecting health. But, in a lengthy aside, taking up roughly one-fourth of the op-ed, Davenport ex-plained that Miller had done so in a way that preserved the constitutional order and blocked policies that would "[drag] the State Governments at the chariot wheels of the National Government."[22]

Prohibition politics, however, made Miller's position a short-lived stance. In the 1922 elections, New Yorkers returned former governor Al Smith to Al-bany, in addition to giving his party narrow control of the Senate.[23]

As the effort to nominate Al Smith—first in 1924 and later in 1928— would later indicate, Smith was widely viewed as a leader in the country's progressive movement, one who had pushed New York to undertake a variety of protective, prolabor regulations and who had successfully remade the state court to protect rather than block progressive legislation. Throughout his ca-reer, from his early days until his marginalization as a Liberty Leaguer, Smith demonstrated a fairly consistent belief in an active, progressive state—and a weak federal government. In other words, Smith epitomized progressive fed-eralism.[24] Although Smith was a committed states' rights man who would end his days as a pariah in opposition to the New Deal expansion of federal power, he and his allies criticized Miller on grounds of economy, and Smith pledged to accept Sheppard-Towner. But even then, and consistent with progressive federalism, Smith conceded the core of the Republican's constitutional claim. Miller was right, Smith suggested, to criticize the principle "that the Federal Government should make appropriations of this kind. . . . The federal govern-ment should [not] in any way subsidize the States for any activity that wholly belongs to the state." But where Smith's predecessor had erred was not the substance of the protest but its venue: as the new governor explained, "If you quarrel with the principle involved, the place to air your argument is at Washington and not in Albany," especially considering New York was sending its tax money to DC either way.[25]

Embedded in Smith's exhortation on behalf of state acceptance of Sheppard-Towner funding were the seeds of one principle and one prudential calculation that would continue to reappear in state Sheppard-Towner debates. The prudential calculation would characterize many a future legislator's thought, eventually swaying, as noted, even states' rights obsessive Texans: the money unjustly taken from the citizens of a state would still be spent, and thus it was irresponsible to punish that state's citizens for the constitutional sins of Washington.

Strikingly, and unlike most of the other state officials debating Sheppard-Towner, Smith also suggested the weak version of an institutional reason to accept Sheppard-Towner, one that some others would make more explicitly (and which Smith would himself eventually reject in the context of Prohibition). Smith argued, in effect, that it is not the province of state officials to interpret the federal Constitution. According to this logic of unitary interpretation, the place for national constitutional issues to be decided is Washington, DC. (In its strongest form, the logic of this argument is such that decision-making is only by the Supreme Court: this is judicial supremacy.)[26] Thus, Smith would accept the already appropriated federal money, even though no one believed that Smith actually endorsed federal grants-in-aid. After all, he and Maryland's Democratic governor Albert Ritchie were regarded as the nation's two most prominent critics of the so-called 50/50 plans, one nickname for grants-in-aid.[27]

In other words, Smith endorsed progressive federalist arguments against the constitutionality of Sheppard-Towner, as one would expect considering his well-established views on behalf of a limited federal government and an expansive state. But, unlike many of the state legislators and governors in the era (including, later, himself), he disagreed that state legislatures and the state appropriation process, rather than Congress or the federal courts, were the appropriate venue for raising that legal argument.

New Jersey governor Edward Edwards, a Democrat in a fairly competitive state, followed the path not of his fellow Democrat Al Smith but of the Republican Nathan Miller—only he did so without any legislative support, as, unlike in New York, the Garden State's Republicans tended to favor

Sheppard-Towner—and the voters had favored them with massive superma-jorities. Edwards initially, if perhaps disingenuously, claimed agnosticism in presenting the bill to the house during the convocation of the legislature, and the legislature initially voted to accept the bill by huge margins (unanimously in the Senate and by a 33–10 spread in the House).[28] Veto-proof margins did not deter the fiercely states' rights Edwards from issuing a veto anyway to de-cry "paternalism."

"As one who believes in the preservation of the rights of the sovereign states as distinguished from centralized government," Edwards explained, "I feel that every measure which tends to weaken or destroy that distinction should be defeated." Regardless of his earlier professed agnosticism, "mature consideration" of Sheppard-Towner convinced him that it was just "another evidence of the rapidly developing tendency of the Federal Government to en-croach upon the police powers of the states."[29] Edwards picked up a handful of votes in the state senate (for an 11–3 spread) but actually *lost* ten votes in the lower chamber's successful override (43–10).[30] New Jersey had signed onto Sheppard-Towner—though Edwards would continue to fight it and the equally centralizing Sheppard Prohibition Amendment—in his new post as one of the state's senators in Washington.[31]

Republicans in Pennsylvania behaved like their copartisans across the Del-aware River: though their congressional delegation resisted Sheppard-Towner, legislators and Governor William Sproul accepted participation with next to no fanfare or controversy—for example, with a 196–1 vote in the house.[32]

New England

Contrary to our association of New England Republicans with centralization and southern Democrats with states' rights, with it was the former, with one ex-ception, who staunchly resisted Sheppard-Towner. In other words, Sheppard-Towner offers support for the argument of Henry Adams—the Harvard histo-rian descended from both John and John Quincy Adams—that states' rights was "as sound and true a doctrine . . . as dear to New England as to Virginia" and one that "Massachusetts [had] appealed to as often and almost as loudly as South Carolina."[33] For example, against the efforts of the zealously proslav-ery, antebellum Deep South denying rights to sojourning free blacks from the North, Massachusetts politicians staked the protection of its citizens as both an obligation and marker of its own state sovereignty.[34]

If New England was the center of the era's Republicanism, Massachusetts was the center of the center in the early 1920s: Vice President Coolidge, House Speaker Frederick Gillett, and the de facto majority leader of the Senate, Henry Cabot Lodge, all hailed from the Bay State.

Massachusetts's politics reflected an odd synthesis perhaps best encapsulated in the future president: a fundamental conservatism that tried to best protect the core logic of a market economy while acknowledging and correcting for structural changes induced by industrialization and the consolidation of capital. As America was changing, Bay State legislators thought seriously about and responded to those changes, but they still remained committed to their old beliefs and were especially hostile to anything hinting of radicalism, centralization, or attacks on the Constitution.

Thus, Massachusetts was the first state to enact a minimum wage commission and the second to enact a worker's compensation plan, but its voters would overrule their legislators and ferociously oppose the federal child labor amendment. (This was true even though the Bay State had already strictly instituted such a domestic policy and arguably would want to suppress competitive disadvantage or a race to the bottom enabling southern child labor to undercut wages.)[35] In other words, while instituting protective legislation at the state level, albeit more cautiously than, say, Wisconsin, Massachusetts embodied the core logic of progressive federalism.

Seemingly pointing toward support of Sheppard-Towner, the state had generously funded maternity health programs—with even the usually frugal Calvin Coolidge urging expanded appropriation.[36] In his second year as governor, Coolidge, having moved from the state house (where, as floor leader, he had shepherded many of those progressive bills through), defended his skepticism of new legislation by explaining that most reforms necessary to update government had already been accomplished in his "stupendous" first year as governor and the years beforehand. In sharp contrast to Coolidge's first message, which had urged legislative innovation before setting forth the list of policy goals that would become his list of accomplishments in the 1920 speech,[37] Coolidge argued it was now simply time to determine if they had worked: "In general, it is time to conserve, to retrench rather than to reform, a time to stabilize the administration of the present laws rather than to seek new legislation."[38]

In short, perhaps Massachusetts's reformers were victims of their own success and reform fatigue: after all, the changes had been implemented, the state's labor unions had been appeased, and moderates and conservatives had

turned hostile to both labor and government in the wake of the Boston Police Strike and the various war measures that induced conservatism in America more generally.[39] Upon taking office, Coolidge's successor Channing
Cox echoed those words, with his first address to the general court explaining that "the needs of Massachusetts today do not so much require great legislative reform . . . [as] reforms and improvement in administration."[40] He
continued, "We are just emerging from years of intense feeling, tremendous
effort, and unusual sacrifice. . . . The people of our Commonwealth . . . are
somewhat weary of the prolonged strain. They desire to return to the normal
scope of daily action."[41] Whether the result of ideological shift or programmatic fulfillment, Massachusetts's political leaders suddenly seemed uninterested in political change—and they registered it in skeptically considering
Sheppard-Towner.

As became apparent during the public meetings and debates on Sheppard-
Towner in the early months of 1922, not all the state's citizens appreciated
its leaders' hesitation, but even many bill supporters expressed palpable discomfort with federal power. The contour of the legislative hearings in Boston were quite similar to the concurrent debate taking place in Albany. Elias
Field, a city attorney for Boston, channeled Al Smith in explaining that the
question was not whether the bill was good or bad, constitutional or not, but
only whether Massachusetts would forfeit the money to other states or take
it—a position Sheppard-Towner supporter Senator Henry Cabot Lodge—
ironically the most conservative of Theodore Roosevelt's inner circle—
endorsed by telegram. Most of the medical personnel and social workers tes-
tifying on its behalf were quite enthused, but the testimony of Dr. Eugene
Kelley, the state commissioner of public health, "plainly represented a conflict of conviction." Kelley believed in the value of maternity information but
shared critics' anxieties about federal intervention in state affairs. Such skeptics could at least take comfort, he said, in knowing that the bill actually had
little possibility for federal control, but, he pleaded, whether Massachusetts
decided to opt into the matching program or run it entirely in house, he hoped
it would be funded at least as generously as the federal plan. Opponents, including the leadership of a women's Catholic organization, offered the standard criticisms, attacking the bill on both constitutional states' rights grounds
and more generic prudential worries about big government precedents. Frank
Dresser, a lawyer representing various manufacturing interests, managed to
blend both strands in offering the most eloquent critique of the testimony. The
general expansion of federal power, he lamented, not only violated the specific

text of the Constitution but made citizens forget "we owe as much to the flag of the Commonwealth in those matters of state sovereignty as to the Stars and Stripes on questions of national sovereignty."[42]

Lodge's pragmatic support for state participation (on top of his own vote for the bill in the US Senate) did not prevent him from being besieged by a cadre of women's activists reviling the conservatism of Massachusetts' congressional delegation in its opposition to Sheppard-Towner, among other things. New York, Connecticut, and Massachusetts, they grumbled, often seemed to be the only holdouts to a progressive legislative agenda popular in the rest of the nation.[43] They were not wrong to think that: congressional voting patterns did show that the stiffest opposition to Sheppard-Towner appeared in Massachusetts and New York, though the usually federalist and relatively conservative Lodge voted to support final passage.[44] Massachusetts's stand against the maternity bill soon would got even lonelier in late 1922, as the fall of Nathan Miller and his allies had made Massachusetts the unquestioned leader in the fight against Sheppard-Towner.

On March 1, 1922, the general court offered its first salvo: a redrafting, first proposed on February 16, of an alternative to the Sheppard-Towner acceptance bill.[45] The new draft made clear that state legislators believed themselves to be participants in and bound to help enforce the US Constitution. As such, the bill began by warning of the "growing tendency in the national Congress to undertake governmental activities which have formerly been solely left to the jurisdiction of the states," particularly through grants-in-aid. Thus, it issued two orders: the first requested that the supervisor of administration collect a list and history of all such grants the state received. The other section was more aggressive: "Doubt exists as to the constitutional right of the federal Congress . . . to enact . . . the Sheppard-Towner Act." Therefore, the attorney general was asked three questions. First, in his opinion, is its enactment within the powers of Congress? Second, would Massachusetts's acceptance "waive its rights as a sovereign state to contest the constitutionality of said act before the Courts of the United States?" And third, what course should Massachusetts take if, in his judgement, "the law is unconstitutional?" The house quickly concurred with this course of action.[46]

A little over two months later, Massachusetts Attorney General Weston Allen submitted a blistering response to the legislature.[47] After a perfunctory acknowledgment that it was "a matter of considerable delicacy" to make an assertion of constitutionality before the US Supreme Court had acted, he offered a distinctly Jeffersonian claim that the powers "expressly granted to

Congress, including the power to make all laws necessary and proper for carrying the powers enumerated into execution, are all stated in Article 1, Section 8." Everything else, he asserted, citing Supreme Court caselaw, was reserved to the people by the Tenth Amendment. Restated another way, "The powers given to the federal government are only those which are necessary to the existence and effective maintenance of the nation."[48]

"Maternity and infancy," Allen concluded, were "manifestly . . . within the scope of the police power," which he again attributed to the Tenth Amendment. The constitutional framework made the allocation of the police power abundantly clear, with the grudging acknowledgment of one recent, unfortunate exception: "There is no grant of power to Congress to regulate the internal affairs of the States (excepting that given by the Eighteenth Amendment)."[49] Those Tenth Amendment police powers were comprehensive and indivisible: "Each state has the right and the duty to provide for the general welfare of its people, and in those respects the authority of the State is complete, unqualified, *and exclusive*."[50] That right and duty—note that Weston insisted it was a state duty—were also unalienable: if the powers "are outside the powers conferred upon Congress by the Constitution, and within the field of the powers reserved to the states, the act is not made constitutional and valid by the circumstance that those powers will be only exercised in or with respect to those states whose legislatures accept it, for Congress cannot assume and the legislatures cannot yield the powers reserved to the States by the Constitution."[51]

The violation was not merely the federal government expanding beyond its authorized powers into the exclusive domain of the states—though, as noted previously, that in itself was objectionable—but, Allen feared, states would soon find themselves beholden to conditional federal demands. Grants-in-aid might begin cooperatively, but they would end coercively. "Every state is required," he explained, "to designate or authorize the designation of a State agency to cooperate with the Children's Bureau. . . . [The state] is required . . . to submit to the Children's Bureau detailed plans for carrying out the provision of the act within such State, such plans to be subject to the approval of the Board."[52] After describing the reporting procedures, Allen warned,

> Thus, in effect, a system is created . . . by which plans are to be
> submitted to federal boards, the nature of which appears to be wholly
> undetermined. . . . Those plans are to be administered by [federal
> agents] . . . and control over the conduct of State Agencies is vested in

the Children's Bureau . . . by the provision authorizing the withholding [of funds when] it is determined . . . [that] funds have not been properly expended.

Allen then expanded on his position that Sheppard-Towner did not derive from an enumerated federal power, largely restating the arguments of Madison and Jefferson against Hamilton. Congressional supporters, he observed, had justified Sheppard-Towner "on the ground that it is a provision for the general welfare of the people of the United States." That phrase appeared twice in the Constitution: once in the preamble, which "contains no grant of power" (according to his citation of the then-recent but now canonical *Jacobson v. Massachusetts* [1905]), and once in the tax power. But the use of general welfare in the tax power, he argued, was not an independent grant of power but a catch-all preview of the list specifically enumerated thereafter. As support for this position, Allen cited the constitutional convention, Madison (both as Publius and president), and a variety of court cases, from Marshall to the present, though he conceded that Hamilton had been momentarily successful in pushing the "contraverted" reading that Congress now advanced.[53] But even if the Hamiltonian reading was the right one, Allen argued, Sheppard-Towner would *still* be unconstitutional because it allocated money for the good of the specific participating states, not the *general* welfare: "It is yet to be determined that Congress has the power to appropriate to the states . . . revenues raised from the people of the United States for national purposes."[54]

After that lengthy discourse on the nature of the tax power, Allen quoted James Monroe's Cumberland Road bill veto message to explain that the acceptance of unconstitutional funds would not preclude constitutional questioning: "Although [the states] may assent to the appropriation of money within their limits for such purposes, they can grant no power of jurisdiction or sovereignty by special compacts with the United States. This power can be granted only by an amendment to the Constitution, and in the mode prescribed by it."[55] In effect, Allen argued, states could not voluntarily waive any aspect of sovereignty—either responsibility to care for their own citizens or control over their welfare policies—short of an Article V modification. Allen hedged his bets, however, asserting that although "whether . . . the state . . . can contract away its sovereign rights . . . is a matter of grave doubt," he nonetheless suggested doing so would weaken the state's case and thus, on prudential grounds, held that Massachusetts ought to reject Sheppard-Towner funding.[56] Allen then interpreted several precedents to suggest that the Commonwealth could serve as a party to such a challenge, especially since he doubted that court precedents allowed citizen challenges to federal expenditures.[57] (On this latter point, he would prove correct.) For good measure, Allen added a policy observation to the state's legislators, urging them to remember that the funding scheme was somewhat equalized across states' disadvantaging net-revenue contributors like Massachusetts and redistributing to poorer states.

In May, Representative Henry L. Shattuck (who had sponsored the initial request for Allen's opinion) moved to authorize Allen to begin the lawsuit; the senate joined as well.[58] Although James Beck, the ultraconservative US solicitor general and future member of Congress (R-PA), accepted the obligation to defend the law in court, it appears that he believed it to be unconstitutional and discreetly encouraged Massachusetts's challenge.[59] Led by Governor Morrow of Kentucky, ten states joined the Association of Land Grant Colleges—presumably defending the agricultural grant-in-aid programs created by the 1914 Smith-Lever Act—and filed countersuits.[60] *Massachusetts v. Mellon* soon began weaving its way through the courts.

The case garnered widespread coverage in local newspapers and spurred a fair amount of public debate, with Woodrow Wilson's former vice president Thomas R. Marshall perhaps the most prominent public backer. Although remembered as a progressive, the Indiana Democrat praised the Massachusetts lawsuit for reminding Americans that the Civil War ended slavery but not states' rights. Engaging one of the major points raised by Sheppard-Towner supporters, Marshall contended that he had long agonized over his administration's decision to fund state road-building but concluded that the power to authorize post roads gave him explicit textual support. Anticipating Justice Robert Jackson's *Wickard v. Filburn* (1942) opinion (or especially Justice Stephen Breyer's 1995 *U.S. v. Lopez* dissent), Marshall feared a loose causal chain for general welfare could result in funding delousing programs on dogs, because dogs give fleas to humans and aggregated human unhappiness affected the general welfare. Such could not, he contended, have been the purpose of the spending clause.[61]

As the case wound its way up the courts, a defensive Governor Channing Cox, echoing the logic of Nathan Miller in New York, used his second inaugural address to make the case for progressive federalism and remind listeners that Massachusetts was implementing analogous maternity legislation even if it had declined the federal grant in Sheppard-Towner.[62] But whether there would be a Sheppard-Towner to decline—or whether the courts would vindicate Allen's challenge—remained to be seen.

A year to the day that Massachusetts instructed Allen to begin his suit, the New Hampshire Senate was again considering Sheppard-Towner, a modified version with a proviso clarifying that the state would still expend its own money should the Supreme Court overturn the program. (New Hampshire had been among those states preemptively approving the program in 1921, which it did on apparently uncontroversial voice votes.)[63] Awareness of that possibility—and warnings about its consequences—had been raised in New Hampshire, with the League of Women Voters distributing a pamphlet that explicitly assuaged states' rights fears but warned that a negative decision in the legal challenges to Sheppard-Towner would wipe out federal participation in vocational education, agriculture, and other policies.[64]

A pair of retired military officers in the New Hampshire House offered heated opposition in "one of the liveliest debates of the session." The Democratic Minority Leader, Colonel James Lyford, and former rear admiral Joseph Murdoch, a Republican, each condemned Sheppard-Towner on states' rights grounds, concluding that the buildup of government in Washington had already "made us the most governed country in the world." The youngest member of the house, Representative Keleher, joined the two old veterans but focused his criticism on the bill's ineffective implementation. Against Murdoch's bill to retract New Hampshire's participation stood the largely progressive Republican leadership, both formal and informal.

Unlike other northeastern states, New Hampshire's progressives lined up fully in support of Sheppard-Towner. Among the other New Hampshire progressives in support of Sheppard-Towner were Majority Leader Stevens, representative Robert Bass (who had served as governor in 1911 and 1912 before being dumped for supporting Theodore Roosevelt over Taft), and future governor John Winant—a powerful base of support that made the Granite State unusually sympathetic for New England.[65]

After killing Murdoch's bill, the house passed a Sheppard-Towner acceptance on a voice vote; the senate followed with 15–5 support two days later. Before the final vote, the senate agreed to modify the bill and incorporate a sanctity of home provision.[66] However, much muted opposition there was in the state—the committee considering Sheppard-Towner was said to be divided—New Hampshire legislators balked at casting votes against it.[67] One could perhaps argue that New Hampshire—after all, a fairly economically libertarian state like its New England neighbors—chose to hide behind the ongoing lawsuit, but the DC circuit had *upheld the bill* a few weeks before.[68] Instead, it appears that the leadership of the party (and in a one-party state, thus the legislature) was simply more supportive of federal action. The 1920s saw the New Hampshire Republican Party at its most bifactional period, with John Winant briefly leading a progressive faction that controlled the party but would soon melt back into the state party's general conservatism.[69] Winant, who sponsored the state's 1921 Sheppard-Towner bill, would later serve as New Hampshire's governor and the first director of the Social Security Board (before quitting in protest of Republican attacks on it).[70] The optics were also overdetermined—it would have taken a particular coldness to spurn representative George Wood, who, in urging support for the bill during the debate, brought his granddaughter to the floor and explained her mother died in childbirth.[71]

The rest of New England would take Massachusetts's lead rather than New Hampshire's, resisting Sheppard-Towner on states' rights grounds and demonstrating the strong strain of northeastern federalism in the era. Rhode Island had declined to act in 1922 and would hold out until 1925. Vermont did likewise, ignoring the bill in 1923 (before approving it by overwhelming margins in 1925).[72] Both houses of the Connecticut legislature quietly approved the enabling act accepting Sheppard-Towner,[73] but Connecticut would become one of three states never to participate when its appropriations committee blocked funding on states' rights grounds.[74] Unfortunately, no roll call data exists, and journalistic interest seemed nonexistent. It is possible that a bipartisan consensus agreed to kill it quietly rather than create an electoral issue.

Although Maine would eventually join Sheppard-Towner during the legislation's dying days, the state long refused participation, largely due to a single individual, Governor Percival Proctor Baxter. Heir to a massive canning fortune (which he would use to personally build Maine's nature preserves), Baxter, then state senate president, assumed the governorship upon the death of his predecessor in 1921 and would remain in office until 1924. Baxter was a lovable crank, and part of that persona included a flinty belief in Maine self-reliance and autonomy from an overweening federal government. At least through the end of the 1920s, Baxter was regarded as a progressive Republican like his frequent correspondent and political ally Herbert Hoover; indeed, he was widely derided as a "socialist" in state politics for his belief in public ownership of Maine's hydropower industry.[75]

As Maine considered the bill in 1922, Franklin Payson, a local landowner, testified to Baxter and his council, arguing that Sheppard-Towner violated the constitutional thinking of America's leading constitutional theorists: Washington, Marshall, Lincoln, Lodge, and Root (with extensive citations also to Massachusetts attorney general Weston Allen's legal opinions and Chief Justice Taft's recent *Bailey v. Drexel Furniture* decision against a punitive federal tax on goods produced with child labor). Henry Shattuck, the Massachusetts state representative leading the charge against the bill in that state's legislature, similarly provided helpful material the state had collected (such as Allen's full reports), lobbying Baxter against the bill in the hopes they could prevent the states "becom[ing] no more than agents of the Federal Government."[76]

Neither was probably necessary. To say that Baxter despised the federal government overstates the matter, but only slightly.[77] In his 1923 inaugural address, Baxter celebrated Prohibition and hailed the state's legacy as "the pioneer Prohibition state"—so far so good for a law-and-order Republican from the state whose name gave birth, and international infamy, to temperance laws.[78] But whereas Winthrop called for Plymouth to be a beacon on behalf of godliness, Baxter proposed Maine set an example of self-government by vigorously enforcing Prohibition free of federal intervention. He thus instructed the legislature to avoid federal aid and show that Prohibition could be enforced without reliance on the federal government.[79] In the same speech, he warned of creeping federal power that would eventually culminate in a "paternalism" that would sap individual dignity and self-reliance.[80]

Finally, his best-remembered legacy and life's work, Baxter State Park, was designed to be a stick in the eye of Washington, DC. Baxter had become fascinated with the Maine wilderness during his youth and, failing to persuade the state to develop the site as a nature preserve, he resolved to preserve it himself. Over the course of several decades, Baxter used his family fortune to accumulate the land around Mount Katahdin by any means necessary, whether simple purchases, trades, or cajoling local timber barons in exchange for land he had purchased elsewhere. Baxter did not hand this over in one big gift, however. Beginning in 1931,[81] Baxter would cede smaller parcels at the opening of most legislative sessions. He did this, he said, in order to make different legislatures, governors, and officials agree to his terms, which he felt would make them even more binding and precedential. Those terms were simple: that the land be preserved "forever . . . in the natural wild state" *by the state of Maine*.[82] Nor was Baxter kidding about the terms: when state officials discussed cooperating with the federal government, Baxter ceased his donations until said officials repented of their mistake and promised to keep the park separate, free of federal control.[83] It remains so today.

But nowhere was this hatred of federal oversight clearer than the politics of Sheppard-Towner. In July 1922, Baxter refused the provisional gubernatorial acceptance authorized by the bill—though, like Miller in New York, he had the state fund an equivalent program (though not as generously). Baxter had the *Kennebec Journal* print a statement declining acceptance, in which he explained that he empathized with supporters' "humanitarian . . . and unselfish" sincerity, and he conceded that the substance of the bill itself was "reasonably moderate." Nonetheless, he explained, backers failed to consider the dangerous precedent it would entail. "Reform by unconstitutional methods cannot be enduring," he reminded his constituents. Baxter then cited an excerpt of Taft's opinion in *Drexel*—the same opinion cited by Payson's testimony—holding that such reform without textual change threatened the very covenant of American governance. Moderate as the bill might be, Baxter insisted, it was an "entering wedge" which he hoped Maine's congressional legislators would not push further. Baxter then used language that hinted at both Elihu Root and compact theory: "Maine will loyally support the Union, in all matters that come under the provisions of the Federal Constitution, but the time has arrived when the people of this State will jealously guard the rights inherent in them as a Sovereign people *and will accept the responsibilities the possession of such rights impose*."[84]

As the next session of the legislature convened, he told its members to consider the bill—after subjecting them to a long-winded tirade about the creep of national government and a passive-aggressive warning that "the principle of the state's sovereignty is involved in this question." Thus, "the action that this Legislature takes on the Sheppard-Towner Bill will be of deep interest to students of government throughout the country."[85] For even more subtlety, Baxter added that "the time has come for the states of the Union to hold to principle and to carefully scrutinize all offers of 'Federal Aid' before accepting them."[86]

Unfortunately for Baxter, his legislators did not take the hint. The committee considering the bill added a sanctity-of-home provision but forwarded it to the house at large.[87] After some debate, Dora Pinkham, the bill's sponsor, rallied support and sent the bill to Baxter's desk, on a 72–65 vote in the house and 17–11 vote in the senate.[88] Since Maine is unfortunately the only state to record its floor debates of Sheppard-Towner in full, it is worth presenting the contour of those discussions.

During these debates, Representative Harold Weeks asserted it to be his duty to vote against the bill for infringing on state prerogative and quoted an earlier speech from Governor Baxter that declared that he would "stand with New York, Massachusetts, and Rhode Island. . . . The State of Maine will not sell its birthright."[89] Weeks added that the physicians he knew, and the women who testified at a local meeting in his small town of Fairfield, had opposed the bill, and he implied that the national lobbying movement purporting otherwise was manufactured (he specifically invoked Congresswoman Alice Robertson's warnings, presumably about the Women's Joint Congressional Committee [WJCC]). Failing to see either the obvious conflict of interest or the false dichotomy he posed, Weeks added that these physicians explained that meeting with a doctor (meaning one of them) was far superior to the pamphlets attached to Sheppard-Towner.[90] Weeks bemoaned inefficient and wasteful, overhead-riddled bureaucracies in DC—which were, moreover, unconstrained, as the bill contained no penalties for meddlesome government officials, rendering the sanctity-of-home provisions hollow.[91] Finally, he described the question in existential terms:

> The really vital point in this matter is not as to whether we are getting something for nothing. It is whether or not we want to surrender the State rights to the Federal Government. [Conceding that Maine had taken funding before] it seems to me that the time has come when we must stop. . . . We should get away from this doctrine of Socialism and Paternalism and Bolshevism. . . . Save us from a bureaucratic state! Save us from a concentration in Washington of numberless bureaus for the regulation of human affairs![92]

This proved too much for one of Weeks's fellow Republicans, Benedict Maher of Augusta, who noted that concerns about centralization had not been raised for road-building, national guard cooperation, or aid to agricultural research at the university. Maher had evidently not read his Henry Adams, as he incredulously asked, "In Heaven's name, when did it occur to invoke this bogey of centralization in northern New England, up here where we have always stood for the Hamiltonian theory, for the bigger, stronger, centralized government?"[93] Perhaps influenced by the now-discredited but then-dominant Lost Cause–understanding of history that conflated federalism exclusively with southern thought, Maher here expressed a sentiment that others would similarly raise: he wondered just when it was that the Northeast accepted apparently southern interpretations of federal power. (The *Portsmouth Herald* observed that, as of the summer of 1923, only New Hampshire deserted New England to sign up for Sheppard-Towner. By way of contrast, Louisiana was the only southern holdout.)[94]

Other defenders of the bill cited support from physicians they knew, as well as a litany of infant mortality statistics to explain the necessity of Sheppard-Towner. Because international observers had participated in Children's Bureau conferences, some of the more paranoid comments from the opposition warned of foreign bureaucrats teaching the "American Christian mother how to bring up her child"[95] or engaged in other forms of red-baiting. The themes of federalism, states' rights, and decentralization, however, continued to be the primary battleground. Supporters clung to a Hamiltonian interpretation of the spending power of Article I, Section 8, as freestanding rather than attached to other enumerated powers, reiterated that states remained free to set their own policy or decline the money, and insisted that no dangerous, centralizing precedent would be set considering the Smith-Lever Act and other grants-in-aid that already existed. Opponents repeatedly disavowed some or all of those programs, hoping to use Sheppard-Towner as the staging ground to reverse centralization.[96]

As one the eight states refusing Sheppard-Towner in 1923, Maine had, like all of the others, accepted the 1914 Smith-Lever Act, the first of the grants-in-aid in the period. But unlike Connecticut, Kansas, and Vermont, the only three to reject the Industrial Rehabilitation Act of 1920, Maine had accepted the most recent such grant-in-aid program—albeit under a different governor.[97]

In Maine's upper house, Republican senator Harmon Allen attempted to offer a principled distinction between federal aid to roads and food efficiency, which he saw as contributing to military readiness and therefore an enumerated power, and Sheppard-Towner, which, as a purely health law, did not; others echoed the military's claims and reminded him that a healthy population was more important to any war-making than even the best roads.[98]

Governor Baxter's veto message was precise and to the point in echoing the critics of centralization:

> My views on the Sheppard-Towner are well known. . . . I protest against
> the passage of this resolve [b]ecause it is an unwarranted invasion by
> the Federal Government of the sovereign rights of the State of Maine;
> because it establishes in Washington a Federal bureaucracy that is not
> likely to be in sympathy with the government of this State and the
> citizens thereof; because it invades the privacy of our homes; because it
> infers that the State of Maine cannot and will not properly care for those
> of its others and children who need assistance; because it pauperizes
> our state. . . . If the State of Maine refuses Federal Aid and sends forth a
> strong protest against the expansion of this dangerous and undermining

doctrine, all lovers of liberty throughout the nation will take heart. The State of Maine then will be hailed as the leader in the movement to return to the fundamental doctrine of our forefathers, that a state is sovereign and will brook no interference in its own internal affairs.

After a brief reminder that under his leadership Maine had itself offered and would continue to offer similar services, Baxter concluded with a blunt and resolute rallying cry: "Maine will not," he thundered, "sell its birthright for a mess of pottage."[99]

Baxter thus argued Sheppard-Towner would damage both parties in the federal-state relationship. By assuming powers not delegated to it, the federal government would cease to be within its constitutionally lawful boundaries and, thus, suffer a loss of legitimacy. In addition to that specifically constitutional argument, Baxter offered two concerns that were not strictly legal but were not mere policy critiques either. Instead, they struck at the heart of the American project of self-government. First, Sheppard-Towner would further the creation of an independent bureaucracy, with its own institutional desires and needs separate from the control of Maine.[100] Second, especially ironically for someone often accused of "socialist" views in the state's domestic politics, Baxter flirted with red-baiting, discreetly insinuating that bureaucracy, especially in such an issue, led to totalitarian interventions in the home.

Baxter was equally concerned with the dispiriting effect he believed that Sheppard-Towner would have on Maine. As Root, Coolidge, and Senator William Thomas (D-CO) had all observed, whenever the people demanded a service, states needed to be prepared to act in order to avert federal intervention. Baxter agreed, and thus supported Maine's in-house effort to provide maternal health assistance. He worried, however, that the opposite would happen with Sheppard-Towner: federal intervention would sap the autonomy and dignity of a state, converting it from a proud and self-reliant body into a "pauper." Rather than become dependent on the will of another body—the DC Children's Bureau—Maine should do precisely the opposite, and thus Baxter urged his fellow citizens to lead the nation in challenging centralization and constitutional decay.

Perhaps not fully recognizing the depth of Baxter's commitments, Florence Kelley took to personally lobbying the governor, who remained unmoved. Kelley's intervention, futile as it may have been, at least was not as counterproductive as a Children's Bureau official whose attack on Baxter mirrored James Reed's sexist comments in the US Senate. Where Reed had declared the best maternal help would be to find husbands for the Children's Bureau, the bureau official dismissively attributed Baxter's views to his (non)marital status.[101]

More serious pressure came from Augusta, where Dora Pinkham attempted to override Baxter's veto with an equally forceful insinuation: treason. After explaining that worries about federal invasion were silly in a cooperative program, Pinkham dropped the hammer. Baxter's dream of Maine leading a movement to insist on sovereign rights was not a guarantee of liberty. Instead, "[It] sounds almost like a declaration of Civil War." Similarly echoing the Lost Cause interpretation of history, she explained: "We once had a war to decide the question of State rights. We hear about that very seldom in the North." At this point, Carl Miliken, Maine's governor during World War I, was escorted to the dais.[102] A few more words followed this theatrical display, and then the vote. The show proved for naught: by a 47–85 vote, Baxter's veto easily survived. (Baxter had vetoed many bills during that legislative session but had been overridden so many times that one representative laughed that passing override bills was "considered the king of indoor sports" in Maine.)[103]

As Baxter had hoped, his stand had already garnered a fair amount of attention outside of Maine, with national papers listing Maine alongside Massachusetts as the vanguard of American freedom and constitutional fidelity.[104] The publishers of two Indiana newspapers praised Baxter, much to their chagrin. The *Goshen Daily Democrat* particularly appreciated Baxter's efforts to popularize states' rights among Republicans when its own party seemed to have lately abandoned the principle. Thus, it admitted with some embarrassment, only these "new friends for states rights" seemed to be making the doctrine's "last stand."[105] Senator William Borah (R-ID), the famously contrarian western states' rights progressive, responded to Baxter's submission of the veto with a private note of congratulation.[106]

All "lovers of liberty" did not, however, take heart as Baxter dreamed. A little over two months later, during the summer of 1923, the Supreme Court unanimously declined to consider the constitutionality of Sheppard-Towner in two companion cases: those of Massachusetts and Harriet Frothingham, the president of the Woman Patriots.[107] As Nathan Miller had feared in declining to have New York join Massachusetts's suit, Justice George Sutherland insisted that the petitioners lacked standing and, in logic that became foundational to twentieth-century jurisprudence, the Court held that paying taxes to a possibly unconstitutional program did not rise to the status of a justiciable harm.[108] Nor could it stand on behalf of its citizens, as Massachusetts' attorney general Weston Allen had argued. Thus, Sutherland concluded, whatever the constitutionality of Sheppard-Towner—and the opinion professed agnosticism on this question—this case was not the proper vehicle to challenge it. Virginia lawyer and Democratic representative Henry St. George Tucker, who had filed a brief in the cases and remained its most dogged congressional opponent on constitutional grounds, continued, in vain, to find a test case that would meet the Court's jurisdictional command.[109]

Since Massachusetts itself was neither forced to expend anything nor suffered direct compulsion of any kind, it was also not directly harmed. "We are called upon to adjudicate not rights of person or property, not rights of dominion over physical domain, not quasi-sovereign rights actually invaded or threatened, but," Sutherland explained, "abstract questions of political power, of sovereignty, of government."[110]

Sheppard-Towner returned to Maine's legislative thicket in 1925, armed not only with an apparent judicial imprimatur but the encouragement of Governor Owen Brewster, Baxter's one-time ally turned bitter rival. The debate was far longer, but the content was similar to the *Congressional Record* and the previous session's exchanges, in both the highs and lows. Dora Pinkham found her position attacked by the conservative Republican Katharine Allen who had joined the legislature since the last vote. There were again discussions of Maine still losing its tax revenue either way and dueling claims that, on the one hand, the federal oversight was really a rubber stamp or that, on the other hand, it advanced dictatorial power and German- or Russian-style paternalism. (This was supposedly centered in the nefarious socialist women of the Children's Bureau who apparently believed children were property of the state.)[111]

The main focus, however, remained federalism. Senator Frederick Hinckley, a Republican, explained that he understood that while he was a citizen of the state of Maine, he was also a "citizen of the United States of America, a group of 48 sovereign states operating independently, but every one of them working together for the good of all"—which this bill would advance.[112] Senator Paul Powers (R) turned Baxter's Maine exceptionalism on itself, gloating that Maine was the "most American of all the states" with the fewest immigrants—thereby making the protection of its old-stock children even more important.[113] Another opponent of Brewster's plan to pass Sheppard-Towner noted northeastern recalcitrance with regional pride: "The good old New England States wish to stand by their State rights."[114] Others noted that it was a similar centralizing effort as the child labor amendment—also reviled as an assault on states' rights, albeit one at least taking proper constitutional form via an amendment.[115] The bill passed in the senate by 16–13 and 19–9 votes, but Baxter's old views held the day in the house, with a stunning 41–89 defeat of the bill.[116] The senate refused to agree with the house and go on record opposing the bill,[117] but that was mere show.

In 1927, Governor Brewster would again call for the reversal of his enemy's signature political stand—and get it. Although Brewster admitted federalism concerns, he told the state's legislators that they ought to accept Sheppard-Towner, along with other federal aid.[118] (At this point, Brewster could argue that there was no principle to vindicate, as Congress, at the urging of Calvin Coolidge, had passed a bill phasing the program out, as will be discussed later in the chapter.) With national support for Sheppard-Towner fading as it neared its sunset, Maine legislators reversed course and signed onto a dying bill as Brewster requested.

Nearly all of the discussion in the house was from Republican representative Fred Greenleaf, the solo dissenting member from the joint committee. (He was opposed by seven other men and two women, including Dora Pinkham.) Greenleaf's lonely screed was futile, tired, and conspiratorial, seemingly resigned to a doleful warning of the inevitable rather than an effort to persuade. He began by explicitly recycling the federalist arguments from the previous two sessions as well as Governor Baxter, at which point he launched into reading the most paranoid, red-baiting excerpts from the petition of the Woman Patriots (which had been redistributed to the states by US Senate opponents, as noted earlier). Thus, Florence Kelley, the "legislative generalissimo of the Socialist campaigns, enlists hosts of sentimentalists . . . [who] for the most part know no more about her revolutionary socialist strategy than Napoleon's mercenaries knew of his military strategy." Kelley, he continued, was following the advice given to her in correspondence with Friedrich Engels, who suggested Americans would never accept explicit socialism but only if slowly and subtly introduced.[119]

Sheppard-Towner, Greenleaf growled, was such an introduction. Interestingly, the Woman Patriots, and Greenleaf in excerpting their argument, did display a rather subtle grasp of contemporary constitutionalism, or perhaps stumbled on one by accident. Seizing on a confession by bill architect Julia Lathrop that Sheppard-Towner was "broader than a simple health measure," he held this to be part of class-conflict legislation instead. Thus, although the argument was not teased out, based on the era's jurisprudence the bill could then be implicitly beyond the police powers since not related to the common good.[120]

The arguments for Sheppard-Towner were the same as before, especially in the senate, only now most ably defended in the lower chamber by Gail Laughlin (R-Portland), a female lawyer serving in Maine's legislature.[121] Laughlin was brief, since the vote was by now inevitable. Clearly stung by Greenleaf's sexist insinuations, Laughlin began by distancing herself from "almost everything" Kelley believed, though she did note that Kelley's father, William "Pig Iron" Kelley, had been a friend of business when serving in Congress. Otherwise, she explained, Greenleaf's position amounted to little other than rejecting freely offered money, especially as DC was phasing the program out. After all, *at Baxter's own doing*, Maine had already set up an equivalent program, and DC was not intervening in other states, so no state coercion occurred. Thus, she said, this was literally only an issue of financial prudence versus stubbornness.[122]

Other legislators were even less kind to those opposing Sheppard-Towner: one said it reminded him of his old college days, when people defeated by facts and logic had only one avenue left: "talk loudly about states' rights, more loudly about the centralization of authority, and howl as loudly as we could about socialism . . . and pour out all the invective at our command on Mrs. Florence Kelley." Maine's senators and representatives in Congress, however bad they might be, "were not so dumb or so dishonest that they had sold out . . . [or] thrown away the rights of the State of Maine."[123] Greenleaf demanded a roll call vote: by a margin of 92–20, with 38 absent, the house approved the dying Sheppard-Towner. The senate approved it soon after, rejecting a redundant provision to phase it out in 1929 (which federal reauthorization already imposed).[124]

Having now tracked the fate of Sheppard-Towner throughout the states of the Union, one may summarize the regional story thus: opposition to Sheppard-Towner was clearly the heaviest in New England, noticeable but generally ineffective in the Midwest, minimal in much of the South, and almost nonexistent in both the Mountain and Pacific states. Media interest followed legislative cues but generally was slight; a typical report in most states—even those where passage was somewhat dicey—merely observed final success, often buried in passing in the middle of perfunctory legislative roundups.[125] (Northeastern papers tended to more carefully cover the constitutional debates.) As the return to Congress for possible renewal will more fully illustrate, further generalizations are quite difficult, as party, ideology, race, and even state per-capita income—all the usual predictors of political action—so poorly account for states' decisions on whether to accept or challenge Sheppard-Towner.[126] But what is clear is that the folk account of a southern Democratic conservative commitment to states' rights contending against a progressive northern Republican commitment to nationalism has an especially hard time accounting for the politics of Sheppard-Towner.

Back to Congress

Due to factors like fears of the electoral consequences for women's suffrage, Sheppard-Towner initially passed despite latent fears of federal encroachments, but the states' rights concerns that had been simmering since its initial consideration reasserted themselves and showed the enduring strength of federalism in the American constitutional culture. As Sheppard-Towner's sunset approached, the old debates flared up but with a different balance of power. By the mid-1920s, many who voted for the bill seemed to suggest that it had fulfilled its objective of an initial nudge. Both Sheppard-Towner states and the half-dozen holdouts seemed to have implemented appropriate maternity programs, and thus there was no need to further fund or intervene in local affairs.[127] (Of course, this offered a convenient face-saving gesture for those who would have opposed the bill years ago before but for their fear of the WJCC.)

The interest-group story during the renewal fights from 1926 to 1928, and again in 1931, was in many ways a replay of 1921, only with the participants fighting at different relative weights. Women's groups backing the bill remained very active, threatening to mobilize four million supporters.[128] The WJCC continued its aggressive lobbying as before, but its power had declined.[129] After endorsing the bill's renewal, the League of Women Voters staged a debate in New York City, where the bill was again attacked on constitutional grounds. In a powerful appeal to the home crowd, the speaker arguing against the bill cited Prohibition as the result of discarding constitutional localism.[130]

What was different, other than Prohibition, was that opponents were not caught off guard. The American Medical Association (AMA) came out strongly against the bill (over internal dissent from its pediatric division), as did more prominent leaders in the Catholic Church.[131] The Woman Patriots came to the fight stronger than they had been in 1921, and in the meantime had closely allied with powerful dissenting US senators (and even reversed the Daughters of the American Republic, which now sided with opponents of the bill). The Woman Patriots issued a thirty-six-page petition denouncing the bill as an unconstitutional expansion of federal power and a socialistic plot by Florence Kelley. The objective, they claimed, was to get the federal government running the lives of mothers and children as a stalking horse for general big government. Senator Bayard inserted the petition into the *Congressional Record* while he and his hard-line allies Wadsworth, Reed, King, and Greene used franking privileges to distribute it widely.[132]

Nearly all of the major papers in the country had turned against Sheppard-Towner in the interim. The *New York Times* continued its bitter condemnation of the bill long after its favorite son Nathan Miller had been chased from politics. In an editorial brimming with contempt, it predicted, "Many lips will still open longingly for Uncle Sam's magic nursing bottle," even after the bill's expiration: "That any Congressman who gives even occasional lip service to state rights could support [the bill's renewal] would be comical if there were not so few Democrats left not willing to leave their states as foundlings at Uncle Sam's doorstop."[133] The *Los Angeles Times* lamented that the effect of women's suffrage seemed to be a more interventionist federal government, as Sheppard-Towner showed.[134] The *Chicago Tribune* cited Sheppard-Towner— and thanked Illinois for refusing it—in worrying that other proposals such as the Sterling-Reed bill (establishing a Department of Education, updating the earlier Sterling-Towner bill) signaled "the end of state governments."[135] By 1931, even more newspapers, such as the *Washington Post* and *New York Sun*, had joined the chorus. But, while the proportion of discussions now tended toward states' rights instead of paranoid red-baiting tirades, the fight in Washington looked like it had before—only now with Calvin Coolidge's thumb on the scale.[136]

As his Massachusetts legislative record demonstrated, Coolidge did not take a laissez-faire view of government. Instead, Coolidge's view of state and federal power matches that of Elihu Root, holding that the former should be active in advancing their citizens' good—and that failure to do so would result in the warping of federalism and its clear limits on federal power. As Coolidge observed, echoing Root's description of the obligations of the states under progressive federalism: "Where the great body of public opinion of the Nation requires action, the States ought to understand that unless they are responsive to such sentiment the national authority will be compelled to intervene. The doctrine of State rights is not a privilege to continue in wrong-doing but a privilege to be free from interference in well-doing."[137]

Thus, Coolidge asked Congress to pass legislation establishing equivalent maternity bureaus in the nation's capital, where Congress obviously had Article I, Section 8, constitutional authority to act—while calling for the withdrawal of federal power from such interventions in state affairs, seeing them as "an insidious practice which sugar-coats the dose of Federal intrusion."[138] In a Memorial Day address delivered at Arlington National Cemetery in 1925, and which offers the most systematic explanation of his views on federalism, Coolidge explained his position on grants-in-aid: "The ardent states' rights advocate sees in this practice a vicious weakening of the State system. . . . The average American, believing in our dual-sovereignty system, must feel that the policy of national doles to the states is bad and may become disastrous."[139] Agreeing that states should be allowed a period to wind down their expectations of federal money, he indicated that he would accept a temporary extension of the program—attached to a final endpoint.[140] This was not good enough for all—Senator Thomas Bayard of Delaware, a Democrat who had joined the Senate since the last fight, condemned Coolidge for what he saw as half-hearted states' rights views, arguing that the president proclaimed commitment to such principles but hedged by endorsing temporary renewal of Sheppard-Towner rather than immediate elimination on federalism grounds.[141]

In April 1926, such a two-year extension had cleared the US House on a 218–44 voice vote, but the bill stalled in the Senate.[142] James Reed, who had led the effort to block Sheppard-Towner's initial passage, now had at least twenty-one allies in the Senate, which was sufficient to obstruct passage.[143] Reed could afford to be nasty: he had brushed off an effort to replace him, led by women angry with his Sheppard-Towner conduct the first time.[144] He was not the only survivor of the first maternity campaign, as seven of the nine dissenters from 1921 remained. In addition to Reed and King, Borah (R-ID), Broussard (D-LA), Moses (R-NH), Warren (R-WY), and Wadsworth (R-NY) were still members. Senators Dilligham (R-VT) and Thomas Watson (D-GA) had died. Three Democrats who had backed the bill in 1921 had now reversed: Peter Gerry (RI), David Walsh (MA), and Carter Glass (VA).[145] Gerry presumably fell in line with Rhode Island's skepticism about Sheppard-Towner, but the other two are worth noting in more detail. David Walsh had been on the progressive side of politics in Massachusetts (and had helped lead the failed effort to condemn the KKK at the infamous 1924 "Klanbake" convention), though he had made a more conservative turn since his defeat in 1924. (He had returned to Washington in a special election in 1926). Carter Glass had unsteady political roots in 1921, only joining the Senate the year before the first vote, but in the interim he had become an integral member of the Byrd machine's archconservative, states' rights politics in Virginia, where he would continue to aggravate FDR until his death.

On the GOP side, George W. Pepper of Pennsylvania, who had helped Solicitor General Beck defend the constitutionality of the statute,[146] and former House Speaker, now senator, Frederick Gillett of Massachusetts flipped and now opposed the bill.[147] Other foes added to Reed's ranks since 1921 included Cole Blease (D-SC), Thomas Bayard (D-DE), William Cabbell Bruce (D-MD), Hiram Bingham (R-CT), Frank Greene (R-VT), David Reed (R-PA), Edwin Edwards (D-NJ), Walter Edge (R-NJ), Jesse Metcalf (R-RI), Lawrence Phipps (R-CO), and Walter George (D-GA).[148] In short, senators of both parties and of various regions (though still retaining the northeastern tilt), mobilized against the bill.

Most states, having seen the national policy climate turn, appeared to stand down during this later debate over maternal aid. As noted in the preceding section, several states had struggled with protests against Sheppard-Towner specifically and grants-in-aid more generally, but few of these ultimately cleared the state houses. Several states were later adopters but seemed to do so only after the eventual death of the bill had been established and their principle vindicated; in this number we can count Maine and Kansas. A couple other states did go on record reiterating their support of the bill in the late 1920s. Michigan, which generally shied away from states' rights claims, repassed Sheppard-Towner cooperation with a massive majority in its state house and voice votes in thesenate.[149] Oklahoma, which had easily passed Sheppard-Towner and was fairly consistent in applying for federal aid, similarly petitioned for its renewal.[150] But the overwhelming support offered by the states in the early 1920s was not to be.

Senator Sheppard and his allies like Florence Kelley realized that Reed's political forces would likely kill the bill altogether, immediately, by the end of 1927. Thus, they cut a deal akin to Coolidge's suggestion, amending their own bill to clarify that Sheppard-Towner would be phased out in 1929 in exchange for a temporary extension (which they hoped could still be extended again). The filibuster ended, the House concurred, and Coolidge signed the bill. As he did so, the president remarked that the contentiousness of the repeal fight—for even a tiny program—proved that the protection of states' rights required

Congress to strenuously avoid such grants-in-aid in the future.[151] The bill once reviled as the "entering wedge" for socialism had been set on a course to extraction and extinction.

Efforts to salvage it in subsequent years went nowhere. Herbert Hoover called for renewal in annual messages in 1929 and 1930, but dejected supporters of the bill, including Florence Kelley, argued that, unlike Harding, Hoover did not try very hard in actually exerting political capital on its behalf.[152] Hoover had run a conference on health to try to encourage passage of a Sheppard-Towner extension, but it rapidly spun out of control due to fights about bureaucratic reorganization and territorial turf wars, even among the bill's supporters.[153] A trio of Democratic senators—David Walsh (MA), Millard Tydings (MD), and Elbert Thomas (King's colleague in Utah)—filibustered a final, tepid renewal attempt in 1931.[154]

Did Sheppard-Towner even succeed in prompting state action as designed? The results are mixed, but they do suggest initial opposition to federal participation on states' rights grounds correlated with maintaining an independent program after the phase-out—in other words, they most fulfilled the logic of robust use of state police powers on behalf of progressive ends. The three states that refused to participate to the bitter end—Connecticut, Massachusetts, and Illinois—continued to operate in-house clinics.[155]

Among the forty-five states that did eventually participate, three basic behaviors emerge. Sixteen states more or less preserved total expenditures on children's health—meaning they made up much or all of the difference in lost federal funds, again fulfilling the logic of progressive federalism by which states acted for the public health without federal intervention. Among this group were a disproportionate number of the skeptical or holdout states: Kansas, Maine, Maryland, New Jersey, Rhode Island, and Vermont. Seventeen states ratified the cuts by reducing the amount spent on children but by less than the amount of the federal grant—they cut the federal grant and did not make up the difference from their own treasuries, but continued to spend funds raised in-house. Twelve states cut their own spending even more—that is, their own activity had been largely bound up only with federal Sheppard-Towner nodding. (These mostly included western states, although Washington, Louisiana, and New York also numbered among them. The latter two holdout states were, ironically, now governed by Huey Long and Franklin Roosevelt—not exactly libertarian skinflints or laissez-faire fanatics.) The best predictors for a state's decision among those three options were spending on childhood health before Sheppard-Towner (as in, an underlying commitment to state spending) and the state's economic condition—states that believed in protecting mothers' and children, and could afford to, continued to spend money on their behalf.[156]

Sheppard-Towner and State
Constitutional Interpretation

Most states accepted Sheppard Towner with unanimous or near-unanimous votes (at least if one discounts the unusually high abstentions); active legislative resistance largely took the form of redundant provisions guaranteeing the sanctity of the home against state officials, using almost identical language as in the original federal bill. Thus, a merely cursory look would suggest that maternity benefits were more or less totally accepted, a few cranks aside.

Instead, the more interesting question is why Sheppard-Towner generated any resistance or nonparticipation whatsoever, much less the contentious constitutional fight that it did. Its passage and implementation seem incredibly *overdetermined* considering the suicidal optics of voting against the health of mothers and newborns. The sums appropriated were indeed so "pitifully small" as to not raise even the hackles of such a fiscal conservative as the notoriously cheap, green-eyeshaded Calvin Coolidge, who agreed to maintain funding for an orderly phaseout.[157] The money was going to be withdrawn as taxes either way, so state participation guaranteed at least some return, a point pressed by many pragmatic state legislators. The interest group effort proved fierce, with the WJCC as powerful as any seen in memory, and was working within a perfect political window that made its threats appear even more credible. The military endorsed it. And to be clear, the optics were terrible: opposing the bill really was easily criticized as voting against motherhood, if not apple pie. Thus, the question is not why Sheppard-Towner passed almost everywhere; the better question is why there was even resistance to it, in spite of all of the above?

In assessing the states' opposition to Sheppard-Towner as a case of constitutional interpretation, and of states' conception of their own police powers obligation to build a protective state, it is worth considering the alternative explanations that were and have continued to be raised.

Critics, both at the time and today, have often noted the seeming incongruity of states accepting grants-in-aid for other things but balking at Sheppard-Towner.[158] (Academic accounts tend to be particularly sneering.)[159] The parallel had first intrigued Lathrop, the architect of the project, who wondered why, if the federal government would give funds for agricultural education (Smith-Lever), it could not be induced to do the same for children?[160] Representative Towner argued that a tighter interpretation of the General Welfare Clause of Article I's spending power, as Massachusetts argued for, would negate not only grant-in-aid plans but federal activities in education, the Children's Bureau, the Smithsonian, and the Department of Agriculture, among other things.[161]

States were not the only ones to suffer charges of hypocrisy: during the reauthorization debates in 1926, Dr. Robert de Normandie of Harvard Medical School argued that the federal government was involved in eight other health bills, but the AMA opposed only the one.[162] Many defenders drew distinctions on constitutional grounds—namely, that federal power in transportation, jobs, and agriculture had been established before, or that those efforts were, alternatively, recent mistaken experiments that were also unconstitutional and should never have been passed in the first place.[163] Whether one finds these to be opportunistic claims or not depends in large part on one's theory of constitutional interpretation; many of the bill's opponents offered what they argued were credible textual distinctions, even if not distinguished by an abstract principle.[164]

Claims of this hypocrisy are somewhat harder to mount against the particularly recalcitrant states, as they supported the ends of maternal and infant health. Constitutional arguments were not the last resort for people afraid to make conservative policy claims, as they supported the same substantive progressive policy when administered by a different organ of government. Nathan Miller, the New York governor who opposed Sheppard-Towner, nonetheless had the legislature spend *more* money on equivalent maternity programs to keep his state out—possibly paying for that decision with his career.[165] As noted previously, those states that had resisted participation with claim of states' rights did indeed seem to believe in state responsibilities, as they were more likely to retain, and generously fund, in-house programs with the expiration of the federal bill.

But even each of the three permanent holdouts also had mini-Sheppard-Towner acts. Grace Abbott, Lathrop's friend and successor as head of the Children's Bureau, credited her organization with spurring Connecticut and Massachusetts to keep pace and noted their mortality rates made noticeable drops; Illinois also set up a program.[166] Thus, it seems that opposition did seem to be largely good-faith efforts to use the state police powers on behalf of the public good—in this case, through financially small expenditures that paid significant dividends for the public health. The worst one can say of some of the wealthy states was that they were long-term strategic actors, spending money now to try to avoid a precedent that would be costly in the long term. That suggests the possibility of interest and ideology interlocking—parsing out precisely what proportion of each animated legislators would be both impossible and unnecessary, but considering identical claims appeared in poor and rich states alike, it is hard to sustain a charge of pure instrumentalism: state per-capita income had no statistical effect on the probability of participation, with a Maine or a Kansas balancing every New York or Massachusetts.[167]

In other words, as these chapters have argued, governors' or legislators' commitment to a vision of federalism with an active state government and limited federal government—in short, the logic of a progressive federalism— seems the best fit in explaining their actions. The difficulty in finding alternative explanations supports this broadly good-faith interpretation as the source of constitutional resistance to Sheppard-Towner in the states.

Political advantage and mobilization do not so easily fit the facts. Opposition to Sheppard-Towner in Washington was not a partisan story; the leadership and vote totals are almost perfectly balanced. Ideologically speaking, members with economically progressive records, joined constitutional lawyers in ferocious criticism. William King (D-UT), one of the two most zealous congressional opponents, hailed from a state whose legislature happily accepted Sheppard-Towner, and appear to have opposed it for ideological and idiosyncratic reasons as much as anything else. King, both a progressive and a constitutional lawyer, declared himself to be obligated to block "Republican heresies" against the Constitution no matter how long the error had been allowed to survive and even if his own party had now been seduced by them. (The Democratic Party had made support for the women's and children's bureau part of the 1924 and 1928 platforms, which the GOP did not.)[168] The platforms did not contrast strongly, and the critics of the bill dismissed it as the machinations—or, in William King's words, "heresies"—of the other party.

At the presidential level, Harding and Hoover backed it; Coolidge approved of the substance of maternity legislation but only if confined to DC. The most hostile governors, however, were Republicans like Nathan Miller and Percival Baxter (who nonetheless were both most closely associated with bill supporter and progressive Republican Herbert Hoover).

What little one can tentatively tell of the state legislators voting against participation has no clear partisan pattern either. This intuition has statistical support in Carolyn Moehling and Melissa Thomasson's work, who explain their results thus: "Perhaps not surprisingly given the narrative accounts of the battles over Sheppard-Towner, the political party in control of the governor's office or either of the legislative houses had no effect on a state's take-up of the federal grants."[169] Indeed, William Allen White lamented that women's groups were mucking up the party system, citing Sheppard-Towner as an example where responsible party government and fidelity to platforms and ideology seemed swamped by lobbying.[170]

States that rejected Sheppard-Towner were all over the country, but the most successful were clearly concentrated in New England, which matches the Senate politics during the Sheppard-Towner renewal fight quite well. Those often bipartisan delegations in opposition had a definite northeastern skew: Connecticut, Massachusetts, New Jersey, Pennsylvania, and Rhode Island. Thus, there is evidence for a regional story, but it is far from a determinative one; the same claims were advanced in much of the country, only in smaller proportions elsewhere.

Moehling and Thomasson provide fairly strong, state-level empirical support for Senator Kenyon's thesis attributing passage to the overwhelming yet untested belief in the power of women's suffrage. Their statistical analysis finds that the best predictor of state participation in Sheppard-Towner was when women's political participation began. States that had granted suffrage earlier were, all else being equal, less likely to offer significant appropriations. Knowing that women's policy preferences were heterogeneous and not single-issue decreased the chance of voting to spend money; those without longer track records of women's voting were more likely to bend to that perceived fear.[171] This change in the electorate is about the strongest explanation for *why* the bill passed and was accepted in many states, but it is less helpful in understanding the fierce opposition in, say, the Northeast (where women's suffrage was late).

Lobbying against the bill—by the AMA, the Sentinels, and the Woman Patriots—was comparatively weak. Such lobbying grew along with those organizations, but the time line suggests that they were growing as a result of the same conservative forces the early resisters cited.[172] But the presence of doctors, AMA affiliation, and other metrics for a medical lobby had a minimal effect, if any, on a state's Sheppard-Towner participation. Perhaps the strongest lobbying group against the bill was the Roman Catholic Church, whose membership rolls did have a predictive effect against adoption.[173] However, this explanation is also somewhat questionable. As noted above, the Jesuits were hostile, and a few other officials criticized the bill (for example, in 1924 Cardinal O'Connell condemned government interference in family affairs, leading others to follow suit). And, by the final debate in 1932, the Jesuits had won over much of the Catholic leadership and allied groups who adopted states' rights positions, including the National Council of Catholic Women.[174] Again, however, the Church was *not* lobbying initially, and its opposition appears to lag behind the protests and nay votes against state participation.

The particular interaction of the WJCC and the fortuitous political window did give an edge to the bill in Congress, but even when mobilized, the AMA was a minor factor at the state level. The Catholic Church did have more of an effect, but this entailed little formal lobbying and instead consisted predominantly of Jesuit opinion leaders writing angry op-eds. Thus, while the passage of Sheppard-Towner cannot be envisioned without the WJCC, the same is not true of the opposition movements, the AMA and Woman Patriots or not.

Theda Skocpol's suggestion that Sheppard-Towner was a racial story—with legislators in the South and West eager to stick the federal government with the tab of unpopular minorities (Indians in the Plains states, Hispanics in the Southwest, and blacks in the South) no doubt has some bearing, but an examination of state legislative histories indicates a more complicated, somewhat less instrumentalist account.[175] Eagerness for the bill was not confined to places with significant minority populations: many basically all-white states in the North and the upper Mountain West were just as ravenous.

Some contemporaries *did* justify the bill on demographic grounds, but the direction cuts the opposite of Skocpol's argument. Instead of getting federal money to pay for marginalized groups, officials wanted it to defend *white Americans*. As noted earlier, Maine legislators often cited the need to protect the fertility of their old-stock population as a reason to support the bill.[176] A South Carolina envoy to a Virginia meeting of health-care workers callously explained regional support for the bill on xenophobic grounds: "We have a very small foreign population. We will preserve our children because they are native Americans. . . . I care less about the death of foreigners in Boston than I care when a baby dies [in the South.]"[177] Moreover, an equal access clause in the bill understood to be a prohibition on racial discrimination had generated at least some skepticism of it, but, even so, the bill itself was largely ignored by black newspapers (as it had been by almost all white-owned ones as well).[178]

The unanimity of passage of analogous state-level programs indicates that, at least aside from a few cranks, opposition to Sheppard-Towner was

not a policy objection masquerading as a more rhetorically appealing constitutionalism. If anything, it was just as much constitutionalism trumping policy commitments. Nor was opposition really a question of self-interest: while
Massachusetts grumbled the program would cost the state more than it would
get back, it would lose that money regardless—participation would cut those
losses.[179] Albany initially spent *more* than it would have had it participated,
simply to remain free from *nominal* federal control that amounted to a rubber stamp.

Nor was it a regional story of surly southerners or westerners feeling far
away and shut out of power by a Yankee industrial core;[180] at the time of its
passage, sons of Massachusetts led each part of the elected national government, and the Northeast would serve as the staging ground of resistance until
the very end. Indeed, much to the bewilderment of Florence Kelley, the supposed doctrines of Dixie seemed to be totally absent among eagerly participating southerners, with decentralist beliefs having migrated north. Instead, the
South was just as eager to accept Sheppard-Towner and its financial assistance
as any region in the country, with the exception of the Far West.

As a result, Sheppard-Towner is something of a hard test for legal realists, taking place where we should least expect it. In an era when both the
courts and Congress were generally considered to be vigorous enforcers of
federalism, state officials *still* felt obligated to inject themselves into constitutional interpretation. As historical institutionalists remind us, institutional constraints shape norms as well.[181] With national parties and the Supreme Court
both zealously guarding federalism in the 1920s, state legislators and governors, even those deeply committed to federalism like Al Smith, could credibly say that Washington—not Albany, Augusta, or Austin—should enforce
constitutional limits. But, even with those generally reliable constraints, holdout states against Sheppard-Towner continued to offer the constitutional objections that much of Congress had seemed scared to deal with and which the
justices of the Supreme Court had notably declined to confront due to jurisdictional concerns.

Looked at in full, Sheppard-Towner seems to present an instance of constitutional principles actually mattering and shaping behavior at the individual level (if not always sufficiently to then shape behavior at the institutional
level).[182] Sheppard-Towner's debate was essentially purely constitutional, as
few objected to the substantive issue on policy grounds and indeed supported
wholly in-state equivalents. Some made the argument more implicitly and ab-
stractly in bemoaning centralization of the government, but the critique was

essentially waged on purely states' rights grounds: Which sovereignty would be responsible for developing a regime of positive rights? Consistent with the attitudes of a progressive federalism, many answered that it should be the states using states' rights to take such a responsibility.

While Vermont Senator Greene's observation that Sheppard-Towner was an "entering wedge" for socialism seems more than a bit overblown, it did represent a marked change as the first real federal social welfare legislation— the beginning of positive rights at the national level, as subsequent commentators have agreed. The twin court cases it brought (*Massachusetts v. Mellon* and *Frothingham v. Mellon*) would indeed serve as precedents upholding sea-change legislation in the New Deal, including Social Security itself. Critics then and now have leveled smug charges of inconsistency, but it is abundantly clear that many understood agriculture, transportation, and defense—the subjects of the other grants-in-aid—to be substantively different from welfare policies in terms of constitutional authorization. Even supporters had some reservations, and the flurry of state resolutions asserting states' rights and pleading for an end to grants-in-aid suggested the early throes of an addict dimly cognizant of his own fall—still possessing the physical power but not the will to kick a developing dependence.

Further indicating that opponents of Sheppard-Towner were within the mainstream understanding of constitutional federalism, those resisting did so with scrupulous constitutional logic akin to the "necessary and proper" measures of mobilization Madison hoped for in the Virginia Resolution. States resisted by declining to accept funding, trying to repeal it legislatively, pursuing communications with like-minded states, and pursuing test cases in the Supreme Court, all of which were forms of disagreement without resorting to Calhounian assertions of sovereignty and nullification or outright resistance. Thus, Sheppard-Towner in some ways represents an ideal type of state constitutional interpretation: principled and by the book. It also, however, suggests that such resistance may be comparatively weak unless organized by pressure groups or partisanship, especially when the opposition is so organized.[183]

Sheppard-Towner, then, illustrates both the aspirations and limits of constitutional discourse taking place in the states. Unlike passage in Congress, which was largely shaped by a single interest group making a credible electoral threat, state refusal to participate in Sheppard-Towner suggested a remarkable display of constitutional principle, animated by largely uninterested and nonpartisan considerations. The weakness of such high-minded disinterest, however, reminds us that incentives and institutions matter. Rejecting federal grants for an abstract principle is a hard sell politically, and in the end all but a handful of states ultimately acceded. Without either partisan mobilization or interest-group pressure, such a stand, however noble and uninterested it may have been, proved difficult to maintain, but in the end, there was enough state opposition to keep the issue from settlement, and state constitutional interpretation successfully shaped federal policy.[184] With 10 percent of the states of the Union refusing to join and openly protesting, Sheppard-Towner's landmark expansion into federal welfare did not become an accepted change in American political development, replacing progressive federalism with a more consolidated nationalism of federal intervention into the domain of health—at least, not until other developments a decade later. Instead, state opposition to the maternity act provided the rhetoric and live conflict that Calvin Coolidge and other critics could rally behind in the later 1920s.

Of course, the state police powers could be threatened not only by federal legislation displacing the states' sovereignty, as in Sheppard-Towner, but by federal judicial actions more directly prohibiting state action. The following chapters will show how minimum wages and injunctions similarly remained live issues of states engaged in constitutional dialogue with the courts throughout the 1920s and 1930s. As with Sheppard-Towner's defeat, in which state efforts also successfully joined with presidential support to reverse federal law in defense of the state's police powers, state enforcement of minimum wage laws and other pressure culminated in the de facto end of the "liberty of contract" and the termination of anti-labor injunctions.

CHAPTER FOUR

The Liberty of Contract:
Federal Intervention in
State Economic Policy

A United States tribunal has thus suddenly become the arbiter of a state's
industrial destiny.
> —George Hunt, Democratic governor of Arizona, criticizing the
> Ninth Circuit's decision to block a protective labor law

Are we to understand, then, that the states are no longer sovereign as to their own
territory and their own internal affairs? Are they to the government at Washington
only as wards to a city?
> —Lorenzo Lewelling, Populist governor of Kansas, criticizing the
> Supreme Court's restrictions on state railroad commissions

The Constitution of the United States has committed the maintenance of peace
and good order to the . . . state governments. If the state government has fallen into
the hands of socialists . . . or . . . imbeciles we do not thereby acquire the right to
assume control.
> —Judge Moses Hallett, federal district judge in Colorado, rejecting
> mine companies' request to intervene in a strike in the 1880s

Although mid- to late twentieth-century Arizona is generally thought of as a
bastion of conservatism—of Barry Goldwater, William Rehnquist, and Sandra
Day O'Connor—in the 1910s and 1920s, shortly after statehood, it was con-

sidered anything but. For the eastern establishment, the Copper State's deserts were a hotbed of frightening radicalism. William Howard Taft believed that he had to block Arizona's initial petition for admission to the Union on the grounds that the territory's proposed state constitution, allowing recall of judges, would destroy the rule of law: "legalized terrorism," he had pronounced it. The state senate voted to undo a century of Madisonian constitutionalism by returning to a unicameral legislature like the Founders so feared and which every state rejected by the early nineteenth century. Arizona's constitution, easily the most progressive in the nation, boasted not only recalls but initiatives and referenda, as well as a wish list of protective labor legislation. The clear leader of Arizona politics was the iconic governor George Hunt, the George Washington of the state, who, like the great general, had served as president of its constitutional convention and then made the smooth transition to its first chief executive. Unlike Washington though, who retired after two terms, Hunt so often ran for—and won—reelection that Will Rogers jokingly pronounced him the state's "hereditary" governor.[1]

While the ardently progressive Hunt supported a robust, active, and definitely not-limited *Arizona* government, he, like other Arizona progressives of his time, was devoutly committed to decentralized federalism and to a fairly strict construction of the Constitution.[2] Hunt, for example, boasted of his states' rights beliefs in refusing to terminate a quarantine when asked by President Coolidge, and in asserting the claim in federal water politics. He also exchanged prostates' rights letters with several fellow governors, among them a then like-minded, prepresidential Franklin Roosevelt.[3] In these letters, Hunt joined a commitment to federalism with what arguably be described today as a form of constitutional originalism:

> While the old idea of the right of a state to nullify federal laws is gone, it does not follow that while the federal government is supreme in its field, the states are not equally supreme in their own. . . . It appears to me that where new questions arise that obviously were not contemplated by the makers of the constitution, they should be handled either by the states, in accordance with the reserve power in the 10th amendment, or granted to the federal government by proper constitutional amendments, rather than by strained legal decisions of the Supreme Court.[4]

Nor was this a one-off thought. In another letter to another gubernatorial colleague, Hunt lamented "the gradual destruction of states rights" aided by "the tendency of the courts to ignore the literal wording of the Constitution and make their decision on what they considered may be the greatest good for the greatest number."[5] Hunt would have objected to his allies being characterized as imbeciles or socialists, as Judge Moses Hallett had suggested of earlier Colorado populists, but he would have appreciated Hallett's underlying point that judges needed to be careful in only enforcing text, not their views of wise or foolish policy.[6]

In this, Hunt reflected a fear that had been raised in the Arizona Constitutional Convention (over which Hunt presided): a failed section in an alternative proposal for a Bill of Rights had proposed banning judicial substitution of the "general intent or spirit" or "public policy" for the text. It would instead have restricted judicial review only to enforcement of "some express provision of this Constitution or necessary implication from such express provision."[7]

That was not the only worry of Arizona progressives, which echoed the constitutional skeptic Brutus.[8] In the same 1788 essay opposing New York's ratification, Brutus feared the Constitution's national institutions would all collaborate in the destruction of decentralized federalism, engaging in a giant logroll expanding federal power.[9] Hunt similarly fretted: "The court is always inclined to validate acts of Congress, while Congress is humanly inclined to extend its own power, beyond constitutional limits. The court likewise is inclined to approve the act of an executive, who appoints members of the court. Popular opinion, therefore, is the only check on the eventual complete federal control of all our intimate and local affairs."[10]

In other words, while much of the rest of Hunt's constitutionalism—supporting unicameralism, initiatives, referenda, and recalls—undoubtedly appalled Elihu Root, Hunt nonetheless fulfilled a key part of Root's progressive federalism: Hunt deeply believed in using the power of the state to check business and protect workers; hence his reputation for radicalism, but he was adamant that this come from the *state*. In his January 1915 speech opening Arizona's second regular legislature, he invoked federalism in defending a protective labor law that was deeply popular with the state's progressive and labor movement at the time, reiterating that states' rights and a robust conception of their police powers were both essential to Arizona's goals.

Hunt protested the Ninth Circuit's recent decision to block Arizona's so-called "80% Measure," arguing the federal government had injected itself into to the state's affairs. This protective law, sought by the organized labor movement of the state, aimed to ensure that every employer in Arizona hired no fewer than 80 percent US citizens and faced penalties for failing to meet that threshold. In addition to possibly conflicting with various treaties, the 80% Measure was assailed as depriving lawfully admitted aliens the ability to earn a living—a dangerous proposition for justices interested in protecting "the liberty of contract," as they would in this case by an almost unanimous vote.[11]

In striking down a progressive law his state had passed to protect its domestic labor force, the federal judiciary, Hunt railed, had usurped for itself the status of "arbiter of a state's industrial destiny." They had banned a state's "expression of the people's attitude toward the wholesale importation of aliens to the virtual exclusion of the citizen from the right to earn his daily bread in the states in which he has take up his residence and is rearing his children."[12] While Hunt did not invoke the talismanic phrase "states' rights," that was the clear undercurrent, as newspaper coverage corroborated.[13] As Hunt biographer David Berman observes of the episode, "In a single swoop [Hunt] was able to combine his dislike of courts with a defense of states' rights, majority rule, the initiative process, and a major policy stand taken by organized labor."[14]

Hunt's battle with the Supreme Court that culminated in *Truax v. Raich* (1915) was in some sense typical of the conflicts between progressive states and federal judges during the era. In the late nineteenth and early twentieth centuries, the federal government almost never intervened against the states concerning rights explicitly enumerated in the Bill of Rights (such as freedom of speech), but this inaction this was not true in the economic realm. With the US Supreme Court still shying away from incorporating (applying) the Bill of Rights against the states via the Fourteenth Amendment, and Republicans largely acceding to the southern nullification of the Fourteenth and Fifteenth Amendments, the key rights conflicts of the late nineteenth and early twentieth century were challenges against protective economic legislation.[15] In the latter sphere, federal courts built up several lines of jurisprudence limiting state regulatory power, the most notorious of which became the so-called "liberty of contract," which served as a battleground throughout much of the first half of the twentieth century.

These judicial interventions, taking place as elements of the populist movement were giving birth to the new Progressive Era, shaped state economic policies and generated constitutional pushback from the states, protesting what they saw as the erosion of their traditional police powers guaranteed by the Tenth Amendment.

The following two chapters will recount a variety of such federal judicial interventions into the states' effort to regulate economic activity and provide protective labor legislation, showing how this was as much or more a question of federal versus state authority and federalism as economic theory. State actors coalesced around and invoked states' rights to push back against what they viewed as unconstitutional national policymaking intervening in the domain the Constitution left to the states. In other words, this is the archetypal model of progressive federalism, in which left-leaning state officials used states' rights language, strikingly similar to that of the era's political mainstream, as well as present-day conservatives, to push back against what those progressives believed was conservative federal overreach. Progressive federalism was understood not just as a sword to enact policy but a shield against federal policymaking—in this case, by federal courts.

These judicial decisions that prompted federalist resistance by progressive state actors broadly came in one of two types. The first type of intervention was the labor injunction, in which a court would issue a judicial order, backed by penalty of law, prohibiting some particular action or set of actions undertaken by workers or labor organizers that the judges held would violate employers' rights. The scope of such orders could be very narrow—perhaps instructing an individual to cease union recruitment—or very far-reaching—blocking a strike or boycott. In the hands of employer-friendly judges, such tools could decimate unionizing or other efforts by organized labor—all without any clear legislative framework guiding or limiting them.

Ostensibly pursuant to the protection of Congress's enumerated commerce and mail powers, injunctions became arguably the most aggressive and widely resented of federal courts' interventions into states' economic policies, leading to their eventual suppression by Congress. After state and lower courts had been experimenting with labor injunctions, the Supreme Court ratified them in the case of *In re Debs* (1895), approving a practice then-circuit court judge William Howard Taft had notably used in the years before, first against the Brotherhood of Locomotive Engineers and then Eugene Debs's American Railway Union (in the Pullman Strike).[16]

As William Forbath observed in his seminal work on labor law, the courts' aggressive claims of equity powers on behalf of employers enabled a form of "government by injunction," to adopt the term used by Illinois governor John Peter Altgeld, until decades of congressional efforts to clamp down on federal injunctions finally saw them ended with the Norris-La Guardia Act of 1932.[17]

The second broad type of federal intervention concerned due process, which itself could be disaggregated into two types of claims. Using the due process clause of the Fourteenth Amendment, courts built up two other clear lines of precedent constraining state regulatory efforts. The first of these, though rooted in due process, was not about protecting fundamental, substantive individual rights and was instead closer to separation-of-powers jurisprudence. In this line of cases, courts limited states' efforts to use commissions or statutory price-fixing on quasiutilities like railroads, with the judges arguing that legislatures either directly asserting, or authorizing commissions to directly assert, prices without judicial review constituted a deprivation of meaningful judicial oversight.

The final line of precedent restricting state economic activity, and certainly the most infamous, was the individualist "liberty of contract" claim, which will make up the bulk of the next two chapters. The legal academy came to dub this the *Lochner* era, one in which purportedly laissez-faire fanatic judges wielded the liberty of contract to strangle economic legislation favored by progressives seeking to blunt the harder edges of industrial capitalism.[18]

Federal judicial intervention in state economic policy, even across all three lines, was narrow enough to counsel against understanding this as the *Lochner* era often mythologized as a time when states were locked out of very broad swaths of their police powers by zealous laissez-faire federal courts. Nonetheless, federal judicial activity in the economic realm was, if not wide-ranging, still deeply consequential, and thus provoked state pushback, especially but not exclusively from progressive governors. It helped forge, at the beginning of the Progressive Era, a significant intellectual linkage between federalism and progressivism. Preserving the states' autonomy to use their police powers—in this case, to regulate corporate and economic power—gave a very strong incentive to embrace the traditional constitutional understanding of decentralized American federalism.

There was relatively little state officials could do about injunctions or the blockage of their railroad commissions, other than loudly protest and tinker with commission procedures in the hopes of meeting the courts' objections. But against liberty of contract—especially in its more radical 1920s guise—states pressed more sharply for minimum wages and other laws.

This long-term struggle between progressive federalism and conservative courts over the liberty of contract ebbed and flowed. After the *Lochner* case, the states temporarily won, using state politics to keep the issue alive until they could reclaim the power to regulate local economic activity from the federal government; this is the story told in the latter half of this chapter. But that victory would be temporary, and the battle over liberty of contract would be rejoined in the 1920s, which is largely what chapter 5 recounts.

Eventually such efforts, joined with the bipartisan support of both parties' presidential wings, succeeded in ending the court-mandated liberty of contract, although both yellow-dog contracts and minimum wages soon folded into *Congress's* ability to regulate interstate commerce in an increasingly national economy.

Injunctions and Due Process: Railroads and Economic Federalism

Before moving to liberty of contract, in which the bulk of progressive federalism state pushback occurred, it is worth briefly turning to the other two broad forms of economic intervention that courts made in blocking state protective regulation: the separation-of-powers, procedural due-process argument and the labor injunctions. For purposes of brevity, this section will focus on railroads, arguably the economic sector in which public outcry for regulation was strongest; a full account of the politics of railroads would generate (and has generated) studies in itself,[19] and what will follow is illustrative rather than comprehensive.

This diversion serves two purposes. First, it offers something of a chronological bridge to the liberty of contract cases and the resurgent wave of constitutional conflict in the 1920s, showing how populists and progressives not only embraced federalism from the beginning of the movement in the 1890s but continued to do so. Second, it suggests that judicial interventions in other economic spheres were understood in broadly the same way, with state officials critical of federal interventions but even the most radical governors declined an open confrontation even hinting at nullification. In other words, radical though these governors' policies may have been, their constitutional understanding of federalism was thoroughly within the mainstream, both in terms of federalism and the appropriate tools to defend it. That the Court itself was not sharply attacked is unsurprising; in most cases, throughout the era, legislators and most commentators treated the Supreme Court as a good-faith actor neutrally applying the law as best as possible, albeit with occasional error.[20]

But not all critics were so sanguine. In the 1890s, when the Progressive Era was just starting to take root, state governors fiercely criticized these judicial interventions, demonstrating that they remained dedicated to both a decentralized constitutional federalism and their own obligation to defend constitutionalism rather than cede it to the courts. This helped set the stage for decades of unimpeachably left-wing governors and activists criticizing what they saw as unconstitutional federal intervention in the states' sovereignty.

John Peter Altgeld, Illinois's Democratic governor during the 1890s, condemned federal courts' use of injunctions during labor disputes, and he specifically assailed his fellow Democrat Grover Cleveland's suppression of the Pullman riots in 1894. Altgeld had deployed the state militia to keep the peace there but repeatedly informed President Cleveland that the state refused its consent for federal intervention.[21] Urged by Attorney General Richard Olney and citing the need to protect delivery of the US mail, President Cleveland— though himself a devout states' rights believer—countered that the federal government retained jurisdiction and could deploy troops to overpower the striking railroad workers. Olney's argument won out, and Cleveland suppressed the riots.

At the next meeting of the Illinois legislature, Altgeld savaged Cleveland's intervention in the state's internal affairs, attempting to situate himself within what he understood the post–Civil War settlement to require. He did not support defiance of constitutional authorities, observing that "the old doctrine of state rights is in no way involved. Nobody for a moment questions the supremacy of the Union." By the "old doctrine," Altgeld, like others at the time, meant the now-discredited compact theory and its corollary of nullification. As his speech makes abundantly clear, Altgeld did not view the Civil War as displacing the nation's federalist order, but instead only marginalizing Calhoun's misunderstanding of it. Implicitly invoking Lincoln's fear of spiraling secession, Altgeld added that "without federal Union there must follow anarchy . . . [and] the Great Civil War settled that we should not have anarchy."

But the American order, Altgeld added, had another "foundation upon which the glory of our whole governmental fabric rests . . . just as sacred, just as inviolable. . . . Without local government there must follow despotism." If the Civil War had eliminated secessionist anarchy—in Altgeld's phrasing, "the old doctrine of state rights"—it now remained to be settled whether the president could destroy local government by unilaterally deploying the military just like "Emperor William or the Czar of Russia." Such federal intervention was a "new departure [and] a violation of the Constitution as it has been understood for over a century."

Altgeld would do nothing to actively obstruct federal power, but he could not allow "the acts of the President . . . to stand unchallenged and thus form a precedent" and consequently "considered it my duty to protest." That Grover Cleveland, a fellow Democrat "placed in power by a party that had made local self-government a cardinal principle for more than a century," committed the offense, made the "stabbing" even harder to bear.[22]

Although largely forgotten now, Altgeld was a major player in the nation's politics in the 1890s, with many lamenting his foreign birth confined him to a kingmaker role within the Democratic Party rather than a presidential candidate able to advance his vision of prolabor localism himself. An able lawyer (who mentored Clarence Darrow), Altgeld was best known for a staunch commitment to civil liberties and sympathy for labor, most notably when he pardoned those convicted of the Haymarket riots on the grounds that the evidence in the case did not justify a conviction.[23] This, in turn, led the GOP to wage an all-out war against the supposedly dangerous leftist radical in 1896, a campaign aiming not only to avert Altgeld's reelection but more importantly to help the national ticket. The GOP was stuck with a candidate (William McKinley) who had until recently been on the wrong side of the metal coinage debate—he had not been for the gold standard that now constituted Republican orthodoxy. As a result, campaign strategist Mark Hanna and the Republican leadership decided to run against Altgeld as much as silver or William Jennings Bryan, with the media following suit. Altgeld, eager to defend his constitutionalism, happily joined the battle.[24]

Thus, Theodore Roosevelt, like many Republican leaders, assailed Altgeld as the power behind the Democratic Party (a not wholly unmerited claim, considering Altgeld's oversized influence on the platform at the convention). What made Altgeld's disproportionate influence dangerous, Roosevelt insisted, was that Altgeld's criticisms of the Supreme Court and judicial interventions showed him to be "free from all the restraints of public morality." Ironically, considering his own radically progressive views on the courts would alienate many of his inner circle—like Root and Taft themselves,[25] Roosevelt thus warned that such a dangerous creature as Altgeld would "bequeath to our sons, a red welter of lawlessness . . . as fantastic and vicious as the Paris commune itself." Altgeld turned the tables on the young Republican: just as Roosevelt had delivered this speech in Chicago; Altgeld journeyed to the Cooper Union in Roosevelt's New York to give a heavily publicized restatement of his 1895 legislative message, decrying federal interference in state affairs and the dangers of "government by injunction."[26]

Nor were such attacks on Altgeld simply confined to the 1896 election, as political figures tried to discredit his populist localism both before and after the election. Taft appeared at the annual meeting of the American Bar Association (ABA) in August 1895, decrying critics like Altgeld and defending his own action in *Debs*, saying, "A public nuisance more complete [than the Pullman Strike] cannot be imagined."[27] Respected judge Thomas Cooley had more explicitly denounced Altgeld at the prior year's ABA meeting, leading Altgeld to liberally quote Cooley's own prior words, an excerpt from his famous treatise, denouncing the dangers of employing a centralized standing army as law enforcement.[28] But such attacks served their purpose—though running well ahead of Bryan, Altgeld nonetheless lost his reelection campaign to the Republican candidate John Tanner.

Tanner began his governorship by making clear that he disapproved of (a caricature of) Altgeld's political thinking, with the newly inaugurated governor portraying his predecessor as a neo-Calhounian secessionist, in contrast to Tanner, who defended the courts, paid homage to law and order, and criticized "a class of politicians [who] . . . favors a species of communism." This included a muddled waving of the bloody shirt to implicitly chastise Altgeld's ostensible states' rights views—though Tanner still paid deference to federalism, which, after all, remained the core of the era's constitutional thought (albeit not Roosevelt's). Tanner warned of any "outside state authorit[ies who would] suspend" the powers of the federal government "on any inch of American soil." As long as people remembered the prison camps of Andersonville and other rebel horrors, "no puffed and bustling representative of the slaughtered heresy of state sovereignty can ever again order Uncle Sam 'to keep off the grass' with the approval of the American people." But yet, even this followed an extended discussion of dual citizenship (state and federal), the observation of enumerated powers, and the promise that "we are proud of our State, and would be quick to resent an infringement upon its just rights."[29]

Thus, even Tanner, who sought to link localist constitutionalism and labor unrest and praised courts for intervening to protect capital, *still* felt obligated to pay homage to the motto inscribed on Illinois's state flag today: "State Sovereignty, National Union"—just as the radical Altgeld had in condemning, but not obstructing, Cleveland's federal intervention. In other words, very little separated the constitutional federalism praised by the conservative and progressive combatants. Both—including, it must be emphasized, the radical progressive—shared the same understanding of traditional constitutional decentralization.

Populist Kansas represents an analogous case of clear but limited state resistance to federal constitutionalism, as hatred of the railroads and their judicial abettors nonetheless translated only to fierce rhetoric joined with acceptance of federal legitimacy.[30]

If not quite the conflict of antebellum Bleeding Kansas, the state was still a tumultuous climate, one in which armed rivals vied for control of the state capitol, the militia was ordered to retake it, and the courts and Republican legislators were seen as usurpers of the people's government by railroads. And yet, surrounded by such turmoil and political radicalism, the zealously states' rights governor leading the Populist Party's protest charge nonetheless urged compliance with the Court's due process holdings—even though the judges had eviscerated the very cornerstone of the Populists' anti-railroad program. In other words, even in the midst of an almost unbelievable state of political unrest, Kansas's ultraprogressive governor linked a dogged belief in states' rights with an unwillingness to use nullification to enforce it.

In 1893, Governor Lorenzo D. Lewelling and the Populist Party moved to take control of Kansas government after winning the previous November elections. Acknowledging the "Scylla and Charybdis" of railroad commissions, the governor insisted the state's legislators solve "the inefficacy of too little power on one hand and the unconstitutionality of too much power on the other hand." He told them to draft legislation consistent with the Court's invalidation of the 1887 Minnesota commission law on due process grounds.[31] (The justices had argued nonjusticiable commission rates deprived railroad owners of due process.)[32]

Although neither Lewelling's victory nor Populist control of the senate were in doubt, a competing slate of Republican candidates claimed victory in enough contested seats in the lower house to tip that chamber to their control. As a result, caucuses of both the railroad-allied Republicans and anti-railroad Populists asserted themselves to be the legitimately elected House of Representatives of Kansas, leading to the "Legislative War" in which each party occupied the halls of government, alternating in a monthlong spectacle in which each "House" conducted its respective business at the same desks at different times of the day. Eventually, the Republicans moved to expel the Populists, who responded by barricading themselves in with armed defenders; the Republicans managed to chase out the Populists and fortify themselves under their own guard.

Armed citizens massed around the capitol from all over Kansas, further adding to the chaos. Governor Lewelling then ordered the state militia to clear the usurping Republicans from the capitol. Citing separation-of-powers grounds, the militia refused the governor's order to act against the legislature, as did the local sheriff. At this point the lawyer for the Atchison, Topeka, and Santa Fe Railroad—whom Lewelling would later derisively refer to as the real "chief executive of the revolutionary state government"[33]—made a proposal—acceptable to Lewelling and the so-called Dunsmore (Populist) and Douglas (Republican) Houses alike—agreeing to defuse the situation by deferring to the state supreme court. After the court sided with the Republicans on the contested seats, the Populist holders of the uncontested seats joined the now-Republican House.[34]

Recognizing the precariousness of their situation, the house Republicans offered a railroad commission bill that did most of what the Populists had sought.[35] The Populist controlled senate, however, held out and refused to go along, unable to agree to holding the railroad commissioners' elections in off-years (which they believed would favor Republican-backed candidates less zealous about regulating the railroads).[36]

In 1895, as he was handing over power to his Republican successor, a frustrated Governor Lewelling scourged the nation's federal courts, which had put Kansas in such a situation. The judges, while "admitting the sovereign power of the state" in theory, nonetheless had in practice "constitute[d] themselves general guardians of the state governments."[37]

This was as true of judicial interventions invoking due process to stop states from setting maximum rates as it was of strike-breaking with injunctions, which, as Altgeld similarly argued, violated the separation of powers as well as federalism, creating instead "government by injunction." Lewelling criticized the federal courts for using deputized marshals to make and enforce law independent of Congress and the president, the same point Samuel Gompers observed in 1902 in holding that anti-labor injunctions were "not upon the statute books of the United States, or any of the sovereign states of the Union."[38] While nodding to the separation-of-powers argument, the governor reserved most of his wrath for the plutocrats seeking to eliminate federalism once they had captured the courts: "Those benefited by these outrageous indignities to sovereign states" now falsely sought to claim that "the doctrine of state's rights went down in the civil war."[39]

Lewelling was having none of this, defending what he saw as the traditional, decentralized constitutionalism that enabled progressive state efforts to act on behalf of the public good—in this case, by patrolling railroads. For

Lewelling, this vigorous Jacksonian states' rights remained the true legacy of the Civil War:

> Are we to understand, then, that the states are no longer sovereign
> as to their own territory and their own internal affairs? Are they to
> the government at Washington only as wards to a city? The doctrine
> disposed of by the fortunes of war was the right of a state to secede and
> assume to be independent of the union; to throw off its allegiance to the
> federal government. The doctrine of internal state sovereignty was not
> invalidated. On the contrary, the reconstruction acts proceeded upon
> the theory that the victorious union was made up, not of a consolidated
> people, but of sovereign states.[40]

The week before, Colorado's outgoing Populist governor Davis Hanson Waite had similarly protested Cleveland's deployment of troops in Illinois and Colorado, arguing Cleveland violated Article IV, Section 4, of the Constitution by sending troops without the state's consent. Like Altgeld and Lewelling, Waite advised only a protest memorial, a futile request in light of the state's incoming Republican legislators.[41]

The examples of Lewelling and Altgeld are not meant to be comprehensive or typical, but their actions (or lack thereof) despite their relatively extreme ideological positions helpfully illustrate two features of state constitutionalism and economic regulation more generally, as well as the strong connections between federalism and the populists and proto-Progressives of the era.

First, a commitment to states' rights and the presumption of state autonomy were compatible not only with populists like William Jennings Bryan but also the far-left flank of that era's politics.[42] Instead, they fit together quite easily, as Theodore Roosevelt bemoaned. Moreover, even as these comparative radicals bitterly condemned the Court's national interventions in railroad and labor affairs of the states, this did not translate to substantive defiance by the states—they offered grudging compliance and protest instead, consistent with the post–Civil War settlement rejecting nullification as a tool to enforce the decentralized federalism they favored.

Although state officials complied—albeit unhappily—with judicial interventions into state railroad affairs, even the specter of criticism coming from the states unnerved nationalists less interested in preserving the sanctity of the courts than of the Union. Perhaps none was more troubled than Theodore

Roosevelt, who, unlike many of his allies in the nascent progressive movement, and even his inner circle of Elihu Root, Henry Cabot Lodge, and William Howard Taft, detested federalism.[43]

The strong connection between economic radicalism and states rights' constitutionalism clearly shaped the young Roosevelt, who had aggressively campaigned against Altgeld by attacking him as a communist. Of Roosevelt, Mark Twain once observed that every time he had met Theodore Roosevelt he had liked him, but as to Roosevelt, "the statesman and politician, I find him destitute of morals and not respectworthy . . . ready to kick the Constitution into the back yard whenever it gets in the way."[44] Roosevelt's later *Autobiography* openly dismissed states' rights and localist constitutionalism, but he held these antipathies even before his postpresidency turn toward the constitutional radicalism that so frightened Root, Taft, and other leading Republicans.[45] Ten years after the defeat of Altgeld, then-President Roosevelt became quite irritated when states passed legislation "in their belief that it can be more radical . . . than the Nation will permit." Presumably thinking of populists like Lewelling, Roosevelt explained that state leaders thus "resent[ed] the Nation's doing anything and spend their energies in getting on the statute books State laws which will be declared unconstitutional or else will amount to nothing."[46]

In response to the Nebraska state GOP platform asking for a federal constitutional amendment ending labor injunctions, Roosevelt privately observed, "This proposal is simply one to abolish the Federal Government; the Federal Judges must have power to prevent the States from nullifying federal laws." The alternative, he dramatically, even theatrically, explained to Nebraska senator Elmer Burkett, "is of course to endorse nullification, secession, and disunion." So distressed was Roosevelt that he told Burkett to keep the letter secret, not out of fear his views would get out but that it would bring more public attention to the dangerous resolution being discussed far from the corridors of national power.[47]

But of course, even the most radical of the states' rights populists did not, despite Roosevelt's hysterical diatribe, "endorse nullification, secession, and disunion," which leads to the second point. Instead, these skirmishes in railroad law illustrated that even radicals largely fell within the broad national consensus—one whose believers, while not embracing a compact theory of state sovereignty, still remained deeply committed to an orthodox understanding of states' rights and were furious about illegitimate federal intervention into the states' domain. State officials did not sit idly by when the federal government stepped into what they believed was the states' internal affairs. They were comfortable offering fierce protests, but they were scrupulous to raise these in respectful protests (or an amendment request in the Nebraska case) rather than defiance—even if they were willing to use force in their own domestic politics.

Liberty of Contract

Arguably the clearest example of progressive federalism in the period between Reconstruction and the New Deal concerned the decades-long fight by states to reject federal courts' liberty of contract doctrine, which, though relatively infrequent, state officials still understood as a serious external intervention into the sphere of constitutional state sovereignty. It was, as the subsequent cases will show, a remarkable exemplar of the tug-of-war between progressive advocates of state authority and conservatives in the federal government. In some cases, it is worth noting, there was also a substantive hook, rather than simply a federalism one, insofar as some state courts began aggressively applying the doctrine within their own domains, forcing reformers to fight not just against overreach by federal judges but efforts by state courts to situate liberty of contract in either the United States or state constitutions.[48]

Although not explicitly using the phrase "liberty of contract," *Allgeyer v. Louisiana* offered the first invocation of the infamous principle in striking down a state law in 1897. The unanimous *Allgeyer* justices held that the state of Louisiana could not prohibit its residents from making a contract, out of state, with an out-of-state insurance company. In so holding, the Court appealed to "the right of the citizen to be free in the enjoyment of all his faculties, to be free to use them in all lawful ways, to live and work where he will, to earn his livelihood by any lawful calling, to pursue any livelihood or avocation, and for that purpose to enter into all contracts which may be proper, necessary, and essential."[49]

According to traditional accounts, such liberties, the court held, though not enumerated in the text of the Constitution, were nonetheless fundamental rights and thus protected by what later came to be known as "substantive due process." Subsequent scholarship has argued that such early "substantive due process" cases were less about "fundamental rights" and more about ensuring governmental deployment of the police powers had a true public purpose rather than being arbitrary or pretextual—and thus beyond legitimate legislative power and against the law of the land.[50]

Like many other liberty of contract cases, *Allgeyer* awkwardly cited that expansive principle while seemingly describing another concept—usually class legislation.[51] In this case, however, it was offering something resembling the Court's dormant commerce clause jurisprudence, as Louisiana was not merely regulating its own insurance laws but striking out beyond its borders at one of its citizens engaged in interstate commerce. However, since the Court had ruled insurance beyond the field of interstate commerce in an 1869 decision, the justices turned away from preexisting dormant commerce clause analysis to formulate a new liberty of contract to strike the law.[52]

The exact breadth of this liberty was unclear in the opaque opinion, but the justices, despite such expansive rhetoric, left states a wide range of authority to tame the power of insurance companies. As if for emphasis on this point, the very first line of Justice Peckham's opinion bluntly asserts, "There is no doubt of the power of the state to prohibit foreign insurance companies from doing business within its limits," full stop.[53] Moreover, the narrowness of *Allgeyer*'s holding—blocking a punishment for citizens making out-of-state contracts—was confirmed in subsequent cases that vindicated aggressive state regulation of insurance and, especially "foreign," insurance companies.[54] In the years after *Allgeyer*, states debated and passed numerous bills trying to tame the industry—evidently interpreting both *Allgeyer* and its progeny as a blessing to do so.

Almost a decade later, Peckham authored *Lochner v. New York* (1905), which overturned a New York law restricting the hours of bakers. *Lochner* became rhetorically notorious, especially after Theodore Roosevelt latched onto it as a source of particular ire and campaign vitriol,[55] but if *Lochner* created an era in which states feared enacting protective labor legislation, states apparently missed the news, as they continued to press on in regulating working conditions pursuant to the states' police powers. They proposed and even passed nearly identical legislation in the years following the decision, suggesting that they did not see themselves trapped by a libertarian ethos. Instead, it seemed, states interpreted *Lochner* as striking down a particularly heinous instance of corrupt political protection—class legislation—rather than legitimate lawmaking protecting the public good.[56]

Thus, like *Allgeyer*, *Lochner* could be easily distinguished without asserting the need for states to engage in direct and confrontational constitutional pushback, and the states could help shape an understanding of the decision as more limited in scope than critics like Roosevelt feared. They unsurprisingly moved to do so. Before *Lochner*, states already confined maximum-hours legislation to cover those understood as physically weaker (in the case of women and children) or those occupations where long hours proved dangerous, with the latter having already garnered a judicial blessing and reaffirmation of the states' broad police powers.[57]

After *Lochner*, the Court reverted to upholding such legislation, and neither states nor the federal government seemed particularly deterred from considering (and sometimes passing) analogous maximum-hours legislation. The *Lochner* decision's shaky foundations appear to have been recognized almost immediately, certainly by the justices themselves. Purportedly only a last-minute switch had converted Justice Harlan's then-majority opinion into a dissent, interrupting a long continuity approving of hours legislation before and after the bake-shop case.[58]

Harlan's dissent, typical of his defenses of a robust police power as noted in chapter 1, effectively laid out the claim for progressive federalism, as far as federal courts were concerned:[59] "Let the State alone in the management of its purely domestic affairs so long as it does not appear beyond all question that it has violated the Federal Constitution . . . [because of] the principle that the health and safety of the people of a State are primarily for the State to guard and protect." New York's law "cannot be held to be in conflict with the Fourteenth Amendment without enlarging the scope of the Amendment far beyond its original purpose." That would, he feared, bring "under the supervision of this court matters which have been supposed to belong exclusively to the legislative departments of the several States when exerting their conceded power to guard the health and safety of their citizens by such regulations as they in their wisdom deem best."[60]

It was essential, Harlan reminded his fellow justices, to remember that "the preservation of the just powers of the States is quite as vital as the preservation of the powers of the General Government." The judiciary could not, rightly, "enter the domain of legislation, and upon grounds merely of justice or reason or wisdom, annul statutes that had received the sanction of the people's representatives." That was outside the courts' domain: "The public interests imperatively demand—that legislative enactments should be recognized and enforced by the courts as embodying the will of the people unless they are plainly and palpably, beyond all question, in violation of the fundamental law of the Constitution."[61] In other words, Harlan said, the courts should make sure to preserve the legitimate authority of the states, under American federalism, to advance the public good.

In his fifth annual message that December, President Roosevelt matter-of-factly called for congressional legislation establishing maximum railroad hours, arguing that "if there are any reasons for limiting by law the hours of labor in any employment, they certainly apply with peculiar force to the employment of those upon whose vigilance and alertness in the performance of their duties the safety of all who travel by rail depends."[62] (Congress would eventually pass such legislation in the form of the Adamson Act in 1916.) Indeed, the Supreme Court seemingly viewed *Lochner* as beneath comment, upholding, for example, a similar law by a per-curiam opinion later that year (*Cantwell v. Missouri*), and making no mention of it in a 1907 federal hours case (*Ellis v. United States*).[63] Even the conservative Nathan Miller, who, unlike Coolidge or Hoover opposed women's minimum wage laws, found maximum-hours laws to be appropriate.[64]

Consistent with an interpretation regarding *Lochner* as either a clear outlier or silently overruled, similar protective legislation appeared up and down the legislative journals and statute books of the states, as miners, railroad workers, and telegraphers achieved eight- or ten-hour restrictions. Legislators continued to pass or seriously consider efforts to restrict maximum hours for a vast swath of employees, further indicating their understanding of *Lochner*'s limited scope before the Supreme Court itself had explicitly offered any such indication.[65] In other words, although the states did not explicitly repudiate or defy the Supreme Court's opinion, they used state government to keep the broader issue alive until the justices might reconsider the issue and, from the states' perspective, restore their police powers to their proper constitutional place.

Supported by the Court's 1908 decision in *Muller v. Oregon* upholding the state's law setting a maximum cap on women's hours,[66] Oregon looked to a general statute providing for maximum hours for men as well.

Although legislators could point to *Muller*, constitutional worries did constrain Salem legislators who initially hesitated on passing maximum-hours legislation for all types of employment. In 1911, when the legislation was first being considered, the bill narrowly passed the state senate (16–13) but stalled in the lower chamber, where the judiciary committee declared it unconstitutional as drafted. Deferring to the warnings of their colleagues, the full house rejected it by a 17–40 vote.[67] Having apparently ironed out the problems to their satisfaction, the next session passed a maximum-hours law easily, by 45–10 and 17–12.[68] The Supreme Court eventually upheld this general maximum-hours law in *Bunting v. Oregon* (1917).[69] The states had thus reclaimed, to the extent it had been threatened, their constitutional authority to protect workers' health by limiting working hours. The federal judicial intervention into the states' police powers had looked more like a fluke than a sustained campaign.

As revisionist literature has rediscovered, the *Lochner* era of economic libertarianism was hardly that. The case, while beloved of law professors and therefore ground firmly into the minds of undergraduates, was largely a nonentity, recognized even at the time as a relative outlier in an era that generally upheld protective economic legislation, at least at the federal level.[70] As Walter Dodd observed soon after, *Lochner* had been an anomaly, a deviation from federal courts largely letting the state police powers adapt to changing needs—in other words, a largely unfettered imprimatur to progressive federalism: "Except for the rather unfortunate lapse in the New York bakeshop case, the Supreme Court has in the main taken a liberal attitude toward legislation aimed to meet new social and industrial needs. . . . Yet there remains the fact that perhaps the greater number of our state courts are illiberal . . . and able to block needed social and industrial legislation."[71] That federal judges in *Lochner* had blocked a state protective law that was anomalous in another way: it was the rare law that would fail federal permission after approval by the more libertarian New York state courts.[72]

Lochner was atypical in this sense because, consistent with the era's ethos of federalism, it was state courts that were also far more economically laissez-faire than their generally noninterventionist national counterparts, and had been for decades. In other words, in these cases, the imposition of laissez-faire was not imposed from above but by the states, and specifically state judges, themselves. While some have argued state courts, though clearly more aggressive than federal courts, were still less libertarian than popularly charged, the indictment clearly holds in New York, most clearly illustrated by the canonical cases *Wynehamer v. New York* (1856) (striking the state's prohibition law), *In re Jacobs* (1885) (overturning a tenement cigar-making ban), and *Ives v. South Buffalo Railway Co.* (1911) (striking down the state's workers compensation law).[73] The middle case, in which New York's court stuck a bill then-Assemblyman Roosevelt had steered to passage, helped establish not only the state's business-friendly jurisprudence but also Roosevelt's long antipathy toward judicial intervention.[74] Not until the mid-1930s, after a decade of gubernatorial control by Al Smith, Franklin Roosevelt, and Herbert Lehman, was New York's judiciary one that vindicated the state's police powers rather than implementing the narrow construction the court had maintained since the mid-nineteenth century.[75]

Moreover, successful federal challenges tended to be grounded less in laissez-faire fanaticism than in a Jacksonian egalitarianism that remained deeply skeptical of corrupt bargains between legislators and political favorites.[76] While *Lochner* author Justice Peckham shied away from that framing, over the preferences of both the lawyers and the marginal justices, David Bernstein's *Rehabilitating Lochner* convincingly demonstrates the maximum-hours legislation specifically at issue in the case was less about safety and more about a cabal of industrial bakers trying to squeeze out smaller, largely immigrant-owned competitors. Thus, although most textualists would deny that fact ultimately justified striking down the legislation, the intuition of the *Lochner* justices in doubting a public purpose in this case was well-founded.[77]

With *Lochner* both largely ignored in subsequent decisions and an unrepresentative case of rent-seeking masquerading as protective legislation, Chief Justice Taft thus had strong reason to believe the Court had gone along with the states and implicitly overruled *Lochner* by the time it handed down *Bunting v. Oregon* in 1917.[78]

In other words, Taft believed that the states' campaign on behalf of progressive federalism had properly been victorious and the states' police powers to regulate working conditions broadly approved. As Taft noted, Justice Joseph McKenna's *Bunting* opinion, upheld by four colleagues (and presumably supported by Louis Brandeis, who previously had represented Oregon and thus recused himself), ignored *Lochner*. As such, *Bunting* supported the states' impression that *Lochner* had never been taken seriously as an expansive precedent. In short, as even commentators at the time noted, *Lochner* was largely stillborn until its negative canonization by progressive law professors and the political actors who decided to rally against it,[79] with even careful judicial observers like William Howard Taft siding with the states' effort to understand *Lochner* as a rather minimalist opinion rather than a striking blow against their police powers and the ability to regulate for the benefit of workers.

Thus, at least for the first two decades of the Progressive Era, the less well-known, but arguably more consequential, liberty of contract caselaw that proscribed prolabor state activity was judicial protection of so-called yellow-dog contracts. In the late nineteenth century, employers seeking to prevent unionization began using what were eventually known as yellow-dog contracts, in which businesses explicitly stated that an employee's decision to join a union (or sometimes a specific union) constituted a firing offense. As part of the general trend toward protective, prolabor legislation, states passed bills sanctioning employers for using these antiunion contracts. Congress did the same in the Erdman Act, its 1898 law regulating railroad labor in response to the Pullman Strike four years earlier. Despite the widespread constitutional skepticism of class legislation and the exposition of a liberty of contract in *Allgeyer v. Louisiana* the year before, members of Congress accustomed to raising constitutional objections to federal bills raised no protests in passing the Erdman Act.[80] Even Richard Olney, Cleveland's attorney general pushing for an injunction in the Pullman Strike, supported congressional regulation of yellow-dog contracts where Congress had power to do so and drafted, based on the recommendations of an anti-strike commission, much of the text.[81]

If members of Congress had seemed unperturbed by the constitutional implication of anti-yellow-dog efforts, the nation's courts were less placid. Beginning with an 1894 Missouri ruling, state courts, including in the very progressive Wisconsin, blocked every yellow-dog law put before them—even before the US Supreme Court considered the issue. (State courts often cited federal decisions such as *Allgeyer* and *Lochner* to justify their own rulings, however.)[82] When the Supreme Court finally heard the issue, though generally more forgiving of protective legislation than state courts, it nonetheless struck down both the federal anti-yellow-dog provision in the Erdman Act (in *Adair v. United States*) and one of the few surviving state provisions (with *Coppage v. Kansas*), invoking liberty of contract in both cases (and federalism in the former).[83]

However, except for those key exceptions, the Supreme Court signed off on the rather significant expansion of state power in the early twentieth century, as states began to regulate and attempt to tame the economic effects of industrialization—progressivism and federalism basically went hand in hand.[84] Between 1920 and 1931, state spending on welfare almost *quadrupled*, and political scientists in the mid-1920s discussed whether laissez-faire was on its way out—hardly what one would expect from a populace cowed by judicial bullying.[85] Nor were these simply the musings of academics safely ensconced in the ivory tower; political figures had been uttering similar sentiments. Illinois governor Frank Lowden would bluntly explain that "an industrial age, whether we desire it or not, imposes new obligations on the state." With the rise of the steam engine and mass production, "the old days of *laissez-faire* have gone, never to return. The State, everywhere, has taken on new functions which it will not relinquish. . . . [S]trict individualism [is] doomed."[86] Just to the south, Missouri governor Frederick Dozier Gardner attributed this change to voter preferences:

We have but to compare the viewpoint the people had of government twenty-five years ago with the viewpoint today to be very forcibly impressed with this fact. Then the individual was the controlling factor in life. . . . The viewpoint of the public has evidently changed, for now we find the government exercising control over commerce, education, society, industry, food, raiment, health, transportation, and domestic affairs. . . . The responsibilities of the government have increased.[87]

Use of the states' police powers to pass worker's compensation laws, part of the effort to undermine the feudal vestiges of American law,[88] always received the US Supreme Court's blessing, and depending on the bill's exact framing, often by unanimous decisions. This favorable reception in the courts seems much less surprising when one realizes that many of the combatants who would eventually grapple over the constitutional validity of New Deal–era legislation nonetheless joined together in backing workers' compensation in the early decades of the twentieth century. Thus, Franklin Roosevelt, Frances Perkins, and Harry Hopkins cut their teeth in early efforts to implement workers' compensation in New York (which Governor Charles Evans Hughes signed). Even constitutional sticklers who would eventually become anti–New Deal Horsemen backed it as well: then-senator George Sutherland pushed for federal regulation on behalf of railroad employees in 1912 (pursuant to the interstate commerce power), while Pierce Butler contributed a brief on behalf of Minnesota's state law.[89]

As a result, few disagreed when Justice Mahlon Pitney, in the 1917 case of *New York Central Railroad Company v. White*, accepted the claim that the preconditions and assumptions that had guaranteed many of the old doctrines did not apply in modern economies. Since these assumptions were mere common-law rules rather than constitutional mandates, legislatures could wield their sovereign police power and reverse fellow-servant and related doctrines to implement workers' compensation laws.[90]

Even federal liability laws largely garnered a judicial imprimatur. In 1908, the Supreme Court struck down a federal law on Tenth Amendment grounds, but only insofar as its overly broad language interfered with what were considered purely intrastate activities. (Only Peckham, Brewer, and Fuller objected, in principle, to congressional laws on workers' compensation, and all of them would leave the court in the next few years.) Once the 1908 modification clarified that such laws only applied to interstate operations like railroads, future conservative Horseman Willis Van Devanter wrote for a unanimous court in approving of the federal workmen's compensation laws in 1912—the federal government could impose protective regulation in the spheres where an enumerated power of Constitution allowed it, but the justices left the states permission to build their own liability regimes.[91]

The contrast between those two decisions on federal workers compensation illustrates an important, often forgotten distinction (although one in which observers can be justified in forgetting, insofar as the Supreme Court justices themselves often did). Even many of the turn-of-the-century cases that sided with business against regulation largely did so on grounds of federalism rather than strictly laissez-faire—questions about the proper *allocation* rather than the *existence* of powers.[92] Thus, while the *E. C. Knight* decision imposed a fairly strict dichotomous test between commerce and manufacturing in measuring federal regulatory power, Melvin Fuller's opinion was mostly devoted to elevating the powers of states to suppress noncommercial monopolies.[93] Other cases, such as the employer's liability cases noted previously, sustained the substance of legislation as long as the distinction between state and federal powers remained divided to the Court's satisfaction.

In short, in addition to their liberal use of injunctions,[94] courts basically interjected themselves in two spheres of legislation designed to limit the excesses of industrial capitalism: national policies they believed exceeded the enumerated powers and thus fell afoul of the Tenth Amendment and anything that smacked them as explicitly anti-employer/prounion, which *Lochner* and the yellow-dog cases did.[95] As Melvin Urofsky and Paul Finkelman have observed, "In other areas of protective legislation, the Progressives could hardly have asked for more from the [federal] courts."[96]

More broadly, they argue that judges appointed by the three Progressive Era presidents—Roosevelt, Taft, and Wilson—were no different than others in their view of economic regulations, especially when the national government was testing the limits of its power. Thus, according to Urofsky and Finkelman, we should think of these progressive judges as a broadly conservative movement still relatively hostile to a centralized, modern state, and one with a healthy respect for states' rights and a robust conception of their police powers.[97]

Thus, although frustrated in odd cases—such as *Lochner*, which the states successfully resisted in vindicating their police powers against federal intervention—states had little need to press back and went about the work of passing protective lawmaking, the sort of progressive federalism that Elihu Root had urged and which the federal courts seemed to have generally blessed.

The 1923 case of *Adkins v. Children's Hospital* changed this, as it and its progeny moved beyond a strict protection of decentralization into the creation of a no-man's land forbidding some commercial regulations altogether. Even progressives had accepted the Court's decision to strike down the child labor tax in *Bailey v. Drexel Furniture* (1922), with Frankfurter himself shrugging and saying, "We must pay a price for federalism."[98] But there was no such federalist return on investment with *Adkins*, and thus the effort by states to reassert their police powers and resist that decision—as well as the Court's jurisprudence on labor injunctions and yellow-dog bans—is the subject of the next chapter.

CHAPTER FIVE

The Liberty of Contract II:
State Resistance

Resort to national action on everything is bound to dry up the sources of a healthy
national life—action by the states. . . . I don't give a damn about "states rights" but I do
about states' responsibilities—the states as organs for legal control for determining
most of our social relations.

—Felix Frankfurter

As the previous chapter showed, the so-called *Lochner* era hardly deserved the
name. The signature decision was largely ignored by political actors, and while
radical governors protested other judicial interventions, these were often on
either procedural grounds and thus correctible or were striking down particularly unusual laws, such as one in which Arizona arguably interfered with federal immigration law. The more substantively consequential line of cases—the
protection of yellow-dog contracts—annoyed labor, but these did not immediately raise the same federalism objections insofar as the Supreme Court's
anti-yellow-dog decisions in *Adair* and *Coppage* accepted and nationalized the
effectively unanimous decisions of state courts (though they themselves were
often just applying earlier federal decisions). Progressive politicians nonetheless objected and needed to convince not only their own state courts but eventually the federal courts that this was an issue that the Constitution rightly left
to the states' police powers. They could not as easily claim this was an issue in
which nine geographically distant robed masters rejected the widespread preferences and jurisprudence of the states and set a national rule from on high.

But that was precisely what the Court did in *Adkins v. Children's Hospital* and its subsequent cases, in which the justices controversially invoked the "liberty of contract" and blocked the states from using the police power to create minimum wages.[1] If there is to be an "era," it ought to instead be "the *Adkins* era," which rejuvenated the liberty of contract and in which state officials sought to reclaim their police powers while labor and its allies tried to use states as toeholds to force reconsideration or narrowing of Supreme Court holdings prohibiting protective labor legislation. In vindicating protective labor laws against these judicial interventions (in the realms of labor injunctions, yellow-dog contracts, and minimum wages), state resistance would eventually succeed in restoring the possibility of progressive federalism.

State Pushback: Yellow-Dog Contracts and Labor Injunctions

As the last chapter explained, yellow-dog contracts—contracts restricting unionizing activities—were a particular target of labor activists who sought to use the states' police powers (and the federal power where appropriate under interstate commerce, such as on railroads) to check them. As state courts echoed the Supreme Court in blocking those bills, progressives' defeat of yellow-dog contracts also necessitated overcoming state courts. But the main target, that would ultimately have to be defeated, remained the federal judiciary and its intervention in the state police power—after all, state courts often cited federal holdings in their own decisions blocking state yellow-dog bans. Overcoming federal courts required both state officials and national institutions to work together to vindicate the states' police powers as well as relying on state legislative politics as a forum in which to keep the issue alive.[2]

Hitchman Coal Company v. Mitchell (1917) merged the issues of yellow-dog contracts and labor injunctions while expanding the use of both—and in turn triggered state backlash against them. Hitchman had insisted on standard yellow-dog language: that his employees would be terminated for joining the United Mine Workers of America (UMWA). UMWA workers sought to unionize the mine's employees by organizing a possible strike (likely after placing sufficient numbers of employees primed to strike for unionization even after agreeing not to within the company's workforce). Hitchman, in turn, sought an injunction against the unionizing efforts, arguing that the labor-organizing efforts were abetting a breach of contract. The Supreme Court agreed, in effect, authorizing labor injunctions as a remedy to enforce yellow-dog contracts. This unsurprisingly made yellow-dog contracts more effective, and thus popular among employers, and prompted even more such injunctions (and perhaps more extreme and even dangerous forms of labor activity).[3]

This escalation provoked state and national figures, not only progressives but also conservatives, to think of ways to pierce the judicially created shield protecting yellow-dog provisions from the states' police powers. The National War Labor Board, with Taft as its chair, attacked employers for using yellow-dog contracts.[4] Experience on the board seems to have nudged Taft—who, after all, had served as an early architect of the labor injunction—toward greater sympathy with labor, as he now saw protective legislation like minimum wages as part of the public good rather than corrupt class legislation in opposition to a presumptive liberty of contract.[5] State judiciaries similarly began turning in favor of greater deference to union activities. In 1923, the Ohio Supreme Court declined to grant an injunction blocking union officials from organizing employees with yellow-dog contracts, distinguishing it from the Supreme Court decision in *Hitchman*, in which the justices granted an injunction under similar circumstances. Two New York cases similarly followed in declining to enforce parts of yellow-dog contracts.[6]

With both the frequency and consequence of yellow-dog contracts expanding, labor and its allies looked to attack the Court's anti-yellow-dog doctrines through state politics. Among these allies was Edwin Witte, the University of Wisconsin economist, who, in advancing the "Wisconsin Idea" bridging academia and politics, also served as the chief of the state's Legislative Research Bureau (and therefore a crucial draftsman of Wisconsin's protective labor legislation). Witte's work, in other words, was essential to the political project of Wisconsin, often held up by politicians across the spectrum as a paragon of progressive federalism. Witte observed that the chief "value of the yellow-dog contracts lie not in enforcement against the workmen who sign them but in injunctions against attempts of unions to organize the employ[ees] or to induce them to join in strikes. No case is known of an employer's suit against a workman violating a non-union agreement."[7]

In 1925, Ohio legislators considered a model anti-yellow-dog contract bill drafted with just that consideration in mind. The bill was the product of a group of labor-allied lawyers and scholars—including Witte, Herman Oliphant, Francis Sayre, Felix Frankfurter, Donald Richberg, and Roscoe Pound—who helped draft and defend a framework for attacking yellow-dog contracts that would start with the states and scale up to eventually become the anti-yellow-dog federal Norris-LaGuardia Act in 1932.[8]

In striking a ban on yellow-dog contracts, *Adair* had conceded that "no contract, whatever its subject matter, can be sustained which the law, upon reasonable grounds, forbids as inconsistent with the public interests or as hurtful to the public order or as detrimental to the common good."[9] The court simply, if questionably, held that "the employer and the employee have equality of right, and any legislation that disturbs that equality is an arbitrary interference with the liberty of contract which no government can legally justify in a free land." In effect, the judges claimed, Congress was not regulating for any sort of public interest—such as the health of workers—but was instead simply practicing a form of class legislation by intervening on behalf of one of two equal parties in negotiations.[10]

To overcome *Adair*'s argument that banning yellow-dog contracts was a form of class legislation aiming for a merely private good, these economists and lawyers joined University of Wisconsin professor John Commons's idea to declare yellow-dog contracts hostile to a public purpose—with Pound's suggestion to employ unenforceability as the means to achieve that purpose.[11] Rather than use criminal sanctions to punish companies using yellow-dog contracts, like the bills overturned in *Adair* and *Coppage*, the model bill insisted on government nonintervention: it declared all *subsequent* yellow-dog provisions contrary to public policy and thus merely unenforceable. *Adair* and *Coppage* likely meant that the Court would strike such a bill down, as Edwin Witte feared, but labor had little to lose. Besides, as Witte observed, perhaps thinking of the growing support even among some like Taft, "no one can be sure what [the courts] will do until such legislation is actually before them."[12]

It took some time to get such legislation before them. A deadlocked Ohio Judiciary Committee vote in 1925 meant its backers would have to wait for the bill's reconsideration in 1927. At that time, the state's Republican attorney general Edward C. Turner issued a lengthy defense of its constitutionality, explaining that the police power allowed the state legislature to regulate contracts for the public, rather than private, good. "Insur[ing] industrial tranquility" by minimizing strikes and lockouts, Turner held, clearly advanced the public good; collective bargaining, in turn, would still lead to contracts that would protect employer and laborer alike. With that imprimatur, answering a constitutional objection raised by the Republican majority leader, the state senate passed the bill by a 29–3 vote in 1927. A majority of the house also voted to approve the bill, but it failed to garner the two-thirds vote necessary to suspend the rules and reach the calendar.[13] The Ohio Federation of Labor nonetheless warned that it would keep Turner's document in hand for future use as a definitive constitutional defense of such legislation.[14] Other industrial states considered the bill in 1927, but these, too, were unable to secure passage. California's assembly approved the bill by a 43–36 spread but lost by two votes in the senate, while an Illinois house committee issued a favorable report but little else.[15]

As would become the case with minimum wage legislation, it was, fittingly, Wisconsin that finally took the lead in pushing back with a bill designed to test the Supreme Court's resolve. In 1925, the progressive John Blaine had used his inaugural address to lament America was increasingly bound by "government by injunction," "the most serious assault on constitutional government since the *Dred Scott* decision."[16] In 1929, the Badger State became the first—and for two years only—state to adopt a law holding future yellow-dog provisions unenforceable in the state courts. (The AFL had sought passage in all forty-eight states.) Offered by socialist senator Thomas Duncan, the anti-yellow-dog proposal garnered the unanimous backing of Wisconsin's socialists, its progressive La Follette faction of the GOP, and even a handful of conservatives.[17] Governor Walter Kohler, a conservative-leaning Republican (and industrialist) who had replaced the progressive Fred Zimmerman, backed the bill (as he had the simultaneous repeal of the state's prohibition laws), garnering both local and national attention in approving such a "drastic" law "rejected by every other state."[18] Although Duncan and the Wisconsin Federation of Labor argued Kohler had merely allowed the bill under duress, Kohler nonetheless made his prolabor record—rooted in the yellow-dog ban and in his business practices as chairman of Kohler—the core of his unsuccessful 1930 reelection case.[19] After Kohler's subsequent defeat in Wisconsin, his successor Phil La Follette approved Duncan's incorporation of the yellow-dog provisions into a more comprehensive labor framework that also banned labor injunctions.[20]

After Wisconsin took the lead, states throughout the country attempted to similarly defang yellow-dog contracts within their borders—and in some cases succeeded. After a coup against the state's Republican leadership, Ohio passed the bill it nearly had backed six years earlier, winning by overwhelming totals in both houses (82–33, 25–1), garnering the signature of Democratic governor George White.[21] Oregon, Colorado, and Arizona also approved nearly identical bills. Indiana's legislature passed it nearly unanimously, but the senate failed to override Republican Harry Leslie's veto following state attorney general James Ogden's warning of unconstitutionality. New York, Massachusetts, Illinois, California, Maine, Kansas, Missouri, and South Dakota also considered yellow-dog bills.[22]

Early judicial consideration, however, suggested that courts remained unconvinced by efforts to draw a distinction between the new anti-yellow-dog efforts and the old. Massachusetts's state legislators, while considering their bill, requested an advisory opinion from the state supreme court in 1930. The judges came back with a no, citing federal decisions in *Adair*, *Coppage*, and *Hitchman*—although, as Witte observed, Bay State justices had done so without hearing arguments and thus some hope remained.[23] (The Massachusetts justices would reiterate their opinion in 1931, with New Hampshire's supreme court issuing a similar advisory opinion in 1933.)[24]

In the meantime, yellow-dog legislation reappeared at the federal level, now joined with injunction politics as a result of the *Hitchman* case linking the two. In other words, this was a sphere in which the states seeking to vindicate progressive federalism against federal courts had some national institutions as allies. Successful anti-injunctive legislation had been long sought since *Debs*. Although President Theodore Roosevelt—and even President Taft—had requested legislation restricting labor injunctions, Republican Congresses repeatedly ignored pleas for anti-injunction bills, thus leading labor to endorse the Democrats who, in 1914, passed the anti-injunction Clayton Act. Drafters of the Clayton Act sought to clamp down on the practice, but federal courts construed it (and its state imitators) narrowly, though perhaps with the approval both of a Congress that intentionally wrote a vague statute and of Wilson, who invoked New Freedom in declining to give an explicit labor protection from antitrust. And in the case of Arizona, federal courts overturned the state law entirely in *Truax v. Corrigan* (1921), over the protest of progressive justices Holmes and Brandeis arguing for the constitutional prerogative of states to experiment. As Brandeis observed, this was simply "an exercise of the police power by which, in the interest of the public and in order to preserve the liberty and the property of the great majority of the citizens of a state, rights of property and the liberty of the individual must be remolded from time to time to meet the changing needs of society."[25]

The American Federation of Labor (AFL) abandoned its apolitical "voluntarist" thinking in 1927 and reengaged the political process, again seeking a federal anti-injunction law that would be tougher than Clayton while *also* incorporating the specific yellow-dog unenforceability provisions pioneered in the state legislation.[26]

Both national parties immediately responded by endorsing anti-injunctive legislation in their 1928 platforms.[27] Labor also flexed its muscles in joining with the NAACP to block Hoover's 1930 nomination of Judge John Parker to the Supreme Court—largely on grounds he had aggressively followed the Supreme Court's *Hitchman* precedent and issued an injunction in the *Red Jacket* case, as well as making seemingly antiblack statements while running for governor ten years earlier.[28]

With the resurgent political salience, anti-injunctive efforts moved to Congress, where they were joined with anti-yellow-dog efforts modeled on the state bill passed in Wisconsin.[29] (In 1928, Senator George Norris had convened many of the same scholars who drafted the state laws to draft his federal equivalent.)[30] Although labor injunctions themselves were defended by, among others, former solicitor general James Beck, who warned their abolition pointed toward Moscow, yellow-dog contracts themselves were, according to Edwin Witte, "almost literally without a friend in either house of Congress." Members of Congress offered near unanimous policy support, albeit tempered by legal reservations, in attacking them in a bill that prevented federal courts from enforcing yellow-dog contracts or issuing most forms of labor injunctions. Even conservative members of Congress invoked the AFL's cause as one they too shared, noting the AFL's conservative views and hostility to communism warranted their support.[31] With such a relatively unified front, Congress passed Norris-La Guardia in 1932, which both severely limited federal courts' ability to issue labor injunctions and made yellow-dog contracts unenforceable in federal court—effectively invalidating them, as far as the federal government's involvement was concerned. President Hoover approved the bill, though expressing some discomfort in his signing statement and suggesting the possibility of court intervention.[32]

Passage of the federal Norris-La Guardia Act meant a unanimous front of Congress, the president, and the states against the Supreme Court, triggering further policy diffusion as states adopted a model anti-injunctive bill drafted by Frankfurter's protégé and coauthor Nathan Greene.[33] (State diffusion was necessary, of course, as Norris-La Guardia could not, consistent with federalism, tell the states what to do with their own courts.) Pennsylvania and California passed anti-yellow-dog legislation akin to Wisconsin's 1929 law while other states passed analogous anti-injunction legislation more broadly.[34]

Aided by allies in Congress and progressive activists, the state legislatures had reclaimed part of their police powers from federal judicial overreach and overcame one prong of the liberty of contract. However, as would be true of minimum wages, the federal government would almost immediately reassert its control of policy, though federal policymaking on labor was now coming from Congress, not the Supreme Court, and on the side of labor rather than employers.[35]

State Pushback: Minimum Wages

Although *Adkins v. Children's Hospital* (1923) overturned congressional handiwork in attacking minimum wages as inconsistent with the liberty of contract, its due process holding clearly threatened the far more numerous and important state laws, as later cases soon confirmed.

Throughout the second decade of the twentieth century, states had been rapidly implementing minimum wages for women; fifteen states, as well as the District of Columbia, had implemented such legislation by 1919. Of these, eleven had created legally binding commissions to set minimum wages for women while Massachusetts (and, briefly, Nebraska) used a commission to set a wage but which only had the power to shame, not formally sanction, any violators. Utah, Arizona, and South Dakota fixed a statutory hourly rate in lieu of commissions.[36]

Even as they diffused throughout the Union, such laws long stood in the shadow of a legal threat while the Court deadlocked in considering the issue: the 1923 decision had actually been the *second* judicial attempt to overturn minimum wage laws.

Stettler v. O'Hara (1917), in which Oregon state courts cited post-*Lochner* precedents to approve their state wage law in 1914, had been the first legal challenge to state minimum wage laws.[37] Unlike other economic issues where state judges proved more skeptical of the proposed government interventions than their federal counterparts, state courts had been and would continue to be almost unanimous in approving minimum wage statutes; of the twenty-nine state judges to hear minimum wage challenges before 1923, only two held it unconstitutional.[38]

After the Supreme Court delayed for several years with rearguments due to changes in membership, the justices finally issued a deadlocked ruling in 1917. (Brandeis recused himself because he had served as initial counsel for Oregon before handing the case off to Felix Frankfurter upon joining the Court.) The frustrating result left the Oregon decision standing, without any opinion as guidance going forward.[39]

Such guidance finally and decisively appeared in 1923 in the form of the notorious *Adkins v. Children's Hospital*. By a 5–3 vote and over the dissent of both Holmes and Taft, the justices overturned a congressional law providing minimum wages for women in the District of Columbia. This was partly because, as Justice George Sutherland argued, the Nineteenth Amendment made women politically equal and thus no longer needing to be treated as wards of the state in bargaining. (Sutherland had championed the amendment as a Republican Senator from Utah.)

Especially because, based on the Supreme Court's seemingly strong deference to the state police powers in recent years, many had expected the opinion to come out the other way; the reception of Sutherland's opinion was decidedly negative and placed the justices out of step even with their usual conservative allies, to say nothing of critics like Arizona's George Hunt.[40] The popular press excoriated Sutherland, declaring that he was naïve in simply looking to the employer-employee relationship rather than acknowledging society was itself involved more broadly through welfare policies. As the *New York Post* declared, "A business which does not pay a living wage is essentially parasitic. It subsists because society pays the difference"[41] Nine months after *Adkins* and in his first annual message since assuming the presidency, Calvin Coolidge announced his support for the overturned DC law, calling for an amendment to overturn the decision, just as he had backed Massachusetts's minimum wage commission a decade before.[42]

New York's governor Al Smith, who perhaps more than any other major political figure of the era linked progressive policy views with traditional constitutional beliefs, was aghast.

In the failed New York Constitutional Convention of 1915, as an assemblyman and finally as governor, Al Smith had strongly championed a state minimum wage law year after year.[43] He had even defended it on precisely constitutional grounds, explaining that it was like fire exits and sanitation— other measures he had championed—in helping women's health, not class legislation, which he also detested.[44] The same Jacksonian streak that led him to bristle at class legislation made him an ardent states' rights believer—in this case, the right and duty to use the state police powers on behalf of the health of citizens.

Indeed, this widely reviled case proved no less infuriating to William Howard Taft.[45] In an incredulous (and rare)[46] dissent, Taft cited a variety of cases, most notably *Bunting v. Oregon*, which had upheld state maximum-hours laws, in explaining that the US Supreme Court had long upheld the principle that police power restrictions on contracts were acceptable provided they were actually targeting abusive or unhealthy working conditions. This was, the precedents held, *especially* true for legislation applying to women—though Taft's opinion remained open to the possibility that men could also benefit from such laws. Uncharacteristically channeling legal realist indictments of his brethren that held them to be doing policy rather than law, Taft reminded his fellow justices that "it is not the function of this Court to hold congressional acts invalid simply because they are passed to carry out economic views which the Court believes to be unwise or unsound."[47]

Unlike *Lochner*, which had not been followed up by the Fuller or White Courts (and hence gave Taft, like the states and many others, the impression that it was effectively a dead letter), the *Adkins* justices clearly applied *Adkins* as more than a one-shot fluke. *Meyer v. Nebraska* (1923) and *Pierce v. Society of Sisters* (1925) used liberty of contract to strike down laws limiting educational choice.[48] (This prospect may reappear in the present day, as will be discussed in the concluding chapter.)[49]

Adkins's fate—and thus the fate of minimum wages (and, perhaps, the fate of various schoolteachers and parents)—largely resulted from flukes of membership. Had Stone replaced McKenna, who had been ailing for a decade, a year and a half earlier, *Adkins* would have come out the other way. Similarly, had an illness on the DC circuit court not forced a rehearing, *Adkins* would have been heard before Butler and Sutherland joined the Court. "Thus," scholar Thomas Reed Powell dryly lamented, "Sometimes it almost seems the Constitution is in part at least dependent upon circumstances but dimly in the vision of its progenitors."[50]

By 1925, a majority of the Court likely backed Taft in believing *Adkins* had been wrongly decided. With the replacement of Joseph McKenna by Harlan Stone, the Supreme Court had five members (Stone and Brandeis, and *Adkins* dissenters Taft, Holmes, and Sanford) who believed *Adkins* had been a mistake.[51]

Perhaps sensing this, litigators quickly urged the Court to look anew at *Adkins*. In the 1925 case of *Murphy v. Sardell*, the state of Arizona, whose minimum wage law was being contested, attempted merely to distinguish its law from the federal rule overturned in *Adkins*. By way of contrast, an amicus brief on behalf of California's Industrial Welfare Commission directly challenged *Adkins*, citing some of Powell's legal scholarship proving the seemingly arbitrary events that gave rise to it.[52] Similarly, the appellants' brief in *Donham v. West Nelson Manufacturing*, an analogous case from Arkansas, directly asked the Supreme Court to overrule *Adkins*.[53] But in neither case did the Court respond favorably: only Brandeis dissented from these later applications, with the others apparently believing themselves bound by its precedent (as Holmes made explicit).[54]

Implementation of *Adkins* spread, with legislatures preemptively acting to comply as federal judges continued to strike at state minimum wage laws. A federal court had blocked Wisconsin's law in 1924. Utah repealed its minimum wage in 1929. The state supreme courts of Kansas and Puerto Rico applied *Adkins* in striking minimum wage laws for women, while Minnesota's attorney general declined to enforce its law except as applied to children (since *Adkins* did not explicitly control that).[55] The Ohio legislature had long refrained from exercising the wage-making authority it received via a 1912 constitutional amendment, waiting for court approval (which had been dragged out during *Stettler*'s protracted case history). *Adkins* obviously denied such approval, and thus Buckeye legislators—who ironically had finally begun implementing such legislation when *Adkins* was decided—shelved their plans until receiving presidential encouragement to resist *Adkins* in 1933.[56]

One minimum wage law did procure a judicial imprimatur but in a way that seemed to mock the idea of a minimum wage actually helping women under economic pressure. Massachusetts courts approved their state's publicity-based minimum wage commission, but states that made wage enforcement compulsory had not fared so well.[57]

After *Adkins* and these follow-ups, a cadre of progressive activists debated how best to restore protective economic legislation, foundering over disagreements about gender equality and federalism. William Borah had avoided criticizing *Adkins* itself but had predicted it would lead to an amendment restoring states' powers.[58] Borah's prediction, however, was not borne out, as an internal division between opponents of the decision stalled progress on a reversing amendment. Florence Kelley proposed a variant of the Equal Rights Amendment that would nonetheless specifically allow protective legislation on behalf of women (generating a split with the more formalist libertarian Alice Paul, an ally of George Sutherland). Felix Frankfurter and his labor-friendly lawyer allies situated *Adkins* at the locus of several constitutional questions, preferring instead to use other cases to overturn it and generally restore due process to a simply procedural question, which a specifically minimum wage focused amendment would not do. If an amendment had to be used, Frankfurter—a devoted acolyte of the decentralist Brandeis—instead joined his mentor in preferring one that would eliminate the due process clause against the states in order to end substantive due process. This would rejuvenate, rather than suppress, the police powers and states' enthusiasm for using them.[59] As Frankfurter observed, "Resort to national action on everything is bound to dry up the sources of a healthy national life—action by the states. . . . I don't give a damn about 'states rights' but I do about states' responsibilities—the states as organs for legal control for determining most of our social relations."[60]

Unfortunately, however, it would take *Adkins* critics several years to agree on their response. To force a test case, the strategists suggested the passage of new state laws that would use the wage-fixing formulas to which Sutherland's opinion had possibly alluded.[61] California's progressive Senator Hiram Johnson attempted to have Congress propose a constitutional amendment after *Murphy*.[62] To Florence Kelley's distress, the National Consumers League argued against Johnson's proposal to overturn the decision by national amendment, fearing that it would give leverage to the Wadsworth-Garrett Amendment movement aiming to require state referenda for all Article V ratifications.[63]

But while labor activists squabbled over how best to draft and legitimate new state legislation, several predominantly but not exclusively western states continued to press on in spite of the *Adkins* and *Murphy* decisions, adopting a variety of tactics to assert their authority to set minimum wages and thus pursue their progressive policy preferences in the face of federal hostility.

The Pacific Western States

Far from the District of Columbia, California, Oregon, and Washington defiantly maintained active wage commissions in the absence of formal federal rulings there, which they did by skillfully preventing cases from reaching federal courts. The western and especially Pacific skew in being the most robust supporters of state-level economic protective legislation was no accident. With the Rockies bisecting transportation networks, the West and especially the Far West were comparatively isolated from the rest of the nation's economic affairs. Higher transportation costs—especially when railroads were king—meant that the region could embark on protective legislation without suffering much of a competitive disadvantage; they simply wanted to be left alone from federal interference (though the three Pacific states would coordinate policy among themselves).[64]

Thus, as jealous contemporary observers in the rest of the country pointed out, mandatory minimum wage policies survived in California, Oregon, and

Washington, since businesses there had much less of an incentive to challenge their own state's minimum wage legislation.[65]

In Washington, courts either avoided rulings or held the minimum wage laws constitutional.[66] Thus, Washington's commission was the most fearless, continuing to issue fines, as it did against two root beer stand proprietors in Walla Walla in 1930.[67] As a result, Washington's law could survive to ultimately become *West Coast Hotel v. Parrish* (1937).[68] This was not in the least bit subtle. As Robert Post explained, "The continuous open defiance of the State of Washington, together with the strong support of the local business community, explains why . . . the Court could marvel that the minimum wage statute of Washington had been 'in force' through the 'entire period' since *Adkins*."[69]

Oregon's attorney general more carefully threaded the needle in maintaining a functioning system of wage controls. After *Murphy*, he conceded that the commission could not issue formal sanctions.[70] However, he also reiterated the commission's legitimacy by explaining that the US Supreme Court decisions had not affected the commission's work on minors, maximum hours, etc. Although the commission ceased printing the wage scales as binding, most employers continued to honor them, as several employers and professional associations had issued statements explicitly disavowing *Adkins*. The Manufacturers' and Merchants' Association of Oregon went a step further, pledging to "use every effort to discourage anyone from testing the validity of the law in the courts" or to "repeal the law by the legislature."[71] The secretary-manager of the Manufacturers Association of Oregon, who opposed the child labor amendment on federalism grounds, nonetheless was celebrated for suppressing his members' efforts to legally challenge the minimum wage after *Adkins*.[72]

As one contemporary observed in 1930, the Oregon labor commission "carries on no prosecutions" for wage violations, but it "does continue its inspections and investigations, it continues to declare the minimum wage, maximum hours, and standard conditions of work. In brief, it continues its operations as before, except that it now depends upon favorable public opinion for its sanctions rather than upon legal prosecutions."[73] The business community clearly did view public opinion as supportive of minimum wage: one advertisement in the *Oregonian* reminded customers "that ours was the first department store in this city . . . to establish a real 8-hour working day—[and] to adopt a minimum wage for men and women."[74]

California adopted two strategies, calling for both a constitutional amendment to overturn the liberty of contract while also seeking to evade the application of that doctrine to the state's laws. With only one legislator dissenting in either house, California had endorsed its senior senator Hiram Johnson's post-*Murphy* effort to amend the Constitution and restore the states' police power to set a minimum wage.[75] (A later attempt, asking for an amendment allowing both minimum wage and maximum hours, died in committee in 1933 after Roosevelt had already come out in support of states' minimum wage laws.)[76]

Like Oregon, California's minimum wage policy similarly operated in a state of plausible deniability, ignoring the spirit of the Court's rulings and preserving a floor for women's wages. After *Adkins*, California's board ceased issuing wage "orders" but continued to publish data and rely on popular enforcement. As one contemporary noted, "The law is deprived of its power of enforcement but it is being applied nonetheless" and even had more teeth following a 1927 amendment.[77]

While California's attorney general had feared that *Murphy* would strike his state's law, as in Oregon, California businesses generally banded together in defense of the state's law immediately after the decision.[78] One had attempted to drum up a false suit against the minimum wage, ostensibly on behalf of an oblivious employee, who then publicly shamed the company and disavowed its effort to make her an unwitting party to the legal challenge, just as the National Consumers League was readying to litigate the issue before the state supreme court.[79] Even massive national companies seemed to refrain from bucking the local business consensus not to challenge the law: the then-conservative *Los Angeles Times* lamented the "open secret" behind General Motors' plan to withdraw a plant from California in 1933 rather than contend with or oppose Sacramento's supposedly voluntary minimum wage law.[80]

Prominent state politicians mocked both *Adkins* and the later, effectively identical *Tipaldo* case. Outgoing governor C. C. Young, a progressive Republican, openly gloated about the success of California's well-funded minimum wage board in his 1931 farewell address.[81] Both California governor Frank Merriam—a conservative-turned-increasingly moderate Republican—and the state's industrial relations director Timothy Reardon similarly shrugged off the *Tipaldo* case, each insisting that the commission would operate until receiving a direct and specific court order blocking their activity. Reardon suggested that differences in the bill made the decision inapplicable while Merriam believed *Tipaldo* likely would strike the California law but he would continue anyway in hope of an amendment correcting the Court's misinterpretation.[82] Other commentators did note that it had teeth nonetheless; for example, both the *Christian Science Monitor* and *New York Times* printed excited summaries of California's wage boards' conclusion that the law did not harm industry but had raised the standard of living for women.[83] Thus, tempered somewhat by prudence, the three Pacific states could maintain commissions by simply ignoring the Court's liberty of contract rulings. Through careful control of standing, these progressive states managed to commit what Mark Graber would dub "partial nullification," evading the implications of court orders without having to invoke John C. Calhoun's formulation explicitly rejecting federal constitutionalism.[84]

The Midwest and East

Other states took one of two tracks in responding to *Adkins*: either maintaining weakened commissions or, in the case of Wisconsin, attempting to draw up a new statute aimed to force a judicial reconsideration. Eventually, in 1933, New York would lead a multistate effort to do just that.

In the Midwest, North and South Dakota repealed or weakened their implementation mechanisms but specifically left the minimum wages nominally on the books—in effect, converting their laws into an even weaker version of the symbolic sort that Massachusetts had pioneered in 1912 and continued to employ.[85] Alone among the states of the Union, only Wisconsin, fulfilling its reputation for a muscular federalist progressivism, took proactive legislative effort to preserve and implement its state law before the election of Franklin Roosevelt and a new nationwide push for minimum wage laws in 1933.

Unlike the western states, which simply had not suffered direct federal court intervention, Wisconsin had seen its law struck by federal action in 1924. Local papers were outraged. One expressed the outside hope that Taft and Brandeis—whom it erroneously dubbed new members since *Adkins*—would help reverse the case. After all, the editors proclaimed, "Wisconsin authorities have proceeded very carefully and employers have been as a rule satisfied with the minimum wage fixed by the commission." But that prudent application was not enough, it grumbled, because "the decision just made is another reminder that the federal constitution governs over all state laws and state authorities. It is bound to be criticized and may become a campaign issue."[86] The *Wisconsin State Journal* cited Taft's condemnation of his peers in related cases and challenged legislators and jurists to limit what it believed to be the Court's zealous, extraconstitutional imposition of economic doctrine on the states (even as the *Journal* concluded that it was nonetheless important to have a strong counter-majoritarian protection and cited separation-of-powers concerns to bitterly condemn Senator Robert La Follette's [R/P-WI] proposal to overturn judicial decisions via congressional vote).[87]

Initially, the state's industrial board offered a defiant, Lincolnian interpretation of the decision: pledging to honor it in the specific case and withdraw action against Folding Furniture Works (the party in the decision) but to zealously enforce the minimum wage otherwise—in effect, treating the decision as a new *Dred Scott*.[88] Even as the state industrial board pledged to press on, within a week of the final district decision, state legislators immediately went about blunting the decision.[89]

In 1925, utilizing a textual hook gleaned from Sutherland's *Adkins* opinion and under the guidance of University of Wisconsin economics professor John Commons, Wisconsin legislators passed a law prohibiting "oppressive" wages "lower than a reasonable and adequate compensation." To nominally comply with the Sutherland opinion (as well as Commons's own views about government merely setting a floor to correct market failure, not creating economic justice itself), these were not defined as "fair" but minimum and defended as equivalent to the sort of "confiscatory" rates that utilities could not charge.[90] Both houses of the Wisconsin legislature passed it without dissent.[91]

The intention was, quite clearly, to challenge the Supreme Court's decision from within its own professed logic. As Edwin Witte, the head of the Wisconsin Legislative Research Library, wrote to an inquiring citizen, the new statute continued the "living wage" principle for minors (which *Adkins* had not touched) but also "throw[s] back to the Supreme Court its own proposition as regards the proper basis" for adult women's wages. "This has the advantage," the author continued, "of forcing the Supreme Court to consider a different settlement."[92] A similar letter six years later was even more blunt in condemning the judiciary: Witte suggested that the authors of the Wisconsin law viewed it primarily as a distraction that would protect the minors' law, resigned to the "probab[ility] that the courts would declare this law unconstitutional." Nonetheless, they hoped that at the very least the courts "would be somewhat embarrassed" since the Sutherland opinion purported to offer a "principle . . . conform[ing] with true ethics" that would justify such legislation.[93]

States soon interpreted the election of President Roosevelt as encouragement to reenact minimum wage laws and not merely commissions. Resistance to the Court's holding quickly expanded from typical progressive holdouts like Wisconsin and a handful of western states to the nation more broadly—

particularly areas in the generally Republican-dominated industrial and cultural core.[94] New York took the lead in passing so-called new design wage legislation in 1933.

Acknowledging unfavorable court precedents, Governor Herbert Lehman, an FDR protégé, followed his predecessor's 1931 address in observing that recommendatory commissions (as in Massachusetts) had never been struck. (Then Governor Roosevelt had initially followed his own mentor Al Smith's lead in grudgingly bowing to *Murphy*.)[95] Moreover, changing economic conditions since *Adkins* might cause the Court to analyze even mandatory wages differently—less as class legislation and more for the public good. Thus, Lehman explained, "The States should exert their authority to discharge their duty." He then charged state legislators to fulfill New York's long-standing, self-appointed role as an opinion leader: "Other states, naturally, are guided by the action of the leading manufacturing states in the Union. . . . Someone must make a start in the endeavor . . . and I covet for our State this leadership. I believe other states will follow our lead."[96]

New York's legislature answered the governor's call. After sifting through several competing bills, its legislators eventually passed two with the assumption that Lehman would make a choice: one, developed by Florence Kelley's National Consumers League and sponsored by Democratic senator Albert Wald, would have established a permanent, binding commission for women and minors. The other, by Republican senator Thomas Desmond (who also backed Wald's bill), would have created a temporary, Massachusetts-style commission but which applied to both men and women. Future Eisenhower attorney general Herbert Brownell had also offered a third, almost identical bill, although its commission would not have promulgated wage targets but simply made findings. He argued that his bill—backed by Alice Paul's National Woman's Party for its application to men and women alike—was better tailored in consideration of the Court and that mandating wages would simply result in the liquidation of female employees.[97]

The Desmond Bill had a few Republican supporters but was primarily a Democratic-backed bill. Republicans claimed that the courts were more likely to approve the Desmond Bill due to its emergency provisions, as well as the gender neutrality (since *Adkins* had, over Holmes's and Taft's protests, declared gendered protection obsolete upon the passage of the Nineteenth Amendment). Frankfurter and the New York branch of the National Consumers' League (NCL) disagreed. Instead, they suggested that Desmond's inclusion of men meant that the authors were "unfamiliar with [the] technical legal problems" and instead were likely the pawns of corporate power seeking a constitutional poison pill. Lehman concluded that the precise drafting of the NCL/Wald bill would withstand constitutional challenge, and its greater effectiveness made it preferable to Desmond's Massachusetts-style commission.[98]

Lehman had thus proved he was willing to press farther than Al Smith had been willing to go, as Smith, though horrified by *Adkins*'s violation of progressive federalism, had not been willing to use the gubernatorial chair to so directly resist a judicial decision (just as he also balked at refusing to accept money Congress had concluded was constitutional in Sheppard-Towner, even as his own progressive federalism led him to reject the constitutionality of grants-in-aid). In 1923, Smith had dispatched his attorney general to argue *Adkins*, then requested a modification of his proposed minimum wage bill to match the unfavorable ruling.[99] He guardedly declared it imprudent to explicitly defy the Court but proposed modified wage legislation trying to work within its constraints as best he could: "*As a practical matter*, I do not think it advisable for the legislature to pass a statute . . . in a form similar to that case which was condemned by the Supreme Court. . . . I feel, however, that some legislation on this subject which will pass the test of judicial scrutiny should be enacted promptly."[100] In his 1924 annual message to the legislature and again in 1927, he reiterated his support for a publicity-based wage commission like Massachusetts had, apparently the best that could be done within precedent: "The Supreme Court has held that the state is without power to impose a penalty . . . but that is no reason why the state should stand idly by and take no action that would, at the very least, discourage the employment of women at starvation wages."[101] Only now, in 1933, did Smith come out for provocative legislation more directly challenging *Adkins/Murphy*, endorsing Lehman's bill in Smith's regular newspaper column.[102]

Upon the bill's passage in Albany, Roosevelt, whose secretary of labor Frances Perkins had been pushing for the federal government to fight the Supreme Court's minimum wage decisions,[103] recommended thirteen other governors follow Lehman's example and endorse such legislation. In addition to those who did succeed in pressing legislation through, Roosevelt contacted Alabama Democrat Benjamin Miller (serving since 1931), Delaware Republican Douglass Buck (1929), Indiana Democrat Paul McNutt (1933), Maryland Democrat Albert Ritchie (1920), Michigan Democrat William Comstock (1933), North Carolina Democrat John Ehringhaus (1933), Pennsylvanian Republican Gifford Pinchot (1931), and Rhode Island Democrat Theodore Greene (1933). Most were newly elected, progressive Democrats swept in during the

Depression, although Roosevelt also contacted his rival (and spurned running mate) in the 1932 race, the conservative (but states' rights obsessed) Democrat Ritchie, the progressive Republican Pinchot (who had returned after being term-limited out in 1927), and conservative Du Pont ally Buck.[104]

Armed with a specific presidential imprimatur, five states (Connecticut, Illinois, New Hampshire, New Jersey, and Ohio) passed legislation for the first time, while Massachusetts, in turn, replaced its toothless commission with a standard law in 1934. Utah (which Roosevelt had not contacted) restored the law it had repealed in 1929 in compliance with *Murphy* and *Donham*.[105] Of these states pressing back against the Court, only New Hampshire's John Winant—head of the state's progressive Republican faction and the future Roosevelt Social Security commissioner—was not a Democratic governor, despite nearly all being Republican-leaning or even Republican strongholds.[106] Nonetheless, passage was not contentious or partisan. New Hampshire passed minimum wage on a voice vote, as did Connecticut (after turning back a housekeeping effort by a handful of Republicans to exempt laundries).[107] Ohio and New Jersey passed theirs on unanimous roll calls.[108]

As Vivien Hart observed, the National Consumers' League and the other architects of the model minimum wage law had combined nearly all the proposed wage standards: adding Florence Kelley's insistence on a health hook and Sutherland's purported "fair wage" to the oppressive minimum standard Wisconsin used in 1925. In effect, they were trying every conceivable option to get the Supreme Court to reverse course.[109]

Buoyed by language in *Nebbia v. New York* (1934) vindicating state police powers to regulate the economy,[110] New York, the other model minimum wage states, and the NCL had reason for optimism in hoping that the liberty of contract had eroded. As Barry Cushman notes, the Hughes Court had effectively (but silently) dispatched *Adair* and the yellow-dog line of cases in 1930, and thus after *Nebbia* in 1934, *Adkins* remained the outlier.[111] While New York's highest court had struck down the new state law by citing *Adkins*, they suggested the national Court might reconsider the precedent in light of changing economic conditions; it was simply not the role of the state justices to make that reconsideration themselves.[112]

The Supreme Court debated whether to uphold the state's new minimum wage law. The Court did not, and five justices reiterated the essence of the *Adkins* opinion and overturned New York's law in *Morehead v. New York ex rel Tipaldo* (1936), vindicating the employers (and their lawyer, former Governor Miller), who had argued the result in *Adkins* dictated the result here.

This decision, coupled with the preexisting declarations of unconstitutionality against analogous congressional laws, frustrated not only progressives but moderates and federalists who, while bristling at such regulatory power in the hands of the national government, nonetheless feared the Court had created the vacuum Elihu Root had dreaded. In a widely covered press conference, Roosevelt observed that the Court had moved beyond federalism concerns to create a paralyzing "no-man's land," but he otherwise remained fairly reserved in his statement. (Reporters suspected he did not want to create another controversy as he had with intemperate comments after *Schecter*.)[113] An aggravated Lehman requested an immediate rehearing, adding that he would support a constitutional amendment authorizing more power to both state *and* federal governments if the Court did not reverse the decision. (He would effectively call for his state's legislators to repass the law at the start of the next session.)[114]

Many in the GOP, even those on the far right of the party, were equally angry since the justices had seemed to undercut Republicans' commitment to states' rights, with which they had been defending both the Court and the Constitution more broadly against Franklin Roosevelt's nationalizing program.[115] Hamilton Fish, an ardently conservative, anti–New Deal Republican from New York, immediately (and angrily) called for an amendment restoring states' regulatory power, as did the moderately progressive Herbert Hoover in his invocation of states' rights and California's successful commission.[116] GOP presidential nominee Alf Landon instructed the Republican convention to move beyond compacts of uniform legislation and now endorse an amendment authorizing the states to regulate labor for women and children—if such laws were not acceptable "within the Constitution as it now stands"—while at the Democratic convention, Kentucky senator Alben Barkley's keynote simply brushed aside the Court's decision as well-intentioned but wrong-headed and suggested a new interpretation was needed to restore the Constitution to its proper, expansive meaning. (If the Court didn't take the hint, an amendment was possible.)[117]

Again striking the states' ability to have a minimum wage, the justices generated, as Barry Cushman summarized, "a public outcry . . . simply of a different order than the criticism" of other anti–New Deal decisions.[118] Gallup polling suggested 70 percent of Americans supported an amendment to overturn the no-man's land and restore the states' ability to set wages, although they remained uncomfortable with an analogous amendment allowing federal power to set wages.[119] (When disaggregated by region, the South was most supportive of an amendment authorizing Congress, not the states, to set wages, with the reverse true in New England, which retained the old Yankee commitment to states' rights.)[120]

Newspapers were equally vicious, with only ten of the 344 editorials that discussed *Tipaldo* defending the decision.[121] The *Washington Post* explained that, unlike salutary decisions that had overturned federal legislation "based upon positive and clear-cut logic deeply imbedded in the Constitution," the *Tipaldo* majority seemed to have forgotten that "the powers of the states are not specifically limited as are those of the Federal Government."[122] Other newspaper editorials expressed a common thread of bewilderment in which commentators sympathized with the states' rights underpinnings of *Schecter* or *Carter Coal* but could not reconcile that with *Tipaldo*'s attack on the states' police powers.[123] The *Baltimore Sun* laughed that the decision had ruined Republicans' efforts to run on a defense of constitutional states' rights and the integrity of the Supreme Court in vindicating them.[124] The *Christian Century* remembered Brandeis's now-famous paean to federalism in "the Oklahoma ice case" and approvingly reminded its readers of the unanimous decision in *Schecter* when the Court's progressives "found no difficulty in accepting [the] restriction of the federal power, because they believed, it still left the power of the states. . . . It is precisely this power . . . which the latest decision of the Supreme Court destroys."[125]

A flurry of amendment proposals appeared in Congress. Two days after the decision was announced, Democratic Representative John Martin of Colorado issued a blistering condemnation of the decision and resurrected a proposal that had been drawn up at the beginning of the 74th Congress by his fellow Colorado Democrat, Senator Edward Costigan.[126]

Section 1: The Congress shall have power to regulate hours and conditions of labor and to establish minimum wages in any employment and to regulate production, industry, business, trade, and commerce to prevent unfair methods and practices therein.

Section 2: The due process of law clauses of the fifth and fourteenth amendments shall be construed to impose no limitations upon legislation by the Congress or by the several states with respect to any of the subjects referred to in section 1, except as to the methods or the procedures for the enforcement of such legislation.

Section 3: Nothing in this section shall be construed to impair the regulatory power of the several States with respect to any of the subjects referred to in section 1, except to the extent that the exercise of such power by a State is in conflict with legislation enacted by the Congress pursuant to this article.

As his colleague Representative Samuel Pettengill (D-IN) feared, such proposals to give Congress intrastate powers only furthered the danger of centralization illustrated by Prohibition. Just as the Eighteenth Amendment overstepped in centralizing power to regulate alcohol, so had the Fourteenth Amendment enabled courts to block state economic prerogative, and thus a clarifying and corrective amendment reenabling state power should follow. Thus, Pettengill declared, "The amendment I would propose would be entirely consistent with the American tradition of States' rights. . . . To grant to the Federal Government new and far-reaching powers is one thing." Instead his amendment, focused on eliminating substantive due process, would "restore to the States powers . . . which they possessed prior to the passage of the Fourteenth Amendment."[127] The states' rights progressive William Borah similarly proposed a modification to the Fourteenth Amendment that would eliminate substantive due process while incorporating some of the First Amendment to the states—akin to Madison's failed Bill of Rights proposal.[128]

Perhaps of all the decisions the Four Horsemen left behind, *Tipaldo* proved the most enraging by departing from a broad federalist consensus bridging conservatives and progressives. Instead, it appeared to impose a substantively reactionary economic vision—seemingly vindicating the paranoid musing from those in Roosevelt's inner circle convinced, as Attorney General Cummings had vented after *Schecter*, that "they mean to destroy you."[129]

While commentators and elected officials were outraged, courts, however, seemed to sense that the resistance offered by Wisconsin, New York, and the other states had pressed the justices to reconsider. New York's state courts had quietly and mechanically applied *Adkins* without agreeing or disagreeing in the case that became *Tipaldo*.[130] A federal court in Ohio allowed that state's new law on grounds that the statute was distinct from the one at issue in *Adkins*.[131] At the very first business session of the fall term in 1936, the justices themselves declined Lehman's request to rehear New York's *Tipaldo* case—but did agree to take a nearly identical case from Washington, *West Coast Hotel v. Parrish*.[132] Washington's state supreme court opinion in *Parrish* challenged its national counterpart to prove minimum wages were a "plain, palpable invasion of right . . . and has no real or substantial relation to the public morals or welfare."[133]

It could not, and the justices reversed course in *West Coast Hotel v. Parrish* (1937), finally approving the constitutionality of state minimum wage laws after two decades of unhappy struggle. *Parrish* traditionally has been attributed to Owen Roberts backing down in the face of court-packing—in effect, recoiling in the face of a presidential threat—but scholars have demonstrated that any "switch in time" took place in chambers before the announcement of any active threat against "nine," although some observers had believed one could be coming in light of the fierce public backlash.[134]

Roberts later contended that he had been prepared to overrule *Adkins* in *Tipaldo* but that New York had instead insisted *Adkins* remained good law and thus the state tried to "disingenuously" distinguish the two almost identical statutes. Roberts claimed he had demanded Butler write a fairly mechanical opinion, simply noting that the statute was the same as *Adkins* and, thus, since New York had contended *Adkins* was different, not wrong, there was little to do but strike the law on strictly precedential grounds. Butler initially agreed but was provoked by Stone's dissent into an opinion defending the Court's decision on grounds of constitutional principle, which Roberts conceded should have triggered him to write a narrow special concurrence.[135]

In effect, Roberts argued a tactical error by New York's and the NCL's lawyers was at fault. If Roberts is credible—and the *Tipaldo* opinion itself does implicitly invite such a reconsideration, as many noted and expected at the time[136]—then more direct, less disingenuous, state resistance could possibly have succeeded in breaking the Supreme Court's post-*Adkins* hold on state power earlier.

More likely, though, it would have failed nonetheless, as more recent scholarship suggests that the states' tactical decisions did not have the impact Roberts claimed, and that it was instead Chief Justice Hughes—ironically, a *Tipaldo* dissenter—who actually remained the implacable obstacle to ending the *Adkins* era.

Barry Cushman's examination of the Court's docket records, while rejecting Roberts's effort to blame the New York legal strategy for *Adkins*'s survival, still largely exonerates Roberts of the charge that he obstinately stood by the precedent until cravenly caving to public pressure. Consistent with Roberts's later memorandum explaining his own reasoning, the docket records show that even in the initial decision to hear *Tipaldo* he had indicated an unwillingness to join an opinion distinguishing it from *Adkins*. These records *also* critically show, however, Roberts's willingness to decisively overrule the case—in 1936. But contrary to Roberts's later memorandum, the states' respective legal strategies did not matter; neither New York (in *Tipaldo*) *nor* Washington (in *Parrish*) formally requested the justices officially overrule *Adkins*, though the question was clearly before the Court in both cases.

What did matter, as Cushman shows, is that the politically sensitive Chief Justice Hughes, a former governor and presidential candidate, gave in to public pressure and shifted *his* thinking. Hughes was notoriously averse to overturning precedents and instead preferred to distinguish them—as he had with *Adair* in 1930—even if, to the exasperation of critics, no clear principle existed for doing so. However much he may have disliked *Adkins*, Hughes had evidently insisted on merely distinguishing it, as the second line of his *Tipaldo* dissent makes clear.[137] (This was true even if doing so left the liberty of contract nominally alive, with the lingering possibility of resurrection, as *Lochner* had undergone after its ostensible silent death in *Bunting*.) Roberts, quite reasonably failing to see a respectable distinction between the two almost identical statutes, wouldn't join an opinion distinguishing *Tipaldo* from *Adkins*, and Hughes wouldn't join one that failed to. But the overwhelmingly negative public reaction to *Tipaldo* forced Hughes to back down and allow the Court to consider overruling *Adkins*, at which point Roberts could join his brethren in finally dispatching the liberty of contract and restoring the states' police powers.[138]

State actors had not sat idly by as the Supreme Court took away their police powers to regulate contracts, either by banning yellow-dog clauses or setting minimum wages, as state actors engaged in a back-and-forth dialogue with the judges' interpretations of liberty of contract. As this history shows, states viewed themselves not merely as laboratories and practitioners of progressive federalism but as participants in constitutional interpretation rather than merely conceding judicial supremacy. Nonetheless, consistent with the constitutional mainstream thought of the era, they were unwilling to cross the line from dialogue to defiance, pushing back hard only when it became the states and executive branch against the courts rather than a nullification-like contest between the states and federal government.

Like today, minimum wages were a widely popular (and fairly easy to understand) issue among the electorate and a core part of progressive and even conservative agendas (if implemented at the state level). Even figures later associated with conservative establishment Republicanism had largely supported state minimum wage laws early and would continue to do so, as Coolidge and Taft illustrated. And yet, evasion of the Court's jurisprudence occurred only in the isolated American periphery and, even then, among fellow partisans (even as out-party Democrats had every incentive to use minimum wages as a political wedge issue).

Three Pacific states pretended *Adkins* never happened, implementing their minimum wage policies with the aid of supportive public opinion but nonetheless avoiding direct confrontation with industry for fear of a judicial loss. These states were economically isolated from market competition, rendering their business communities supportive or, at the very least, compliant with efforts to implement minimum wage policies. The Dakotas charted a middle course, similar to the symbolic power exercised in Massachusetts. Only Wisconsin issued legislation to push back. However, its legislators publicly framed it as a mere accommodation of the Supreme Court's opinion, even as its head of the legislative research bureau, involved with the drafting, confessed otherwise. Each of the states that resisted *Adkins* and *Murphy* before 1933 was a one-party, largely progressive but GOP state. (And, as best one can tell, conservatives in Wisconsin and the Pacific states played along, if nothing else.)

In 1933, this changed, as an intrepid New York governor, and his political mentor in the White House, urged states to pass legislation in light of an economic climate radically different than the 1920s—and yet even the New York response was deferential to the Court, largely arguing that minimum wage laws had ceased to be, if ever they were, "class legislation" and such regulations were argued as necessary uses of the state police powers to restart the economy for the good of all. In short, while states were willing to engage in constitutional dialogue with the courts in defense of progressive federalism, state resistance, even to a widely and wildly condemned decision, proved surprisingly tame, consistent with the era's respect for judicial decision-making and constitutionalism.

Root's fear had been that states would be corrupt and/or lazy in using their police powers for the public good. On the issue of minimum wage, however, a few had tried to provide for their people in the face of court shackles (and, based on the trends both before *Adkins* and after *Tipaldo*, others likely would have followed).

After a few years of give and take with the courts—prolonged by a year due to a refusal to confront them directly—the states finally succeeded in clawing back the power to issue a minimum wage (and in the process solidified the states' police powers more generally against at least one kind of unenumerated rights claim).[139] It was, however, a power that mattered less when the federal government also, almost concurrently, received judicial permission to assume that responsibility, thus undermining a critical component of progressive federalism and rendering the states' hard-won ground somewhat scorched earth.

CHAPTER SIX

Popular Constitutionalism, the States, and the New Deal Revolution: The Fall of Progressive Federalism

Whereas, the national government of the United States has during the past several years assumed the exercise of powers . . . [that are] destroying the rights of the people of the several states and striking at the foundation of the fundamental principles on which the republic was established. . . . The underlying principles on which the republic was founded are being cast aside, and the flag of national domination has been raised as a standard, in the place of the self-reliant flag of home rule. . . . Federal officials are found in every quarter of the land whose duties have heretofore been unheard of. . . . The day of awakening has arrived and the growing power of the national government must be further curtailed.

Resolved by the Senate, the Assembly Concurring, that [the] Legislature . . . call upon the legislatures of the several states . . . to call a convention . . . [with] the purpose of the preservation of the self-governing right of the states . . . and to restore to the states and to the people certain rights now exercised by the national government . . . contrary to the intent of the federal constitution.

—Wisconsin legislature, 1921

While twenty-eight states now have laws providing for some form of old age security, the lack of uniformity, the restrictions upon eligibility . . . together with the absence of any legislation in nearly one-half of the states, indicates the necessity of federal legislation.

—Wisconsin legislature, 1935

Only fourteen years separate the first quote, which began this book, and Wisconsin's plea to the federal government to take up social welfare in 1935.[1] In 1921, Wisconsin had joined its progressive, prolabor policies with a protest against grants-in-aid like the Sheppard-Towner Act. But rather than offering a robust states' rights charge that all but echoed James Madison's Virginia Resolution, as it had before, in 1935 Wisconsin legislators instead begged Washington to displace the state's just-passed 1934 pension law with a national standard, before it had even really had a chance to test its own.

How did this happen? After briefly summarizing the legal and intellectual climate of the old constitutional regime, this chapter will consider the states' reaction to and interpretation of Franklin Roosevelt's constitutional revolution. Unlike the other cases, state governing officers largely refrained from offering any constitutional arguments, resignedly ceding the field in what was effectively a negative case of extrajudicial constitutional interpretation by the states. Yet far from being delegitimated by the New Deal's political transformation, state interpretation retreated, declining but not disappearing from the American political order and, after a few years in abeyance, slowly reappearing.

Such a retreat and return is not true, however, for the deep affinity many progressives had held for federalism since the start of their movement, one which joined states' rights and a robust conception of their police powers. This decades-long connection between progressive politics and conservative, decentralist states' rights–oriented constitutionalism was fairly and decisively sundered by the New Deal's constitutional revolution. That it *was* sundered, however, would have seemed all but inexplicable to an observer of politics in the 1920s and even the early 1930s.

Constitutional Conservatism at Its High Tide

The incapacitating stroke of one president (Woodrow Wilson) and the death of another (Theodore Roosevelt) had prevented the very real possibility that in 1920 both major American parties would rally under the banners of ardent progressives seeking *third* terms. Instead, both parties nominated candidates from their right flanks, perhaps better reflecting a public fatigued by political reform and war.[2] Warren Harding campaigned on a return to "normalcy," nebulously promising a return from wartime mobilization and perhaps some of the progressive excesses that had preceded it. Thus, a conservative defeated a conservative and assumed the presidency in 1921, setting the stage for a broadly conservative decade.

The New Mexico House's celebratory public telegram echoed the hopes of many in moving on from Wilson's presidency, with Harding bringing "the return of a sane and representative government."[3] Even Oliver Wendell Holmes would give voice to a spirit that seemed uninterested in political crusades and instead just wanted to be let alone. "While I don't expect anything very astonishing from [Coolidge]," Holmes observed in 1924, "I don't want anything very astonishing."[4]

Such a sentiment was shared by much of the Democratic leadership: all three of the party's nominees during the 1920s (James Cox, John W. Davis, and Al Smith) were broadly Jeffersonian in sentiment, even if, like Calvin Coolidge, they had seen the need for progressive protective legislation at the state level.[5] The vestiges of Theodore Roosevelt's Progressive Party, now led by Robert La Follette, as well as wings within both the GOP and the Democrats, called for a more active government, but these progressive voices remained marginal—better able to obstruct legislation than pass their own. As Scot Powe suggests, between the 1870s and 1930s, tariffs and metals were the basic fault lines of politics; elites of both parties were essentially for limited government and against "class" legislation—unlike the wishes of many of their voters.[6]

The 1924 election had offered particularly interchangeable choices (other than Robert La Follette's third-party challenge), but even 1920 had suggested a conservative confluence.[7] Cox held similar views to his fellow Ohioan Harding—for example, hostile to federal education aid and worker's compensation, earning the grudging respect of the archconservative former speaker Joseph Cannon, who pronounced that Cox "would make a damn good Republican if he weren't a Democrat."[8] And if Harding himself was not quite the reactionary of caricature—for example, endorsing the maternity bill pushed by Children's Bureau progressives[9]—he captured an element of stability in an unsettled age.

This nostalgic turn also brought with it a distinct constitutional conservatism. As Maxwell Bloomfield writes in his study of 1920s political culture, "One important aspect of 'normalcy' proved to be a revival of Constitution worship in the postwar decade."[10] This manifested itself in several mutually reinforcing ways: a cottage industry of literature on behalf of decentralized government, mobilization by groups like the Sons and Daughters of the American Revolution pushing for Constitution commemorations, the proliferation of civics courses, and even Treasury Secretary Andrew Mellon passing out copies of Solicitor General and future Congressman James Beck's conservative constitutional treatise in schools.[11] After all, as the American Bar Association solemnly warned in 1922, "The schools of America should no more consider graduating a student who lacks faith in our government than a school of theology should consider graduating a minister who lacks faith in God."[12] It was in this context that W. E. B. Du Bois, writing *Black Reconstruction* in the late 1920s, could shake his head at the pervasive constitutional "fetich worship" that surrounded him.[13]

As part of that conversation, President Calvin Coolidge, although far from a legal theorist, repeatedly and publicly invoked a traditional vision of federalism that emphasized the primacy of states. Although rebuttable, Coolidge believed that there should be a strong "presumption . . . that [political remedies are] the business of local and state governments. Such national action results in encroaching upon the salutary independence of the States."[14] In a radio address celebrating the fiftieth anniversary of Colorado's statehood, Coolidge attempted to educate Americans about his belief in federalism, which would demand more of states and less of the federal government. The president admonishing his fellow citizens for being "inclined to disregard altogether too much both the function and the duties of the states" and, in a moment of civic education, he instead reminded listeners that states "are much more than subdivisions of the federal government. They are also endowed with sovereignty in their own right."[15]

Such retrenchment of power from DC was not a mission undertaken only by congressmembers and the Harding and Coolidge administrations, as state officials moved to claw back power, or resist Washington's decisions in a variety of ways and across a variety of issues. Memorials to Congress appealing to states' rights and decentralization appear sporadically but broadly during the period. In explaining its rejection of the child labor amendment despite having its own tough laws on the subject, Vermont passed, by almost comical margins, a resolution explicitly citing the Tenth Amendment.[16] Northwestern legislators petitioned Harding to pardon political prisoners caught by the Espionage Act, holding it to be a violation of free speech once the war was over. (Neither passed, as the committees argued Harding already was taking care of it.)[17] Perhaps the most widely circulated was a protest against proposed policies that would have phased out the wartime federal estate tax but constrained states' autonomy in imposing them on their own citizens. In at least a dozen states, one or both houses protested the estate tax policy on states' rights grounds.[18] Suggesting the diffusion of such resolutions (and the activity of business interest groups), nearly all of these were identical or very similar, warning that the recent change to the tax code "menaces the rights of states, because its object is to persuade them to abandon their inheritance law."[19]

In addition to the detailed cases covered in the preceding chapters, other topics in which federalist resolutions were considered or passed included a federal public shooting range bill (Colorado), Esch-Cummins railroad policies (Ohio and Oklahoma), farm transportation regulation (Minnesota), and an Interstate Commerce Commission decision (Missouri).[20] Utah's governor condemned nationalistic rhetoric coming out of DC in a water dispute with Arizona—even though that nationalistic rhetoric aided Utah's claim to a greater share of Colorado River water.[21]

This list is meant to be merely illustrative, since most of the issues were considered merely in passing, often in an isolated state. But what this list does suggest, however, was the ease with which states' rights claims were and could be offered, whether during the early stages of the Depression or the supposed good times that preceded it, and the institutional legitimacy that state actors felt in offering a constitutional argument through the political process and not merely the courts. Appealing to such claims, in short, was a perfectly acceptable discourse, regardless of region or partisanship.

The installation of Charles Evans Hughes as chief justice in 1930 perhaps most clearly embodied the consensus. The chief justice brought an especially compelling biography: a former two-term governor of New York, associate justice of the Supreme Court, a presidential candidate who lost that office by a mere three thousand California votes, and secretary of state. And if that resume was not enough, he was held to be an extremely powerful presence. As then Roosevelt legal adviser and future justice Robert Jackson would later explain to Roosevelt, any Supreme Court choice must be extremely intellectually confident around Hughes: "Any man you would be likely to appoint from the west would be possessed of an inferiority complex in the presence of the Chief Justice, who looks like God and talks like God."[22]

But Hughes was also nominated because he was believed to be in harmony with the constitutional values of Taft and Hoover, who blended a traditional concern with constitutional forms with a progressive recognition of the need to cabin markets. Both as president and chief justice, Taft had tried to fill the Court with men who shared those views rather than men with the substantive libertarianism of the Court that existed when he was president or ones who endorsed the attacks on the Constitution's structure, as had Theodore Roosevelt and Woodrow Wilson.[23]

That is why, for example, Taft had sought to have the states' rights committed Sheppard-Towner foe Nathan Miller installed on the Court, which Miller regretfully declined—though not as regretfully as his decision to later turn down Coolidge's offer of attorney general. That, Miller later obliquely lamented, set in motion the destruction of constitutional enforcement—insofar as it enabled the rise of Harlan Stone whose pivotal fifth vote and advice to the Roosevelt administration later proved essential to upholding the New Deal–constitutional revolution.

As Miller's governorship was ending, Taft inquired of Miller's interest in a Supreme Court seat, telling the New Yorker he would recommend him to Harding. Miller confessed to wanting it as his highest ambition, but embarrassedly admitted that he had actually gone into debt as governor and needed the continued revenue of his corporate salary to support his seven children. Coolidge subsequently offered Miller the attorney general position after the fall of the corrupt Harry Daugherty, even explaining he would be able to secure Borah's permission (and thus the support of the judiciary committee). But even though it was assumed to be fast-tracking him for the Supreme Court, Miller declined. As Miller understatedly lamented later in life, "I put ambition aside and did not then know what was to happen to the Supreme Court," wistfully observing that after he turned down the attorney general position, "Dean Stone was appointed. He became an associate justice of the Supreme Court and when he died was its Chief Justice." (Stone had been elevated by Roosevelt as a reward for supporting the president's program to reinterpret the Constitution and massively expand federal power.)[24]

In fact, fears of precisely such an outcome had led a dying Taft, fearful that those whom he called "the Bolsheviki" would seize the Supreme Court, to hesitate to leave it until Hoover promised to replace him with the satisfactory Hughes, whom Taft had once appointed as associate justice, rather than Coolidge appointee Harlan Stone whom Taft had initially endorsed for the Supreme Court but whose judicial flexibility and seeming contempt for federalism rapidly disillusioned his former patron and almost certainly would have given Coolidge regret.[25]

In a widely covered August 1930 address to the American Bar Association (and one largely repeating themes in his recent book), the newly confirmed chief justice Charles Evans Hughes charged his fellow lawyers with the defense of states' rights. In the book, he explicitly disagreed with Holmes's argument that the ability to declare federal laws unconstitutional was perhaps unnecessary to a working federalism. Instead, Hughes argued, courts must carefully enforce dual federalism: "Theories of state autonomy, strongly held so far as profession goes, may easily yield to the demands of interests seeking Federal support [and] many of our citizens in their zeal for particular measures have little regard for any of the limitations of federal authority." Thus, he insisted, "judicial review [in] "maintaining . . . our dual system" . . . is likely to be of increasing value."[26]

In speaking to the bar, the now-chief justice recognized that Congress could easily destroy the power of the states (and vice versa) if the justices did not ensure the balance of constitutional federalism. Hughes recognized that there would be difficult cases at the margins, especially as more commerce became national. Nonetheless, "the balance between state and national authority is of the essence of American institutions that it should be preserved so far as human wisdom makes this possible." He charged the lawyers—not simply the judges—to remember that "encroachments on state authority should be resisted with the same intelligent determination as that which demands that the national authority be fully exercised to meet national needs."[27]

That also, he alluded, meant leaving the states alone to enforce their police powers. Hughes lamented that the overuse of the Fourteenth Amendment's due process clause has "kept our courts busy, most of the time without much reason for its invocation."[28] This was an old theme for Hughes. Although worded diplomatically, in the wake of the deadlocked *Stettler* minimum wage case, Hughes gave a 1918 presidential lecture to the New York Bar implicitly criticizing judicial overreach against the police powers: "Failure to deal with these problems with the adequacy demanded by good sense and the spirit of fairness will not be due to lack of power so far as the Federal Constitution is concerned, but to the mis-use or non-use of the power which the nation and the states respectively possess."[29] In other words, Hughes called for states to be allowed to exercise their police powers without unjustified federal oversight and for the legal community to ensure the federal government remained confined to its constitutionally authorized powers.

Hughes's exhortation was remarkable only for its speaker, not its speech. As James Patterson's history of the states and the New Deal argues, voters were fairly happy with the conservative 1920s and, perhaps more surprisingly, state officials were on the whole similarly satisfied with the constitutionally conservative, strict federalism that carried over into the Great Depression. Governors and state legislatures applied fairly little pressure on Hoover other than to have him increase the speed and quantity of road stimulus funding. Few sought to have the federal government expand its constitutional prerogative by wading into welfare or more local commercial regulation.[30] Thus Hoover, whose desire for active government was tempered by a constitutional conservatism, was arguably well in line with the constitutional thinking in the states.[31]

The 1932 Democratic Party platform called for most policy development to happen at the state level and more aggressive loans to the states or federal infrastructure spending, matching what was coming from below.[32] Most memorials and resolutions from states in the early years of the Depression had been variants asking Congress or the president to be more liberal with or faster in disbursing interstate highway funds, a traditionally accepted (if once controversial)[33] use of the Commerce Clause (or spending power) to fund infrastructure necessary for interstate commerce. This was hardly the stuff of a budding constitutional revolution.[34]

Roosevelt, Ritchie, and the End of Progressive Federalism

In May 1932, Maryland social workers delivered a report to Governor Albert Ritchie that doubtlessly pleased the hardened states' rightser. Ritchie had, as ever, been insisting on minimal federal intervention in local affairs, even with the Depression raging. The social workers' report indicated that the people of Maryland did not appear to want significant federal or even state intervention—largely vindicating the governor's position during the summer in which he would undertake his presidential campaign.[35]

At the start of the Democratic election in 1932, the three leading presidential contenders were Franklin Roosevelt and Al Smith of New York and Ritchie of Maryland—the widely perceived consensus' second choice, including by Ritchie himself.[36] Though Ritchie was the most conservative of the three, all of them seemed to endorse a progressive federalism, joining a robust and active state government with a limited federal government, typified by their shared hostility to the Eighteenth Amendment, which all three could run against as big-government Republicanism. Thus, for the powerbrokers who made up the Association against the Prohibition Amendment (AAPA), which was on the verge of defeating the Eighteenth Amendment on federalism grounds, states' rights seemed to be in good hands, with one of the three almost certain to be the next president of the United States.[37]

Ironically, Franklin Roosevelt had been among the most eloquent proponents of progressive federalism in the early 1930s, as he dueled not only Ritchie but Roosevelt's former mentor Smith in trying to claim that mantle for the Democratic Party and the entire country.[38] Because New York was such an essential and Republican-leaning swing state, and Roosevelt had demonstrated his electoral prowess there in the 1930 midterms, he entered the race as the clear favorite.

Roosevelt had spent much of his governorship posturing himself to run to the constitutional right of Hoover by appealing to the traditional Democratic norms of states' rights, joined with his reputation for pursuing an active New York government advancing the interests of labor and the economically downtrodden. This was not only in private correspondence—for example, in a series of prostates' rights letters traded with the ultraprogressive but doggedly federalist Arizona governor George Hunt—but in public as well.[39] In his proclamation of Constitution Day in New York, Roosevelt added that it was "of particular importance that we study the special powers which have been given over to the Federal government by the sovereign states which form our Union, remembering that all powers not so delegated still vest in the states themselves."[40]

Similarly, in March 1930, Roosevelt delivered an extended radio address extolling states' rights and educating citizens about them, one that may as well have been delivered by Ritchie. After walking through both the Ninth and Tenth Amendments and the very limited list of enumerated federal powers—specifically augmented, he noted, by the Eighteenth Amendment—Roosevelt observed that the difference and boundaries between limited federal powers and preexisting, expansive state powers were "by implication so plain as to have been recognized by the people generally" and clearly established "by judicial interpretation . . . during many years." Thus, he confidently asserted, "We are safe from the danger of any such departure from the principles on which this country was founded just so long as the individual home rule of the states is scrupulously preserved and fought for whenever it seems in danger"[41]—not the words of an aspiring constitutional revolutionary.

These states' rights themes—and the need to zealously defend them—had been even more aggressive in Roosevelt's speech convening a meeting of the states' governors, when he not only reiterated his commitment to enumerated powers but sounded positively Madisonian in demanding strict construction of those powers lest the division between the constitutional authority of the states and the federal government be erased. Previewing the words of the Four Horsemen striking at his New Deal seven years later, FDR lamented that "the elastic theory of interstate commerce, for instance, has been stretched almost to the breaking point to cover certain regulatory powers desired by Washington."[42]

Roosevelt joined this sharp attack on federal overreach with a similarly sharp criticism of state neglect that had enabled it—allowing him to continue to hedge on Prohibition in 1931. He dismissed the "cowardly" action of states "evading our responsibility" to pass laws tailored for their specific political and legal climates and which instead sought uniform federal laws.[43] Roosevelt even sounded like Nathan Miller, the state's former Republican governor and an opponent of Prohibition turned reluctant functional dry who had feared states needed to do more aggressive criminal enforcement to avoid federal intervention. Roosevelt warned that "if our states do not themselves . . . remedy the condition of affairs, we shall find the heavy hand of Washington laid on us by federal legislation and the people of our commonwealths will raise no voice in protest, because their own state governments have been inefficient, stupid, or negligent."[44] These laws would, in many cases, be uniform and model legislation shared among the states, but they would be passed by the states themselves, as Elihu Root and the movement for uniform legislation had insisted decades before.[45]

In coming out with an early endorsement in 1930, the *Atlanta Constitution* hopefully fawned over Roosevelt's record as that of a "cool and authoritative apostle of Jeffersonian and Jacksonian Democracy, the Democracy of delegated and limited Federalism, sovereign state rights, and the inalienable American privilege of home rule."[46]

Even the collection of criminal records, Roosevelt insisted, should not be shunted off as something "for the census bureau to do. The evasion of state sovereignty has not yet reached the point, thank God, when the federal government can issue orders to state officials as to what they shall and shall not do in keeping records, or anything else."[47] Ritchie, too, had been in the newspapers in 1931 for a federal–state squabble over record-keeping, but he had made his name as a states' rights fanatic long before balking at handing state records over to the Hoover administration.

The long-serving Maryland governor, a former state attorney general, remained devoutly committed to federalism and the Tenth Amendment throughout his career and had more than a decade defending states' rights against national power at nearly every opportunity. While he had focused on internal government reorganization and had not been especially states' rights–oriented in his first term, after achieving most of his in-house platform, he became increasingly irate with what he saw as GOP attacks on states' rights, especially through grants-in-aid and Prohibition.[48]

Though Ritchie hatched various schemes to defend states' rights—including, at one point, a congressional house of governors akin to the original role of the Senate—his most aggressive battleground had been Prohibition (which he also hoped to use to realign the parties into a nationalist and a federalist divide), and where he had become somewhat infamous for his repeated disruptions of presidential conferences on enforcement.[49] Nonetheless, as he accurately characterized his views, "Volstead . . . is only part of a federal invasion of the rights of states."[50] He had also attacked the Sheppard-Towner maternity bill and grants-in-aid more generally.[51] He had bluntly refused Harding's request to call up state troops to suppress a strike in Maryland.[52] He attacked proposals for federal education policy.[53] He even refused President Hoover's request for data to help deal with the Depression in 1931 (though he initially and grudgingly cooperated with the Roosevelt administration to ensure Maryland received its share of economic recovery aid in 1933).[54]

Like New York's Republican governor, the equally states' rights–committed Nathan Miller, Ritchie linked his rigid constitutional textualism with the recognition that the changing economy made more commerce interstate and thus changed the applicability and scope of federal power without changing its text or meaning.[55]

Ritchie had long hoped for a political realignment that would see believers in states' rights and constitutional fidelity assemble in one party and nationalists in the other, a theme he advocated most prominently in his well-publicized 1924 Jefferson Day dinner address.[56] The Maryland governor sounded like Martin Van Buren, fearing that a bipartisan consensus on behalf of national power had marginalized constitutional defenders who needed to reorganize to vindicate the nation's founding principles—the most of important of which, for Ritchie, was federalism, and his vehicle for achieving this would be Prohibition.[57]

Ritchie had seized on the satirical name of Maryland as the "Free State" (holding out against national Prohibition) and helped develop a reputation of himself and his state as the nation's vanguard defending of states' rights. Already building a brand, he had embarked on a nationwide states' rights speaking tour after the 1924 election, leading the *New York Times* to call him "the foremost advocate of the old Democratic doctrine of states' rights in the country" while contemporary political journalist (and future *New York Times* editorial board manager) Charles Merz observed that he gave more speeches in more of America than anyone "save Lindbergh and Will Rogers."[58] The most detailed study of Maryland during Prohibition led its author to conclude that among the state's political class, "the advocacy of states' rights seems to have been genuine," with an honest and deeply held commitment linking Ritchie to both Maryland's Democrats and Republicans in fighting the growth of federal power.[59]

As the Maryland legislature observed in recommending him for the presidency, Ritchie's dogged defense of states' rights was the core of his appeal.[60] While Roosevelt was the obvious favorite, with his former mentor Al Smith the next most common choice, Roosevelt nonetheless recognized the potential threat of Ritchie's extreme states' rights appeal when Prohibition would be perhaps the leading issue. Thus, akin to his strategy in 1930, arranging for an extreme wet Democratic platform in New York in 1930 to run against as a relative alcohol moderate, Roosevelt had his campaign manager James Farley seek an extreme wet platform to eliminate the distinctive appeal of Albert Ritchie by letting FDR run simply to execute the platform.[61]

In short, the extreme state's rights fanatic Ritchie and Al Smith, paragon of progressive federalism, both suffered defeat in the 1932 Democratic primary election but only to someone who had taken an arguably stiffer line on the interstate Commerce Clause, endorsed the hard-line states' rights attack on Prohibition and widely criticized the states for a passivity that in turn threatened to bring federal power upon them. In 1932, it was far from obvious that Roosevelt himself would be the one to bring that federal power—and make signing off on it an article of faith among Democrats. Indeed, the campaign arguably pointed the opposite. As George Lovell observed, Norris-LaGuardia was signed by Hoover "at a time when FDR's campaign vision was that balancing the federal budget was the key to recovery!" The *Chicago Tribune* summarized Roosevelt's campaign as "Hoover the radical, Roosevelt the conservative."[62]

The constitutionalist, states' rights opponents of Prohibition—the nascent movement toward Ritchie's realignment—soon turned on Roosevelt, as it became apparent that his opposition to national Prohibition came more from an opportunistic disagreement with alcohol suppression as a policy (or as a political loser) rather than as part of a consistent vision of decentralization like his Democratic rival (and first vice presidential choice) Albert Ritchie. The leadership of the Association against the Prohibition Amendment, designed to contest Texas senator Morris Sheppard's Eighteenth Amendment on states' rights grounds, largely transferred into the Liberty League working to fight Franklin Roosevelt's efforts toward a more nation-oriented government, both in terms of more aggressive federal regulation and the establishment of a national welfare state.[63] They believed that they had seen, as Barry Goldwater later acidly described it, "Franklin Roosevelt's rapid conversion from constitutionalism to the doctrine of unlimited government."[64] But, in a series of well-known cases—*Schecter*, *Carter Coal*, and the like—the Supreme Court objected to the expansion and consolidation of federal power brought by much of the New Deal.

Felix Frankfurter advised Roosevelt that he would be best served letting the Court keep overturning legislation in order to build pressure for a constitutional amendment (or preferably appointments) that would remake the federal–state balance of powers by giving the federal government wide power to deal with national conditions. This was not exactly a secret. *New York Times* columnist Arthur Krock reported on that strategy and that the White House believed "only through a full set of judicial reverses can the people be induced to extend the Federal power sufficiently to make room for the New Deal," and indeed they had begun allowing constitutionally dubious bills through to stage such a fight.[65] As Roosevelt aide Harry Hopkins boasted, "I want to assure you that we are not afraid of exploring anything within the law, and we have a lawyer who will declare anything you want to do legal."[66]

The libertarian political columnist H. L. Mencken bitterly predicted that the Roosevelt administration would follow Hopkins's course: "That he will appoint men who actually believe in the Constitution is hardly likely," he lamented. Nor would Roosevelt "waste . . . time trying to change [the Constitution] by the orderly process of amendment." Instead, to defend the New Deal, Roosevelt would choose "revisionists" and sic "juridic stooges upon [the Constitution], asking them only to make a thorough job."[67]

Between 1935 and early 1937, Roosevelt deliberated whether to pursue an amendment granting the federal government new economic regulatory powers (and confirming a Hamiltonian interpretation of the Spending Power) but concluded—almost certainly incorrectly—that even a humbled Liberty League would be able to mobilize sufficient support to stop ratification of an amendment. As Roosevelt ally Senator Burton Wheeler (D-MT) observed, blockage of an amendment in state legislatures was doubtful in the wake of the sweeping 1936 election that had brought Democrats in control of state governments. It would be even more unlikely that the other Article V option, popularly elected ratifying conventions, which had been used to eliminate the Eighteenth Amendment, would have opposed a Roosevelt-backed amendment. With Roosevelt in control of three-fourths of Congress, members of the administration and allies outside of it began drafting possible texts.[68]

Nonetheless, at the urging of Attorney General Homer Cummings and National Recovery Administration (NRA) counsel Donald Richberg, and bolstered by dissents from Justice Harlan Stone, Roosevelt decided to argue that these federal powers *already* existed and were simply being denied by an economically reactionary Court—though, as David Kyvig notes, Roosevelt also grumbled about the Constitution's inherent inflexibility, which, as Kyvig suggests, indicates Roosevelt believed the Constitution was "fundamentally irrelevant to his problem . . . [something] to be worshipped from afar, but up close it was a stumbling block to be circumvented, not a structure to be lived in and remodeled to suit."[69] Ironically, Cummings also worried an amendment to the Commerce or Spending Power's General Welfare Clauses would overshoot and dangerously expand federal power.[70]

Stone had laid the groundwork for the growth of cooperative federalism by grants-in-aid by advising the Roosevelt administration on the possible breadth of the tax power already in the Constitution. Although a Coolidge appointee who apparently considered his political preferences to be conservative, Stone had a capacious interpretation of federal power granted under the Constitution.[71] Labor secretary Frances Perkins, helping to draw up Social Security, bumped into the justice at a tea party hosted by Mrs. Stone and fretted that she found it difficult to constitutionally justify the program—the Commerce Clause was insufficient—and thus feared the Court would strike it down as it had so much of the New Deal already. Stone purportedly cupped his mouth and whispered, *"The taxing power of the Federal Government, my dear*; the taxing power is sufficient for everything you want"—hinting that he, at least, adopted Hamilton's position that the taxing and spending power was freestanding rather than, as Madison had insisted, limited to the enumerated powers.[72] In effect, Stone was siding with Sheppard-Towner—and, in a way, with those who had feared its vindication would lay the groundwork for massive expansion of federal power through grants-in-aid.

But rather than provide a basis for support as the AAPA and Liberty League or James Madison might have hoped,[73] and as many states had done with Sheppard-Towner, now states offered little objection to this vast expansion of federal power, instead accepting it as a complement (or replacement) rather than a rival to the policies they had been developing.

The States and the New Deal

In the late 1920s and early 1930s, the old progressive federalism was beginning to slowly enact, at the state level, the skeleton of what would soon become fleshed into the federal Social Security state. Old-age pensions were
expanding rapidly, though systems of unemployment insurance were much
slower to develop, with only Wisconsin having actually established such a
program by 1933; others, as in Massachusetts, failed in the legislature.[74] By
1933, more than half of the states in the Union had enacted an in-house old-
age pension, with the bulk added between 1929 and 1933. Members of Congress, citing the example of the now-defunct Sheppard-Towner, had begun
pushing first for similar grant-in-aid programs and then for more direct federal pensions.[75] At the same time, Dr. Charles Townsend had amassed millions
of members of his Townsend club, publicly advocating his plan to use old-age
pensions as a form of Depression-era economic stimulus, with state legislatures often receiving (and sometimes forwarding on) memorials and petitions
for Congress to adopt Townsend's plan.[76] While the 1932 Democratic Party
platform had only "advocate[d] unemployment and old-age insurance under *state* laws," in a 1934 June message to Congress, Roosevelt explained he
would be rolling out a national Social Security plan, which Congress passed
in 1935.[77] Thus, the states themselves were building up old-age pension systems on their own, but state-run unemployment insurance had farther to go.
As Edwin Witte, one of the architects of Social Security, observed, the Roosevelt administration used old-age pensions—which in 1933 state legislators
increasingly recognized their voters wanted but could not pay for in the Depression—as leverage to push through the rest of Social Security.[78]

Once Roosevelt had made known that something resembling Social Security would be coming, states began passing legislation complying with federal
mandates for grants-in-aid rather than rejecting desperately needed federal
money in the interim. As the deadline for compliance at the end of 1936 drew
closer, this became an outright rush.[79] Even for many sympathetic to the old
order, it became harder to resist Sherman Minton's pithy but somewhat apoc-
ryphal dismissal: "You can't eat the Constitution"—especially as his like-
minded allies won elections under the Roosevelt banner in 1934 and 1936.[80]

In a 1936 address at Madison Square Garden, the Republican Alfred
Landon insisted that it was incumbent on elected officials to enforce the Constitution as written, not as they wished it to be, until an amendment changed
the text (with Landon himself sympathetic to doing just that).[81] Roosevelt,

by contrast, used an equivalent preelection Madison Square Garden speech to argue that anyone who objected to the New Deal was fundamentally un-American, "already aliens to the spirit of American democracy," who, as enemies of the polity, should consider leaving the country: "Let them emigrate and try their lot under some foreign flag in which they have more confidence."[82]

Few legislatures regularly met in 1936, but after the November election, nearly all quickly convened and pushed through provisions putting their states in compliance, especially with the unemployment provisions, which they had been slower to enact. Four states had passed unemployment legislation in 1935 while Social Security was being debated in Congress, with Alabama and Oregon passing their legislation in the months after congressional enactment. Another twenty-eight passed them by the end of 1936, ensuring they did not lose access to federal funds, with the bulk of these enactments (eighteen) in rushed December special sessions. Another ten passed theirs as their sessions met in the early months of 1937. Florida, Missouri, and Illinois held out until the very end, not passing unemployment insurance until after the US Supreme Court, in a series of cases handed down on May 24, swept aside all constitutional challengers to the federal enactment of the various parts of the Social Security system.[83]

The comparatively poor legislative history of the states in the 1930s makes it hard to form firm conclusions about any state ratification of the kind that would add normative force to a popular constitutional revolution; the sequencing and threatened loss of funds indicate grudging compliance, especially with unemployment insurance, rather than enthusiasm—much as with Sheppard-Towner. Reduced to a simply binary vote, the voting records of hostile Maine (where even most Republicans signed onto Social Security, albeit with explicit reservations, acknowledgments of an emergency, and odes to states' rights) and Mississippi (where loyal Democrats sought even more federal expansion if it meant more federal money) appear nearly identical, with overwhelming support. Governor's addresses give only slightly more with which to work, but, outside from southern Democrats tightly linked to FDR, even those tended to be brusque, simply matter-of-fact, actuarial descriptions of the fiscal savings that would come from cooperation.

While a handful of Republicans and conservative Democrats maintained their opposition to the New Deal in the state legislatures until the bitter end, the extremely lopsided roll calls show few had any meaningful chance of success when it came to a final vote; indeed, the ferocity of these critics often came from the futility of their cause. As with Sheppard-Towner, once successful enactment of the federal repeal plan seemed inevitable, state opposition virtually collapsed. Unlike with Sheppard-Towner, there was not a sympathetic, states' rights–oriented president who might leverage his political power, and thus there was comparatively little reason not to simply vote for the acceptance and rely on the courts, which had thus far robustly resisted Roosevelt's expansions. In addition to complying with the requirements of the federal law, progressive states passed memorials and resolutions calling for the expansion of federal power (on behalf of what we think of as the most enduring and central features of the New Deal, especially old-age pensions). Some protested the expansion of national power (in other issues like oil production), but only one state's legislature truly resisted Franklin Roosevelt—and threatened to bring back nullification to do it.

The New Deal in the State Legislatures

As the preceding chapters and recent work have shown in various ways, southern states' rights and constitutional conservatism were heavily confined to racial hierarchy; robust acceptance of Social Security, like Sheppard-Towner before it, was no outlier in a poor South willing to take federal aid even as it invoked "states' rights" to protect its racist social structure.[84] With the partial exceptions of Maryland and Texas, where a minority of legislators offered states' rights protests, and Florida, where legislators waited to pass unemployment, southern governors and legislatures were most enthusiastic in embracing the idea of a constitutional revolution transferring the welfare protections of the states' police powers to the (better funded) auspices of the federal government.

Several governors simply recognized the actions of their states' voters. In January 1935, Missouri governor Guy Park instructed state legislators to pass state old-age pensions to fulfill the demands of a state constitutional amendment passed by initiative, adding that delay might perhaps be prudent so that they could coordinate with the coming federal program.[85] Park's successor, fellow Democrat Lloyd Stark, argued that the "voice of the people, not only of Missouri but of the entire nation, was overwhelmingly in favor of the new humanitarian policies originated and now being carried out by our national administration. Therefore I construe it to be our first duty" to help implement those policies.[86]

Although Senator Harry Byrd was among the leading Democrats opposing

Franklin Roosevelt's program on states' rights grounds,[87] his Byrd machine ally George Peery took a more conciliatory tone, interpreting the election as changing the citizenry's expectations. The emergency of the Depression changed the perception of the people, moving old-age pensions from an "obligation regarded as . . . resting upon the states and localities" to one reset to the federal level. Though America was now "near the end of the emergency," and the federal government would be withdrawing from most direct aid, this new perception remained, and thus, Peery argued, Virginia needed to cooperate with the new federalism and maximize grants-in-aid, which it did.[88] Kentucky did almost the same, amending its constitution to create an in-house old age pension system in 1934 and modifying its state law for compliance two years later.[89]

South Carolina, despite its state sovereignty positions defending white supremacy, was among the most committed defenders of federal power in vindicating the New Deal. Early in Roosevelt's first term, Governor Ira Blackwood sent a special message to the legislature, noting that the "National Administration has requested . . . South Carolina [pass] an act on the order of the National Industrial Recovery Act," asking them to do as Washington requested.[90] Pursuant to Governor Blackwood's request for cooperation with the NRA, in 1934, South Carolina's legislature implemented an analogous code "as affecting intra-state commerce within this state"—over the objections of one-fifth of the members to what one called "nefarious legislation . . . being rammed down the throats of the people of South Carolina."[91] But most legislators called for even more direct federal involvement, passing resolutions seeking federal aid to induce citizens to return to farms and to establish an old-age pension system, which they held to be "an appropriate function of the federal government which has adequate resources to establish and maintain the same."[92]

Governor Olin Johnston's inaugural address cited the general election results in perceiving an electorate interested in "bring[ing] all the benefits of the broad national program of social security to the doors of all deserving South Carolinians."[93] The state legislature agreed, again passing a resolution in 1935 calling for the creation of a federal old-age pension.[94] Unlike those who explain the exclusion of agriculture from Social Security as the product of southern senators' interest in white supremacy, Johnston pleaded with South Carolina's legislators to memorialize Congress to amend the bill and include agricultural workers, as well as to approve all legislation necessary to achieve full Social Security compliance as they had not in 1936.[95] Johnston similarly pressed the state's legislature to demand Congress pass "legislation . . . necessary for the stabilization of hours and wages," which, Johnston insisted," is a federal obligation."[96] Burnet Maybank, who followed Johnston as governor, criticized Social Security's cooperative federalism model for remaining nominally state-centered, which had the effect of offering more money to rich states able to get a higher match rate—in short, he wanted it *more centralized* in order to more aggressively subsidize antipoverty efforts in South Carolina.[97]

Mississippi's governor Martin Conner had agreed, grumbling about the limited redistribution brought by federalism in his session's 1935 special session called to pass state legislation. It was appalling, he said, to have different standards in different states; instead, the entire economic system should be redistributive and centrally run from Washington.[98] Nor were Mississippians pleased with *U.S. v. Butler*'s attack on the Roosevelt's Agricultural Adjustment Act, passing a resolution condemning the decision (though focusing on its policy effects rather than constitutionalism).[99] A Georgia states' rights protest asking to repeal the NRA was swiftly killed, further showing the Deep South's embrace of a constitutional revolution.[100]

In 1935, North Carolina's governor John Ehringhaus boasted of his state's cooperation with the NRA and urged the state to comply with the imminent passage of federal unemployment insurance, even as he observed more study needed to be done on old-age pensions.[101] Two years later, his successor, Governor Clyde Hoey, delivered an inaugural address that was an extended ode to the New Deal.

Hoey exhorted state legislators to take an active role lest, as Elihu Root and other had warned, the federal government would fill the void: "If we do not wish the federal government to regulate all of our internal affairs, we should assume that duty and responsibility for ourselves."[102] Beyond that passing aside, Hoey was robust in defending cooperation between active governments at the state and national level. He was pleased that North Carolinians seemed to be honoring the NRA codes even after the courts had scratched them, observed the need to realize and appreciate that government had now become active in providing for social needs, and hailed "the adoption of the whole social security program as the most forward and advanced step in this generation and the most humane enactment of any legislative body in all the history of the nation."[103] Four years later, North Carolina's governor Joseph Melville Broughton Jr. pledged to continue gubernatorial support of the New Deal and asked the state legislators to continue theirs, on account of the wild popularity of and "overwhelming support of that great humanitarian and brilliant exponent of social reform . . . Franklin D. Roosevelt."[104]

Only three southern states constituted real exceptions to the examples listed above, offering even some defense of the old order: Texas, Maryland, and Florida.

Unlike most other southern states, Texas legislators invoked states' rights commonly on nonracial matters. For example, like California, in 1935, the Texas legislature strongly objected to the administration's oil regulations, especially in light of the state electoral platform, helpfully and liberally quoted in the resolution. According to the Texas legislature, the proposed bill was "contrary to the [states' rights] principles contained in the platform of the Texas democracy and contrary to the principles of our dual form of government in that it is an attempted invasion of the sovereign powers of this state."[105]

On the other hand, its senior senator Morris Sheppard arguably did more than any early twentieth-century legislator to expand federal power, pressing through both the Sheppard Prohibition Amendment and the Sheppard-Towner Act. As many Texas legislatures had repeatedly protested when considering (and eventually acceding to) the Sheppard-Towner bill a decade earlier, it was difficult to reject a grant-in-aid offer even if legislators objected to the underlying proposal, either on policy or constitutional grounds.

So it was with Social Security. The state constitutional amendment authorizing the state to run an old-age pension, including in cooperation with the federal government, passed all but unanimously in the 1935 legislature,[106] but accepting the requirements imposed by the actual bill proved more divisive. The initial, nearly unanimous house vote foundered in conference, with opposition in both houses ranging from a third to a fifth in its tangled legislative history.[107] Of these, however, most protested on grounds that the eligibility requirements were too strict, but others protested on account of the inclusion of "negroes and Mexicans . . . as recipients" of some of the states' benefits. Several argued that it allowed too much federal oversight and thus, in the words of one senator, "surrenders the rights of this state to the Federal Government and particularly to the Social Security Board" when the amendment ratified by the people had called for a *state* old-age pension system.[108] A member of the house agreed, adding that he was for "complying with the Constitutional Amendment [and providing] a real pension for the old people of Texas," but he remained "opposed to the Federal Government dictating in the affairs of Texas. I will not for a 'sop' bargain away the rights of the people of Texas."[109] But these solitary protests, uncharacteristically entered in the records of the journal (which did not otherwise include their debates), indicate the weakness rather than strength of federalist opposition to Texas's participation in Social Security.

In Maryland, Albert Ritchie briefly bowed to the earliest parts of Roosevelt's New Deal to ensure Maryland received its reconstruction funds, but he reverted to his Jeffersonian states' rights fanaticism and become a Liberty League ally and vocal critic of the administration between his electoral defeat in 1934 and early death two years later.[110]

That defeat had, many felt, resulted from Ritchie's commitments to a now bygone era. Republican governor-elect Harry Nice had narrowly lost to Ritchie in 1919 but had defeated the once invincible governor in 1934. Several factors contributed to a slide in Ritchie's popularity: his extremely long tenure (fourteen years in a state where reelection was seen as unusual), his awkward handling of a lynching on the eastern shore, the end of Prohibition (his signature issue and the core of his strength in Baltimore), and finally, his resistance, albeit somewhat muted, to Roosevelt's regime. In fact, Nice had campaigned as that strange Republican who would be a better ally to Roosevelt than the man who once spurned his offer of the vice presidency.[111]

In his 1935 inaugural address, Governor Nice condemned "reactionary" GOP hardliners angry that the party didn't go after Roosevelt, but he did gently criticize the more ambitious, "inexperienced," "appalling," and "bold" "theorists who experimented at will" and who wanted to see the federal government assume vast new powers.[112] At the same time, Nice hedged his bets by dismissing those who feared the expansion of federal power, specifically executive power, would result in a "weakening authority of the states, [the] undermining and destroying of the stability of the Federal Union, and [the] destr[uction] of the permanency of the States themselves." Judicial decisions had expanded federal power before, Nice argued, without such catastrophes.[113] Maryland's Tenth Amendment-fanatic legislators, who a decade before had incessantly protested grants-in-aid and Sheppard-Towner and pushed for the Wadsworth-Garrett amendment making nationalizing amendments more difficult, now followed the lead of Harry Nice rather than the man whose stands had led them to commend him as the ideal choice for president. State old-age pensions complying with Social Security unanimously sailed through both houses and again easily passed in the subsequent special session for unemployment after Nice hailed that as a nonpartisan and admirable policy to be instituted regardless of "federal compulsion."[114]

Florida's legislators were strategic in their participation, like many states.

They were among the most enthusiastic early backers of old-age pensions but among the last waiting out possible participation in unemployment. On the one hand, they had been among the trio of states quietly waiting for the courts to sign off on Social Security before implementing their own unemployment plan. On the other hand, they showed unwavering support for the old-age pension part of federal Social Security, unanimously amending their constitution to comply and passing a bill cooperating with the program in 1935—passing a resolution reiterating their fidelity to it two years later.[115]

Outside the South, state legislative and gubernatorial support proved less effusive, with more vocal protests but equally firm support in the end.

The Pacific northwestern states sounded like Dixie in clamoring for a federal takeover of old-age pensions. In the spring of 1935, Washington's outgoing governor Clarence Martin argued that the state's old-age pension system was not working because it depended too heavily on the counties, urging the legislators to transfer the obligation to the state until the federal government took over.[116] The legislature agreed, passing a memorial to Congress pleading for a federal Social Security old-age program (with an overwhelming 43–2 vote in the senate) and shortly thereafter passing a bill that preemptively accepted whatever program the federal government passed.[117] Oregon's house similarly sought a federal program, though in this case favoring the alternative Townsend plan being widely circulated.[118] (The 1935 Oregon House session seemed especially receptive to federal power, with a majority of the lower chamber petitioning Congress to pass national eugenics marriage laws as well.)[119]

California legislators were less enthused about the expansion of federal power than were their other Pacific neighbors, but they too accepted its key features and resisted only a specific regulation perceived as harming their specific industry. Nonetheless, they pitched this critique on decidedly high-minded terms. A unanimous legislature insisted that "the past history of the sovereign state of California [demonstrates] its earnest endeavors to jealously guard the States rights' prerogatives granted under the Constitution"—which in this case meant fighting against a bill regulating oil production and therefore "is contrary to the principles of our dual form of government in that it provides for an attempted invasion of the sovereign powers of California and would permit Federal encroachment upon the exclusive power this state to control the production of its natural resources."[120] As with the rest of the country, however, that stiff defense of federalism did not translate to rejecting federal entry into the realm of welfare, which it accepted during the special session later in the year. Nonetheless, almost a fifth of California's senate, including future conservative stalwart William Knowland, voted against complying with Social Security, demonstrating a stronger hostility to federal power than in most of the country.[121]

Colorado's governor observed in his 1935 inaugural address that Congress would likely pass an old-age pension law, adding that he was especially eager to have the state cooperate with the federal government.[122] The legislators obliged, passing memorials endorsing both federal operation of old-age pensions and a federally mandated six-hour work day in 1935, with all but two senators approving of state implementation of Social Security in the special session that followed.[123] To the Southwest, Arizona's legislators pushed through Social Security in special sessions in 1936 and 1937—ignoring as frivolous an Arizona legislator's proposal to repeal the state's federal Social Security participation and revert to a solely in-house model.[124]

In his 1936 campaign for president in 1936, Kansas governor Alf Landon delivered several bracing, widely covered speeches condemning Roosevelt's Social Security program—but not, it must be noted (as by an unhappy *New York Times*) on constitutional grounds, instead proposing an alternative, ostensibly more efficient grant-in-aid program.[125] (Landon did, however, later argue that the 1936 Democrats broadly sought "the destruction of states' rights and home rule," also criticizing in his acceptance speech Democrats forgetting the federal division of and enumeration of powers.)[126] But this defense of a federal role in a Social Security-like system was not an election-year turn. Landon—who soon after quietly trembled about a Roosevelt dictatorship—called for cooperating with Social Security as early as January 1935, and the complicated legislative history of an amendment authorizing Kansas to participate was not due to opposition to the proposal but partisan fighting to claim credit, with both Landon and the Democrats laying claim to its passage.[127] In short, Kansas legislators believed a revolution was coming and wanted to be remembered on its right side come the next election. Landon's successor, Democrat Walter Huxman, reiterated that theme, urging the state's legislators to engage in "active and wholehearted cooperation between the state and the national government," adding that doing so "is not a question of surrendering any state rights or state functions to national government."[128]

Although Connecticut's governor Wilbur Cross had been elected on a hardline states' rights agenda (especially targeting Prohibition), he took a more conciliatory tone in considering the New Deal. Cross, formerly the dean of Yale's Graduate School, once observed, "I associate largely with Republicans and when I come down to the fundamentals of government I find but little disagreement; we all stand for the rights of the state against federal government control."[129] Soon, however, Cross wondered aloud whether Republicans reviling Roosevelt's activism were really prepared to hike state taxes to provide for recovery once they blocked federal payments: as for him, "In the emergency I am ready to lay aside the ghost of state sovereignty."[130]

As he inaugurated the state's 1936 special session, Cross suggested complying with the Social Security Act but, in a nod to state sovereignty, added that this would be fairly minimal since the state's preexisting in-house old-age pension was more or less already in compliance with the federal rules and thus the state need merely establish the unemployment provisions.[131] In 1937, Cross recognized the threat posed by the cases that became *Steward Machine v. Davis* (1937) and its companion case *Helvering v. Davis*, observing that many lawyers believed the Social Security program unconstitutional.[132] Like many other such programs, Connecticut's unemployment law contained a provision ceasing the program should the federal law be invalidated (as many expected). Cross requested the state create an unemployment commission to study (and presumably recreate) unemployment legislation in-house should that occur.[133]

Illinois, while one of the three holdouts to the passage of unemployment legislation, delayed passage not on constitutional grounds but simply factional politics. Illinois's houses had unanimously passed an in-house old-age pension system in 1935, with only one vote dissenting from modifying the program to comply with Social Security in the state's special session the following year.[134] The delay in passing unemployment insurance until after the program began, however, was less about constitutional objections and more about internal Democratic Party fighting in the wake of Anton Cermak's death in the failed attempt to assassinate Roosevelt, with his handpicked governor and other Democratic officials fighting for control of the state party.[135]

Although Ohio Democrat Martin Davey fell out with the administration and later resisted its anti-Depression efforts, he and the legislature supported federal efforts on Social Security. As Davey observed in commenting on state passage of its old-age pension, "This humanitarian and forward looking legislation is so obviously necessary that the national Congress" was likely to pass the same and he looked forward to cooperating, which a nearly unanimous legislature did in a special session soon after—only after agreeing to discontinue the program should the federal contribution end.[136]

Massachusetts had long served as an innovator for prolabor policies, as even its conservatives like Calvin Coolidge had proven to be relatively supportive of such reforms during the Progressive Era. Its legislators, however, had often had a strongly states' rights streak, one which had been bolstered by a popular referendum's rejection of the federal child labor amendment even as the citizens insisted on a state analogue—a strong case against a purely reductive view of federalism as a cloak for self-interest. Even these northeasterners, rooted in industry and with an interest in suppressing the South's comparative advantage, resolutely turned against the amendment.

Thus, they rejected participation in Sheppard-Towner until the program's sunset had been locked in, and the state's resistance to Prohibition had resulted in the creation of aggressive federalist apparatus of lobbying groups like the Sentinels of the Republic and the Constitutional Liberty League (not to be confused with the Liberty League opposed to Roosevelt). While it had been tilting Democratic in recent statewide elections, these had been conservative states' rightsers, many of whom became, like Joseph Ely, anti-Roosevelt Democrats, but this was slowly changing, as the election of Roosevelt ally James Curley indicated.[137]

Massachusetts's Leveret Saltonstall, a Republican succeeding two Democrats for the first time in decades, worked to position his GOP as a different one than the Coolidge states' rights party who had governed the Bay State before the New Deal realignment. Saltonstall's public papers nonetheless reveal someone who recognized how incomplete the constitutional revolution actually was and how much of that old order remained.

Saltonstall's 1939 inaugural address called for extensive federal cooperation, including with housing, old-age pensions (which he called "predominantly a national problem [that] must be solved by our federal government"), and even a call for Congress to respond to the wishes of Massachusetts citizens and take up the even more radical Townsend plan.[138] While a speech to the American Civil Liberties Union (ACLU) some months later did obliquely attack Roosevelt for Court packing, he nonetheless downplayed states' rights and declared it especially essential to have the Bill of Rights checking the states, especially in protecting freedom of speech.[139] While we now know this was probably correct as an original matter, and that even many devoutly states' rights–committed Republican framers believed the Fourteenth Amendment applied the Bill of Rights to the states,[140] such a position was a radical attack on state power at the time Saltonstall adopted it. His second inaugural address made a prudential case for states as better representing local knowledge—in effect, a plea for subsidiarity—but the speech was notable in its fawning sense of cooperation with national power. For Saltonstall, states no longer had constitutional rights but simply ought to "insist upon the independence of our local and state governments" to retain their "own initiative and self-reliance."[141]

Three weeks later, Saltonstall delivered an address to a gathering of Republicans seeking to create "an immense centralization of control" to begin military mobilization. Saltonstall made a passing nod in which he proclaimed himself "a firm believer in state's rights," but again only because "this country is too big to be controlled from one city . . . but at the same time, no country is too big for concentrated leadership when it must act as a nation . . . promptly and unitedly." In short, surrounded by old-guard Massachusetts Republicans, Saltonstall was willing to make a rhetorical concession to federalism, but only in the service of justifying federal expansion.[142] Two years later, in a commencement address he gave at Williams College's sesquicentennial, Saltonstall was even more dismissive. Williams had been the recipient of a large bequest from the now-disbanded Sentinels of the Republic, a states' rights–focused lobby group who turned over their assets to endow an essay contest devoted to constitutional fidelity,[143] but one would not know that from Saltonstall's address. Saltonstall again dismissed constitutional federalism, declaring that "the states must not seek to preserve moth-eaten prerogatives." Instead, Saltonstall focused on purely utilitarian calculations: when the war ended, "the question will be *which branch* of government can *best perform* the services to which our citizens are entitled." States seeking to claw back power from the federal government "must seek only the restoration of the chance to do those jobs which can be done better by them than by remote control."[144]

Vermont, the bastion of Coolidge conservatism and (with Maine) one of two holdouts in the 1936 election, called a perfunctory special session in 1935 and 1936, approving the modification of its old-age pension to Social Security with voice votes in both houses.[145] Governor George Aiken grumbled about federal interference but nonetheless shepherded through old-age pensions and other progressive policies.[146]

In the wake of the 1936 election, FDR's election manager James Farley famously paraphrased the old electoral slogan to hold, that "As Maine goes, so goes Vermont," but some in Maine seemed willing to go very far indeed. In a strange and forgotten document, Maine's house of representatives declared their state, along with Vermont, to be the only two enclaves in an otherwise post-constitutional America. After recounting the nation's history of fighting tyranny and centralization, Maine's house explained that "46 of the 48 former sovereign states of this allegedly inseparable Union have indicated their wish to depart from the principles of self-government laid down by Washington, Jefferson, Jackson and Lincoln [and] . . . in our mature judgment these 46 vassal states have traded their birthright of self-government, having committed a veritable act of Secession."

As a result, the legislators requested their governor consult with "the sole remaining sovereign state of Vermont to join with Maine in the . . . preservation of our Constitution and a return to the United States of our forefathers." What that would have entailed—a protest? A consultation? Secession?—is unclear. Although the house passed it without objection, the state senate killed it, and grumbling state legislators resigned themselves to compliance with the Social Security Act, hoping that the US Supreme Court would strike it down and save state sovereignty.[147]

Maine's floor debates, which, during the 1930s, were the most thoroughly recorded of any state, show a marked tension between that loudly professed allegiance to states' rights and the pressure of the federal inducement, with many reluctantly agreeing to accept the federal money in the interim but hoping that the courts would declare the program unconstitutional. It also demonstrates far more widespread support for states' rights than the state's lopsided roll call votes indicate (which, in turn, suggests perhaps more grudging acceptance in other states whose floor debates were not recorded).

Maine legislators debating accepting the two-part Social Security fought almost entirely on federalism grounds (as well as budgetary worries for old-age pensions) before reluctantly accepting the bills—only to have the Social Security Board reject the old-age pension plan and the governor thus veto it.[148]

One member engaged in an extended Jeffersonian defense of a narrow construction of federal power and firm adherence to the division between the powers of the two governments, citing examples from his past voting record, conceding that the bill looked similar to "coercion." He wanted to join "any attempt that can be made, within the limits of our Constitution, to improve the condition of the laboring man and prevent unemployment. This method," he weakly noted in grudgingly accepting a bill, "may do it." But in light of his basic commitment to federalism, he could endorse the bill only "very reluctantly," and only because he feared "the whole union. . . . [to be] greatly endangered" otherwise and in the knowledge that many regarded his "position [as] inconsistent."[149] A usual ally said he understood his friend's sympathies but he could not adopt them: "While I have been a Republican, there has been one principle for which the Democratic Party once stood in which I have always believed, and in which I believe today . . . states' rights. I believe in the sovereignty of the individual state." In this case, accepting the bill would violate his own actions: "Two years ago, standing where I now stand, with hand upraised, acknowledging my Maker, I registered an oath" to the constitutions of the United States and Maine. Supporting this bill, "thoroughly contrary to the principles of our federal Constitution," he lamented, would mean treachery to that oath.[150]

Republican after Republican offered similar odes to federalism—with even one *supporter* observing that he considered his endorsement of the bill "the most disagreeable and offensive public act of my short career" and which was forcing members to "be placed in the position...[to have] violated [their] oath" taken to the Constitution. He had, he feared, enabled a "reprehensible" precedent "surrendering our state rights [to] dictatorial powers from Washington," But, he weakly added, "Let us cross that bridge when we come to it," and he hoped that in the future, he and his colleagues would "stand up and fight for the oath which we have taken, fight for our sovereign rights, and refuse to surrender our state rights."[151] This, from a *supporter* of the bill!

After the legislature passed the bill (over the governor's veto on grounds that the Social Security Board seemed displeased by the plan), the legislators in the following session moved to modify it to placate the board—while several, even those proposing modification in the interim, took a pleased tone in seeing Social Security declared unconstitutional in the lower court.[152] Thus, for legislators in Maine, something of a division of labor pushed through Social Security: they could vote to receive funding while believing the Constitution (as they understood it) would in the end be vindicated.

Indiana offers the next most thorough legislative record of state constitutional analysis of the New Deal, since several of its members insisted on their lengthy speeches being entered into the record.

In its 1936 special session, Indiana, with Senator Sherman Minton and Governor Paul McNutt, had overwhelming Democratic majorities in both houses and passed Social Security with ease—yet it generated perhaps the most blistering dissents registered in any state legislative record that year. The trio of bills passed with approximately four-fifths support of both houses. (For example, House Bill 564, the old-age bill, passed with forty-one supporters, with seven Republicans and one Democrat in opposition.)[153]

Three Republicans asked for permission to record their positions in the house journal, offering among the most extended evidence of state political thought criticizing the New Deal. Representative William Babcock's was a temperate observation to his constituents that the grain dealer had done his best to preserve "home rule" in the bill but financial necessity required a final aye vote to secure much needed federal aid.[154]

Two of his colleagues were less temperate. Herbert Evans delivered a ferocious tirade filling up a full five pages, attacking the bill on financial grounds, for altering the relationship of the individual to the state, and for subverting the Constitution, as the new law would "inva[de] . . . states' rights, . . . destroy home rule," and convert Indiana "into a province of the national government."[155]

Guy Dausman, a lawyer serving as a Republican legislator in Indiana, delivered a shorter but even more blistering attack on what he saw as his colleagues' failure to enforce the Constitution and its mandate of states' rights. Instead, he raged, they had rolled over for the developing regime of positive federal rights being rammed through by overreaching executives, in both Washington and Indianapolis, with the mere indication that a law was "an administration measure" resulting in lockstep support. By voting to have Indiana join with national unemployment and old-age pension plans, they had followed the governor in an "utter lack of conception of the meaning of his oath," ignoring the "the constitutional right to self-government" so basic that "every American citizen, even an Indiana lawmaker, is supposed to have some glimmering, however crude." Only the justices of the Marble Palace offered any hope: "Should our courts fail to . . . reject this vicious, destructive legislation, we have seen the beginning of the end of our Government." Dausman's declaration was, as he knew better than any, a jeremiad following legislative defeat.[156]

The acquiescence and Wisconsin's aggressive championing of the New Deal offers perhaps the most concise illustration of the collapse of the old vision of a state-oriented progressivism. If Oregon had served as the innovator for labor legislation in the 1910s, Wisconsin had served as the model for welfare legislation while also robustly defending a vision of progressive federalism—an active state left alone by the federal government. Yet, as Justice Butler noted in his *Steward Machine* dissent as evidence of federal coercion, even Wisconsin, the state best modeling a Social Security program, had been forced to modify its law to comply with federal command.[157] Yet as the epigraph to this chapter showed, Wisconsin, rather than jealously protest such interference as it might have a decade before, positively called for it,[158] reiterating in 1939 the state's interest in the federal government having the robust ability to provide for the general welfare.[159]

In a companion case to *Steward Machine v. Davis* (1937), which confirmed the loose Hamiltonian construction of the tax power rhetorically hinted at in *U.S. v. Butler* and which served as the authorization for Social Security, the justices also specifically upheld the unemployment provisions. In *Carmichael v. Southern Coal and Coke Co*, handed down the same day as *Steward*, the justices perfunctorily turned back the federalism charge against Social Security, spending the bulk of the opinion defending the state's implementing taxes and machinery as within the state's police powers discretion and also not a violation of the due process clause.[160] With the end of any possibility of blockage from above, the last holdouts complied. The Constitution, the justices concluded, authorized cooperative federalism between the federal and state governments, anchored by a liberal use of federal tax and spending powers.

Nullification and the New Deal

Only one state aggressively fought back against the New Deal—reaching back to antebellum efforts to block federal power. As in the 1890s and 1900s, the most aggressive states' right claim (on nonracial issues) came not from reactionary conservatives but from economic populists of the left. Although nullification had been discredited by the Civil War even as states' rights remained the dominant constitutional argument, forcing anti-Prohibitionists to vigorously deny any connection to Calhoun,[161] Huey Long's Louisiana passed a decidedly antebellum, orthodox nullification law closer to the 1832 South Carolina ordinance than to other states' rights politics. Unlike massive resistance two decades later, however, its aim was not to maintain white supremacy but instead as part of a Long game for the presidency that depended on unquestioned control of Louisiana.

Article IV, Section 4, of the Constitution holds that "the United States shall guarantee to every State in this Union a Republican Form of Government," and, according to many Americans, Huey Long's dictatorial regime had ceased to be one. In a popular constitutionalist campaign on behalf of the Guarantee Clause, citizens and journalists peppered the Roosevelt administration with pleas to intervene against a state government that contemporaries increasingly compared to Hitler's fascist state. Now a US senator, Long continued to rule the state through his puppet governor, nicknamed "O.K." Allen, after his purported response to any order from Long.[162] Long not only dominated the governor's mansion but had converted the legislature into a mere rubber stamp and controlled the courts, negating the separation of powers. A 1934 law gave the state's attorney general power to take over any local case and prosecute or try it as he saw fit.[163] He had clamped down on freedom of speech and used the state police to threaten any electoral or political rivals—including his own lieutenant governor, who staged a failed effort to force Long out of office. A later Long biographer summarized his record thus: "[Long] ordered [the legislature] to slavishly pass hundreds of bills that increased his power, destroyed his enemies, and stretched the very limits of constitutionalism."[164] As Long observed to a rival who threw a copy of the Louisiana state constitution at Long to protest his lawbreaking, "I am the Constitution just now."[165] Such was not, the critics pleaded with Roosevelt, the stuff of which republican governments were made.

Nonetheless, after the Roosevelt administration became less optimistic about the probability that a Guarantee Clause would succeed, Roosevelt aide Harold Ickes declared in April 1935 that the federal government would terminate federal funding to Louisiana unless Senator Long withdrew his efforts to control it. Long replied that Louisiana was sovereign and Ickes could go "slambang to hell"; on April 22, he offered a somewhat more measured speech to Congress doubling down on Louisiana and states' rights.[166] In the April and July special legislative sessions, Long provided his legislators with various bill seeking to quash local governments from direct involvement with federal money, ensure all elections officials had to be selected by the governor, and strip New Orleans of most revenue and finally bring the Crescent City, which had held out against Long, to heel. Back in Congress, Long tried to filibuster the renewal of the National Recovery Act in 1935 (particularly to stop its federal appointments); Long mocked Roosevelt by offering an annotated reading and analysis of the Constitution for hours.[167]

More seriously, and perhaps most controversially, in response to concerns that the federal government would use the Guarantee Clause to move against his government, Long's legislators proposed (and, after his shooting, passed) two neonullification bills nominally designed to enforce the Tenth Amendment, agreeing with almost 80 percent support in both houses.[168] Illustrating just how lawless Long's regime had become, and how much it differed from the constitutional scruples of most progressive federalists, the bill was, in the words of the *Washington Post*, "considered the broadest and boldest defiance of Federal authority since the Civil War."[169] Long had personally ordered his legal adviser George Wallace to draft the nullification bills. Wallace balked, insisting the legislation was obviously unconstitutional, but Long ordered him to "draw it up anyway," figuring that if the Supreme Court struck it all down (which he would not fight) Long would at least be able to control patronage in the state in the meantime.[170]

Long, through O. K. Allen, had summoned the special session to consider twenty-one issues, including "to legislate for the preservation . . . of the powers reserved . . . by the 10th Amendment." Though the controversial bill was widely anticipated (receiving front-page coverage in most national newspapers) and staged as a fight against Roosevelt, Long flippantly dismissed the session as considering "nothing very important or political."[171] The senator's presentation of the bill to what that the *Baltimore Sun* euphemized as "his responsive Louisiana legislature" (as opposed to "under complete control of [Long]," as the *Times* reported), went as expected, with Long delivering a harangue against federal overreach violating the Constitution. When asked what federal activities would trigger the bill's punitive measures, Long responded, "That would be for a lawyer to say," though—perhaps speaking as such a lawyer—he then added that the act's provisions would come into effect if Washington "laid a concrete street, and that violated the Federal Constitution" or interfered with elections, or involved itself with education. He also flippantly responded, when asked to interpret the Tenth Amendment, that he did not even know what it was—obvious nonsense from someone both Taft and Brandeis considered a brilliant lawyer.[172]

The first of the two bills, House Bill 28, authorized the hiring of special counsel "to preserve and protect the powers reserved to the State of Louisiana by the Tenth Amendment to the Constitution." The purpose of this was to guarantee resistance to efforts by the president, Congress, or government corporations or agencies to engage in acts held to violate the Tenth Amendment in Louisiana. Anything not authorized by the Constitution, be it a direct exercise of power or even the mere appropriation of funds, warranted a potential suit.[173] But seeking to have judicial enforcement of a constitutional guarantee —in this case, of federalism—was still well within the norms of American constitutionalism.

The second bill, by contrast, sought to do what even the most radical opponents of the Reconstruction Amendments had not: mobilize state forces to proactively obstruct federal policy, even it meant the arrest of federal officials, in order to "preserve and protect the powers reserved to the State of Louisiana . . . by the Tenth Amendment."[174]

Long's death the day after its passage, followed soon after by O. K. Allen's fatal brain hemorrhage (thereby preventing him from following his boss's footsteps in taking over the machine), not only spared Franklin Roosevelt the trouble of Long's planned third-party run but the specter of armed conflict between Louisiana and Washington.

Louisiana legislators had called for Louisiana (and Congress) to surpass Roosevelt's old-age pension plan with Long's more generous version, perhaps the Share Our Wealth plan Long had been using to catapult himself to national prominence.[175] After Long's death (and that of senator-elect and former governor Allen), Louisiana fell in line passing the necessary legislation to implement Social Security in its 1936 session.[176] Four years later, its incoming governor agreed that the Long regime had been dictatorial, but even as a member of the anti-Long faction, he had to concede it had been so because Long understood poverty. As in other poor Deep South states, Governor Sam Houston Jones wanted an even less decentralized Social Security, one which would be even more redistributive by dropping the state contribution that disproportionately hurt southern states like Louisiana. This was because "we of the South have paid our toll and tribute to Wall Street" and thus "the great wealth of this nation is centered in the North and East," producing a "system [that] is economically wrong."[177]

In sum, then, Louisiana's opposition to the increase in federal power under Roosevelt was purely idiosyncratic—more about who wielded power than power itself. It does not appear that Long particularly believed in the dangerous constitutional theory he was opportunistically adopting, but his death nonetheless had put Louisiana back in line with mainstream southern thought and its support for federal power. Such support, of course, would be withdrawn when they realized their pact with Roosevelt had resulted in the quiet creation of strong institutions that would bring power to bear in destroying a Southern regime of formalized white supremacy.[178]

Constitutional Revolution?

By the end of the New Deal, as Patterson observed, federal-state relations had been transformed. Governors used to ignoring DC other than through highway and agricultural funding and the occasional photo-op now had to be intimately involved with the federal government, carefully coordinating to collect grants-in-aid lest constituents feel cheated. The reach of the federal government not only grew but grasped state legislatures into bowing to that expansion: "Most galling to states-rightsers, the New Deal cornucopia led states to fit their spending and tax policies to federal stipulations."[179]

Even before *Wickard v. Filburn*'s massive expansion of Washington's authority, Wendell Wilkie argued that Supreme Court decisions "have made the United States a national and no longer a Federal government." (A resigned Wilkie would focus his campaign less against FDR's consolidation of national power than executive power.)[180]

The "constitutional moments" theory of constitutional developed by Bruce Ackerman in his *We the People* trilogy argues that this drastic change could occur because the New Deal modified the process for amending the Constitution, with a particular sequence of elections and political practice eventually supplanting Article V's state-based model. In Ackerman's account, most precisely elaborated in the concluding third volume, particular elections, especially the elections surrounding 1936 and 1964, have served as popular referenda on de facto constitutional change independent of an amendment.[181]

Ackerman's account has been widely challenged both normatively (for example, by originalists) but also empirically.[182] Sounding like a political scientist critiquing the idea of electoral mandates, New Deal historian William Leuchtenberg has argued that these elections, especially 1936, covered far more issues than the simple referendum Ackerman tried to frame it as and thus it is impossible to impute voter support of sweeping away Article V and federalism as opposed to, say, simply endorsing what was perceived as more effective economic stewardship.[183] (John Hamilton, the head of the Republican National Convention, echoed the idea of an overdetermined election, lamenting, "The Lord couldn't have beaten Roosevelt in 1936, much less the Liberty League.")[184] Barry Cushman argues against a popular constitutional revolution and mandate on behalf of the New Deal, looking at opinion polls to hold that voters did not seem to adopt any changed constitutional vision.[185]

But if Cushman is right that voters' preferences had not changed, many state legislators ended up voting exactly as if they had read and fully believed Ackerman's account but who, when engaging in constitutional reasoning, also often spoke as if they rejected its underpinnings entirely. In short, they offered provisional compliance with an act many viewed as dubiously constitutional while assuming the Court would strike it down—much as they had with the Sheppard-Towner Act in the 1920s, when even a devout states' rights believer like Al Smith condemned Sheppard-Towner but explained he would have New York take its fair share of the money until the program ended. Others who might have had private reservations generally praised and endorsed the Social Security program, reinforcing the idea that extrajudicial and popular constitutionalist support for Roosevelt's reforms had the sanction of a politically incontestable new order—that the overwhelming success of Democrats in recent elections was precisely the constitutional mandate Ackerman claims.

While uneven implementation and filtering through state machines limited some of the more revolutionary and reconstructive possibilities of the New Deal,[186] state-level resistance was indirect and passive. Unlike with Sheppard-Towner, where most states complied but obviously grudgingly and with protests hoping for the program's end, state legislators' and governors' constitutional opposition to the drastic expansion of federal power with the New Deal was functionally irrelevant, confined to a handful of safely ignored speeches from holdouts attempting to shame their colleagues or wait for the Supreme Court, which did not come to their rescue.

As Patterson observed, the prospect of cutting off federal funds to defend the abstract principle of federalism was a position "which no humane and politically astute governor could afford to ignore [and hence] . . . most attacks on the social security system came not from governors waving the banner of states rights but from [progressives]" who wanted an even more national system such as Huey Long—the lone nullificationist of the era.[187] If even Albert Ritchie, who had wanted to remake both the structure of Congress and the American party system to defend states' rights, was willing to bow down, no other governor hoping for a political future realistically would do otherwise.

The immediate aftermath of the New Deal thus appears consistent with *both* a constitutional revolution as well as the tight-fisted fiscal prudence of the decade that preceded it, in which many state legislators and officials abstained from acting as independent constitutional interpreters if it meant costing their state revenue.

The clear constitutional revolution, however, was not in erasing federalism but in finally sundering progressivism from states' rights, which long linked conservative constitutional beliefs with a policy preference for an active state government. James Patterson argued that the New Deal "transformed the nature of argument. Before the New Deal, states' rights remained a vital if negative dogma which enabled people like Byrd of Virginia and Ritchie of Maryland to achieve national prominence. . . . But in showing what positive government could do, the New Deal forced politicians to recognize that states' rights without state activism must perish."[188] As an example of this, he cites governor Olin Johnston of South Carolina, who warned his colleagues

in 1935 of the need to have active state government: "There has been a continuous decrease of state powers because . . . the states have not used them,
and the people wanted government. If a government does not measure up to
its responsibility by the exercise of its powers . . . they will be exercised by
the mobs, by the rabble, or something. It is God's and nature's law."[189] But
this was exactly the argument that had *already* existed, on both right and left
alike—connecting Altgeld, Lewelling, and Root from the turn of the twentieth century with Frankfurter, Smith, Baxter, Coolidge, and Hunt in the 1920s,
and manifested itself through their combination of states' rights and a robust
conception of their police powers on behalf of citizens, as well as the interstate compact movement in which states agreed to make uniform standards
for criminal law, traffic rules, and the like. Due to business opposition, free-
dom-of-contract, and even, at the margins, courts' due process reasoning,
states were perhaps slower to implement such active governments that voters
were coming to want, but the nature of the argument was already as Patterson
described, *before* the New Deal, and it largely ceased to be afterward.

As the preceding chapter showed, even ardently conservative Republicans
supported an amendment that would override (and, in their mind, correct) the
Court's interpretation of the due process clause that had limited *state* power.
But Roosevelt chose to pursue no amendment: neither a limited state-centered
one that would pare back substantive due process and enable robust police
powers regulation of economic affairs, nor amendments modifying the commerce clause to allow federal regulation of some parts of intrastate commerce
as well. The end result is *Wickard v. Filburn* (1942), which, through its loose
causal chain of things affecting interstate commerce, plausibly gives the federal government something close to a police power.

Indeed, one wonders about the counter-factual history[190] had the Court offered a vigorous defense of state economic power earlier—in effect, issuing
the same admonition to go back to the states that Justice Brandeis offered when
joining his brethren in overturning the National Recovery Act in *Schecter* in
1935. Moments after Chief Justice Hughes announced the unanimous decision
in *Schecter*, Brandeis summoned Roosevelt aide Thomas Corcoran, a Frankfurter protégé (and one of several Harvard Law acolytes serving in the White
House). Brandeis deputized Corcoran to deliver a message: "This is the end of
this business of centralization, and I want you to go back and tell the President
that we're not going to let this government centralize everything. It's come to
an end. As for your young men, you call them together and tell them to get out

of Washington—tell them to go back home, back to the states. That is where they must do their work."[191]

Though the Court had clearly wanted to move in that direction since *Nebbia*, under *Adkins* (and its restatement in *Morehead v. Tipaldo*, as discussed in chapter 5), Roosevelt could and did plausibly argue states could not: the justices had created a no-man's land, and thus Roosevelt could easily discredit what appeared a brittle and irrational jurisprudential theory. As Elihu Root had worried long before, state inaction on desired legislation would eventually generate societal pressure that would blur the distinction between powers allocated to the state and federal governments.

As chapters 4 and 5 recounted, the states had finally been able to claw back the authority to regulate wages—but the reinvigorated police powers were irrelevant. The Court had reversed itself by more broadly approving both state *and federal* powers, such as with the 1938 Fair Labor Standards Act, rendering the effects of *West Coast*—and the long struggle to achieve it—largely redundant.

Unlike the subsequent cases of *Darby* in 1941 or especially *Wickard* a year later, Hughes's *Jones and Laughlin v. NLRB* (1937) still professed to be deeply committed to dual federalism but simply ordered a slight nudge in the line between intrastate and interstate commerce (by way of contrast Hughes, in conference, had objected to the reasoning in *Darby*, fearing "our dual system of government would be at an end," and seriously debated dissenting before resigning himself to the defeat of his cherished constitutional value).[192] Thus, *Jones and Laughlin* could theoretically have been consistent with a dual federalist structure (with Jones and Laughlin's distinctive size and role as a backbone of national industry requiring federal intervention) or, at worst, distinguished away since it offered no clear principle, but the decision clearly empowered the trajectory that led to the end of dual federalism.

Hughes's effort at statecraft may have backfired another way. As Bruce Ackerman has argued, the Court itself—and thus, by virtue of his pivotal vote, Chief Justice Hughes—perhaps helped legitimate the idea of flexible jurisprudence, not Article V, as the source of constitutional change. By bowing to Roosevelt rather than forcing him, over his preferences, to go to one or more of the many amendments being poured out by his congressional allies (and even endorsed by some of his conservative foes)—adding to federal enumerated powers, weakening substantive due process, or requiring supermajority decisions of the Supreme Court—the Court offered support to those arguing

for a more flexible method of constitutional change rather than the exclusiv-
ity of Article V.[193]

Shortly after his installation as chief justice during the Great Depression,
Charles Evans Hughes had aggressively praised states' rights and dual federalism—in short, formulating the case for a progressive federalism. And, as
James Stoner has argued, Hughes may have sought to apply the Constitution, even its original meaning, as faithfully as possible in light of contemporary political needs—as his pained *Jones and Laughlin* decision, insisting on
the importance of federalism even as it expanded federal authority in light of
the Depression, makes clear.[194] But, whatever his devotion to federalism, he
may very well have helped bury it with his obstinacy to reconsider *Adkins*,
suppressing the states' efforts to reclaim their police powers until they were
meaningless in the face of a massively enlarged federal authority he had little
choice but to also nominally bless.

In the Wake of the New Deal

After the 1936 election—which many feared as having precisely the revolutionary meaning Bruce Ackerman later attributed to it—national Republicans
halted in making arguments about federalism. A semihistrionic Alf Landon—
not exactly a fire-breathing conservative—bemoaned the end of the old constitutional order but told his brethren to hold their fire from such controversies in
the hope there would still be free elections someday. Republicans in the United
States Senate similarly laid down their arms on the separation of powers, leaving it to Democrats like Burton Wheeler and the Supreme Court itself to take
the lead in defeating Franklin Roosevelt's court-packing plan in 1937.[195] A
very different Congress than Florence Kelley saw in 1927 meant that she finally had her victory with Sheppard-Towner. The state bureaus that survived
the 1929 expiration enabled an institutional core that the federal government
could draw on when, under the direction of Secretary of Labor Frances Perkins (an old ally of Kelley), it restored the program in the Social Security Act
of 1935 after the Court came down on behalf of a Hamiltonian understanding
of the taxing and spending power. There would be no Nathan Millers or Percival Baxters this time; all states would take the funds by 1936.[196] The New
Deal coalition, and the Supreme Court's approval of expansive interpretations
of federal powers, most notably the commerce and spending powers, left the

once-unifying force of federalism a much less useful argument, deemphasized in constitutional discourse.

This was institutionally reinforced in a variety of ways, which have proved heavily path-dependent, if not determinative: from rapid change in the party's platforms and membership, to Roosevelt's appointments to the Supreme Court (after a threat of court-packing to secure that judicial philosophy) resulted in cases that anchor almost all of contemporary progressive lawmaking, to his efforts, albeit with relatively little success, to use the 1938 elections to attempt to purge remaining Jeffersonian Democrats (while tolerating those who invoked states' rights on race but otherwise supported his government-building). That Republicans appeared to remain faithful to federalism, while Franklin Roosevelt and his allies had perhaps ceased to be, meant that the bulk of the surviving leadership of the 1920s Democratic Party sided with the GOP in the 1936 election.[197]

But states' rights discourse was not eliminated, as its halting return a few years later indicates. State behavior is thus profoundly inconclusive in trying to assess how and whether states interpreted the 1930s as an enduring constitutional revolution. Some, especially Roosevelt allies, cited language very similar to those of an Ackermanian constitutional revolution, arguing for a mandate of constitutional change. Some complied in citing a vision of specialization of labor and judicial supremacy—that the venue for constitutional objections was in the court system and that the legislators' jobs were not to interpret the federal Constitution but only assess if laws offered a good deal for the state or not. Not constitutional fidelity but fiscal prudence was to be such state legislators' goal, especially in an era when frugal "economy" was the watchword of all governing officials, and state-level governing officials frantically sought ways to cut their budgets drastically.

Still others complied with Roosevelt's reforms as a one-off, perhaps temporally bound emergency, but not a modification of the beliefs underlying the polity—beliefs that legislators would return to within a decade. And finally, a few hardliner legislators who believed the New Deal was unconstitutional scourged their colleagues as oathbreakers for voting to cooperate (or abstain from constitutional judgement) but proved ineffective.

Thus, evidence from the states is of an incomplete constitutional revolution: one which remade the practiced powers of the federal government but which was not so conclusively discrediting as to prevent a subsequent rediscovery of constitutional federalism, both for racial supremacy (in federalism's most public if perhaps not most representative face) as well as the far more numerous deployments in less public issues.

Even as the Supreme Court was offering something close to a blank check on federal power in *Steward Machine* and *Wickard*, state legislators and governors resumed memorializing protests against federal overreach, though almost solely among conservative states dominated by Republicans or outlier Democrats like Byrd's Virginia. As such, after a few years in abeyance, by the 1940s states' rights and Tenth Amendment rhetoric began creeping back in, and not just among southerners fighting the Fair Employment Practice Committee, other legislation against white supremacy, or judicial rulings threatening their very social order, but among more mundane issues and throughout the country.

During the late 1930s and early 1940s, Vermont's legislature and governor renewed states' rights protests on issues that did not make the news, such as dams or domestic airline routes.[198] Maine legislators unsuccessfully raised the same with forests.[199] Harry Byrd's Virginia protested federal regulations on electrical power and automobile weights.[200]

Harry Nice's farewell address to the Maryland legislature softly backpedaled on his 1935 speech, warning that America seemed increasingly smitten with foreign ideologies of centralized power at the expense of constitutional and individual freedom—with Maryland fortunately less "utopian" and centralizing than the federal government and other state governments.[201] Not a full vindication for Albert Ritchie, but perhaps a tacit bow of respect.

Ohio's Martin Davey concluded his career with a 1939 farewell address serving as an especially bitter "Jeffersonian" tirade against the centralization of power in the US federal bureaucracy and its "snoopers," with the departing governor seething against grants-in-aid as the core of his Tenth Amendment tirade against what he portrayed as a relentless campaign of the Roosevelt administration to "destroy the rights of the states." The "bait . . . which some people look upon as free, is the seductive power by which the states surrender many of their basic and important rights, [as they soon] no longer control [their own] affairs but immediately becom[e] the victim of the theories or caprice of the Federal Bureau."[202]

In 1941, Nebraska's governor Dwight Griswold called for more federal centralization of Social Security rather than the awkward mixed administrative system but, he otherwise observed with some resentment, that the federal government had recently become more important than the states and he would do his utmost to fight for Nebraska's states' rights instead of allowing the federal government "telling us how we shall operate our [various programs.]"[203]

In 1947, Indiana's senate overwhelmingly adopted a resolution defending the states' sovereignty and police powers by calling for the end of grants-in-aid not specifically tied to an enumerated power.[204] Interestingly, and suggesting the possibility of connecting a commitment to constitutionally enacted Reconstruction and federalism, among its supporters were the two sponsors—one Republican, one Democrat—of several procivil rights exhortations to Congress, a call for enforcement of the Fifteenth Amendment, anti-lynching law by the South, and a ban on racially discriminatory employment practices involved in interstate commerce.[205] While the grant-in-aid resolution died in the house, a nearly identical resolution passed in 1969.[206]

Even Massachusetts's Leveret Saltonstall, who had spent much of the preceding five years dismissing federalism, now sounded almost identical to Coolidge. In a 1944 speech to the Massachusetts Selectmen's Association, Saltonstall admonished them not to rely on federal aid and to instead remember that "while we insist upon states' rights, we must not overlook states' responsibilities"—a classic formulation of the old progressive federalism.[207]

The 1941 turnover in New Hampshire's executive perhaps most concisely illustrates the slow resurgence of states' rights rhetoric. The Granite State's outgoing governor Francis Murphy, a Winant ally who would join the Democrats, gloated that he had been vindicated in dismissing states' rights claims against federal flood control.[208] His successor, Governor Robert Blood, by contrast, argued that the federal government's increasing use of grants-in-aid threatened to undo the American Revolution itself.[209] While these grants had brought many wonderful things, Blood noted, the emergency had passed and New Hampshire should begin to more seriously examine such grants "if she wishes to retain her right of self-government so dearly bought in the Revolutionary War and as a result of which, in part at least, the Federal government took its existence."[210]

Thus, if, as Bruce Ackerman contends, the mid-1930s comprised a constitutional revolution, sweeping aside federalism for a new faith in Washington, it was evidently a short-lived one, as within a decade states and state officials had pulled the totems of their old political religion from their places of hiding,[211] and even the president of the United States would soon feel no shame in defending the old creed.

Conclusion:
Progressive Federalism's
End ... and Beginning?

I believe deeply in States' rights. I believe that the preservation of our States as
vigorous, powerful governmental units is essential to permanent individual freedom
and the growth of our national strength.
> —Dwight Eisenhower, address to governors

The United States government has become too big, too centralized, too powerful,
too intrusive, too materialistic, too impersonal, too grasping, too militarized, too
imperialistic, too violent, too undemocratic, too corrupt, and too unresponsive to
the needs of individual citizens and small communities. National and Congressional
elections are sold to the highest bidder. State and local governments assume too
little responsibility for the well-being of their citizens—too often abdicating their
responsibilities to Washington.
> —Second Vermont Republic, "Declaration of Independence"

Decades after Calvin Coolidge, Al Smith, and Felix Frankfurter picked up
Elihu Root's plea for states to assert their responsibilities as part of decentralization and "states' rights," one can hear the same sentiment from Dwight Eisenhower—the same Eisenhower who, after all, rejected southern violation of
the Fourteenth Amendment. After saluting the Tenth Amendment, Eisenhower
gave the ode to states' rights in the epigraph, before proceeding to Root's logic
and its hope of preserving constitutional federalism: "But it is idle to cham-

pion States' rights without upholding States' responsibilities as well. . . . By inadequate action . . . the states can create new vacuums into which the federal government will plunge ever more deeply, impelled by popular pressures."[1] Eisenhower's declaration makes clear that the constitutional revolution of his predecessor, Franklin D. Roosevelt, had not permanently erased federalism from the American political landscape. Rather, FDR had destroyed its support on the left, marking the clear and (perhaps permanent) fissure between progressivism and a deep commitment to states' rights. Under Roosevelt, the intellectual core of the progressive left had rapidly switched from one where many progressives—including Roosevelt himself—held strongly federalist views to one where few do. (Indeed, as noted in previous chapters, Roosevelt himself had decried as un-American the very same interpretations of the commerce and taxing powers that would anchor his New Deal.)

The language of robust state activity trying to keep ahead of—and ward off—federal intervention had been erased when the federal government assumed for itself the privilege of first mover. Thus, far from being the sort of rhetoric created by the New Deal, this states' rights progressivism was the language *displaced* by it.[2] That is why, as will be elaborated in this chapter, Mitt Romney's later defense of "Romneycare" in Massachusetts as the sort of policy the Tenth Amendment authorized states to do, but which should be opposed in its variant of "Obamacare," sounded so alien to our ears (and completely ineffective in placating the Left and Right alike): he was speaking to the states' rights progressive tradition destroyed by the New Deal.

After a few years in hiding among conservatives, the states' rights language slowly crept back into more mainstream political dialogue, eventually taking control, at least rhetorically, of one major political party, as Albert Ritchie had long hoped (though, from his perspective, the wrong party). Thus, the New Deal constitutional revolution succeeded in making federalism itself a partisan notion rather than an ideal to which both parties could successively appeal to, as had been the case a decade before. As Frederick Rudolph observed in his study of the Liberty League, even in 1950—at the high point of deference to federal power under Roosevelt's Democratic successor Harry Truman—the existence of organizations devoted to a strict constitutionalism and states' rights could not simply be written off as a self-interested pressure group of a handful of plutocrats hiding behind nice rhetoric: however ignorant of political realities constitutional federalism might be (as Rudolph contended), such a set of values was rooted deeply in American thought even if out of favor with the current New Deal regime.[3]

In short, far from federalism or state constitutional interpretation disappearing or being discredited, only the most extreme forms of state constitutional interpretation became illegitimate after the Civil War, and several of the most significant constitutional conflicts in the subsequent decade were waged at the state level. While the Civil War delegitimized states' resort to secession and (largely) did the same for nullification, the cases considered demonstrate that both invocations of federalism and state participation in constitutional politics—not merely lawsuits—remained acceptable courses of action between Reconstruction and the New Deal, and the brief sketches in the previous chapter show that it survived, albeit in weakened form.

These conflicts reveal several features of the American constitutional order: (1a) Federalism is more than southern racial conservatism. The notion that federalism equates to southern racial conservatism is perhaps most closely, but by no means exclusively, associated with William Riker's 1964 book *Federalism* and its memorable aphorism that "if one disapproves of racism, one should disapprove of federalism."[4] His observation matches the sentiments expressed by many of America's mid-century political leaders. As Scot Powe notes, the justices of the Warren Court widely held the belief that "federalism served no ascertainable purposes except to authorize local—and typically southern—oligarchies to impose their backward . . . views on those unfortunate enough to live within their jurisdictions."[5] Bradley Hays similarly observes that "it should be no surprise that constitutional scholars who lived and worked in the shadow of the civil rights era . . . rejected state-based constitutional engagement . . . as illegitimate," doubly so since these invocations of federalism operated at the same time as the expansion of federal power more broadly under the Great Society was the norm.[6] Robert Schapiro summarizes this bluntly: "States' rights . . . became tarred for a generation by its association with racism" and "the civil rights era represented a defeat not only for particular claims of state autonomy but also for the very idea of decentralization," finishing off whatever of dual federalism remained after the New Deal.[7] Other scholars have pointed out various racially inegalitarian consequences of federalism, from the local administration of Social Security to criminal justice.[8] Decades of southern-influenced historiography encouraged Americans to remember the Civil War not as a war over slavery but about states' rights resisting centralization.

Even a sympathetic federalist like Martha Derthick concedes, "Racism has tainted American federalism for most of the nation's history," while Pauline Maier agrees that "it now takes historical imagination to understand how people could have understood the preservation of the rights of states as a way of protecting individual rights. . . . 'States rights' today seem more firmly associated with the defense of slavery, disenfranchisement of black voters, and resistance to integration."[9]

There is no doubt that federalism, and especially "states rights," has often most strongly been associated with racism—certainly in popular understanding. Southern resistance to the Reconstruction Amendments and efforts to enforce them (such as the Lodge Bill or anti-lynching laws), the nominal "States Rights" Dixiecrat Party, and the Southern Manifesto rejecting *Brown v. Board of Education of Topeka* all were defended through invocations of states' rights. The most successful and proactive resistance of federal power by state governments in American constitutional history was the effort of southern Democrats to maintain white supremacy, in which party and region interlocked in such a way as to encourage clear defiance of federal constitutional law (and incentivize northern copartisans to look the other way).

However, there are reasons to think that the creation of national mythology has resulted in a counterproductive oversimplification. Just as the civil rights movement was more than *Brown* so too does federalism have a historical import that risks being overdetermined by a single issue.

Southern apologists were, after all, not federalism's first claimants, nor its most consistent.

Calhoun's turn from nationalist to state sovereignty theorist is well known, but a mere seven years before nullifying the tariff, the South Carolina legislature passed a memorial insisting that the Bank of the United States—the bane of strict constructionist states' rightsers for three decades—was not only constitutional in Washington, DC, but that its branches throughout the United States were also.[10] In the 1850s, southerners increasingly judged every federal development not by its trespass upon states' rights but by its implications for slavery. In the 1890s, Dixie's support for the federal Blair Bill (to subsidize education), for example, predictably waxed and waned in lockstep with northern efforts to achieve a modicum of racial justice. After the *Civil Rights Cases* and seeming federal disengagement in civil rights enforcement, southerners sought any Blair Bill aid they could get, and their congressional delegations were key supporters of the bill up to 1888. When Republicans took control of the government, however, and the Lodge Bill threatened Yankee intervention in southern elections to enforce the Fifteenth Amendment, support for the otherwise unrelated Blair Bill evaporated.[11] Likewise, many have argued that in the decades to follow, southern support for Prohibition also tracked beliefs about its racial implications rather than concerns about federalism.[12] And perhaps most telling about their supposed states' rights convictions, when southerners finally took control of Congress during the Wilson administration, they sought *federal* bans on interracial marriage.[13]

Recent scholarship has thoroughly demolished the so-called Lost Cause understanding of history (developed beginning in the 1880s and dominant through the mid-twentieth century), which framed federalism as the primary motivation for southern secession. (The corollary of this narrative then was that a victorious North had embraced Hamiltonian nationalism with southerners and racial conservatives defending a Jeffersonian states' rights posture.)

One might argue that the victors of the early twentieth-century Lost Cause historiography—reinterpreting the Civil War to be about federalism rather than race—were southern white supremacists and progressives, while the losers were black Americans and constitutionalists/federalists. The whitewashing away of slavery to absolve the South (and preserve Jim Crow), while also marginalizing the importance of black equality, is well-known. But it is also worth noting that it had the more subtle secondary effect of rationalizing the turn toward national power popular among the wing of progressives represented by Woodrow Wilson, Herbert Croly, and Theodore Roosevelt. By portraying southerners as fighting for a more noble but nonetheless *defeated* cause of states' rights, it made it easier to portray federalism as a lamentably obsolete —but obsolete nonetheless—doctrine fit for America's past rather than future. But that understanding of history—which most of the figures of this era would have grown up with—has been thoroughly debunked by work showing that *slavery*, not states' rights, was Dixie's lodestar, and that antebellum southerners were more than happy to decry federalism when used by northerners to protect free states against slavery.[14]

And of course, constitutional federalism does not always mean states' rights is the overriding principle in all legal controversies; a commitment to American constitutional federalism (or, relatedly, to a constitutional conservatism) is compatible with support for constitutional civil rights—indeed, from one perspective, it requires it. The structure of the Constitution creates strong presumptions on behalf of federalism, but even by its own text that presumption is not supreme, and the Constitution sometimes places other rights or powers ahead of it, whether in the original Constitution (and restrictions on states in Article I, Section 10) or the amended, especially post-Reconstruction Constitution (such as the various guarantees of the Fourteenth Amendment). So, a presumptive commitment to states' rights does not mean endorsing every invocation of it; in this case, the Fourteenth Amendment has banned the states from racially discriminatory policy and empowered the federal government to pass "appropriate legislation" to suppress it.

The conventional wisdom is right this far: it should not be surprising that invoking federalism as a form of constitutional resistance was both the most intense and most frequent within the domain of white supremacy, and legislators and officials were often blunt in describing their efforts as undermining federal interventions into their social hierarchies. As scholars have observed, the entire structure of southern politics and its abnormal party system was designed to achieve and maintain this singular goal.[15]

The case of Sheppard-Towner perhaps most concisely reveals how crudely oversimplified—if not outright inaccurate—modern conceptions of Civil War–era constitutionalism are and can be in distorting our understanding of politics. To whatever extent the Confederacy and its successor regime in the South had been more zealous about federalism than the North—a historically dubious assertion—that reputation was at the very least overstated.

As the cases in this book have shown, despite federalism's occasionally checkered past, it would be, in the worlds of Lawrence Moore, "an improper leap to conclude that all proponents of federalism are crypto-racists. . . . The mere fact that some misuse federalism ought not to banish the concept from the national dialogue. If federalism is part of the constitutional scheme, it would be a double loss to abandon federalism to racists."[16]

Heather Gerken, the scholar most prominently working to rehabilitate federalism's appeal beyond conservatives, agrees, arguing that while "many think 'federalism' is just a code word for letting racists be racist"—an interpretation she concedes is not without merit—"it is a mistake to equate federalism's past with its future."[17] Instead, she argues, provided a basic floor of rights existed and was credibly enforced—such as by Supreme Court implementation of the Bill of Rights and Fourteenth Amendment—federalism (and localism) offered minorities a greater level of political influence, self-government, and the capacity to dissent.[18] Contemporary defenses of federalism by progressives remain far less prominent than on the right, but the case is being made.[19]

It is, perhaps, not an accident that subsequent generations of progressives may have a stronger interest in federalism than those who came of age in the 1950s and 1960s. There are historically good reasons that "states rights" sound like dirty words to progressives, as there is no denying that it was the loudly bleated call of a segregationist South in its death throes. For a generation growing up then, in the wake of the bipartisan New Deal that had temporarily banished other uses of federalism from our political and legal discourse and thus whose primary associations with federalism would have been segregationists' last-ditch attempt to frame their goals in more appealing language, it is not surprising that massive resistance would further discredit federalism in the eyes and ears of progressives.[20] But we should also be careful to avoid telescoping the wide sweep of history to be that which one encountered in one's formative years but which may not be representative of broader trends in American political development and thought. As Gerken argues, neither should we reject a chastened and modified federalism because of one application out of countless in the past.

This study suggests that we should invert our thinking. Rehabilitating federalism is not downplaying or ignoring the importance of race in American constitutional development but rather giving it a central place. Yet showing the centrality of federalism to American politics—in cases separate from race—in turn shows us why southerners unsurprisingly enlisted the central feature of American constitutionalism in defending their highest goal: white supremacy. Southerners used whatever means were at hand, whether states' rights or other features to preserve their social and legal regime. That meant decrying federalism when necessary in the 1850s and latching onto it as a perfectly respectable tool later (or, at least, in the post–New Deal 1950s, one with a more respectable historical pedigree than open invocation of white supremacy). One could say the same things about presidential control of the executive—the executive branch resegregated under Wilson, the army desegregated under Truman—or freedom of speech, shrugged off in pursuit of the "gag rules" in the 1830s through the 1850s, vindicated in the protection of the NAACP in the mid-twentieth century.[21] Federalism has been a tool that has been successfully and repeatedly leveraged by white supremacists, but in this it is like other tools: it could be successful only because it was so widely internalized among northerners, progressives, and others who had not only an intellectual commitment to it but their own eminently reasonable and innocuous incentives to adopt it.

Stated more bluntly, racial supremacy doesn't tell us much more about American federalism than it tells us anything inherent about congressional committee structures (and the goal of organizing unruly Congresses), or consensus-seeking supermajority nomination rules, to use examples of other procedural rules with perfectly defensible good-government justifications but which also were hijacked to preserve the South's particular way of life. Ditto the American welfare state and its racist birth, such as the exclusion of what was then predominantly nonwhite labor (domestic and agricultural labor) from the benefits of Social Security as a way to appease the southern Democrats who served as the backbone of Franklin Roosevelt's congressional caucus.[22] It tells us about *race* and the central importance it played and continues to play in American politics.

In short, then, this history leads us to see that federalism is far more than, as simplistic accounts would hold, an instrumental cover for racism. It was put into the Constitution for other reasons and has been deployed across the political spectrum—including, crucially, after the Civil War—for perfectly honorable and admirable causes, including those progressives embraced.

That leads to a related, and arguably separate, normative corollary, that (1b) progressives need not cede their historical claim to constitutional federalism. Partly because federalism has been so heavily reduced to southern racism, progressives have been uneasy in embracing the doctrine. By recreating the intellectual debates from the period preceding the New Deal, this work offers a history of earlier progressives' embrace of federalism. Especially if national politics continues to remain polarized and thus political gridlock ensues, policymaking will, for good or ill, increasingly turn to the states. Thus, this history helps us not only understand one of America's key moments of state-building but also offers potentially useful lessons for today. To say that progressive hostility to federalism has been deeply rooted since the Roosevelt administration—with that antipathy reinforced in the civil rights era—is not to say that progressive opposition to decentralization is an inherent and permanent part of American politics. There are, perhaps, flickering signs that it may not be.

Obama's solicitor general Walter Dellinger agreed that until the New Deal, and especially the civil rights era, states' rights was usually seen as more strongly associated with the American Left.[23] But unlike conservatives, who continued to hold to and discuss federalism among themselves, post–New Deal progressives had little experience with it other than southerners' invocations of "states' rights" in defense of their old racial order. (Moreover, given that many of these same southerners had happily accommodated massive federal expansion under the Roosevelt Revolution, their calls for states' rights rang hollow, serving as little more than a rationalization for that racial order.)

In the late 1970s and 1980s, progressives made a limited rediscovery of the virtues of decentralization, after decades of indifference, with the so-called New Federalism movement. New Federalism, often associated with a seminal William Brennan piece, served as a largely left-wing backlash against the increasing conservatism of the Burger and then Rehnquist Courts. As the justices became increasingly skeptical of rights claims, some progressives proposed individuals make greater recourse to largely forgotten state constitutions as independent bastions of civil liberties, whether through easier amendments or more expansive judicial interpretation of analogous provisions.[24] Federalism has similarly played a critical role in the movement for same-sex marriage: not only in letting states serve as innovators, proposing and experimenting with more egalitarian visions of marriage, but also in serving as a justification for the Supreme Court's ruling against a heterosexual definition of marriage for purposes of federal law.[25]

While many allege federalism to be simply a cover for a desire to protect racism, the wide range of states' rights fears and the wide distribution of those invoking them in the 1920s counsel against such an interpretation. Prohibition especially had demonstrated the danger of national power to a variety of interests, both business and advocates of state regulation alike, one that diffused through other issues. Indeed, many groups could see how national power could be wielded against them. Thus, the ideologues of the Association Against the Prohibition Amendment waged a decade-long battle against Prohibition, which transferred to the conservative wing of the Democratic Party, and in turn served as the backbone of the Liberty League. This example also hardened resolve in other issues: the northern business elite of the industrial core cited states' rights in protesting estate taxes and opposing Sheppard-Towner and federal child labor restrictions. The latter is especially striking since it was arguably against their economic interests, since child labor restrictions had been opposed most zealously by *southern* manufacturers hoping to use their comparative advantage of cheap labor to catch up with the industrialized North, which banned the practice at the state level.

Just as southerners had wondered "what next?" in fearing the power of the national government to disturb their social order, so did a variety of others: those who opposed a national welfare state, a national libertarian state, or a national moral state (such as congressional blue laws like the Blair Sunday-Rest Bill) all feared the implications for their deviations from the national norms of federalism. Sheppard-Towner's states' rights opposition was led by Yankees and, often, as with Percival Baxter, by zealously pro-Prohibition Yankees. What made Marylanders resent the federal government (Prohibition) was the grandest achievement of a strange coalition of southern populists and moralists from the Midwest and upper New England; what made Boston shudder at Leviathan was the specter of subsidizing development of the long-impoverished South and the developing West. What made Westerners and Midwesterners tremble was the possible imposition of laissez-faire capitalism trumping their own progressive state governments.

If we look at most of the sustained constitutional dialogues in which states objected to and resisted federal authority, it is not southern Democrats but the sons of the Grand Army of the Republic pushing back against federal power. With the admittedly important case of race aside, the South was more supportive or tolerant of a stronger central government, whether looking to Sheppard-Towner (and federal funding in general), the ability to strike at state minimum wages, or Prohibition. Indeed, during this era, the *Northeast* appears to be the most consistent in defending a vision of decentralization—one that a bipartisan, indeed ideologically broad, coalition of its political elite nonetheless often joined with progressive policy commitments at the state level.

What we see unifying these cases is a significant, far-reaching thread of constitutional thought: a serious commitment to both sides of federalism—crudely stated as states' rights and state responsibilities—perfectly compatible with a strong progressive, decentralist tradition. The American governing elite did not insist on a laissez-faire libertarianism across all levels of government.[26] (Of course, as discussed in chapters 4 and 5, some judges, state and federal, did.) Instead, state officials, like the Supreme Court and Congress, held to something closer to Elihu Root's vision of active states protecting rights and the public good. The movement for uniform legislation, protective economic regulations, and decentralization were not in tension but seen by practitioners as part of a single tradition.

However polarized the two parties were across many issues[27]—tariffs, monopoly regulation, or immigration—their constitutional visions were harder to distinguish. As Barry Cushman has observed in disputing regime theory analysis of the pre–New Deal Court, constitutional vision was poorly sorted among the legal elite.[28]

Instead, a Jacksonian ethos trying to steer a states' rights course between a consolidationist nationalism and nullifying state sovereignty served as the core ideological understanding. Republicans and Democrats alike, from both conservative and progressive wings, invoked that tradition in resisting federal constitutional development across a wide set of issues.

In short, active and visible state governments aggressively wielded their sovereign police powers to advance the public good in a variety of ways. Some of these (such as economically protective legislation or defenses of their citizens) are fondly remembered, and others obviously less so. Thus, while not all shared the almost moral devotion to a dual federalism held by constitutional thinkers, a framework of states' rights and a presumption of the distribution of powers nonetheless structured the boundaries of political thought and behavior throughout the country.[29]

At the very least, progressives, moderates, and any others traditionally skeptical of federalism can incorporate a fuller historical picture—one that includes their ideological forebears—in any possible reassessment of federalism.

Returning to the other major lessons of this study: it is clear that (2) state constitutional debates offer evidence of high-quality extrajudicial constitutional interpretation and clear constraints on behavior, even against electoral incentives; and (3) states provide a venue to keep political conflicts alive, and this is no less true of the constitutional sphere than in more conventional policy debates.

Disregarding state-level developments has distorted both the empirical findings and normative prescriptions of extrajudicial and popular constitutionalists.[30] For example, Larry Kramer partly attributes "the all-but-complete disappearance of public challenges to the Justices' supremacy over constitutional law" to "histories that ignore resistance to the Court's view of the Constitution, unless it is to demonize and disparage the opposition as populist excess or political opportunism."[31] Thus, taking account of state constitutional interpretation, as this book does, shows that nonjudicial constitutionalism nonetheless survived far longer than some of its advocates have claimed (to say nothing of its possible survival today). One hope is that exposing some of these debates will encourage future researchers to help us learn more about underappreciated state constitutional thinkers like Nathan Miller, Percival Baxter, or Al Smith, to whom extrajudicial constitutionalists can point in urging contemporary elected officials to uphold their duty to constitutional fidelity.

Scholars of extrajudicial interpretation and popular constitutionalism would be well-served to include the states in their searches for constitutional interpreters, as state officials have engaged in lengthy, substantive, and serious debates on constitutional grounds, keeping issues alive after seeming settlement at the federal level. Some of these cases have fairly scanty evidentiary records or were held in fairly isolated venues, but others were widely circulated and debated in newspapers and other public fora. Like the concurrent Prohibition debates, Sheppard-Towner in particular spurred constitutional dialogue as impressive as any in Congress or the presidency.

Recovering states' constitutional forays into federal debates thus offers support for Madisonian critics of judicial supremacy and the courts as the exclusive guardians of the Constitution. The incorporation of state politics offers significant support to those who charge both the people and their elected representatives—federal and state—to be bound by and enforce the Constitution. States and state officials help rebut a critique often raised against much of the popular constitutionalist literature, as both wispy and even potentially lawless, by providing institutional embodiments of nonjudicial constitutional thought.[32] In short, popular and extrajudicial constitutionalist theories must take state constitutionalism into account.[33]

Against legal realists, state constitutional politics indicates that constitutional commitments *could* constrain behavior. For the state officials who believed their oaths to the Constitution required them to independently enforce it and provide a redundant check when courts and Congress failed, such a specialization of labor was an abdication of their duty—a duty that some were willing to sacrifice for in making obviously politically unwise decisions.

Thus, to the extent there is also a normative takeaway here for an old-fashioned political lesson, it is that elected officials have taken their constitutional oaths and obligations seriously before, even when politically unpopular. It is thus not unreasonable to expect them to do so today, or at least to try to build a political culture that rewards them for taking constitutionalism seriously and speak about constitutional powers and limits to their constituents rather than simply pandering to electoral or partisan pressures. It is admittedly idealistic but not an impossibility: this study shows it has been possible in our history.

The Future of Progressive Federalism

Does progressive federalism matter today, other than as a scholarly artifact, a curiosity of intellectual history? The obvious reason it might is that forms of localism have been offering underutilized resources even to contemporary progressives, whether out of conviction or necessity.[34]

Many of the progressive policies that began this book—California's environmental standards, sanctuary city policies prohibiting state government cooperation with federal immigration, expanding the categories of protected classes, and the like—have depended on states' prerogative to make policy and, in some cases, limiting federal power in some way or another. The so-called neo-Brandeisian efforts of Barry Lynn and now Federal Trade Commission chair Lina Khan to update and apply antitrust enforcement against big tech draw far more from the Jacksonian decentralization that also gave rise to progressive federalism than they do from contemporary Left politics.[35] And, as Sanford Levinson's recent treatment of the return of secessionist thinking to American politics observes, the progressive Vermont secession movement—once endorsed by establishmentarian George Kennan—justifies its claims as necessary to combat the power of American imperialism and late capitalism.[36]

Although a thorough public-policy undertaking is beyond a book of political history, constitutional development, and American political thought, it is worth briefly considering why contemporary Americans might (or might not be) interested in federalism and what these contemporary understandings might look like. There are, of course, a variety of possible understandings, but they likely would fall into one of three broad clusters:[37]

1. Administrative decentralization in which the states are active political actors, but no structural limits exist on federal power against the states.
2. "Opportunistic federalism" utilizing doctrines like the noncommandeering doctrine to prevent the federal government from demanding states implement its policies, but not limiting the spheres or ends of federal power, only some of its means.
3. A constitutional or states' rights federalism—that is to say, one that places substantive limits on the federal government and is based on, but modified from, the progressive federalism that existed before the New Deal.

Some progressives, largely rejecting a decentralized, constitutional federalism that limits the domain of federal power, instead favor a multiplicity of decentralized policymaking, with the states and the federal government exercising robust concurrent powers: administrative decentralization. In this model, states may act until the federal government then does. The existence of multiple policymakers allows for policy experimentation and political agency but for the federal government to clear the field and implement whatever is ultimately deemed an optimal policy. This is a model in which the federal government protects liberties, and the states act for the public good, but the federal government ultimately, in practice, wields something equivalent to police powers to act for the public welfare rather than be blocked from action by structural limits. Moreover, as scholars Malcolm Feeley and Edward Rubin have demonstrated, many of the classic defenses of federalism, such as additional opportunities for political participation or policy experimentation, can be secured through such decentralized administration rather than a constitutional federalism that imposes substantive limits on the central government.[38]

As Alexander Hertel-Fernandez's study of the American Legislative Exchange Council, Americans for Prosperity, and the State Policy Network has suggested, the business-friendly interest groups have been especially successful in policy diffusion by providing model legislation to make it easier for less professionalized and resource-constrained legislatures (such as those lacking in legislative staff support) to pass probusiness legislation in conservative states.[39] But, as Hertel-Fernandez himself has pointed out, part of the reason for this is that progressive elites, donors, and staffers are less interested in states and federalism except as grudging fallbacks when shut out of national power, whereas conservatives' ideological embrace of federalism predisposes them to maintain the infrastructure to achieve policy successes at that level.[40] In other words, even a very mild form of progressive federalism—one in which progressives seek to exercise power at the state level without also checking federal authority—could help break that feedback loop.

Alternatively, as even progressive critics of traditional constitutional federalism have noted, an "opportunistic federalism" is perhaps a reasonable second-order alternative in light of the increasing inability to pass legislation at the federal level.[41] Such gridlocking of national institutions will likely grow ever more true in light of increasing polarization, especially if exacerbated by so-called affective or negative polarization among voters.[42] As Kevin Baker observed in the *New Republic* in 2017, progressives might well be better served by a regime in which taxation primarily shifted from federal to state governments so that progressive states could use their own resources to build a more generous welfare state, expand environmental protection, and the like.[43] Such a federalism would recognize that polarization and the nationalization of the electoral processes have resulted not in gridlock at the state level but increasingly divergent policies, as polarized states secured policy changes.[44]

Relatedly, after decades of trying, and connecting to the *Sebelius* case with which the book began, constitutional originalists have plausibly secured control of the Supreme Court and may begin to more aggressively insist on the much more decentralized federalism established under the original understanding of the Constitution. Until progressives either amend the Constitution or, like Franklin Roosevelt, secure sufficient nominations to again defeat the original understanding and recentralize power, they will likely again have to contend with its judicial enforcement and may as well use it strategically.[45]

Thus, one feature of constitutional federalism—that is to say, a federalism that not only empowers states but limits the federal government—that many progressive federalists have embraced is the concept that the federal government cannot make the state governments enforce federal policy. (This variant of progressive federalism is most closely associated with Heather Gerken.)[46] This is the sort of opportunistic federalism invoked, of late, by Californians in opposition to federal rules on immigration and drug laws, to use two recent examples.

There are a variety of related doctrines—the noncommandeering doctrine (in the regulatory sphere) or the coercion doctrine (in the spending one)—but what they have in common is the idea that the states are not tools of the federal government. Drawing on Sandra Day O'Connor's opinion in *New York v. United States* (1992), Justice Scalia's in *Printz v. United States* (1997), and the various conservative opinions in *Sebelius* (as well as to the antebellum liberty laws avoiding state enforcement of federal slavery laws and Prohibition), these defenders of progressive federalism have argued that the states need not enforce federal policies—most notably, federal drug and immigration laws.[47]

Such a move is consistent with a traditional states' rights federalism (hence the conservative judges expounding it it) and thus is compelling to judicial originalists or conservative politicians.[48] However, it can also be separated from limits on the scope of federal authority that progressives mostly discarded during the New Deal. It does not step the federal government from doing anything directly, only ensures that the federal government and not the states are responsible for its implementation.[49] In other words, by limiting only means rather than ends, noncommandeering and anticoercion offer particularly appealing ways to instrumentally deploy federalism without more broadly endangering progressives' general commitment to an expansive central government or interfering with robust use of the states' police powers.

But if participation and policy experimentation can be secured with mere decentralization, and noncommandeering imposes resource constraints on a federal government implementing policies a state doesn't want, why might one desire substantive limits on federal power of the kind that characterized traditional constitutional federalism?

Conservatives already sympathetic to federalism have argued for its return—not just out of constitutional fidelity but as a necessary condition to maintain civic functioning and peace in light of ever-hardening polarization. Echoing James Madison's warnings that the tendency of consolidation of national power to bring with it a consolidation of executive power culminated in "monarchy,"[50] such conservatives fret that centralized federal power more easily enables authoritarian or dictatorial governance or rapid and unilateral policy pivots from one extreme ideology to the next. (Trump-skeptical conservatives often pointed to Donald Trump as precisely what they wanted pro- gressives to help them join in stopping.)[51] Polarization, they argue, makes this a much different political era than the previous decades of the mid to late twentieth century and raises the need to consider federalism something of a climbdown and deescalation. For example, in a nod to Vermont's thinking, then-*National Review* writer David French argued, "It's time to get busy de- centralizing or get busy dividing."[52]

Conservative federalists would point to the many diverse peoples of this country, arguing they quite simply have not only different needs—from the difference between the water rights regimes of dry Arizona and the wet East— but also different policy views and preferences, such as what to do about mari- juana (or, earlier, Prohibition).[53] American federalism recognizes this diversity and means that, within the backstop limits of the Constitution, "most political activity takes place at the state level of government, where there is more likely to be a consensus, and so varying government policies will both be more re- sponsive to and better reflect the values of the country's diverse communities —rather than feel like policy imposed from afar."[54] Indeed, "by de-scaling our politics from winner-take-all slugfests for control of national institutions such as the presidency and Supreme Court, our resentment of coastal elites or fly- over rubes would perhaps dissipate. The other side would cease to be one's oppressor and instead become merely one's amusingly backward or bohemian neighbor."[55]

But while progressives champion other kinds of diversity, largely related to personal identities, most today tend to be less persuaded of the need to accommodate geographic diversity, such as of communities or states (some- times even suggesting such diversity is largely fictional). They are instead more comfortable with more uniform public policy, which, at least since the New Deal, they have argued brings with it other advantages: more efficiency and less friction from consistent national policies (for example, having a sin- gle rather than multiple old-age pensions), avoiding the problems of unjust lo- cal communities (not just those which may have histories of, say, racism or sexism but of providing insufficient welfare or other spending policies) or the related fear of corporate capture of state or local governments and races to the bottom on public policy. States' rights advocates, they have also noted, are of- ten opportunistic or hypocritical, invoking it when useful and quietly ignor- ing it when not.[56]

Excessively tilting toward the states can and has allowed violations of in- dividual rights of minorities of all kinds. But, as even the Founders recognized in the original Constitution (and whose logic Madison explained in *Federalist* 51 and his 1792 *National Gazette* article and sought to further implement with his state-limiting version of the Bill of Rights), American federalism has always recognized the need to set substantive limits on and guarantee individual rights against the states, not just the federal government. As will be elaborated later in the chapter, this list of restrictions has grown longer over time, from largely economic rights in Article I, Section 10, through equal protection and the privileges and immunities in the Fourteenth Amendment and beyond; thus this objection is more about precise line-drawing than American federalism per se.[57]

Progressive scholars skeptical of federalism—most notably Malcolm Feeley, Edward Rubin, and Sotirios Barber—criticize those who defend federalism on grounds it will generate economic efficiency by discovering optimum policies to then be adopted more widely. Such "fiscal federalism" or "competitive federalism" favored by economic libertarians or business conservatives, they note, often presumes and desires a single good—market efficiency—and a uniform outcome rather than sustained state diversity. The result, then, is often characterized as a "race to the bottom." Barber, in particular, is especially critical of states' rights defenders who would merely "weaken Congress not to strengthen the states but to enhance corporate power."[58] That is indeed a very different understanding of federalism, a purely negative force on behalf of economic efficiency interested neither in states' rights nor a robust conception of their police powers, than the traditional constitutional federalism of George Hunt or Al Smith that saw local actors working for the public good.[59]

The most fundamental objection raised since the early twentieth century is that decentralized constitutional federalism fails to recognize that most Americans consider (or perhaps even always have considered) themselves as either exclusively or primarily a member of a broader national political community, which, in such accounts, is also more likely to have a shared conception of the national common good. Like Feeley and Rubin, Barber extends this claim to argue that dual federalism, by reserving some spheres to the states, violates the idea of a national community and is based on a moral skepticism of the idea of a *national* public good. More confident that agreement on such national goods—both their ends *and* their means—can be identified, Barber would thus read federal power as sufficient to fulfill them, especially the broad ends outlined in the Constitution's preamble. Thus, he views the Constitution as a positive document primarily empowering the government to act for the public good rather than one restraining exercises of power (for example, by creating institutional checks) and preserving spheres of disagreement and diversity. He argues that it is pointless, even immoral, to not empower the national government to act where conducive to these national public goods — and, unlike those he derides as moral skeptics, Barber is much more confident that *national* public goods can be identified and broadly agreeable policies implemented as a result.[60]

These objections will be sufficient to convince many, perhaps even most progressives, not to legitimate constitutional federalism beyond either administrative decentralization or the most necessary instrumentalist or opportunistic cases, if even that. There is a long pedigree in American political thought going back to Roosevelt, Croly, and others of progressives concluding that a commitment to their policy preferences' unbridled implementation nationwide is preferable to constitutional constraint — and indeed perhaps that the Constitution itself is fundamentally unsound and its structures archaic, a relic, etc.[61]

But perhaps more fundamentally, as polarization hardens and a combination of populist and post-liberal conservatism strands develop and propose replacing the Right's traditional view of federalism with a much more aggressive exercise of national power, progressives and moderates may find not just the sword but the shield side of constitutional federalism appealing in ways it hasn't been for almost a century. It was one thing for progressives to think of federalism the way that scholars, to use a different metaphor, speak of state constitutions as providing floors but not ceilings, in which states, under administrative decentralization, could offer additional protections or policies but which does not then limit the authority of the federal government.

For a variety of reasons, progressives could be confident that an empowered federal government would primarily empower them, and much more sparingly be used against them. One such reason was the asymmetric federalism views between the parties. Most conservative policies have been focused on limiting the power or footprint of the national government (and to the extent they weren't, they were often compromising to achieve progressive objectives, such as on No Child Left Behind, Medicare Part D, etc.). Criticism for betraying states' rights thus came almost exclusively from the right itself. Support for national power was also a much easier calculation in an age of Democratic political dominance between the 1940s and 1970s or, more recently, with the prospect of an "Emerging Democratic Majority" in which progressives were more confident of presumptive political dominance, an assumption that has appeared more questionable of late.[62]

Thus, progressives have not had as much to fear from losing control of federal government power when it came to their rights and preferences being squashed—ignored or not advanced, yes, but not retrenched.

But perhaps they do now, and those tempted to throw out the Constitution and its central pillars (including federalism) can already see what happens when either side embraces a willingness to jettison constitutional constraints for their ends.

Some of the more populist elements of the Right seem to be displacing some of the more procedurally inclined elements of the conservative movement, which possibly includes jettisoning the presumptive posture toward constitutional states' rights. If a populist conservative congressional majority and presidential administration were to sweep into Congress in 2024 (or anytime thereafter), the political landscape *would* quite possibly be *very* ripe for progressives to turn to federalism to limit a populist Right government. It is not too hard to see a world where conservatives attempt to impose robust religious-exercise claims against, say, state antidiscrimination laws or target "woke" corporations, as various conservative-leaning states have done within their own borders.[63] These are just some of the most obvious ones that might deeply unsettle progressives.

For example, Republican members of Congress recently proposed requiring all K–12 schools accepting federal funding to include curriculum on communism.[64] That school policy, and especially school curriculum, was long the constitutional domain of the states used to conservative orthodoxy. Now some are considering imposing conservative curricula on the country. One can imagine similar congressional bills regarding race or gender in schools (critical race theory) or ones that would use conditional federal K–12 spending to defund schools that used the 1619 Project versus, say, Hillsdale College's 1776 curriculum. Even putting aside such curricular battles and resorting purely to financial ones, Congress could pressure states to implement school vouchers, education savings accounts (ESAs), or the like. The primary obstacles to these, just as it was with efforts to punish so-called sanctuary cities, would be a combination of the states' rights noncommandeering or coercive-conditions doctrines, both of which would disappear under contemporary progressive theories of nationalism.[65]

Connected to education, but going beyond it, the fierce polarization that developed over health policy is another where we could also envision national imposition of some of the policies implemented in more conservative states: prohibitions banning states from having mask or vaccine mandates; banning employers, restaurants, or others from requiring masks or vaccinations (banning "vaccine passports"); etc. Additional Medicaid conditions fulfilling social conservative ends, the mirror of the Affordable Care Act, is another possibility.

Even more notable, perhaps, is abortion. Historically, conservatives have argued that abortion was a states' rights issue—for example, continuing from Justice Antonin Scalia's famous argument in *Planned Parenthood v. Casey* (1992), Justices Thomas and Scalia seemed unsympathetic to the constitutionality of the federal partial-birth abortion ban in 2003.[66]

But, since the Fourteenth Amendment authorizes federal action when states have failed to protect core civil rights,[67] some conservatives, perhaps most notably Robby George and his allies, have argued the amendment's enforcement power against state neglect of civil rights enables federal suppression of abortion.[68] George and John Finnis offered an amicus brief in *Dobbs v. Jackson Women's Health* (2022), arguing that the Fourteenth Amendment, properly read on originalist grounds, not only allowed the states to regulate abortion but that the amendment actually *prohibited* abortion by its own terms.[69] The majority acknowledged but brushed aside this argument, with Justice Kavanaugh's concurrence specifically rejecting it; instead, they concluded that there was no federal right to an abortion and thus the state police powers could regulate it.[70]

The Fourteenth Amendment position, to be clear, remains a distinct minority among originalists, most of whom argue that the original meaning of personhood under the Fourteenth Amendment does not extend to the unborn and thus the issue remains with the states. However, it has become prominent enough that it is seriously debated among conservative intellectuals, and, in September 2022, Senator Lindsay Graham (R-SC) proposed a *federal* bill prohibiting abortions after fifteen weeks.[71]

If one takes the *National Review* as the center of conservative opinion (as do many scholars of conservative thought),[72] the issue of federalism and abortion fiercely divided conservatives in the wake of *Dobbs*. The official *National Review* editorial (likely written by Ramesh Ponnuru, a former Robby George student who had recently become the magazine's editor and had earlier called for a federal ban on all late-term abortions) endorsed Graham's federal proposal. This led, within days, to blistering dissents from Andrew McCarthy (*National Review*'s primary legal writer, as well as Charles C. W. Cooke and Phillip Klein, the former and current online editors). Ed Whelan, *National Review*'s other primary legal writer, had similarly adopted the states' rights position in a symposium the year before.[73] Senator Mitch McConnell, the Republican majority leader, quickly dismissed Graham's bill, noting that most of his coalition—and presumably himself—preferred it be a state issue.[74] The point, however, is that a growing number of prominent conservatives seem willing to use federal power to dictate abortion policy, and progressives hoping to stop that may have to rely on, and support, the traditional states' rights–oriented wing of the conservative movement.

Perhaps the next fierce divide in our politics will be the debate over the extent to which the Free Exercise Clause constrains the police powers of the states. Three Supreme Court justices recently endorsed reinterpreting the First Amendment to require the states to be bound by the more expansive religious liberty rights developed by progressive justices in the 1960s and detailed in the Religious Freedom Restoration Act (RFRA); this would reverse the previous conservative states' rights positions in the 1990 *Smith* case (also written by Scalia) and the 1997 *Boerne* case.[75] It is worth noting that progressive victory in either of these cases would depend on convincing originalist judges like Brett Kavanaugh and Amy Coney Barrett, like Scalia before them, that the Constitution, faithfully read on originalist grounds, leaves one or both of these issues within the sphere of states' rights and thus the will of the people within those states, rather than national settlements (to be made by conservatives judges or congressional majorities), ought to govern the issue.[76]

Although George and these other originalists made a proceduralist, historical case to claim that abortion is a specific textual exception to states' rights (as do scholars arguing for incorporation of an expansive free exercise),[77] others making such cases are less concerned about constitutional nicety, procedure, or structure. There is, instead, a growing tendency of more hard-line conservatives to argue that the positivist, states' rights position on abortion (or other social issues) enables substantive injustice and there must be a national settlement on behalf of conservative policy goals.

Such arguments appear in the form of so-called common-good constitutionalism being floated by theorists like Adrian Vermeule, which seeks to altogether displace originalism, including its states' rights, as too narrowly proceduralist rather than what Vermeule considers substantively just.[78] One can imagine additional congressional regulations on abortion rooted in expansive and loosely causal readings of the Commerce Clause, where children not born would affect interstate commerce, akin to the sweeping power that would have been upheld by Justice Stephen Breyer's dissent in *U.S. v. Lopez* (1995) and against Scalia's and Thomas's position as noted previously. Vermeule's reasoning is not, of course, limited to abortion but a host of socially conservative ends. How widespread it is, or will be, among younger conservative intellectuals of the kind who will be filling policy positions in this country in the next couple decades is hard to say.

The related National Conservatism could, depending on how it evolves, similarly dislodge conservatives' traditional fondness for states' rights. The official "Statement of Principles" put out by the Edmund Burke Foundation (the primary intellectual nucleus of the movement) rejects the anti-statism of much recent conservatism and calls for a much more robust effort to use government power to impose conservative policy aims on a variety of issues. It does acknowledge, in passing, a "recommend[ation of] the federalist principle," albeit with several notable caveats that, due to their vagueness, either could simply acknowledge the limits on states under the American system (those under the Fourteenth Amendment) or which could be cited as pretexts to sweep federalism away altogether.[79]

To be clear, states' rights need not be inconsistent with either populism *or* nationalism. States' rights populism against a disliked federal government has been a recurrent theme in American politics (see the Jeffersonians, the Jacksonians, the Reagan Revolution, the Tea Party), even as populists' former progressive allies discarded the doctrine, just as the two have arguably split on the Constitution itself (with populists often celebrating the Constitution and criticizing elite or governmental—or progressive–disdain for it).[80] Similarly, to the extent nationalism means something more like patriotism and is often about embracing the distinctiveness of the American tradition, then that tradition's constitutional federalism is a key part; hence, the post–Civil War "states' rights nationalism" ideology discussed in chapter 1. But to the extent populism can call for the displacement of all procedures that get in the way of direct democracy, or that nationalism seeks merely to use consolidated power on behalf of a monolithic American people, then both populism and nationalism, so understood, would be in tension with federalism.

In short, possible trajectories in conservative thought, away from their traditional position of presumptive localism and toward a much more muscular federal imposition of conservative priorities, might give progressives a new reason to reconsider federalism's protections in not merely empowering states but also limiting federal authority.

Political practitioners will continue to be tempted to invoke federalism instrumentally, utilizing tactical and ad hoc deployments of federalism, not just the decentralized policymaking of state police powers but also the anti-commandeering and coercion doctrines preventing the federal government from conscripting state actors. Others may raise enumerated powers objections to undesirable federal legislation, though progressive lawyers have historically and reasonably been shy about doing this due to the possibility of backfiring on other issues.[81]

Most progressives, and almost certainly most progressive intellectuals of the sort offering stark critiques of the Constitution,[82] will likely continue to dismiss federalism as, at best, a relic, looking at such a move as a step backward from the robust government developed over the course of the twentieth century, especially by the New Deal. They would assume that any risk from such conservative governance is fleeting and be unpersuaded by the need to reinvigorate not just state activity but state autonomy. They would, in short, weigh the drawbacks of conservative federal power less than they do the costs to progressive governance. This hesitation to resist constitutional states' rights would seem likely, at least in the short to medium term. In the long term, a sustained nationalist conservatism, coupled with electoral success, could inculcate, in response, a more enduring commitment to federalism on the Left.

Others may weigh the costs and benefits of federalism differently—if not today, then a few years from now. Some might be tempted, in light of recent political developments and greater political caution, to reconsider a broader commitment to states' rights more akin to that recounted in this book, one which imposed real limits on federal power. Moderates and those on the center-Left, in particular, will have rather different calculations of cost-benefit from progressive intellectuals. For example, those near the center, prizing stability and only slow change from a status quo, might find the risk-aversion of limited federal power more appealing than do progressives, especially in light of polarization of the two parties' intellectuals and the seeming concentration of federal power in the executive, which leads to rapid and stark changes in policy.

In order to assess what such a revivified Progressive Era–style federalism could entail, and thus whether it is desirable or not, the next few pages sketch a framework for applying a synthesis of both the basic ideas of early twentieth-century progressive federalism and subsequent constitutional development.

Sketching Out a Common Denominator Constitutional Federalism

Such a constitutionalism would be rooted in the text of the Constitution, including, it should be emphasized, the Reconstruction Amendments. This might seem obvious, but this offers a useful starting point that can provide both progressives and conservatives a common source of authority to appeal to.

The basic framework might be broadly similar to the so-called dual federalism of pre–New Deal constitutionalism, but with some important differences. Most importantly, this approach would confine rights protection largely to those rights enumerated in the Bill of Rights, equal protection, and voting rights—but would also entail meaningfully enforcing those rights. Ken Kersch, for example, described the Old Right dual federalist constitutionalism as "a public philosophy holding a narrow conception of the powers of the national government, an expansive understanding of the powers of the states, where constitutionally protected rights are not involved, and a robust conception of rights and prerogatives of private property."[83] Other than to the extent that conservatives understood property to mean largely laissez-faire economics, that characterization of Old Right dual federalism shares much with the era's progressive federalist constitutionalism as well.

This offers a useful starting point for an attempt at a consensus constitutionalism. It is a federalism that does not privilege states in all circumstances but recognizes the partial commitment of Madison's system. Thus, the political communities of states have rights, but these are circumscribed by the federal Constitution. On the other side, the powers of the central government are somewhat more limited than today but still embody a federal government strong enough to achieve national aims, including many progressive policy aims—in other words, a narrower than present, but not especially narrow, conception of the powers of the national government. And, while such a federalism would create a no-man's land blocking both the states and the federal government from regulating a few policy domains (for example, in the Bill of Rights and equal protection), by more tightly confining these rights to the text of the Constitution, the domain of this no-man's land would be arguably much more narrowly and precisely defined than it was under dual federalism in the early twentieth century and be much more cognizable by the average American insofar as they would be much more textually rooted.

Federal Powers: Commerce

A renewed progressive federalism of the sort sketched out here would likely end up with the federal government's economic powers somewhat close to the 1930s reallocation of federal power—that is, of a wide federal scope for economic powers, especially economic regulatory powers but not progressives' subsequent cultivation of presumptive federal power more generally.[84] The federal government would not be able to use the Commerce Clause to regulate the health, welfare, safety, or morals, except as part of regulating actual commercial operations of this country (such as in setting the maximum hours of interstate railroad workers, as under the classic progressive Adamson Act of 1916).[85] In other words, it would take seriously decisions such as *U.S. v. Lopez* (1995), reiterating that there is no general police power in the federal government.

While that requires paring back contemporary progressives' understandings of the commerce power (such as Justice Stephen Breyer's sweeping *Lopez* dissent), and possibly some of the New Deal caselaw, that does not mean, however, adopting the most crabbed interpretations of the federal Commerce Clause power either.

After the claim that it has been a tool of racism, arguably the most common progressive objection raised to federalism is that it can spur a "race to the bottom": that states (or nation-states) will be induced to deregulate (such as on child labor or safety conditions or environmental regulations) or to minimize welfare benefits, either to attract businesses or to avoid becoming magnets for benefit-seekers. (Conversely, others argue that there can be a race-to-the-top effect putting upward pressure on states.)[86] From a constitutional perspective, policing economic spillover effects is a classic case for federal regulation complementing state policymaking, even under a fairly strict definition of federalism.[87]

The Supreme Court, of course, notably once held otherwise, striking down an effort to prevent a race to the bottom of child labor in the controversial case of *Hammer v. Dagenhart* (1918). It is worth observing, however, that that decision was not only later overturned and atypical from other contemporary cases allowing federal regulation of the interstate movement of goods—suggesting a general sympathy for policing spillover—but it was also made over the dissent of four justices. These included the progressive federalist Louis Brandeis—who, as chapter 6 recounts, applied the traditional use of the direct-indirect commerce test in *Schecter* and bitterly condemned the New Dealers for usurping state authority. The balance of federal commerce power articulated in Holmes's *Hammer* dissent, joined by Brandeis, fits well within both a serious commitment to constitutional federalism and a functional ability of Congress to regulate the modern American economy.[88] In other words, this makes a good marker of a progressive federalism that offers a robust but not unlimited federal power and that even some conservative originalists argue is closer to the constitutional text as well.

As even the conservative Nathan Miller[89] had observed, the increasingly integrated economy, and the desire by companies to participate in that economy, would result in a lot more federal control even under a relatively strict or largely originalist understanding of federal commerce powers. In the age of the Internet and even much more integrated economy, almost all producers and manufacturers seeking access to the interstate market would need to comply. Thus, even a commitment to a fairly strict and decentralized federalism does not mean crippling the federal government from policing spillover effects from the national economy or leaving the states at the mercy of massive multinational corporations.

Originalists contend there is a need to return to the more limited vision of the commerce power advocated by *Governor* Roosevelt and other pre–New Deal progressive federalists—namely, by overturning *Wickard v. Filburn* and replacing it with a more focused constitutional amendment of the kind *President* Roosevelt's New Deal allies subsequently proposed but which he waved off, as discussed in chapter 6. This would explicitly allow the federal government to regulate manufacturing and agricultural (or, more broadly, labor) conditions, wages, etc. in ways that recognized the increasing interconnectedness of the American economy without giving such a wide-sweeping power.[90] But doing so, while perhaps positive for constitutional hygiene and fidelity, would likely be impractical to achieve and almost certainly be a nonstarter for progressives today.

Moreover, the most significant effects of such an overturn-and-replace are largely (but not totally) accomplished by Chief Justice William Rehnquist's concession in *U.S. v. Lopez* (1995)—that the Court would henceforth tolerate, based on precedents like *Wickard*, congressional regulation of fundamentally economic (rather than merely traditionally "commercial") and even *in-state* economic activities.

But, Rehnquist insisted—making *Lopez* an important case—*Wickard* must be read as applying only to economic issues, not all possible policies, and the Court would hold the line and insist that for such a federal regulation to be a valid exercise of the federal commerce power, the underlying activity must be truly economic and not pretextual ways to regulate health, crime, or other domains left to the states.[91] Agreement on and enforcement of this framework might be appealing to progressives as a way to preclude possible conservative efforts to use the commerce clause to legislate nationally on cultural issues but without threatening progressives' economic regulations or undoing decades of established political practice that largely defined what it means to be a progressive in the decades after the 1930s.

Conversely, a progressive-federalist understanding of the commerce power would significantly pare back one aspect of federal power in a way that is especially appealing to progressives, especially on the environmental domain: creating a Left–Right alliance seeking to overturn the so-called Dormant Commerce Clause. This is a very old nineteenth-century doctrine—with origins dating back to the Marshall Court—of judicial nationalism in which federal courts strike down state laws regulating the economy on the grounds that they impair interstate commerce even if the laws do not conflict with congressional commercial legislation or any explicit protectionist bias on behalf of in-state commerce. In other words, the Dormant Commerce Clause approach converts the Congress' power to regulate interstate commerce into a *judicial* restriction on the states' ability to regulate businesses operating within their borders.[92]

This doctrine, long disfavored by textualists and originalists, historically was used against various populist and progressive efforts to check growing corporate power, especially the railroads.[93] More recently, however, the Dormant Commerce Clause threatens to significantly limit states' ability to deal with environmental issues.[94] Especially with a strict separation-of-powers interpretation favored by conservative Supreme Court justices that would limit executive agencies from acting without fairly explicit congressional authorization, coupled with an often gridlocked Congress that lessens federal activity here, Dormant Commerce Clause conflicts are indeed likely to be an important part of environmental policy going forward.

Federal Rights: The Bill of Rights and Equal Protection

American federalism does not mean unencumbered state sovereignty, just as it didn't at the Founding. Taming state overreach of fundamental rights was one of the causes of the Convention—with the Constitution aiming to protect liberty from both states and the federal government while also ensuring sufficient power to the respective governments to achieve their assigned ends.[95] In other words, it protects some rights against the states while still leaving them general discretion elsewhere.

Although Louis Brandeis was skeptical of the application of the Bill of Rights to the states (for reasons elaborated on further), and although the application of the Bill of Rights to the states theoretically is a major intervention into the states' police powers, no functioning modern American federalism could operate without it (certainly no federalism that would be minimally popular or acceptable today).

The incorporation of the Bill of Rights' protections against the states is also almost certainly required by the Fourteenth Amendment (albeit more likely under its Privileges and Immunities Clause). This is, perhaps, the sharpest break between a progressive federalism of the present or future and the Progressive federalism of the early twentieth century. To the extent a no-man's land of rights exists in which certain rights cannot be interfered with by states nor the federal government, it would be these rights, alongside other guarantees (such as the Reconstruction Amendments, especially the Fourteenth, and the handful of rights guaranteed in both Article I, Sections 9 and 10). Again, disagreement might exist about the scope of some of the rights, but they would be those with clear legibility in the text of the Constitution and thus a broader base of popular support, from Left and Right alike.

Dual federalism as practiced in the Progressive Era did not enforce the Bill of Rights against the states (although John Harlan I had pressed for it). The process of incorporating the core protections enumerated in the Bill of Rights began, awkwardly, during the 1920s, but is basically a product of the New Deal and Warren Courts, and especially the agitations of Hugo Black and William Douglas.

Unlike some of the other cases mentioned here, conservatives have basically made their peace with and embraced these progressive decisions and incorporation itself.[96] For example, Justice Ruth Bader Ginsburg's 2019 *Timbs v. Indiana*, which argued that law enforcement had illegally confiscated the vehicle of a drug dealer, correcting a long-standing progressive critique of the justice system, had unanimous support from the Left and Right. The only separate opinions were Justices Neil Gorsuch suggesting and Clarence Thomas insisting that such incorporation should properly come through the Fourteenth Amendment's Privileges and Immunities Clause, not substantive due process.[97] Indeed, contemporary conservatives have effectively endorsed Hugo Black's theory of total incorporation of the Bill of Rights—one that scandalized the deferential Felix Frankfurter and the conservative John Harlan II. Thus, progressives who are interested in federalism, but also in continuing to secure the incorporation of the Bill of Rights, would do well to imitate older progressives like Black in defending them on grounds of textualism (and by defending textualist constitutional theory more broadly).[98]

Just as conservatives have embraced incorporation of the Bill of Rights, so too have they with *Brown v. Board of Education of Topeka* and *Loving v. Virginia*. Indeed, to the extent progressives seek to resist conservative enthusiasm for the Fourteenth Amendment's Equal Protection Clause in the latter's adoption of Harlan's understanding of the Fourteenth Amendment, progressives will, ironically, have to rely on a form of an originalist and states' rights argument (contending that the meaning of the Fourteenth Amendment is narrower than the color-blind standard and thus state institutions are allowed to undertake ameliorative racial classifications and policies, which conservatives believe are banned to states under the Equal Protection Clause).[99]

Beyond the Bill of Rights

As noted in chapter 5, Louis Brandeis and Felix Frankfurter became so disgusted by substantive due process being used to invalidate labor legislation and empower conservative judicial policymaking that they privately discussed whether the Fourteenth Amendment ought to be eliminated altogether.[100] Brandeis continued to seethe about the illegitimacy of substantive due process in *Whitney v. California* in 1927, only grudgingly going along with its use as the vehicle to incorporate freedom of speech.

Brandeis's speculation of eliminating the Fourteenth Amendment is obviously grossly overkill—with equal protection and incorporation of the Bill of Rights (under Privileges and Immunities) unacceptable casualties and would overly empower the states to a level repelling even most states' rights conservatives. But Brandeis's goal, shared with Hugo Black, of eliminating substantive due process of *unenumerated* rights applied against the states may warrant a revisiting from progressives today and looks different than it has in the past. If, as critics of substantive due process have long insisted, it creates an opportunity for judges to roam beyond the text and impose their policy preferences of what they wish the Constitution included, instead of what it does, it now primarily empowers conservatives.

Post *Dobbs*, almost all progressive anxiety about substantive due process refers to *Loving v. Virginia* (1967, holding the Fourteenth Amendment prohibits state bans on interracial marriage), *Griswold v. Connecticut* (1965, holding a right of privacy guarantees the right to use contraception), *Lawrence v.*

Texas (2003, holding *Griswold*'s right to privacy prohibits state bans on "sodomy"), and *Obergefell v. Hodges* (2015, holding the Equal Protection Clause prohibits denying marriages to same-sex couples), and their corollary cases.

Yet each of the policy outcomes favored by progressives in these other cases likely would be sustained under a constitutional federalism even without substantive due process. *Loving*, for instance, is dealt with easily as a straightforward application of the Equal Protection Clause (even under a relatively narrow reading), blocking explicit racial hierarchies in law. Excising the brief substantive due process aside from the opinion's focus on equal protection makes no difference.[101]

Even if the courts were to reject substantive due process, it is rather unlikely the Court would take any of the other cases for reconsideration. Nonetheless, let us posit the consequences of the Court taking up all three cases *and* explicitly rejecting the substantive due process reasoning in each. The practical implications for the contraception at issue in *Griswold* are almost certainly minimal. It should be remembered how anomalous the laws of Connecticut and Massachusetts limiting contraceptive use were even at the time, and it is hard to believe even the most socially conservative legislature in the country would vote to enact such laws, or those at issue in *Lawrence*, today. Like *Lawrence*, *Obergefell* would have much stronger claims under equal protection than substantive due process.[102] As both Chief Justice Roberts (writing in dissent) and Anthony Kennedy (writing for the majority) agreed, *Obergefell* also has far less support under the Court's *Washington v. Glucksberg* substantive due process test, which has long been cherished by Roberts and has again become the Court's standard in assessing claims of unenumerated rights against the states.

Under *Glucksberg* (1997), written by Chief Justice William Rehnquist, the only unenumerated rights guaranteed by substantive due process are those "objectively, deeply rooted in the nation's history and tradition," a compromise to eliminating the doctrine altogether but that would still limit the judicial policymaking Rehnquist so often decried. Borrowing language from some of the earliest substantive due process cases, *Glucksberg* keeps substantive due process but with a decidedly conservative tilt emphasizing that the only rights that did not make it to constitutional text but are still eligible for judicial enforcement as "fundamental" are those that could be clearly shown to have been traditionally valued by society.[103]

The second Justice Harlan's reasoning in the contraceptive cases illustrates why substantive due process so cabined by tradition offers little to progressives. Harlan objected to the law in *Griswold* because Connecticut's restriction on use interfered with *marital* privacy; the clear implication of Harlan's opinions was that unmarried persons were not covered under historical tradition. "Adultery, homosexuality, and the like," as well as "extramarital sexual activity," Harlan had previously declared, were "intimacies which the law has always forbidden and which can have no claim to social protection."[104]

Thus, to the extent substantive due process survives today via *Glucksberg*, it empowers tradition as the fount of judicially discerned rights, creating an asymmetric advantage in which conservatives can discern unenumerated rights that they find amenable but progressives, unable to cite such a long tradition for their rights, cannot. *Dobbs*, relying on the *Glucksberg* framework, illustrates this concisely.

In short, with progressive policies previously delivered by substantive due process now secured by a combination of political support, the Equal Protection Clause, and substantial stare decisis reliance interests, substantive due process thus actually offers relatively little to contemporary progressives going forward. The end of *Roe* means progressives have *already* paid the heaviest cost of such a doctrinal shift.

So, what would conservatives, and especially libertarians, protect of unenumerated rights under *Glucksberg* substantive due process? Calls are out to revivify the family and educational autonomy from the heyday of substantive due process—for instance, using *Pierce* and *Meyer* frameworks to have courts guarantee various forms of school choice.[105] A few libertarian legal thinkers—some now sitting federal judges—have even floated resurrecting the liberty of contract against a variety of regulations.[106] So, although progressives have long vigorously defended substantive due process (against critiques, for example, from Justice Hugo Black), ironically in the future they might find more kinship with Justice Scalia's *Troxel v. Granville* (2000) dissent and its clear rejection of substantive due process.[107]

In sum, a revivified progressive federalism would neither revert to an antebellum model in which no core rights are nationally enforced, nor would it have a federal government shorn of its enumerated powers to regulate truly national issues. Instead, it would be one in which as close to a consensus set of fundamental rights are enforced while leaving the federal government robust but limited.

In some ways, the closest figure representing this position might be, if not Louis Brandeis himself, then the first John Harlan. Harlan famously sought to prevent state-based racial castes under the Fourteenth Amendment (for example, his *Plessy* and *Civil Rights Cases* dissents), enforce the incorporation of the first eight amendments of the Bill of Rights, provide a robust but limited federal commerce power, and not allow federal courts to intervene or decline to intervene in state laws they found merely unwise or unjust. Harlan, for example, would have upheld the mandatory vaccination regime in *Jacobson v. Massachusetts* (1905) while rejecting the Court's effort to uphold separate-but-equal as sufficiently reasonable, as it did in *Plessy*. Rather than assess the reasonableness or unreasonabless of the segregation statute, a judicial practice Harlan decried as inconsistent with both federalism and separation of powers, Harlan would have blocked it as in violation of the Fourteenth Amendment's text and original purpose.[108]

Harlan similarly took a robust but still fairly limited scope for federal commerce power, like federal powers more generally.[109] Fearing a "vast centralized government,"[110] as he explained in his law lectures,

> There are some who believe that it is competent for the government of the United States, through Congress, to do anything, pass any law which appertains to the general welfare. Who think that the government, by the Congress of the United States, is competent to govern anything that may be acquired by legislation at all. Who shut their eyes to the idea that there are states in this country. And who forget that the government created by this instrument is not a government of all powers, but limited to the extent of powers to be exercised. That class of man is a dangerous man, if in public life.[111]

While he argued the specifics of a multistate sugar trust inherently triggered the commerce power in his *E. C. Knight* dissent, part of his concern was that the alternative would disempower states' rights, as massive corporations would escape state regulatory authority. This opinion is sometimes taken as proof of Harlan having an extremely nationalist view of the federal commerce power, but he did not—striking down, for example, the regulation of railroad contract negotiations in *Adair v. United States* (1908) as violating states' rights.

The match isn't perfect: somewhat in tension with his reasoning in the *Jacobson* case and *Plessy* dissents, Harlan adopted liberty of contract,[112] albeit of a far more limited form than the *Lochner* majority. Nonetheless, Harlan offers a reasonably coherent vision of American federalism that broadly speaks to Americans today—one that takes seriously civil rights, civil liberties, and caution about federal government power.

This is, of course, just one version of what a future progressive federalism might look like, adopting some features of the various understanding of federalism held by progressives in the early twentieth century, the mid-twentieth century, and today. The contours of the federalism sketched previously in this chapter require progressives to accept several things they obviously do not favor while perhaps securing other things they or others, especially moderates, might increasingly prize. Just as with federalism itself—which balances between the consolidation of a unitary government and the state sovereignty maximization of a league—determining the exact contours of a progressive federalism would be complicated process requiring negotiating political and constitutional possibilities and trade-offs. But, as James Madison observed, the difficulty of drawing some of the lines should not in itself negate the importance of carefully defending federalism should it be otherwise desirable.[113]

But whether out of a reclamation of the old, pre–New Deal progressive belief in decentralization—a strain apparent in Lynn's Jacksonianism and Vermont's hostility to neoliberalism—or a mere grudging acceptance on purely prudential grounds, or a more sustained interest in a states' rights federalism, progressives have cause to reconsider decentralization in achieving their policy goals as well as fending off those on the political Right—which brings up a final point.

Any successful *and sustained* resurgence of progressive federalism would require a reinvigoration of constitutional discourse and fidelity, not just from the Left but from the American political Right as well.

Of course, although some research has tended to find Republican and conservative voters are more consistent and stable in endorsing federalism regardless of the party in power compared to progressives' more opportunistic endorsements only invoking federalism against Republican officeholders,[114] the Right's consistency on federalism has its own gaps.

Contemporary American conservatives have been criticized for infidelity to their oft-stated principle of federalism in expanding federal power with, for example, national prohibition of partial-birth abortion, marijuana laws,[115] and George W. Bush's No Child Left Behind initiative—a far cry from calls to disband the federal Department of Education as unauthorized by the Constitution, as President Reagan had argued.[116] And, as noted at the beginning of this chapter, some strands of conservatives are succumbing to the temptation to jettison even lip service to decentralized federalism.

But even independent of the temptation of elected officials to relax on principles when in power—to wield power as strongly as possible when one can—

even when *following* their principles, Republicans and conservatives have at times been complicit in the erosion of federalism. They have done so by treating states' rights merely as a cudgel to be used against federal power but without acknowledging the robust state powers that once came with constitutional federalism. Forgetting the wisdom of one of its revered conservative heroes—Calvin Coolidge—as well as forgotten champions like Elihu Root, contemporary conservatives often not only disagree with but delegitimate protective or regulatory policies at the state level.[117]

Perhaps nowhere was this clearer than in the Republican primaries preceding the 2012 presidential election, when presidential candidate Mitt Romney was assailed for hypocrisy in criticizing Obamacare as unconstitutional. Why? Because as governor of Massachusetts, Romney had shepherded through "Romneycare," a legislative package of health-care policies—most notably the combination of an individual mandate and coverage for preexisting conditions, which served as a model for the later federal policy.[118] Minnesota representative Michelle Bachman, for instance, objected that neither the states nor federal government could mandate coverage, and when asked by Robby George in a later debate to explain what provision in the Constitution rendered Romneycare unconstitutional, Bachman instead demurred that "it's inherent in the Constitution." Romney, by contrast, had countered that the policy was indeed unconstitutional at the federal level because of the Tenth Amendment but *was* authorized at the state level. This position would have sounded familiar and eminently defensible for most of American political history—certainly to Coolidge, his predecessor as Massachusetts governor. But Romney's only defender was the long-shot libertarian gadfly Ron Paul (TX), who agreed with his fellow Republicans in attacking Romneycare as a bad *policy* idea but who also vigorously echoed Romney's constitutional defense of the state's individual mandate as falling well within the states' police powers.[119]

To the extent such exchanges are typical, conservatives' reflexive hostility to government may threaten to create the no-man's land so loathed by conservative opponents of *Lochner* and *Adkins*—and which perceptive observers like Root feared would ultimately destroy constitutional federalism. That is not to say that they must endorse every progressive policy, but conservatives should perhaps be more willing to defend those—whether progressives or conservatives—offering a policy at the state level that would be unacceptable at the federal level. Otherwise, they risk further eroding an already weakened discourse of federalism in political culture, one in which states' rights is merely used as a smoke screen to oppose policy rather than an organizing principle safeguarding what the states and the federal government are each authorized to do—and not do.[120] As Andrew Busch glumly observed, "Americans prefer to hear about rights (even states' rights) [rather] than about limits. . . . Much of the discussion about federalism has represented a form of limited government on the cheap—an overwhelmingly implicit nod to decentralization unaccompanied by the hard commitment to enumerated federal powers that would be necessary to protect that decentralization."[121]

After a rhetorical resurgence among Republicans in the last few decades, GOP primary voters in 2016 rejected the most ardently federalist candidates in decades (and instead selected arguably the least). Ted Cruz, Rand Paul, and the so-called constitutional conservative wing of the Tea Party may have made federalism a cornerstone of their recent campaigns,[122] but, as many conservative commentators lamented, much of their electorate instead seemed to prefer a consolidationist in the form of Donald Trump (albeit one whose policies—if not always his rhetoric—appeared more conventionally conservative, including on federalism, than the campaign would have indicated).

Perhaps that was a one-off moment from a one-off figure uniquely uninterested in the specifics of constitutionalism, and conservatives will, in turn, reembrace constitutional federalism. Perhaps not. Perhaps we are witnessing the meaningful demise of federalism, as conservatives join post–New Deal progressives in viewing it as an obsolete doctrine, thinking—as did a young Theodore Roosevelt—it was merely an opportunity for left-wing mischief. Perhaps the Right's turn toward nationalism will generate sympathy toward consolidation and away from states' rights, and the Left will in turn react by reembracing progressive federalism. Or perhaps, in the wake of polarization, federalism will become a unifying détente, much as it did in the 1920s.

Each of these represent possible futures. But in the end, this is a book of political history—one whose readers across the political spectrum may have encountered in it a story different from what they've long assumed. Perhaps, it can start—but certainly not conclude—increasingly important conversations about our Constitution, and it hopefully offers a history that suggests progressives, moderates, and conservatives might each have reasons to look at old debates about states' rights anew. As long as the United States retains its constitutional government, our system leaves the powerful tool of federalism in any hands, good or ill, that would use it.

Abbreviations

State legislative journals are in the form of *JS [State Initial]*, year, page. Congressional journals are in the form of [numbered Congress.Session *CR*], page.

Legislative Records

A.B.	Assembly Bill
A.J.R.	Assembly Joint Resolution
Cong. Rec.	*Congressional Record*
H.B.	House Bill
H.C.R.	House Concurrent Resolution
H.F.	House File
H.J.R.	House Joint Resolution
H.J.M.	House Joint Memorial
J.A.	*Journal of the Assembly*
J.H.R.	*Journal of the House of Representatives*
J.S.	*Journal of the Senate*
Min. Assem.	Minutes of the Assembly
Maine Leg. Rec.	*Maine Legislative Record*
S.B.	Senate Bill
S.C.R.	Senate Concurrent Resolution
S.F.	Senate File
S.J.M.	Senate Joint Memorial
S.J.R.	Senate Joint Resolution

Archival and Secondary Sources

NMP	Nathan Lewis Miller Papers
PBP	Percival Baxter Papers
PCSR	*Prohibition, the Constitution, and States' Rights*
PPAS	*Public Papers of Alfred E. Smith*
PPFDR	*Public Papers of Franklin D. Roosevelt, 48th Governor*

Foreword

1 New State Ice Co. v. Liebmann, 285 U.S. 262 (1932), 311.
2 G. Alan Tarr, "Laboratories of Democracy? Brandeis, Federalism, and Scientific Management," *Publius* 31, no. 1 (2001): 37–46.

3 For a more thorough discussion of the difference between federalism and decentralization see Edward L. Rubin and Malcolm Feeley, "Federalism: Some Notes on a National Neurosis," *UCLA Law Review* 41 (1993): 903.
4 Howard Gillman, *The Constitution Besieged: The Rise and Demise of Lochner Era Police Powers Jurisprudence* (Durham, NC: Duke University Press, 1993).
5 Joseph E. Lowndes, *From the New Deal to the New Right: Race and the Southern Origins of Modern Conservatism* (New Haven, CT: Yale University Press, 2008).

Acknowledgments

1 Wilson Carey McWilliams, "The Search for a Public Philosophy," in *The Democratic Soul*, ed. Patrick Deneen and Susan McWilliams (Lexington: University Press of Kentucky, 2011), 336–352, 348.

Introduction: States' Rights Returns

1 S.J.R. 26, in *Laws WI*, 1921, 1170. The specific objections in the document chronicle both Woodrow Wilson's Esch-Cummins Act (in controlling national railroad rates) and the grant-in-aid programs that would reach their apex with Warren Harding's signature on the Sheppard-Towner Act later that year.
2 *JS WI*, 1921, January 13, 1921, 50. Of course, to what extent railroads were within the power left in the hands of the states was more questionable. The 1886 case of *Wabash, St. Louis and Pacific Railway Co. v. Illinois* (118 U.S. 557) struck down a state railroad regulation on grounds it was an interference with interstate commerce—the so-called dormant or negative commerce clause (in which state laws interfering with interstate commerce were blocked, even in the absence of conflict with a federal statute). This doctrine, its scope, and its complicated applications were all deeply contested. In *Wabash* itself, for example, three justices argued that the majority's opinion conflicted with other cases allowing the states to regulate parts of the transportation network (such as the grain elevators in the recent *Munn v. Illinois* in 1876), and even the majority itself explicitly conceded that Illinois could regulate purely intrastate railroad journeys. The federal government then enacted the Interstate Commerce Commission, which was less active than the states had been. This created something of a no-man's land, where the federal government had the authority to regulate but did not wield it aggressively, to the frustration of state activists like in Wisconsin. Generally speaking, though, courts have been particularly skeptical of state regulation of railroad networks. Even under a more limited understanding of interstate commerce they tended to give the federal government, whether Congress or courts, a significant amount of latitude in that domain (e.g., the *Shreveport Rate Case* in 1914 and *Southern Pacific v. Arizona* in 1945). That the commerce clause could be not just a power of Congress (backed by the supremacy clause) but a judicial shield wielded against state

power even without statutory conflict has continued to be criticized, discussed further in the concluding chapter.

3 Ableman v. Booth, 62 U.S. 506 (1859); "Wisconsin's Labor Code," *Christian Science Monitor*, August 31, 1931, 14. On Wisconsin's flirtation even with nullification, see James H. Read and Neal Allen, "Living, Dead, and Undead: Nullification Past and Present," in *Nullification and Secession in Modern Constitutional Thought*, ed. Sanford Levinson (Lawrence: University Press of Kansas, 2016), 91–123; and Sanford Levinson, "The 21st Century Rediscovery of Nullification and Secession in American Political Rhetoric," in *Nullification and Secession*; Sean Beienburg, *Prohibition, the Constitution, and States' Rights* (Chicago: University of Chicago Press, 2019), 22, hereafter cited as *PCSR*.

4 Most famously, William H. Riker, *Federalism: Origin, Operation, Significance* (New York: Little Brown, 1964), 139–145.

5 Cooper v. Aaron, 358 U.S. 1 (1958); City of Boerne v. Flores, 521 U.S. 507 (1997); Larry Alexander and Frederick Schauer, "On Extrajudicial Constitutional Interpretation," *Harvard Law Review* 110 (1997): 1359–1387. Contrast with Keith E. Whittington, *Political Foundations of Judicial Supremacy* (Princeton, NJ: Princeton University Press, 2007); and Keith E. Whittington, "Extrajudicial Constitutional Interpretation: Three Objections and Responses," *North Carolina Law Review* 80 (2002): 774–852.

6 On the Gold Clause Cases, see Gerard N. Magliocca, "The Gold Clause Causes and Constitutional Necessity," *Florida Law Review* 64 (2012): 1243–1278, esp. 1275–1278; and David Glick, "Conditional Strategic Retreat: The Court's Concession in the 1935 Gold Clause Cases," *Journal of Politics* 71 (2009): 800–816.

7 Julie Novkov, "Bringing the States Back In: Understanding Legal Subordination and Identity through Political Development," *Polity* 40 (2008): 24–48; Walter F. Murphy, "Who Shall Interpret? The Quest for an Ultimate Constitutional Interpreter," *Review of Politics* 48 (1986): 401–423; Neil Devins and Louis Fisher, *The Democratic Constitution* (New York: Oxford University Press, 2004); J. Mitchell Pickerill, *Constitutional Deliberation in Congress* (Durham, NC: Duke University Press, 2004); George Thomas, *The Madisonian Constitution* (Baltimore, MD: Johns Hopkins University Press, 2008); Barry Friedman, *The Will of the People: How Public Opinion Has Influenced the Supreme Court and Shaped the Meaning of the Constitution* (New York: Farrar, Straus, and Giroux, 2009); Andrew Busch, *The Constitution on the Campaign Trail: The Surprising Political Career of America's Founding Document* (Lanham, MD: Rowman & Littlefield, 2007); Whittington, "Extrajudicial Constitutional Interpretation" and *Political Foundations of Judicial Supremacy*; Richard Primus, "The Riddle of Hiram Revels," *Harvard Law Review* 119 (2006): 1680–1734; Elizabeth Beaumont, *The Civic Constitution* (New York: Oxford University Press, 2014); and John Finn, *Peopling the Constitution* (Lawrence: University Press of Kansas, 2014).

8 For counter-examples of state constitutionalism, see John Dinan, *State Constitutional Politics* (Chicago: University of Chicago Press, 2018); John Dinan, *The American State Constitutional Tradition* (Lawrence: University Press of Kansas,

2006); G. Alan Tarr, "Popular Constitutionalism in State and Nation," *Ohio State Law Journal* 77 (2016): 237–280; G. Alan Tarr, *Understanding State Constitutions* (Princeton, NJ: Princeton University Press, 1998); Amy Bridges, *Democratic Beginnings: Founding the Western States* (Lawrence: University Press of Kansas, 2015); Emily Zackin, *Looking for Rights in All the Wrong Places: Why State Constitutions Contain America's Positive Rights* (Princeton, NJ: Princeton University Press, 2013); Jeffrey Sutton, *Who Decides? States as Laboratories of Constitutional Experimentation* (New York: Oxford University Press, 2021); Jeffrey Sutton, *51 Imperfect Solutions: States and the Making of American Constitutional Law* (New York: Oxford University Press, 2018); Robinson Woodward-Burns, *Hidden Laws: How State Constitutions Stabilize American Politics* (New Haven, CT: Yale University Press, 2021); Sean Beienburg, "Contesting the U.S. Constitution through State Amendments: The 2011 and 2012 Elections," *Political Science Quarterly* 129 (2014): 55–85; Paul Herron, *Framing the Solid South: The State Constitutional Conventions of Secession, Reconstruction, and Redemption, 1860–1902* (Lawrence: University Press of Kansas, 2017); and Christian G. Fritz, "The American Constitutional Tradition Revisited: Preliminary Observations on State Constitution-Making in the Nineteenth-Century West," *Rutgers Law Journal* 25 (1994): 946–998. For scholarship on how state politics and not just state constitutionalism is part of constitutional dialogue, see Bradley D. Hays, *States in American Constitutionalism: Interpretation, Authority, and Politics* (New York: Routledge, 2019); Bradley D. Hays, "Nullification and the Political, Legal, and Quasi-Legal Constitutions," *Publius: The Journal of Federalism* 43 (2013): 205–226; *PCSR*; Sean Beienburg, "Progressivism and States' Rights: Constitutional Dialogue between the States and Federal Courts on Minimum Wages and Liberty of Contract," *American Political Thought* 8 (2019): 25–53.

9 See chapter 1, note 15.

10 Donald S. Lutz, *The Origins of American Constitutionalism* (Baton Rouge: Louisiana State University Press, 1988), 153; Gary Gerstle, "The Resilient Power of the States Across the Long Nineteenth Century: An Inquiry into a Pattern of American Governance," in *The Unsustainable American State*, ed. Lawrence Jacobs and Desmond King (Oxford: Oxford University Press, 2009), 63. See also James R. Rogers, "The Forgotten Power of States," Law & Liberty, October 27, 2020, https://lawliberty.org/the-forgotten-power-of-states/.

11 NFIB v. Sebelius, 567 U.S. 519 (2012). It is also worth noting that even the saving construction of the tax power brought with it a standard preventing coercion of the states. On law professors' bewilderment in the face of a serious federalism challenge to the ACA, see David A. Hyman, "Something Went Wrong on the Way to the Courthouse," *Journal of Health Politics, Policy and Law* 38 (2013): 243–253. On the need for scholars to take seriously the role of ideas in shaping constitutional development, see George Thomas, "What Is Political Development? A Constitutional Perspective," *Review of Politics* 73 (2011): 275–294; and Ken I. Kersch, "The Talking Cure: How Constitutional Argument Drives Constitutional Development," *Boston University Law Review* 94 (2014): 1083–1108.

12 Paul Nolette, *Federalism on Trial: State Attorneys General and National Policy-making in Contemporary America* (Lawrence: University Press of Kansas, 2015); Sean Beienburg, "States Rights' Gone Wrong? Secession, Nullification, and Reverse-Nullification in Contemporary America," *Tulsa Law Review* 52 (2018): 191–204.

13 Rick Perry, *Fed Up! Our Fight to Save America from Washington* (New York: Little Brown, 2010), 163–164; Todd J. Gillman, "Ted Cruz Picks Chief of Staff: Chip Roy, Chief Ghostwriter on Rick Perry's Anti-Washington Tome *Fed Up!*," *Dallas Morning News*, November 28, 2012, http://trailblazersblog.dallasnews .com/2012/11/ted-cruz-picks-chief-of-staff-chip-roy-chief-ghostwriter-on-rick -perrys-anti-washington-tome-fed-up.html/.

14 Printz v. United States, 521 U.S. 898 (1997).

15 Perry, *Fed Up!*, 165, 177.

16 Perry, 178–180.

17 Heather Gerken, "We're About to See States' Rights Used Defensively against Trump," Vox, January 20, 2017, https://www.vox.com/the-big-idea/2016/12/12 /13915990/federalism-trump-progressive-uncooperative. See conclusion, notes 17–19.

18 For a list of such efforts, see Jeffrey Rosen, "Federalism for the Left and the Right," *Wall Street Journal*, May 19, 2017, https://www.wsj.com/articles/federalism-for -the-left-and-the-right-1495210904; and Ilya Somin, "How Liberals Learned to Love Federalism," *Washington Post*, July 7, 2019, https://www.washingtonpost .com/outlook/how-liberals-learned-to-love-federalism/2019/07/12/babd9f52 –8c5f-11e9-b162–8f6f41ec3c04_story.html?utm_term=.12b53365003b.

19 Dan Walters, "California Writing a New Chapter in Centuries-Old 'States Rights' Conflict," *Sacramento Bee*, August 20, 2017, http://www.sacbee.com/opinion /california-forum/article167895902.html; David Siders, "Jerry Brown, President of the Independent Republic of California," *Politico*, November 11, 2017, https:// www.politico.com/magazine/story/2017/11/11/jerry-brown-california-profile -215812; Daniela Blei, "From California, A Progressive Cry for States' Rights," *New Republic*, February 14, 2017, https://newrepublic.com/article/140606/cali fornia-progressive-cry-states-rights.

20 David Savage, "Supreme Court's Embrace of States' Rights Could Aid Califor-nia," *Los Angeles Times,* May 15, 2018, https://www.latimes.com/politics/la-na -pol-supreme-court-states-rights-20180515-story.html; Sean Beienburg, "The Lessons in Federalism that Prohibition Taught Us," *National Review Online*, De-cember 13, 2019, https://www.nationalreview.com/2019/12/prohibition-lessons -in-federalism/.

21 Natasha Geiling, "Donald Trump Doesn't Care about States' Rights," Sierra Club, August 29, 2018, https://www.sierraclub.org/sierra/donald-trump-doesn-t -care-about-states-rights.

22 Sam Wang, "If the Supreme Court Won't Prevent Gerrymandering, Who Will?" *New York Times*, August 13, 2019, https://www.nytimes.com/2019/07/13/opinion /sunday/partisan-gerrymandering.html.

23 Laura Tyson and Lenny Mendonca, "Progressive Federalism to Combat Judicial Extremism," Project Syndicate, August 19, 2022, https://www.project-syndicate .org/commentary/tenth-amendment-answer-to-supreme-court-extremism-by -laura-tyson-and-lenny-mendonca-2022–08.

24 New State Ice Co. v. Liebmann, 285 U.S. 262 (1932), 311.

25 On Vermont's secession, see Levinson, "The 21st Century Rediscovery of Nullification and Secession," 46–50.

26 Hays, *States in American Constitutionalism*, 79–92; Read and Allen, "Living, Dead, and Undead"; Beienburg, "Contesting the U.S. Constitution through State Amendments"; Sean Beienburg, "Neither Nullification nor Nationalism: The Battle for the States' Rights Middle Ground During Prohibition," *American Political Thought* 7 (2018): 299; John Dinan, "Contemporary Assertions of State Sovereignty and the Safeguards of American Federalism," *Albany Law Review* 74 (2011): 1635–1667.

27 Martha Derthick, *Keeping the Compound Republic: Essays on Federalism* (Washington, DC: Brookings, 2001), 41. She suggests, in passing, that this may be happening, too, with states becoming more active in suing before the US Supreme Court.

28 Dinan, "Contemporary Assertions of State Sovereignty"; Beienburg, "Contesting the U.S. Constitution through State Amendments."

29 But see Hays, *States in American Constitutionalism*; *PCSR*.

30 V. O. Key Jr. with Alexander Heard, *Southern Politics in State and Nation* (New York: Alfred A. Knopf, 1949); Robert Mickey, *Paths Out of Dixie: The Democratization of Authoritarian Enclaves in America's Deep South, 1944–1972* (Princeton, NJ: Princeton University Press, 2015). As David Bateman, Ira Katznelson, and John Lapinski have demonstrated, building off earlier insights from Key, southern politics was distinctively shaped by the need to maintain white supremacy, which, in turn, shaped the composition of Congress, which, in turn, then shaped the scope of national activity. Congress would work to protect the autonomy of the states to maintain their enclaves of racial hierarchy, successfully blocking federal measures, even those, authorized by the Constitution, that had aimed to dismantle those enclaves. Members of the Democratic Party in the South could hold heterodox views on a variety of issues—and, in fact, as the authors show, the South was arguably more supportive of federal state-building on issues that could be cabined off from or did not have racial implications (and, hence, southerners were not consistent defenders of federalism)—but the maintenance of white supremacy was the non-negotiable condition to maintain power. David Bateman, Ira Katznelson, and John Lapinski, *Southern Nation: Congress and White Supremacy after Reconstruction* (Princeton, NJ: Princeton University Press, 2018).

31 Howard Gillman, "The Collapse of Constitutional Originalism and the Rise of the Notion of the 'Living Constitution' in the Course of American State-Building," *Studies in American Political Development* 11 (1997): 191–247; Randy Barnett, *Restoring the Lost Constitution: The Presumption of Liberty* (Princeton, NJ: Princeton University Press, 2004); Johnathan O'Neill, *Originalism in Law and*

Politics: A Constitutional History (Baltimore, MD: Johns Hopkins University Press, 2007); Edward S. Corwin, "The Passing of Dual Federalism," *Virginia Law Review* 36 (1950): 1–24.

32 Gillman, "Collapse of Constitutional Originalism." See also Ken I. Kersch, *Conservatives and the Constitution: Imagining Constitutional Restoration in the Heyday of American Liberalism* (Cambridge: Cambridge University Press, 2019), 60, 230; O'Neill, *Originalism in Law and Politics*; Johnathan O'Neill, *Conservative Thought and American Constitutionalism Since the New Deal* (Baltimore, MD: Johns Hopkins University Press, 2023).

33 Heather K. Gerken, "A New Progressive Federalism," *Democracy: A Journal of Ideas*, 2012, http://www.democracyjournal.org/24/a-new-progressive-federalism .php?page=all; and, more broadly, conclusion, notes 17–19.

34 On dual federalism and its mid-twentieth-century collapse, see Corwin, "The Passing of Dual Federalism." Others were not so celebratory about what they feared was the end of decentralized government. Though best known for his theory that the political processes were better primed to enforce federalism—often taken as rationalization for an indifference to it—Herbert Wechsler lamented "the virtual abandonment of limits" on the commerce clause that enabled a weakening of federalism. Herbert Wechsler, "Toward Neutral Principles of Constitutional Law," Harvard *Law Review* 73 (1959): 23. For similar lamentations, see Phillip Kurland, *Politics, the Constitution and the Warren Court* (Chicago: University of Chicago Press, 1970), 96; and Phillip Kurland, "Impotence of Reticence," *Duke Law Journal* 4 (1968): 634–635.

35 Marshall Trimble, *In Old Arizona* (Phoenix: Golden West Publishers, 1985), 101.

36 "A Decision for Liberty," *New York World*, June 6, 1923, 12, quoted in Robert Post, "Social and Economic Legislation and the Taft Court," Holmes Devise, ch. 5 (n.p.: n.d.), manuscript on file with author. Lippmann was siding with Brandeis, another defender of progressive federalism, in agreeing with the Court's jurisprudentially controversial decision in *Meyer v. Nebraska*, 262 U.S. 390 (1923), rather than with Justice Holmes's dissent (in the companion case) and its more typical defense of the states' police powers.

37 As Ken Kersch has chronicled, there has been a recent wave of histories by conservatives indicting Wilson, Roosevelt, and other progressives (but often not the Populists) as being deeply hostile to the Madisonian system—its federalism and separation of powers in particular. One of the goals of this book is to show that many—perhaps most?—of their progressive contemporaries did not believe one had to radically modify the American constitutional order, and instead believed that even a strict, quasioriginalist understanding of the Constitution was sufficient to achieve most progressives' policy goals. See Ken I. Kersch, "Constitutional Conservatives Remember the Progressive Era," in *The Progressives' Century: Democratic Reform and Constitutional Government in the United States*, ed. Stephen Skowronek, Stephen Engel, and Bruce Ackerman (New Haven, CT: Yale University Press, 2016), esp. 136.

38 See chapter 1 on Wilson, Roosevelt, and other key players in the 1912 election.

39 Gerstle, "The Resilient Power of the States," 63.

40 Keith E. Whittington, "The Political Constitution of Federalism in Antebellum America: The Nullification Debate as an Illustration of Informal Mechanisms of Constitutional Change," *Publius: The Journal of Federalism* 26 (1996): 14–17; Beienburg, "Neither Nullification." The core of both Richard Ellis's *Union at Risk* and *Aggressive Nationalism* aims to show that this philosophy, which he frames as states-rights majoritarianism, represented the predominant thread in antebellum American thought. See Richard E. Ellis, *Aggressive Nationalism:* McCulloch v. Maryland *and the Foundation of Federal Authority in the Young Republic* (Oxford: Oxford University Press, 2007); and Richard E. Ellis, *The Union at Risk: Jacksonian Democracy, States' Rights, and the Nullification Crisis* (Oxford: Oxford University Press, 1987). For accounts of its eventual transmission not only to Democratic but Republican thought, see Eric Foner, *Free Soil, Free Labor, Free Men: The Ideology of the Republican Party before the Civil War* (New York: Oxford University Press, 1995); Mark Graber, "Jacksonian Origins of Chase Court Activism," *Journal of Supreme Court History* 25 (2000): 17–39.

41 For an elaboration on this survival in the wake of the Civil War, especially in the North, see Gerstle, "The Resilient Power of the States"; *PCSR*, 7, 17–24, 76; Kurt T. Lash, The *Fourteenth Amendment and the Privileges and Immunities of American Citizenship* (New York: Cambridge University Press, 2014), 3–8, 79–83; Earl Maltz, "Reconstruction without Revolution: Republican Civil Rights Theory in the Era of the Fourteenth Amendment," *Houston Law Review* 24 (1997): 221–279; Pamela Brandwein, *Rethinking the Judicial Settlement of Reconstruction* (Cambridge: Cambridge University Press, 2011); Mark Wahlgren Summers, *The Ordeal of the Reunion: A New History of Reconstruction* (Chapel Hill: University of North Carolina Press, 2014); Michael Les Benedict, "Preserving the Constitution: The Conservative Basis of Radical Reconstruction," *Journal of American History* 61 (1974): 65–90; "Preserving Federalism: Reconstruction and the Waite Court," *Supreme Court Review* 1 (1978): 39–79; and Forrest Nabors, *From Oligarchy to Republicanism: The Great Task of Reconstruction* (Columbia: University of Missouri, 2017), 16–18, 155–159, 327–328. More broadly, see chapter 1.

42 This theme, which will be elaborated on later, was a main finding of my previous study; although some northerners had flirted with it at times, nullification was held to be the discredited southern heresy and distortion of American constitutional federalism. See *PCSR*.

43 *PCSR*, 235–239.

44 Larry Kramer, *The People Themselves* (New York: Oxford University Press, 2005); Bruce Ackerman, *We the People*, vol. 1: *Foundations* (Cambridge, MA: Harvard University Press, 1991) ; *We the People*, vol 2: *Transformations* (Cambridge, MA: Harvard University Press, 2000); and *We the People*, vol 3: *The Civil Rights Revolution* (Cambridge, MA: Harvard University Press, 2014); Mark Tushnet, *Taking the Constitution Away from the Courts* (Princeton, NJ: Princeton University Press, 2000). See also this chapter, note 7.

45 I am not the first to make this point. As Robert Nagel observes, Tushnet does

not propose looking to states in formulating his vision of popular constitutionalism. See Robert Nagel, *The Implosion of American Federalism* (New York: Oxford University Press, 2001), 57. The omission of states and state officials seems doubly strange when members of Congress have such a decidedly spotty record in creating the serious nonjudicial constitutional debate that popular constitutionalists favor. Andrew Busch suggests that members of Congress have displayed a particular interest in constitutional debate when appealing for votes, but studies by Neil Devins, Louis Fisher, and Mitchell Pickerill of congressional politics gives us less reason for optimism on this front once they actually take their seats. See Busch, *Constitution on the Campaign Trail*; Devins and Fisher, *Democratic Constitution*, esp. 125–126; Pickerill, *Constitutional Deliberation in Congress*; Keith E. Whittington, "James Madison Has Left the Building: A Review of J. Mitchell Pickerill, Constitutional Deliberation in Congress," *University of Chicago Law Review* 72 (2005): 1137–1158; Whittington, *Political Foundations of Judicial Supremacy*; and Neil Devins, "Why Congress Did Not Think about the Constitution When Enacting the Affordable Care Act," *Northwestern University Law Review*, colloquy 261 (2012), http://scholarlycommons.law.northwestern.edu/cgi/viewcontent.cgi?article=1046&context=nulr_online. This has not always been the case: for examples of Congress taking its obligations for substantive constitutional debate seriously and engaging in extrajudicial constitutional interpretation, independent of policy utility, see the discussion of antebellum internal improvements in chapter 1, the Keating-Owen Act regulating child labor: Stephen Wood, *Constitutional Politics in the Progressive Era: Child Labor and the Law* (Chicago: University of Chicago Press, 1968), esp. 70–75; and Prohibition and federalism, *PCSR*.

46 There is a wide variety in usage in the scholarly literature. Some use popular constitutionalism as an alternative to extrajudicial constitutionalism, with the former referring exclusively to citizens or the public, while others use extrajudicial constitutional interpretation as a subset of popular constitutionalism, with the latter referring to state legislators as well as the public citizenry. My usage, as should be clear, is in line with the latter viewing it as a subset. So for those who draw a stricter intellectual boundary, this book is covering extrajudicial constitutionalism. See also *PCSR*; Sean Beienburg and Paul Frymer, "The People against Themselves: Rethinking Popular Constitutionalism," *Law and Social Inquiry* 41 (2016): 242–266; and conclusion, notes 32-33.

47 On oaths, see *PCSR*, esp. 83–85, 95–101, 162–165. For an argument as to why oaths bind governing officials to enforce the Constitution, including its original meaning, see Barnett, *Restoring the Lost Constitution*, 117–118; Evan Bernick and Christopher R. Green, "What Is the Object of the Article VI Oath?" (working paper, Northern Illinois University and University of Mississippi, August 9, 2022), https://papers.ssrn.com/sol3/papers.cfm?abstract_id=3441234.

48 Thus, this offers a powerful illustration of historical institutionalist accounts of political behavior. See Rogers Smith, "Historical Institutionalism and the Study of Law," in *Oxford Handbook of Law and Politics*, ed. Keith Whittington,

R. Daniel Kelemen, and Gregory A. Caldeira (Oxford: Oxford University Press, 2010), 47–59; Barry Friedman, "Taking Law Seriously," *Perspectives on Politics* 4 (2006): 261–276.

49 For the argument that they always are insincere or opportunistic, see Edward L. Rubin and Malcolm Feeley, "Federalism: Some Notes on a National Neurosis," *UCLA Law Review* 41 (1994): 903–952, esp. 935.

50 John Gerring, "APD from a Methodological Point of View," *Studies in American Political Development* 17 (2003): 84.

51 For surveys of APD literature and its national orientation, see, for example, Ira Katznelson and John Lapinski, "At the Crossroads: Congress and American Political Development," *Perspectives on Politics* 4 (2006): 243–260; Paul Frymer, "Law and American Political Development," *Law and Social Inquiry* 33 (2008): 780–781.

52 E. E. Schattschneider, *The Semi-Sovereign People* (New York: Holt, Rinehart, and Winston, 1960); Zackin, *Looking for Rights*, 124, 209–210.

53 Heather K. Gerken, "The Loyal Opposition," *Yale Law Journal* 123 (2013): 1958–1994, esp. 1988–1993.

54 States intervened in national constitution interpretation in three broad domains in this era. First, as is well known, is race, both in nullifying the Fourteenth and Fifteenth Amendments as well as in expanding state public accommodations law after the Civil Rights Cases (on the latter, see Sean Beienburg and Ben Johnson, "Black Popular Constitutionalism and Federalism after the *Civil Rights Cases*" *Arizona Law Review* 65 (forthcoming). I consider race beyond the scope of this inquiry—not because I believe the issue is unimportant but precisely the opposite: the centrality of the southern effort to maintain white supremacy by rendering the amendment a dead letter warrants, and thus has received, far more attention in the form of the work done by Morgan Kousser, Rick Vallely, and others who have devoted entire manuscripts and even careers to efforts to studying this, arguably one of two key faults in American political development (along with the divide between national and state power). See, e.g., Morgan Kousser, *The Shaping of Southern Politics: Suffrage Restrictions and the Establishment of the One Party South, 1880–1910* (New Haven, CT: Yale University Press, 1974); Rick Vallely, *The Two Reconstructions* (Chicago: University of Chicago Press, 2004). The second major domain in this era in which states intervened in constitutional politics is Prohibition, which I have written about in a previous study. See *PCSR*. The third, which comprises this study, is in economics, in which states pushed back both against expanding a national welfare state as well as in defending their ability to use their police powers to tame modern industrial capitalism.

55 See chapter 5, note 60.

56 In that case, states' decisions whether to have or not have legal alcohol were trumped by the Eighteenth Amendment's authorization of the federal government to enforce uniform dry laws. See *PCSR*.

57 *Steward Machine v. Davis* (1937) (discussed further in chapter 6), and more recently, the different outcomes in the "relatively mild encouragement" allowed in

South Dakota v. Dole (1986), but the "gun to the head" of the states prohibited in *Sebelius* (2012). On the differences between cooperative and coercive federalism, see John Kincaid, 'From Cooperative to Coercive Federalism," *Annals of the American Academy of Political and Social Science* 509 (1990): 139–152.

Chapter 1. State Constitutional Interpretation in American Political Thought before the New Deal

1 Bernard Bailyn, *The Ideological Origins of the American Revolution* (Cambridge: Harvard University Press, 1967); Forrest McDonald, *States' Rights and the Union: Imperium in Imperio, 1776–1876* (Lawrence: University Press of Kansas, 2000); Jack P. Greene, *The Constitutional Origins of the American Revolution* (Cambridge: Cambridge University Press, 2010); Mary Sarah Bilder, *The Transatlantic Constitution: Colonial Legal Culture and the Empire* (Cambridge, MA: Harvard University Press, 2008); Alison LaCroix, *The Ideological Origins of American Federalism* (Cambridge, MA: Harvard University Press, 2011); Aaron N. Coleman, *The American Revolution, State Sovereignty, and the American Constitutional Settlement, 1765–1800* (Lanham, MD: Lexington, 2016); Alexis de Tocqueville, *Democracy in America*, ed. Harvey Mansfield and Delba Winthrop (Chicago: University of Chicago Press, [1840] 2000), 106–108, 351–354.
2 "Declaration and Resolves of the First Continental Congress," Avalon Project, Yale Law School, October 14, 1774, http://avalon.law.yale.edu/18th_century /resolves.asp. These themes, of course, reappeared in the Declaration of Independence itself, such as the first few charges protesting obstruction of their local legislatures.
3 Alexander Hamilton, "Conjectures about the New Constitution," September 1787, Founders Online, https://founders.archives.gov/documents/Hamilton/01 -04-02-0139.
4 Jay to Washington, "Deficiencies of the Confederation," January 7, 1787, *The Founders' Constitution*, University of Chicago Press, https://press-pubs.uchicago .edu/founders/print_documents/v1ch5s15.html.
5 Madison to Washington, "Federal v. Consolidated Government," April 16, 1787, *The Founders' Constitution*, University of Chicago Press, accessed July 8, 2023, https://press-pubs.uchicago.edu/founders/documents/v1ch8s6.html.
6 In perhaps his most famous address, the State House Yard Speech (October 6, 1787), Wilson, trying to secure ratification, argued that "in delegating [federal] powers ... the congressional authority is to be collected, not from tacit implication, but from the positive grant expressed in the instrument of union. Hence it is evident, that in the former case every thing which is not reserved is given, but in the latter the reverse of the proposition prevails, and every thing which is not given, is reserved." See Kermit L. Hall and Mark David Hall, eds., *Collected Works of James Wilson*, vol. 1 (Indianapolis, IN: Liberty Fund, 2007), 171. On Wilson at the Convention, see James Ewald, "James Wilson and the Draft-

ing of the Constitution," *Journal of Constitutional Law* 10 (2008): 901–1009, esp. 975. Jonathan Gienapp has argued Wilson's subsequent constitutionalism remained closer to his preferred unitary nationalism and that such a consolidationist nationalism was much more widespread at the time of the Founding than is generally understood, until erased by "enumerationism" in the decade following. Strikingly, he argues, even Alexander Hamilton did not defend such unitary nationalism, after ratification at least publicly, and instead strategically adopted the language of the enumerated powers, albeit capaciously, as a way to rebut James Madison's constitutionalism on its own terms. See Jonathan Gienapp, "The Myth of the Constitutional Given: Enumeration and National Power at the Founding," *American University Law Review Forum* 69 (2020): 183–211. Theodore Roosevelt similarly interpreted Wilson in arguing for his own nationalist constitutional theory. See Martha Derthick and John J. Dinan, "Progressivism and Federalism," in *Keeping the Compound Republic: Essays on Federalism* (Washington, DC: Brookings, 2001), 109–110.

7 David Brian Robertson, "Madison's Opponents and Constitutional Design," *American Political Science Review* 99 (2005): 225–243; Mark David Hall, *Roger Sherman and the Creation of the American Republic* (New York: Oxford University Press, 2015), 92–122.

8 Pauline Maier, *Ratification: The People Debate the Constitution, 1787–1788* (New York: Simon & Schuster, 2010). See also Daniel Faber, "The Federal Union Paradigm of 1788: Three Anti-Federalists Who Changed Their Minds," *American Political Thought* 4 (2015): 527–556.

9 "Experiments in Government and the Essentials of the Constitution II," *North American Review* 198 (1913): 264.

10 On the conventions and the many demands for a proto-Tenth Amendment as a necessary recommendatory amendment from almost half the states, see Maier, *Ratification*.

11 Mass. Dec. R., art. IV (1780); N.H. Dec. R., art. 7; Ver. Dec. R., art. I (on slavery) and art. V (on federalism); Penn. Dec. R. (1776), art. III. New York's 1777 Constitution has a more oblique reference to exclusive state governing in the first numbered point in its constitution, but it is clear this is what is meant considering its preface earlier alludes to the problem of clarifying where the police power lies, quoting the Continental Congress's resolution asking the states to set up constitutions to establish police powers. No such language appears in the 1776 New Jersey Constitution.

12 Md. Dec. R., art. II (1776); and N.C. Dec. R., art. II (1776). No similar language appears in the 1776 Virginia Constitution, the 1776 or 1792 Delaware Constitutions, the 1777 or 1789 Georgia Constitutions, or the 1778 or 1790 South Carolina Constitutions.

13 For an elaboration of this argument, see Sean Beienburg, "Teaching Federalism: State Sovereignty Declarations in State Constitutions," *American Political Thought* 11 (2022): 232–252.

14 The extent to which pre-Constitution Madison was a Hamiltonian consolidation-

ist, a consistent skeptic of governmental power who also wanted additional limits on the states, or shifted his position, is an entire historical literature that I will not attempt to adjudicate. Whatever the explanation, what is clear is that *after* the enactment of the Constitution, while Hamilton still pushed for centralized authority, setting the stage for their many clashes in the 1790s, Madison interpreted national power much more narrowly—in line with his pitch in the *Federalist* and what he believed the ratifying conventions had agreed to.

15 On the fundamentally federal nature of the polity in its division of powers, see *Federalist* 39, and on the possible enforcement of that division of powers by the states see 44 and 46. Those are not the only *Federalist Papers* that discuss states asserting authority to interpret the Constitution and check federal power; they are merely the most thorough. Allusions to state participation in federal constitutionalism are also made in *Federalist* 16, 17, 28, 31, 55, and 84, and of course the notion of institutional competition on behalf of liberty is deeply embedded in the most famous *Federalist Papers*, 10 and 51.

16 James Madison, "Government of the United States," February 4, 1792, Founders Online, accessed May 28, 2023, https://founders.archives.gov/documents/Madison/01–14–02–0190.

17 Keith E. Whittington, "The Political Constitution of Federalism in Antebellum America: The Nullification Debate as an Illustration of Informal Mechanisms of Constitutional Change," *Publius: The Journal of Federalism* 26 (1996): 4–5.

18 Jonathan Gienapp, "How to Maintain a Constitution: The Virginia and Kentucky Resolutions and James Madison's Struggle with the Problem of Constitutional Maintenance," in *Nullification and Secession in Modern Constitutional Thought*, ed. Sanford Levinson (Lawrence: University Press of Kansas, 2016); Drew McCoy, *The Last of the Fathers: James Madison and the Republican Legacy* (Cambridge: Cambridge University Press, 1989), 130–150; Christian Fritz, *American Sovereigns: The People and America's Constitutional Tradition before the Civil War* (New York: Cambridge University Press, 2008); Wayne D. Moore, *Constitutional Rights and Powers of the People* (Princeton, NJ: Princeton University Press, 1996), 346–365. Madison strongly endorsed the idea that the Constitution's binding meaning was that understood by those who ratified it. See James Madison, "Speech on the Jay Treaty," April 6, 1796, Founders Online, accessed May 28, 2023, https://founders.archives.gov/documents/Madison/01–16–02–0195; James Madison, "Letter to John Jackson," December 28, 1821, Founders Online, accessed May 28, 2023, https://founders.archives.gov/documents/Madison/04–02–02–0367; James Madison, "Letter to Thomas Ritchie," September 15, 1821, Founders Online, accessed May 28, 2023, https://founders.archives.gov/documents/Madison/04–02–02–0321; James Madison, "Letter to Henry Lee," June 25, 1824, Founders Online, accessed May 28, 2023, https://founders.archives.gov/documents/Madison/04–03–02–0333.

19 John C. Calhoun, *Union and Liberty: The Political Philosophy of John C. Calhoun*, ed. Ross M. Lence (Indianapolis, IN: Liberty Fund, 1992).

20 James H. Read, *Majority Rule versus Consensus: The Political Thought of John*

C. Calhoun (Lawrence: University of Kansas Press, 2009); this chapter, notes 18 and 19; Beienburg, "States Rights Gone Wrong." Even then, as Read suggests, Calhoun's goals were not simply diverse localism but a more substantive protection of slavery, one that checked states' antislavery activities. On distinguishing Madison from Calhoun, see Fritz, *American Sovereigns*, 220–231, 291, 296; McDonald, *States' Rights and the Union*; Sean Beienburg, *Prohibition, the Constitution, and States' Rights* (Chicago: University of Chicago Press, 2019), 262n33, hereafter cited as *PCSR*, 18–27.

21   For example, see Gibbons v. Ogden, 22 U.S. 1, 195 (1824): "The enumeration presupposes something not enumerated"; *PCSR*, 262n33; Michael Les Benedict, "Abraham Lincoln and Federalism," *Journal of the Abraham Lincoln Association* 10 (1988): 1–46.

22   Emily Pears, *Cords of Affection: Construction Constitutional Union in Early American History* (Lawrence: University Press of Kansas, 2022).

23   See introduction, note 40, and *PCSR*, chapter 2.

24   Henry Clay, "Speech on Internal Improvements," March 7, 1818, in James F. Hopkins, ed., *Papers of Henry Clay*, vol. 2 (Lexington: University Press of Kentucky, 1961), 450, 463.

25   Ironically, Clay, in fact, had been skeptical of the first bank recharter in 1811 on such grounds, when his Jeffersonian ally, Treasury Secretary Gallatin, had defended it. Clay later conceded, like Madison, its essential role in American currency (from the enumerated power to coin) and to help collect taxes, especially in light of other economic developments, which served as constitutional justifications. See David P. Currie, *Constitution in Congress: The Jeffersonians, 1801–1829* (Chicago: University of Chicago Press), 253–255.

26   Merrill D. Peterson, *The Great Triumvirate: Webster, Clay, and Calhoun* (Oxford: Oxford University Press, 1988), 79–82; Benedict, "Lincoln and Federalism"; Clay, "Speech on Internal Improvements," 450, 453; Henry Clay, "Speech on the Maysville Road Veto" ("On Nullification and other Topics"), August 3, 1830, in Calvin Colton, ed., *The Life, Correspondence, and Speeches of Henry Clay*, vol. 5 (New York: A. S. Barnes, 1857), esp. 402: "The doctrines of that day, and they are as true at this, were that the federal government is a limited government; that it has no powers, but the granted powers."

27   Clay, "Speech on Internal Improvements," 453–458.

28   Clay, 463.

29   Quoted in Currie, *Constitution in Congress: Jeffersonians*, 281.

30   Daniel Webster, "The Landing at Plymouth," December 22, 1843, in *Works of Daniel Webster*, vol. 2. (Boston: Charles C. Little and James Brown, 1851), 205–209; Peterson, *Great Triumvirate*, 398, 103.

31   Clay, "Speech on Internal Improvements," 452; Herman Belz, ed., *The Webster-Hayne Debate on the Nature of the Constitution* (Indianapolis, IN: Liberty Fund, 2000), 110, 111. Madison similarly distinguished between the meaning of "the word 'consolidate' in the address of the Convention prefixed to the Constitution. It then and there meant to give strength and solidity to the Union of the

States. In its current & controversial application it means a destruction of the States, by transfusing their powers into the government of the Union." James Madison, "Letter to Henry Lee," June 25, 1824, Founders Online, accessed May 28, 2023, https://founders.archives.gov/documents/Madison/04–03–02–0333.

32 For examples, see Madison, "Bonus Bill Veto," 1817, American Presidency Project, accessed July 8, 2023, https://www.presidency.ucsb.edu/documents/veto -message-246 (arguing no); James Monroe, "Cumberland Road Veto (and its addendum, "Views of the President on Internal Improvements)," 1822, American Presidency Project, accessed July 8, 2023, https://www.presidency.ucsb .edu/documents/veto-message and https://www.presidency.ucsb.edu/documents /special-message-the-house-representatives-containing-the-views-the-president -the-united (suggesting the tax power gave some but limited powers); Andrew Jackson, "Maysville Road Veto," 1830, American Presidency Project, accessed July 8, 2023, https://www.presidency.ucsb.edu/documents/veto-message-471 (arguing no), and Henry Clay's Response, "Speech on the Maysville Road Veto," 1830 (arguing yes, from enumerated powers and post-roads). See Alison L. LaCroix, "The Interbellum Constitution: Federalism in the Long Founding Moment," *Stanford Law Review* 67 (2015): 397–445, Currie, *Constitution in Congress: Jeffersonians*, 250–281; and David P. Currie, *The Constitution in Congress: Democrats and Whigs, 1829–1861* (Chicago: University of Chicago Press, 2005), 3–37.

33 On South Carolina's secession protest of Wisconsin states' rights, see James H. Read and Neal Allen, "Living, Dead, and Undead: Nullification Past and Present," in *Nullification and Secession*.

34 On federalism's continued importance, not just for Whigs but also post-Whig Republicans such as Lincoln, see *PCSR*, esp. 23–25, 262; and Beienburg, "Neither Nullification nor Nationalism," 275–77; Sidney Milkis, *Theodore Roosevelt, the Progressive Party, and the Transformation of American Democracy* (Lawrence: University Press of Kansas, 2009), 93 (agreeing with Taft that Lincoln and the Republicans viewed federal power as seriously limited outside of wartime); Benedict, "Abraham Lincoln and Federalism" (distinguishing between Lincoln's ideological or aspirational nationalism and his firm rejection of "constitutional nationalism," which did not exist until the twentieth century); and more broadly, for a review of this historical literature on postwar Republican commitment to federalism, see introduction, note 41. On incorporation of the Bill of Rights and other changes from the Fourteenth Amendment, see chapter 4, note 15.

35 On Sumner, see Cong. Globe 42.2 (January 31, 1872), 727–730.

36 See also the *Slaughterhouse Cases*, 83 U.S. 36 (1873), 82. For the argument that the decision's federalism nonetheless allowed the possibility of more federal protection of civil rights than is commonly understood, see Michael W. McConnell, "Originalism and the Desegregation Decisions," *Virginia Law Review* 81 (1995) 1090–1091; and Sean Beienburg and Ben Johnson, "Black Popular Constitutionalism and Federalism after the *Civil Rights Cases*," *Arizona Law Review* 65 (forthcoming).

37 For judicial review of federal legislation, see Keith Whittington, *Repugnant*

Laws: Judicial Review of Acts of Congress from the Founding to the Present (Lawrence: University Press of Kansas, 2019).

38 U.S. v. Carolene Products, 304 U.S. 144 (1938); introduction, note 34.

39 Robert Post, "Federalism, Positive Law, and the Emergence of the American Administrative State: Prohibition in the Taft Court Era," *William and Mary Law Review* 48 (2006): 50. Even Sotirios Barber, a harsh critic of robust states' rights, concedes that in the 1910s or 1920s, "all sides of the states' rights debate seemed to accept a proposition that remained axiomatic"—that "the national government was one of 'limited powers.'" See Sotirios A. Barber, *The Fallacies of States' Rights* (Cambridge, MA: Harvard University Press, 2013), 64.

40 John Tyler, "Veto Message Regarding the Bank of the United States," August 16, 1841, Miller Center, accessed May 28, 2023, https://millercenter.org/the-presidency/presidential-speeches/august-16–1841-veto-message-regarding-bank-united-states; Grover Cleveland, "Veto of Texas Secd Bill," February 16, 1887, Miller Center, accessed May 28, 2023, https://millercenter.org/the-presidency/presidential-speeches/february-16–1887-veto-texas-seed-bill.

41 Emily Pears, "Visible States and Invisible Nation: Newspaper Coverage of Nineteenth Century Lawmaking," *Journal of Policy History* 31 (2019): 354–381.

42 This was especially true since perverse electoral incentives motivated both parties to ignore the Fourteenth and Fifteenth Amendment's protections, which did remove states' constitutional rights in those fields by creating national obligations and powers against the states. Democrats needed to suppress black votes to ensure southern support for their presidential candidates, while Republicans' northern electorates had shown a clear disinterest in the effort necessary to ensure implementation of those amendments. See J. Morgan Kousser, "The Voting Rights Act and the Two Reconstructions," in *Controversies in Minority Voting: A Twenty-Five Year Perspective on the Voting Rights Act of 1965*, ed. Chandler Davidson and Bernard Grofman (Washington, DC: Brookings Institution, 1992). Southern interest in maintaining their racial order obviously created an additional incentive to have Congress block national legislation, at least any that might be later used to destabilize the system of white supremacy. See introduction, note 30.

43 Sidney Milkis, *The President and the Parties* (Oxford: Oxford University Press, 1993); Sidney Milkis, *Political Parties and Constitutional Government* (Baltimore, MD: Johns Hopkins University Press, 1999); Gerald Leonard, *The Invention of Party Politics: Federalism, Popular Sovereignty, and Constitutional Development in Jacksonian Illinois* (Chapel Hill: University of North Carolina Press, 2002), esp. 18–50 outlining Van Buren's doctrines; also this chapter, note 18, on Madison's analogous efforts. See also Larry Kramer, *The People Themselves* (New York: Oxford University Press, 2005), 168, 193–195, 202 (agreeing that both Van Buren and the Whigs anticipated parties would enforce constitutionalism).

44 William J. Novak, *The People's Welfare: Law and Regulation in Nineteenth Century America* (Chapel Hill: University of North Carolina Press, 1996); Emily Zackin, *Looking for Rights in All the Wrong Places: Why State Constitutions*

Contain America's Positive Rights (Princeton, NJ: Princeton University Press, 2013); Kurt T. Lash, *The Lost History of the Ninth Amendment* (New York: Oxford University Press, 2009); James R. Stoner, *Common-Law Liberty* (Lawrence: University Press of Kansas, 2003), 125–149; also introduction, note 10. On the religious communitarian roots of this idea that merged into constitutional thought, see Barry Shain, *The Myth of American Individualism: The Protestant Origins of American Political Thought* (Princeton, NJ: Princeton University Press, 1994); and Wilson Carey McWilliams, *The Idea of Fraternity in America* (Berkeley: University of California Press, 1973).

45 Some pedants thus reject the term *states' rights* on these grounds, though I find the term perfectly acceptable insofar as the federal government exercising a power not given to it thereby usurps the states' right to exercise said power free of constraint from above.

46 On the etymology and development of the term and concept both before and within American constitutionalism, see Santiago Legarre, "The Historical Background of the Police Power," *University of Pennsylvania Journal of Constitutional Law* 9 (2007): 745–796.

47 Tocqueville, *Democracy in America*, 641.

48 Jacobson v. Massachusetts, 197 U.S. 11 (1905), 25.

49 *Jacobson*, 31, quoting Mugler v. Kansas, 123 U.S. 623 (1887), 661. See also chapter 4, note 50.

50 *Jacobson*, 38.

51 Tyson & Brother v. Banton, 273 U.S. 418 (1927), 445–446; Robert Post, "Social and Economic Legislation and the Taft Court," Taft entry in the Holmes Devise (n.p.: n.d.), chapter 5, 141, manuscript on file with author. Holmes's reputation as the quintessential progressive justice who upheld most progressive legislation, however, did not necessarily translate to his economic or political philosophy, as he was skeptical of redistributionist politics on their merits. G. Edward White, *Oliver Wendell Holmes, Law and the Inner Self* (New York: Oxford University Press, 1995), 378–411, esp. 390–391; Robert M. Berry, "From Unsettled Sterilization to Genetic Enhancement: The Unsettled Legacy *of Buck v. Bell*," *Notre Dame Journal of Law, Ethics, and Public Policy* 12 (2001): 432; also *PCSR*, 147.

52 See, e.g., Munn v. Illinois, 94 U.S. 113 (1876).

53 United States v. E. C. Knight, 156 U.S. 1 (1895). For Harlan's dissent, see, esp. 41, 64, 66–70. See also chapter 7 on Harlan's federalism.

54 Hammer v. Dagenhart, 247 U.S. 251 (1918). Even later conservative scholars skeptical of the New Deal's expansion of the commerce power suggest *Hammer* was wrongly decided in tilting too far toward state sovereignty even when issues created spillover or race-to-the-bottom effects. *Hammer*, in this account, overly constrained federal power. Perhaps the direct ban on production in the subsequent 1941 U.S. v. *Darby* case exceeded federal power, but a narrower restriction on actually shipping and transporting such goods in the first case was well within the scope of the commerce clause, even under its narrower direct-effects test. For originalist critics of *Hammer*, see, for example, Robert Natelson, who argues that

the direct ban upheld pursuant to the commerce clause in *Darby* was unconstitutional but that the interstate shipping ban prohibited in *Hammer* (but now also allowed by *Darby*) was constitutional. Robert Natelson, "Tempering the Commerce Power," *Montana Law Review* 68 (2007):121–122. See also Steven Calabresi, "The Originalist and Normative Case Against Judicial Activism," *Michigan Law Review* 103 (2005): 1082–1086; Michael Ramsey, "Was *Hammer v. Dagenhart* Wrongly Decided?" *Originalism Blog*, July 11, 2019, https://originalismblog.typepad.com/the-originalism-blog/2019/07/was-hammer-v-dagenhart-wrongly-decidedmichael-ramsey.html.

55 Brandeis and Holmes, while outraged about *Hammer*, nonetheless agreed with the majority in *Bailey v. Drexel Furniture* in blocking Congress's crude effort to subsequently use the tax power to directly coerce the end of child labor (259 U.S. 20 [1922]). In *Drexel*, Chief Justice Taft decried this an abusive twisting of the tax power that intruded on state police powers. In other words, for them, Congress could stop interstate shipping but not in-state production. Melvin I. Urofsky and Paul Finkelman, *A March of Liberty: A Constitutional History of the United States*, vol. 2: *From 1877 to the Present* (New York: Oxford University Press, 2001), 549–551. For a contrast between the more limited views of federal power of Holmes and those of Theodore Roosevelt who appointed him, see Jean Yarbrough, *Theodore Roosevelt and the American Political Tradition* (Lawrence: University Press of Kansas, 2012), 153.

56 The act made it generally illegal to move alcohol into a state that had deemed itself dry, which the Supreme Court approved almost unanimously. See *PCSR*, 27–28. For similar cases in other domains, see chapter 4, note 92.

57 William Graebner, "Federalism in the Progressive Era: A Structural Interpretation of Reform," *Journal of American History* 64 (1977):354–355.

58 On Root's status as Roosevelt's preferred choice, see William Schambra, "Elihu Root," in *American Political Thought: The Philosophic Dimensions of American Statesmanship*, 3rd ed. (New York: Routledge, 2017), 294. Roosevelt certainly preferred Root but feared his corporate law background would hurt his electability. Edmund Morris, *Theodore Rex* (New York: Random House, 2010), 458–459. Root had been writing letters to his friends in 1906 and 1907 that he would not consider the presidency, and similarly rejected Roosevelt's alternative idea of him running for governor. Philip C. Jessup, *Elihu Root: 1905–1937* (Hamden, CT: Archon Books, 1964), 123. John Milton Cooper suggests that Root, like Lodge, preempted Roosevelt and declined any consideration. John Milton Cooper, *Pivotal Decades: The United States, 1900–1920* (New York: Random House, 1990), 115–116.

59 Elihu Root, "How to Preserve the Local Government of the States: A Brief Study of National Tendencies," Speech to the Pennsylvania Society in New York, Wednesday, December 12, 1906, printed as *How to Preserve the Local Government of the States* (New York: Brentano's, 1907), 12. See also "Experiments in Government," 262–263. For a sympathetic take on Elihu Root's constitutional thought, see William Schambra, "The Saviors of the Constitution," *National Af-*

fairs 10 (Winter 2012), reprinted as "The Election of 1912 and the Origins of Constitutional Conservatism," in *Toward an American Conservatism: Constitutional Conservatism During the Progressive Era*, eds. Joseph Postell and Jonathan O'Neill (New York: Palgrave MacMillan 2013), 95–121; and "Elihu Root," 293–323. On Root's mix of progressive policy views and robust national power alongside a conservative view of the Constitution's limits, especially federalism, see also Milkis, *Theodore Roosevelt*, 116–117. For a discussion of Root's passionate advocacy as a lawyer defending states' rights, see *PCSR*, 44–52.

60 Root, "Preserved," 12.

61 Root, 13.

62 Root, 14.

63 Root, 14.

64 Root, 14.

65 Quoted (albeit with an error omitting "local") in *PCSR*, 229.

66 I was unable to find a comment from Root on *Hammer* itself, but two decades later, he opposed ratification of the resulting Child Labor Amendment that would have overturned *Hammer*. "Root Denounces Child Labor Act," *New York Times*, March 4, 1934, N1; "68 Leaders Fight Law on Child Labor," *New York Times*, April 16, 1934, 1. Logan Sawyer argues that Root then likely shared the same position as his usually like-minded ally Philander Knox—who was Roosevelt's attorney general while Root was secretary of war—even though such a position seems "under-inclusive." Logan E. Sawyer III, "Creating Hammer v. Dagenhart," *William and Mary Bill of Rights Journal* 21 (2012):117–118. It is possible that the earlier, somewhat more nationalist and progressive Root thought differently, before being radicalized by federalism issues raised by Prohibition, which he explicitly cited as an additional reason to reject the amendment lest federal power continue to grow.

67 See Milkis, *Theodore Roosevelt*, 113–120 (discussing Root's pivotal role as RNC chair and procedural enforcer for Taft); Schambra, "Saviors of the Constitution."

68 Lewis Gould, *Four Hats in the Ring: The 1912 Election and the Birth of Modern American Politics* (Lawrence: University Press of Kansas, 2008), 63. For an account of the 1912 election focused on the relationship of those three to Roosevelt, see Schambra, "Saviors of the Constitution"; for how Prohibition showed their commitment to federalism, see *PCSR*.

69 On Taft's progressive policy sympathies, see Kevin J. Burns, *William Howard Taft's Constitutional Progressivism* (Lawrence: University Press of Kansas, 2021); and Milkis, *Theodore Roosevelt*.

70 Milkis, *Theodore Roosevelt*, 191, 108, 192; Schambra, "Saviors of the Constitution"; Gould, *Four Hats*.

71 William Howard Taft, "Progressive Party Platform of 1912," November 5, 1912, American Presidency Project, accessed May 14, 2023, https://www.presidency.ucsb.edu/documents/progressive-party-platform-1912. This illustrates a major strain of progressivism—its desire to concentrate political power both laterally, in

an executive against Congress, and vertically, the nation against the states. Milkis argues this was one of the three most common features of the progressive movement, but tertiary to the primary desire to check concentrated wealth and the secondary desire to rethink of politics as less about individual rights and more about communities exercising meaningful control over their futures. The particular interest in a stronger executive serves as one of the fissures between progressives and the semiantecedent populists. The divide over whether to consolidate power in the federal government between different variants of progressives—such as Roosevelt and Croly versus Wilson and/Brandeis—is, as he notes, another, as well as one that internally divided more populist Progressives from less populist ones. My minor point of disagreement with Milkis is that, although he frequently discusses the decentralizing streak of some progressives (e.g., Milkis, *Theodore Roosevelt*, 41), Milkis occasionally suggests that New Freedom progressives as a group were wary of centralized administrative government but did not celebrate local government (17). I think this treatment of state politics, as well as broadening the horizon beyond to include secondary political figures, suggests many of these kinds of progressives did indeed accept the traditional states' rights view as part of their ideology, even if Milkis is correct in assessing the more famous ones, especially capital *P* Progressives who signed off on the third party, and their antipathy to old constitutional limits (10–26, 31). But this is largely a question of emphasis and how one either lumps or splits the movement's core versus periphery.

72 For Roosevelt's increasingly contemptuous treatment of constitutional federalism see Yarbrough, *Theodore Roosevelt and the American Political Tradition*, 141–151, 164, 191, 202, 212–213, 221, 250; Milkis, *Theodore Roosevelt*, 36–42, 250 (quoting the October speech); "The Herbert Croly, "Presidency; Making an Old Party Progressive," in *Theodore Roosevelt: An Autobiography* (New York: MacMillan, 1913), chapter 10 and esp. 381–382. Of the influence of Croly, see Yarbrough, *Theodore Roosevelt and the American Political Tradition*; also Gould, *Four Hats*, 162–165.

73 Gould, 156, 176–179.

74 See Wilson, First Inaugural Address, printed in Gould, 195; and Lewis L. Gould, *The First Modern Clash over Federal Power: Wilson versus Hughes in the Presidential Election of 1916* (Lawrence: University Press of Kansas, 2016), 14, 29–30.

75 Gould, *Four Hats*, 80.

76 Yarbrough, *Theodore Roosevelt and the American Political Tradition*, 248.

77 Gould suggests this text helped position him as a states' rights committed politician in line with Democratic thinking. Gould, *Four Hats*, 19.

78 Contrast the federalism chapter ("The States and the Federal Government") with "The President of the United States," 54–81, and its famous discussion of a Darwinian versus Newtonian understanding of institutional development. Woodrow Wilson, *Constitutional Government in the United States* (New York: Columbia University Press, 1908).

79 Wilson, *Constitutional Government in the United States*, 195–196.

80 Wilson, 192, 187–188.
81 Gould, *Four Hats*, 163–164. On the extent to which Brandeis influenced Wilson's thought versus joining with it, see Milkis, *Theodore Roosevelt*, 204–217.
82 Milkis, 134–135.
83 Milkis, 136, 219.
84 Gould, *Four Hats*, 156.
85 Milkis, *Theodore Roosevelt*, 177–181; Yarbrough, *Theodore Roosevelt and the American Political Tradition*,154–515, 216, 246–249.
86 On Underwood's commitment to states' rights, which led him to be seen as a leading conservative Democrat ten years later, see *PCSR*, 55–57, 144–146.
87 Milkis, *Theodore Roosevelt*, 271 (quoting Croly), 25, 271–278; Gould, *Four Hats*, 183; and Gould, *First Modern Clash*, esp. 56–57, 121; George W. Ruiz, "The Ideological Convergence of Theodore Roosevelt and Woodrow Wilson," *Presidential Studies Quarterly* 19 (1989): 159–177. For examples of latter conservative critics, see Charles Kesler, *I am the Change: Barack Obama and the Crisis of Liberalism* (New York: Broadside Books, 2012), 33; Ronald Pestritto, *Woodrow Wilson and the Roots of Modern Liberalism* (Lanham, MD: Rowman & Littlefield, 2005); Ronald J. Pestritto and William J. Atto, eds., *American Progressivism: A Reader* (Lanham, MD: Lexington Books, 2008), 25; Yarbrough, *Theodore Roosevelt and the American Political Tradition*, 248; Ken I. Kersch, "Constitutional Conservatives Remember the Progressive Era," in *The Progressives' Century: Democratic Reform and Constitutional Government in the United States*, eds. Stephen Skowronek, Stephen Engel, and Bruce Ackerman (New Haven, CT: Yale University Press, 2016) (surveying conservative historiography of Wilson).
88 Ralph Rossum, *Federalism, the Supreme Court, and the Seventeenth Amendment* (Lanham, MD: Lexington Books, 2001), 94.
89 William Riker, "The Senate and American Federalism," *APSR* 49 (1955): 468–469. For a review of this literature, see Sean Beienburg, "Constitutional Resistance in the States between the Reconstruction and New Deal Eras" (PhD diss., Princeton, 2015), 11–13; and for an example of a popular critique of the Seventeenth Amendment on states' rights grounds, see Rick Perry, *Fed Up! Our Fight to Save America from Washington* (New York: Little Brown, 2010), 38–43.
90 Robert Nagel argues that legal scholars have aggressively participated in this project to close, suppress, or render obsolete many of the national institutional structures by which states once acted as or were expected to act as constitutional interpreters. Nagel, *The Implosion of American Federalism* (New York: Oxford University Press, 2001), 52–54, 78.

Chapter 2. Against Motherhood and Apple Pie: The Sheppard-Towner Maternity and Infancy Protection Act of 1921

1 Though Civil War veterans' pensions functionally served a similar role, albeit one that followed from Congress's war-making powers. Theda Skocpol, *Protect-*

ing Soldiers and Mothers: Political Origins of Social Policy in the United States (Cambridge, MA: Harvard University Press, 1992).

2 For example, Medicaid (and its expansion under Obamacare) is only the most prominent of many today; similarly, many of the provisions of the New Deal were launched as grant-in-aid programs. Use of grants-in-aid particularly exploded in the 1960s, as many Great Society programs made use of them. For a recent treatment criticizing the use of such conditional spending as an unconstitutional way to bypass the enumerated powers, see Philip Hamburger, *Purchasing Submission* (Cambridge, MA: Harvard University Press, 2021). See also John Kincaid, "The Eclipse of Dual Federalism by One-Way Cooperative Federalism," *Arizona State Law Journal* 49 (2017): 1062.

3 See David P. Currie, *Constitution in Congress: The Jeffersonians, 1801–1829* (Chicago: University of Chicago Press, 2001), 116–117, 273.

4 See introduction, notes 7 and 42–45.

5 It is true that forward-thinking executives of net contributor states often warned about their treasuries being drafted into the service of Washington, but they were joined in nearly identical rhetoric by those in net recipient states. Moreover, as will be shown, in the short term, such officials appeared to be punished at the ballot box, though this probably ended up being related to other issues (such as Prohibition). Finally, as will be discussed further in the chapter, there was some correlation between a strong presence of Catholics and a state's hostility to the bill at the end, but opposition by Catholics hardened only relatively late in the debate so should not be overstated as a causal factor.

6 Jan Dolittle Wilson, *The Women's Joint Congressional Committee and the Politics of Maternalism* (Urbana: University of Illinois Press, 2007), 28–29. For more on the Children's Bureau's creation and debates over its scope, see also Elizabeth Sanders, *Roots of Reform* (Chicago: University of Chicago Press, 1999), 342–349.

7 Joseph Chepaitis, "The First Federal Social Welfare Measure: The Sheppard-Towner Maternity and Infancy Act, 1918–1932" (PhD diss., Georgetown University, 1968), 5–7.

8 Chepaitis, "First Federal Social Welfare Measure," 18–19.

9 For the politics of Sheppard-Towner on the federal level, I rely heavily on the account of Joseph Chepaitis, whose dissertation is the only volume-length treatment of the bill and by far the most thorough.

10 Skocpol, *Protecting Soldiers and Mothers*, 501–503.

11 Chepaitis, "First Federal Social Welfare Measure," 38; William Carr, "Place in Cabinet for Education," *New York Times*, February 11, 1923, X16. For more on the controversy over Towner's bill and its part in debates over grants-in-aid, federal roles in schools, and educational nationalism, see Ken I. Kersch, *Constructing Civil Liberties* (New York: Cambridge University Press, 2004), 260–267.

12 Sheppard was an immensely popular congressman elected to the Senate in 1912 after three terms in Congress but who quickly became unpopular with conservative party regulars for the bills that made him beloved by labor. Wilson, *Politics*

of Maternalism, 35–36. On Sheppard's leadership of the Eighteenth Amendment, see Sean Beienburg, *Prohibition, the Constitution, and States' Rights* (Chicago: University of Chicago Press, 2019), 22, hereafter cited as *PCSR*.

13 See, for example, Franklin Pierce's 1854 veto of a federal land grant to fund support for the indigent mentally ill, which Pierce argued the Constitution assigned to the states via their police powers on May 3, 1854. Franklin Pierce, "Veto Message," American Presidency Project, accessed May 7, 2023, https://www.presidency.ucsb.edu/node/202307 . In 1859, James Buchanan similarly vetoed what later became the Morrill Act. James Buchanan, "Veto Message," February 24, 1859, American Presidency Project, accessed May 7, 2023, https://www.presidency.ucsb.edu/documents/veto-message-444.

14 Alexander Hamilton, "Alexander Hamilton's Final Version of the Report on the Subject of Manufactures, [5 December 1791]," Founders Online, accessed May 28, 2023, https://founders.archives.gov/documents/Hamilton/01–10–02–0001–0007.

15 Carson Holloway, *Hamilton versus Jefferson in the Washington Administration: Completing the Founding or Betraying the Founding* (New York: Cambridge University Press, 2015), 155–157. Holloway argues that Hamilton's interpretation of federal power was nonetheless much more limited than his critics have alleged (132–136).

16 See chapter 1, note 18.

17 James Madison, "Speech on Bounty Payments for Cod Fisheries, [6 February 6] 1792," Founders Online, accessed May 28, 2023, https://founders.archives.gov/documents/Madison/01–14–02–0192. See also James Madison, "From James Madison to Edmund Pendleton, 21 January 1792," Founders Online, accessed, May 7, 2023, https://founders.archives.gov/documents/Madison/01–14–02–0174; James Madison, "1791: Madison, Speech on the Bank Bill," February 2, 1791, Liberty Fund, accessed May 7, 2023, http://oll.libertyfund.org/index.php?Itemid=264&id=1060&option=com_content&task=view.

18 Thomas Jefferson, "Jefferson's Opinion on the Constitutionality of a National Bank: 1791," Avalon Project, Yale Law School, accessed May 7, 2023, http://avalon.law.yale.edu/18th_century/bank-tj.asp.

19 On the defeat of the bounties, see Douglas A. Irwin, "The Aftermath of Hamilton's Report on Manufactures," *Journal of Economic History* 64 (2004): 802–808.

20 This number does not include a number of categorical grants, mostly for pest control. "States Resent 'Super Rule' of Uncle Sam: Heed Warning Sounded by Coolidge of Peril," *Chicago Tribune*, December 28, 1924, 12; "Curb Favored on Federal Aid," *Los Angels Times*, December 29, 1924, 6. (These misstate Smith-Hughes as 1919, not 1917.) As of 1902, the five grants were an 1879 bill providing one-time grants-in-aid for teaching materials for the blind, the 1887 Hatch Act funding agricultural stations (which later became attached to agricultural colleges), an 1888 bill funding support for disabled veterans, and a second Morrill Act (of 1890) providing additional funding for the colleges created by the

Morrill land grants. "Federal Grants to State and Local Governments: A Historical Perspective," Congressional Research Service, May 22, 2019, 15–17, https://sgp.fas.org/crs/misc/R40638.pdf. See also Kersch, *Constructing Civil Liberties*, 242–243; and concerning the failed educational grants, 260–267. As noted earlier, Congress also considered others (such as Sterling-Towner for educational grants-in-aid) but these were much more controversial after Sheppard-Towner's controversy. Kimberly Johnson argues that grants-in-aid were a major building block of the first "New Federalism," transitioning from the old "dual federalist" system toward the nationalism of the New Deal. See Kimberly Johnson, *Governing the American State: Congress and the New Federalism, 1877–1929* (Princeton, NJ: Princeton University Press, 2007).

21 Johnson, *Governing the American State*, 30–31, 66–67.

22 See introduction, note 37.

23 Johnson, *Governing the American State*, 23, 178–179.

24 Chepaitis, "First Federal Social Welfare Measure," 40.

25 Stanley Lemons, "The Sheppard Towner Act: Progressivism in the 1920s," *Journal of American History* 55 (1969): 777–778; "Gives President's Stand on Maternity Measure," *Washington Post*, November 1, 1921, 9; Anna L. Harvey, *Votes without Leverage: Women in American Electoral Politics, 1920–1970* (New York: Cambridge University Press, 1998), 195.

26 Chepaitis, "First Federal Social Welfare Measure," 47; 67 Cong. Rec., 1st Sess., 4216. DW-Nominate rank orders of the 104 men who served in the Senate during the 67th Congress suggests the ideological breadth of the nine opponents in the upper chamber. From most to least progressive by rank order: Watson, 4; King, 26; Reed, 31; Broussard, 39; Borah, 45; Wadsworth, 73; Warren, 79; Dillingam, 95; Moses, 104. Royce Carroll, Jeff Lewis, James Lo, Nolan McCarty, Keith Poole, and Howard Rosenthal, "SENATE_SORT67 Rank Ordering," Vote View, accessed May 7, 2023, http://voteview.com/SENATE_SORT67.HTM.

27 On Reed, see *PCSR*, 70–71.

28 Chepaitis, "First Federal Social Welfare Measure," 54–55.

29 Chepaitis, 59, 229, 284.

30 Wilson, *Politics of Maternalism*, 46. On Wadsworth and Borah's federalism, see *PCSR*, 102, 231.

31 *PCSR*, 95, 91.

32 Schecter Poultry v. U.S, 295 U.S. 495 (1935); "Roosevelt Due to Reveal New Plan Today: Borah Is Applauded for His Stand," *New York Times*, June 4, 1935, 1; "Borah Challenges 'Menders' to Risk Constitutional Poll, People Alone Should Decide if States Are to Lose Powers," *New York Times*, June 3, 1935, 1.

33 John Braeman, "The American Polity in the Age of Normalcy," in *Calvin Coolidge and the Coolidge Era*, ed. John Earl Haynes (Washington, DC: Library of Congress, 1998), 35–36.

34 Chepaitis, "First Federal Social Welfare Measure," 125–129, 143.

35 See chapter 1.

36 Chepaitis, "First Federal Social Welfare Measure," 134.

37 Chepaitis, 135–136. Lathrop also made sure to quiet fears about creeping socialism by disavowing maternity benefits and explicitly distancing herself from over-
eager Sheppard-Towner supporters in the print world who also called for such
mother's pensions.

38 Chepaitis, "First Federal Social Welfare Measure," 63.

39 Carr, "Place in Cabinet for Education," X16; "The Smith-Towner Bill," *Elemen-
tary School Journal* 20 (1920): 575–583. See also this chapter, note 20.

40 Chepaitis, "First Federal Social Welfare Measure," 140. Whether there was much
justification for such concerns, or whether they could be dismissed, as Chepaitis does, is another story. As Ken Kersch has noted, this was a moment when the
growing power of the state and traditional understandings of the domain of family
autonomy and local community came into conflict, typified not just by the possible passage of Smith-Towner but also by several cases discussed more in chapters
4 and 5. Kersch, *Constructing Civil Liberties*, chapter 4.

41 Kersch, 267.

42 As the bill allotted only relatively small sums and the operation was fairly straightforward, economy and inefficiency, the usual watchwords of the day, were only
occasionally raised in Congress and the legislatures; the arguments were predominantly either constitutional or about the sanctity of the home against the power
of the government. For a survey of such arguments, see Chepaitis, "First Federal
Social Welfare Measure," 140–143.

43 *JH AZ*, 1923, 439. Nearly verbatim sections appear in almost all of the state bills.

44 Chepaitis, "First Federal Social Welfare Measure," 73–75.

45 Chepaitis, 75; Wilson, *Politics of Maternalism*, 47; Lemons, "The Sheppard
Towner Act," 776–786; "Maternity Bill Is Object of Derision," *Ogden* (UT) *Standard Examiner*, August 11, 1921, 7.

46 "Not Here for Fight but to Aid Veterans," *Muskogee* (OK) *Times Democrat*, August 27, 1921, 1.

47 The later widely used phrase was that of Republican Frank Greene of Vermont,
one of the aforementioned implacable congressional foes. Wilson, *Politics of Maternalism*, 46–47.

48 Wilson, 38–45; Chepaitis, "First Federal Social Welfare Measure," 75–77.

49 Robert Sobel, *Coolidge: An American Enigma* (Washington, DC: Regnery, 1998);
PCSR, 194.

50 "Women as Lobbyists," *Lowell* (MA) *Sun*, January 27, 1921, 6. The paper took
pride in the fact Massachusetts and other industrial states took their duties to citizens seriously and already had similar provisions.

51 "Women Line Up on Baby Bill Battle," *Oshkosh* (WI) *Daily Northwestern*, May
6, 1921, 1.

52 Carolyn M. Moehling and Melissa A. Thomasson, "The Political Economy of
Saving Mothers and Babies: The Politics of State Participation in the Sheppard-Towner Program," *Journal of Economic History* 72 (2012):75–103.

53 Lemons, "The Sheppard Towner Act," 778; Skocpol, *Protecting Soldiers and
Mothers*, 505. Skocpol suggests that Congress took the wrong lesson in the late

1920s, underestimating the women's vote when reauthorization was blocked (Skocpol, 521). The creation of the Children's Bureau under Taft a decade before likely passed with similar anxiety about optics, as the extremely high abstention rate—more than voted aye—suggests. See Skocpol, 304, 484.

54 Indeed, the power of women's groups was at its apex, before partisan organizations assimilated the newly enfranchised women into their long-standing machinery. Harvey, *Votes without Leverage*.

55 Chepaitis, "First Federal Social Welfare Measure," 100–105.

56 Sheila M. Rothman, *Woman's Proper Place: A History of Changing Ideals and Practices, 1870 to the Present* (New York: Basic Books, 1978), 137–146.

57 Leslie J. Reagan, *When Abortion Was a Crime: Women, Medicine, and Law in the United States 1867–1973* (Berkeley: University of California Press, 1998).

58 Chepaitis, "First Federal Social Welfare Measure," 85–87.

59 *America*, September 6, 1924, 21, quoted in Maxwell Bloomfield, *Peaceful Revolution: Constitutional Change and American Culture from Progressivism to the New Deal* (Cambridge, MA: Harvard University Press, 2001), 90.

60 Moehling and Thomasson, "Political Economy," 82.

61 Wilson, *Politics of Maternalism*, 53–54, 61, 100–106. On the Sentinels, see *PCSR*, 82.

62 See previous note. On NAM, Stephen Wood, *Constitutional Politics in the Progressive Era: Child Labor and the Law* (Chicago: University of Chicago Press, 1968).

63 Chepaitis, "First Federal Social Welfare Measure," 14–16.

64 Chepaitis, 31, 120–125.

65 Chepaitis, 163–165; Grace Abbot, "The Federal Government in Relation to Maternity and Infancy," *Annals of the American Academy of Political and Social Science* 151 (1930): 99.

66 While some states had already been implementing women's suffrage even before the Nineteenth Amendment, the South had not, and they too had little evidence with which to refute the WJCC's electoral prophecies of backlash against those who would oppose the bill.

67 35–0 in senate, 57–7 in house. *JS VA*, 1922, 212–213; *JH VA*, 1922, 432–433; V. O. Key Jr. with Alexander Heard, *Southern Politics in State and Nation* (New York: Alfred A Knopf, 1949), 19–36. Unfortunately, Virginia's journals do not record any floor debate, and newspaper coverage discussing its reception in Virginia comports with Florence Kelley's exasperated sigh to Nathan Miller that passage in Virginia had been painless.

68 On Maryland and states' rights, see *PCSR*, 57–65, 100–103, 114–117, 131, 139–144.

69 "Child Hygiene Bill to be Supported by United Women," *Baltimore Sun*, January 13, 1922, 4.

70 I found a dozen articles, mostly in the *Baltimore Sun*. Although that paper's conservative editorial board would have an incentive to play up a women's movement hostile to the bill, other newspapers covered them at some length, and the

WCL criticized the *Sun*'s coverage of them as unfair. "Representatives of the Women's Constitutional League Want It Understood that They Cast No Slurs Upon the Men in Our Legislature," *Baltimore Sun*, January 28, 1922, 6. See "Sheppard Towner Bill Dictatorial: Maryland Women's League Terms Measure 'Vicious Type of Federal Aid,'" *Christian Science Monitor*, January 3, 1922, 5; "Women Take Stand on Ratification of Maternity Bill: Forerunner of Doctrine of Birth Control, Constitution League Declares," *Baltimore Sun*, January 17, 1922, 4; "Constitutional League Opens Fire on State Child Hygiene Bill," *Baltimore Sun*, January 19, 1922, 5; "Constitutional League Declares War on Ritchie, Linthicum, and Lee, " *Baltimore Sun*, January 26, 1922, 5. On Phyllis Schlafly, see Donald T. Critchlow, *Phyllis Schlafly and Grassroots Activism* (Princeton, NJ: Princeton University Press, 2005).

71 "Says Child Hygiene Means Bureaucracy," *Baltimore Sun*, February 15, 1922, 5. For the list of these, see this chapter, note 20.

72 Cordelia Gibbs, "Masked Paternalism," *New York Tribune*, March 9, 1922, 10.

73 Florence Kelley, "Mothers' Federal Aid: Reply to Opponent Who Terms It 'Masked Paternalism,'" *New York Tribune*, March 11, 1922, 10.

74 Cordelia Gibbs, "Mothers' Federal Aid: Not Analogous to Defense, Says Maryland Spokesman," *New York Tribune*, March 14, 1922, 10.

75 "House Falls in Line for Child Hygiene," *Baltimore Sun*, March 29, 1922, 7; "Child Hygiene Bill Passed by House," *Baltimore Sun*, March 31, 1922, 6. The fragments of floor debate appearing in press coverage suggest less subtle arguments than during the Women's Constitutional League exchanges, but it is impossible to tell without the committee reports or nonexistent transcripts.

76 *JH MD*, 1922, 1043–1045, 1178–1180; *JS MD*, 1922, 1110–1111; "House Gets in Snarl over Child Hygiene," *Baltimore Sun*, March 30, 1922, 6. Voting no on the final senate vote were Democratic senators Brady, Fox, and Harrison. Of those, Harrison voted to advance the bill to final consideration but opposed final passage. The five senators who voted no on second passage but abstained from the final vote were Republican Goodell and Democrats Biggs, Frick, McIntosh, and Legg.

77 Biggs worked Prohibition into the speech as well, decrying his fellow legislators for being hypocritical moralists who backed Prohibition but drank in private. "Booze in Legislature," *Gettysburg* (PA) *Times*, March 10, 1922, 3.

78 "Baby Bill Passes, Action Held Illegal," *Baltimore Sun*, April 4, 1922, 1; "General Assembly Ends 1922 Session; Senate Delayed by Filibuster," *Baltimore Sun*, April 4, 1922, 1.

79 "Baby Bill's Passage Likely to Stand: Governor Is Expected to Sign Measure," *Baltimore Sun*, April 5, 1922, 9; "Ritchie to Approve Child Hygiene Bill," *Baltimore Sun*, April 11, 1922, 26; Diane E. Weaver, "Maryland Women and the Transformation of Politics, 1890s–1930" (PhD diss., University of Maryland, 1992), 265.

80 Douglas B. Craig, *After Wilson: The Struggle for the Democratic Party, 1920–1934* (Chapel Hill: University of North Carolina Press, 1992), 237–238. Ritchie

was instrumental in preventing Maryland from ever passing Volstead enforcement—the only state in the Union never to do so—and constantly condemning it as an invasion of states' rights. See *PCSR*.

81 "Ritchie Cites States' Rights as Chief National Issue," *Baltimore Sun*, April 23, 1924, 7; Craig, *After Wilson*; James B. Levin, "Albert C. Ritchie: A Political Biography" (PhD diss., City University of New York, 1970).

82 *PCSR*, 304n10

83 H.J.R. 11, in *JH MD*, 1931, 353.

84 "Pinchot Charges Collapse of Dry Law Enforcing; Ritchie Urges States Rights," *Chicago Tribune*, April 27, 1924, 12.

85 On the purge, see chapter 6, note 197. Tydings's voting behavior is somewhat strange; he opposed the bill up to its final passage. This was perhaps involving a motion to reconsider, but on the final vote he and bill opponent Harrison (who had voted to proceed) switched.

86 Tyding's biographer summarizes his political philosophy by observing that whatever the issue, "he judged it by the effect on individuals' and states' rights" with a remarkably brittle consistency. Caroline H. Keith, *For Hell and a Brown Mule: The Biography of Senator Millard E. Tydings* (Lanham, MD: Madison Books, 1991), 169. Unfortunately, Keith ignores Sheppard-Towner entirely, but the portrayal of Tydings as an immensely ambitious World War I veteran immediately angling for Congress suggests the possibility of electoral concerns (Keith, 168–75). Alternatively, as with Carter Glass, perhaps Tydings simply later became more interested in federalism, perhaps aggravated by the states' rights implications of Prohibition and then of the Federal Emergency Relief Administration (Keith, 174, 202). In the 1934 elections, the Republican Senatorial Committee would commend Tydings, Al Smith, John Davis, Glass, and Byrd for their anti–New Deal, federalist postures (Keith, 201). Tydings, as a member of Congress, later would try to block renewal of Sheppard-Towner by adjourning the House in 1926 (Chepaitis, "First Federal Social Welfare Measure," 223), and would join fellow Democrats Elbert Thomas (UT) and David Walsh (MA) in filibustering another renewal plan in 1931. Lemons, "The Sheppard Towner Act," 785–786.

87 Lemons, 785–786.

88 *JS MD*, 1924, 312, 895–96; "Sheppard Towner Recall Move Fails," *Baltimore Sun*, March 26, 1924, 4.

89 *JS MD*, 1924, 1130–1131.

90 *JS MD*, 1924, 1131.

91 "Jersey Governor Opens 'Wet' Fight," *New York Times*, January 21, 1920, 5. This was despite Runyon being the chief sponsor of the ASL's Volstead implementation in New Jersey. "McCran Backs Jersey's Right to Define Beer," *New York Tribune*, February 10, 1920, 5.

92 Wilson, *Politics of Maternalism*, 103–104, 201.

93 *JH MD*, 1927, 397–98; *JS MD*, 1927, 132–133. Nor was states' rights restlessness confined to the senate in 1924; the house appealed to the same principle in passing an anti-Prohibition resolution. *JH MD*, 1924, 293.

94 J.R. 16, in *Laws MD*, 1927, 1650; *JS MD*, 1927, 1051.

95 *JH GA*, 1922, 1032–1033; *JS GA*, 1922, 334–335.

96 Senate vote: 27–0–3, in *JS WV*, 1923, 296–297; house vote: 88–0–6, in *JH WV*, 1923, 634–635. The state also voted for a resolution endorsing the Sterling-Towner Bill to establish a federal Department of Education; the house passed it on a voice vote, while just two senators actually put their names to votes against it. *JS WV*, 1923, 123; *JH WV*, 1923, 220.

97 *JH AR*, 1923, 204–205, 245; *JS AR*, 1923, 332–333.

98 H.J.R. 21, in *JH AL*, 1923, 541–542; *JS AL*, 1923, 508.

99 "Biennial Address," printed in *JS MS*, 1922, 22–23.

100 "The Maternity Bill Suit," *Hattiesburg-American* (MS), April 17, 1923, 1.

101 *JS TN*, 1923, 557; *JH TN*, 1923, 651–652.

102 "Sheppard-Towner Aid Rejected by Florida," *Washington Post*, May 26, 1923, 3. *JH FL*, 1923, 2182–2183; *JS FL*, 1923, 2533–2534.

103 Key Jr. and Heard, *Southern Politics in State and Nation*, 156–183.

104 "Women Leaguers Denounce Defeat of Pension Bill," *Times-Picayune* (LA), June 28, 1924, 2. Other news stories featured local activists complaining that the bill had been bogged down, but none seemed to cover its passage, only its implementation.

105 *JS LA*, 1924, 885; *JH LA*, 1924, 1165–1166.

106 "House Passes Bill to Help Enforce Law," *San Antonio Evening News*, February 9, 1923, 15.

107 "Senate Accepts Maternity Act," *San Antonio Express*, February 13, 1923, 10.

108 *JH TX*, 1923, 492–493; *JS TX*, 1923, 470–471. This vote total includes paired votes. Technically another senate vote was held in adopting the house version of the bill, but the tallies were the same, only with a few noes having departed to absence (492); "Sheppard-Towner Act Attacked by Davis," *San Antonio Express*, May 3, 1923, 1. Texas legislative makeup and histories found at "Party Affiliation — 38th Legislature," Legislative Reference Library of Texas, accessed May 7, 2023, http://www.lrl.state.tx.us/legeLeaders/members/partyListSession.cfm ?leg=38.

109 *JS TX*, 1923, 87, 128; *JH TX*, 1923, 289–290. The vote was 92–31.

110 Joint no votes can arguably be reconciled as well; for example, one opposes symbolic resolutions or, in the case of the Republican Wessels, declines to endorse a Democratic Party document even if they share its states' rights principles.

111 Again, for purposes of analysis, this paragraph omits all those who abstained or were not present for *either* bill.

112 "New York Sets an Example," *St. Louis Post-Dispatch*, March 13, 1922, 14.

113 "States' Rights Uppermost," February 8, 1925, 4.

114 "Ignorant Mothers, Helpless Babies, and States Rights," *Wichita* (TX) *Daily Times,* September 17, 1922, 2.

115 *JS TX*, 1923, 45, 116; *JH TX*, 1923, 298. It seems likely that the sentiment of that memorial is closer to the truer preferences of the legislators than it is to cheap position-taking (unlike, for example, the populist Democratic Party platform of

sovereignty resolution). Kentucky's house, once the home of the Kentucky Resolution, echoed Henry Clay's support of roadbuilding while rejecting a loose interpretation of the spending power, and similarly protested all grants-in-aid other than roads in 1922, even as the state government moved Sheppard-Towner's acceptance through without event. *JH KY* (1922), 968–971.

116 "Women Aroused over Threat to Stop All Work in State Under Sheppard-Towner Maternity Act," *San Antonio Express*, January 29, 1925, 11.

117 On Maryland and Prohibition, see *PCSR*.

118 "Welfare Aid Is Barred," *Oregonian*, July 1, 1922, 5; "Inaugural Address," January 10, 1923, in *JS WA*, 1923, 47, 50; *JS WA*, 1923, 498; *JH WA*, 1923, 440, 638. In describing Hart's involvement with Sheppard-Towner, Lemons says that he was "unalterably opposed, and only the election of a new chief executive allowed the state to join the program," but the veto message does not suggest this, nor do any other secondary sources list Washington as outside the program after 1923. See Lemons, "The Sheppard Towner Act," 782.

119 A search of newspapers and gubernatorial addresses found no reference to substantive discussion whatsoever in any of those states.

120 In Oregon, Republicans cast all votes in opposition or in absence; the combined three Democrats and two Independents of both houses backed the bill. New Mexico's appropriations committees similarly passed preemptive, uncontested funding. *JH/S OR*, 1921 (special session), 61, 91–92; *JH NM*, 1921, 600, 605; *JS NM*, 1921, 422, 427; *JH AZ*, 1923, 439; *JS AZ*, 1923, 681; *JH WY*, 1923, 358–359; *JS WY*, 1923, 183.

121 "Arizona Plan Ready to Aid Its Mothers and Infants," *Arizona Republican*, July 17, 1922, 1; "Many Ask Benefit of New Law to Aid Mother and Baby," *Arizona Republican*, July 6, 1922, 3. I was unable to find any equivalent mention of federalism in other digitized newspapers I searched as well.

122 *JH UT*, 1923, 279–80; *JS UT*, 1923, 433; *JH WY*, 1923, 358–359; *JS WY*, 1923, 183. Utah and Wyoming both approved without opposition: by votes of 52–0-3 and 14–0-6 in Salt Lake City; and in Cheyenne a house vote of 25 in favor, 0 against, 8 not voting, and a spread of 19–0-6 in its senate. Arizona's two houses approved without dissent.

123 *JH ID*, 1923, 208–209; *JS ID*, 1923, 395. It was about 3:1 in the senate and 5:1 in the house. Eight representatives voted against the bill (compared to fifty-three in favor and four absent/excused), joined by ten dissenting senators (to thirty-two yeas and two not voting).

124 A.B. 283, in *JA CA*, 1923, 866; *JS CA*, 1923, 1127. Representative Dozier (R-Shasta) was the only holdout in the House while Dennet (R-D, Stanislaus) and Republican Egbert Gates opposed it in the Senate. "Block Federal Child Aid," *Los Angeles Times*, April 19, 1923, 12.

125 *JS CO*, 1923, 1080–1081; *JH CO*, 1923, 1532. There were fifty-three for, six abstentions, and five nays.

126 *JS NV*, 1923, 106; "Child Welfare Workers to be Barred by Parents," *Reno Evening Gazette*, February 16, 1923, 2. Senators Dressler and Getchell opposed the

bill, making the final vote 15–2. Getchell was a mining tycoon and Republican leader, serving as an Arizona state senator in 1917–1918 before moving to Nevada, where he served from 1923–1942, in addition to a stint as head of the Nevada state GOP. "Nobel Getchell Taken by Death," *Reno Evening Gazette*, February 10, 1960, 1. "Joint Session Is Held on Sheppard-Towner Act," *Reno Evening Gazette*, February 14, 1923, 2; *JH NV*, 1923, 175 (34–0-2). Representatives Stites and Towle abstained; Stites appears to have been legitimately absent, but Towle voted no on bills before and after passage, suggesting he opposed the bill but declined to go on the record as such. "Sheppard Towner Measure Approved," *Nevada State Journal*, February 27, 1923, 2.

127 *JS MO*, 1923, 967; *JH MO*, 1923, 167; "Will Missouri Join?" *St. Louis Post-Dispatch*, May 21, 1922, A2; "New York Sets an Example," *St. Louis Post-Dispatch*, March 13, 1922, 14.

128 H.F. 1098, in *JH MN*, 1921, 1389, *JS MN*, 1921, 1214.

129 *JH MI*, 1923, 370–371, 1200; *JS MI*, 1923, 398–399; "Doctors Favor Maternity Act," *Traverse City* (MI) *Record Eagle*, March 2, 1923, 16.

130 *JH OH*, 1923, 620–621; *JS OH*, 715–716. One tiny paper lamented that all too few states understood federal aid as coercive federal inducement, but support in Ohio otherwise appeared strong. "'Federal Aid' Bunk," *Lima* (OH) *News*, May 7, 1923, 4; "The Sheppard-Towner Act," *Sandusky* (OH) *Star Journal*, December 1, 1925, 12.

131 On Blaine's progressivism and federalism, see *PCSR*, 74–75, 129.

132 See introduction, note 1; "Address to the Legislature," January 13, 1921, in *JS WI*, 1921, 46–48.

133 *JS WI*, 1921, 50–51.

134 Unsigned Editorial, *Janesville* (WI) *Gazette*, March 27, 1923, 6.

135 *JS WI*, 1923, 780–781; *JA WI*, 1923, 774–775, 1073.

136 *JS NE*, 1923, 1272–1273; *JH NE*, 1923, 1103.

137 *JS NE*, 1922, 48–49; *JH NE*, 1922, 135–136.

138 *JS NE*, 1923, 357–358; *JH NE*, 1925, 1364.

139 The *Cedar Rapids Gazette* condemned those who portrayed the bill as a "maudlin sentimental experiment" for ignoring the pressing need, while the *LeMars Globe Post* praised Massachusetts for fighting back against centralization against the Tenth Amendment. "Needless Sacrifice," *Cedar Rapids Evening Gazette*, August 22, 1921, 4; "Massachusetts Trying to Curb a Bureaucratic Congress," *LeMars Globe Post*, October 2, 1922, 4.

140 "Highways Battle Is On," *Iowa Recorder*, January 24, 1923, 1; "Under the Golden Dome," *Oxford* (MI) *Leader*, February 1, 1923, 6. This does not appear in the legislative journal, likely because Iowa's journal ignored bills that failed to clear a committee.

141 "Federal Government Extends Its Power: Iowa Accepts Sheppard Towner Act," *LeMars Globe Post*, March 29, 1923, 1. A local Iowa paper reprinted the story from the *Hattiesburg American* (MS) on the Massachusetts suit, only replacing the Mississippi endorsement of Sheppard-Towner with the observation that the

Iowa legislative session indicated Iowans' fatigue with federal power. "The Maternity Bill Suit," *Burlington* (IA) *Hawkeye*, May 5, 1923.

142 Only a very slim 21–19 margin had voted in favor in the early vote, but that was insufficient due to senate procedure. *JH IA*, 1923, 618, 1065; *JS IA*, 1923, 343–343, 467. There was an ill-fated effort by Democratic Representative O'Donnell (H.B. 277) to repeal the bill in the Iowa house in 1925. "Lauer Pleads for Support of Maternity Law," *Iowa City Press Citizen*, March 11, 1925, 7. It, too, did not appear in the journal.

143 A 28–9 senate margin was insufficient to clear a two-thirds expedited procedure; a revote taken later in the day added several abstentions to the aye vote and cleared the bill. (The house had already approved it with a 76–9 vote.) *JS SD*, 1923, 1032, 1071; *JH SD*, 1923, 476.

144 "Address to the Legislature," January 2, 1923, reprinted in *JH SD*, 1923, 38.

145 *Laws ND*, 1921, 245.

146 *JS ND*, 1923, 607.

147 *JH ND*, 1923, 1311. With twenty abstaining or not voting, the bill failed on a 46–47 vote; Craig's initial vote would have put it at a majority, but the bill evidently failed to clear a supermajoritarian procedural threshold.

148 The final vote was 81–21–11. *JH ND*, 1923, 1318.

149 *JS IN*, 1923, 343, 467; *JH IN*, 1923, 618. Party data from *JS IN*, 1923, 931; *JH IN*, 1923, 889.

150 *JS IL*, 1923 ,908–909; *JH IL*, 1923, 1097.

151 "Sheppard-Towner Bill Denounced: American Medical Liberty League Advises Prompt Action by the People to Prevent its Final Passage in Congress," *Christian Science Monitor*, November 12, 1921, 1; "Illinois Doctors Oppose Federal or State Medicine: Sheppard Towner Act and Growing Washington Bureaucracy Strongly Condemned in Resolutions," *Christian Science Monitor*, May 20, 1922, 5; Chepaitis, "First Federal Social Welfare Measure," 168.

152 "Delusion of Federal Aid," *Chicago Tribune*, March 29, 1923, 8.

153 "Endorse Roberts Bill," *Decatur* (IL) *Daily Review*, May 10, 1923, 1; "Illinois Needs No Federal Nurse," *Chicago Tribune*, April 22, 1923, 8.

154 *JS KS*, 1923, 564–565; *JH KS*, 1923, 612.

155 *JH KS*, 1927, 450–451. The senate vote was a 30–4–6 vote. *JS KS*, 1927, 453.

156 *JH KS*, 1927, 231.

157 *Annual Report to Congress of the Federal Board for Vocational Education*, vol. 5 (Washington, DC: Government Printing Office, 1921), 325–336, https://books .google.com/books?id=UCwTAAAAIAAJ&printsec=frontcover&source=gbs _atb#v=onepage&q&f=false.

Chapter 3. Sheppard-Towner II: Yankee States' Rights

1 See Richard B. Bernstein and Jerome Agel, *Amending America: If We Love the Constitution So Much, Why Do We Keep Trying to Change It?* (University of Kan-

sas Press, 1995), 126–128; Christopher Terranova, "The Constitutional Life of Legislative Instructions in America," *NYU Law Review* 84 (2009): 1331–1373. For discussion of how the Seventeenth Amendment affected state sovereignty signals originally expected to come from the US Senate, see chapter 1.

2 Nathan Lewis Miller, *Recollections*, 1953, 27, box 2, Nathan Lewis Miller Papers, Special Collections Research Center, Syracuse University Libraries, Syracuse, New York, hereafter cited as NLMP. Miller had opposed the prohibition amendment on states' rights grounds even if he grudgingly enforced it after ratification. See Sean Beienburg, *Prohibition, the Constitution, and States' Rights* (Chicago: University of Chicago Press, 2019), 22, hereafter cited as *PCSR*. On his actions against federal power regulation, see "The Basis of the Water Power Issue," *Lewiston* (ME) *Journal*, February 3, 1921; "Recommending Maximum Development of Water Power of the State," March 11, 1921, Oversize 1, NLMP, 87.

3 Miller had fallen ill at the time of the oral arguments so had hired John Davis to do those. Miller, *Recollections*, 36.

4 "New York and Maine," *Portland Press Herald*, April 21, 1921, Scrapbook 1.126, Percival Baxter Papers, Maine State Library, Augusta, Maine, hereafter cited as PBP.

5 "Staten Island Speech," November 4, 1922, Box 4, NLMP; Miller, *Recollections*, 37. On class legislation, see Howard Gillman, *The Constitution Besieged: The Rise and Demise of Lochner Era Police Powers Jurisprudence* (Durham, NC: Duke University Press, 1993).

6 "Newspaper Interview at Syracuse," October 21, 1922, box 3, vol. 2, NLMP.

7 "Staten Island Speech"; Miller, *Recollections*, 37.

8 "Newspaper Interview," October 14, 1922; and "Address at Poughkeepsie," October 6, 1922, box 3, vol. 1, 1922 Speeches, NLMP; "Staten Island Speech." Miller rejected the label of a stand-pat, laissez-faire Republican, noting he had significantly raised teacher pay and school spending, regulated predatory landlords and coal gouging, hired more nurses and beds for wards of state, developed training and education for the blind and handicapped, opened children's courts to keep them out of regular criminal justice process, passed a law regulating power gouging to ensure New Yorkers could afford energy in the winter, shepherded a workmen's comp law endorsed by labor as the best version, and gotten water power regulated to the benefit of the state.

9 "New York Man to Nominate Hoover to Name Hoover in Convention," *Los Angeles Times*, June 6, 1920, 11; "Hoover Named by Judge Miller," *Los Angeles Times*, June 12, 1920, I2; "Hoover Makes Strong Plea for Judge Miller," *New York Tribune*, October 23, 1920, 3. The two would continue an epistolary friendship and trade books. See, e.g., Letters on December 19, 1922, and January 1929, box 1, NLMP; "Obituary," *US Steel Quarterly*, box 2, NLMP.

10 "Address to the Annual Dinner of the New York Bar Association," January 22, 1922, *Public Papers of Nathan L. Miller, Forty-Sixth Governor of the State of New York* (Albany, NY: J. B. Lyon, 1924), 365; "Miller Demands State Home Rule," *New York Times*, January 22, 1922, 19.

11 "Address to the Annual Dinner of the New York Bar."

12 "Address to the Annual Dinner of the New York Bar."

13 "Repudiates Federal Care for Mothers," *New York Times*, February 21, 1922, 6; Carolyn M. Moehling and Melissa A. Thomasson, "The Political Economy of Saving Mothers and Babies: The Politics of State Participation in the Sheppard-Towner Program," *Journal of Economic History* 72 (2012): 83–84; Joseph Chepaitis, "The First Federal Social Welfare Measure: The Sheppard-Towner Maternity and Infancy Act, 1918–1932" (PhD diss., Georgetown University, 1968), 166–167.

14 Miller further drew a contrast between this and proposals for national- and state-run health insurance in the late 1940s: "Now the socialization of medicine is proposed." Miller, *Recollections*, 27.

15 Jan Dolittle Wilson, *The Women's Joint Congressional Committee and the Politics of Maternalism* (Urbana: University of Illinois Press, 2007), 58.

16 "Back to the Constitution," *New York Times*, January 23, 1922, 8.

17 Narcissa Cox Vanderlip, "The Sheppard Towner Bill: A Plea for Its Acceptance by Present Legislature of New York," *New York Times*, April 4, 1923, 14.

18 "Miller Is Queried on His Opposition to Maternity Bill," *New York Times*, February 25, 1922, 6; "Women Open Drive to Pass Maternity Bill," *New York Tribune*, February 20, 1922, 3; "Women Voice Plea for Duell Maternity Bill," *New York Tribune*, March 9, 1922, 3.

19 Miller had never been especially enthused to be governor; he'd been dragooned into it by the state party and always had an eye on returning to corporate law in order to support his huge family, as he lamented repeatedly in his *Recollections*.

20 "Miller Decries Polls of Public Sentiment," *New York Times*, March 9, 1922, 17.

21 "Women Withdraw Support from Sheppard-Towner Bill," *Christian Science Monitor*, March 2, 1922, 8.

22 Frederick Davenport, "What Governor Miller Has Done," *New York Times*, April 23, 1922, 97.

23 In short, Miller and friends ran hard on a constitutionalist platform, emphasizing states' rights and law-and-order prohibition, as long as the latter was part of the text of the Constitution (which Miller conceded he disagreed should be the case). In addition to running on competence, as he had been a fairly popular, fairly successful former governor, Al Smith made Prohibition enforcement a campaign issue, though his allies also made note of Miller's Sheppard-Towner position. *PCSR*, 97–98, 281n12.

24 I side with scholars who suggest continuity in Smith's ideas and actions. See *PCSR*, esp. 106–107, 293n99; Douglas B. Craig, *After Wilson: The Struggle for the Democratic Party, 1920–1934* (Chapel Hill: University of North Carolina Press, 1992; Robert K. Murray, *The 103rd Ballot: Democrats and the Disaster in Madison Square Garden* (New York: Harper & Row, 1976); Louis Zucarello, "The Political Thought of Alfred Smith" (PhD diss., Fordham University, 1970). For an interpretation seeing Smith as more consistently progressive until a switch at the end of his political career, Robert A. Slayton, *Empire Statesman: Rise and Redemption of Al Smith* (New York: Free Press, 2001). On Smith's remaking of

the New York court to uphold progressive state legislation, see William E. Nelson, *The Legalist Reformation: Law, Politics, and Ideology in New York, 1920–1980* (Chapel Hill: University of North Carolina Press, 2001), 13–91. The unfamiliarity of later observers to progressive federalism is arguably why Smith, although perfectly comprehensible in his own time, has puzzled some later, especially progressive writers, who struggled to understand how he could seem so progressive in state politics and conservative in federal ones.

25 Al Smith, "Speech Recommending Passage by the Senate of Bill Providing the State's Share of Appropriation for the Promotion of Welfare and Hygiene of Maternity and Infancy," May 4, 1923, *Public Papers of Alfred E. Smith* Albany, NY: J. B. Lyon, 1924), 213, hereafter cited as *PPAS*.

26 See introduction, note 5.

27 Chepaitis, "The First Federal Social Welfare Measure," 271.

28 *JS NJ*, 1922, 20; *JS NJ*, 1922, 503–504; *MA NJ*, 1922, 753.

29 "Sheppard Towner Veto Message," March 14, 1922, printed in *MA NJ*, 1922, 939.

30 *JS NJ*, 1922, 805–806.

31 On Edwards's federalism in the context of Prohibition, see *PCSR*, 87–94, 112, 144, 156–158.

32 *JH PA*, 1923, 2321.

33 Henry Adams, *John Randolph* (Boston: Houghton Mifflin, 1883), 281–283; *PCSR*, 76.

34 Maeve Glass, "These United States" (PhD diss., Princeton University, 2016).

35 In response to *Hammer v. Dagenhart*, which blocked congressional bans on shipping (but not manufacturing) of child-labor-made goods across state lines made as a way to both preserve federalism while avoiding a "race to the bottom," Massachusetts legislators initially endorsed a federal amendment to overturn it and proposed federal taxation of goods by abusive labor. In other words, they called for the solution that the federal government would employ before *Bailey v. Drexel Furniture* (1922) subsequently blocked that. *JS MA*, 1919, 267. On *Hammer* and *Drexel*, see chapter 1, notes 54–55. This would change in 1925, with state legislators turning on the child-labor amendment by huge margins (1–33 in the senate) following a failed popular referendum. See W. A. Robinson, "Advisory Referendum in Massachusetts," *American Political Science Review* 19 (1925): 69–73; *JS MA*, 1925, 245.

36 *JS MA*, 1920, 893; *JH MA*, 1920, 1151.

37 Robert Ferrell, *The Presidency of Calvin Coolidge* (Lawrence: University Press of Kansas, 1998), 11. For a further catalog of Coolidge's progressive sympathies in state government, see also James R. Rogers, "Silent Cal Speaks," Law & Liberty, June 8, 2021, https://lawliberty.org/book-review/silent-cal-speaks/.

38 Calvin Coolidge, "Inaugural Address," January 8, 1920, in *Addresses and Messages to the General Court, Proclamations, Official Addresses, Correspondence, and Statements of His Excellency Governor Calvin Coolidge* (n.p.: Commonwealth of Massachusetts, 1920), 154, 1; Robert Ferrell, *The Presidency of Calvin Coolidge* (Lawrence: University Press of Kansas, 1998), 11.

39 Chepaitis, "First Federal Social Welfare Measure," 171–173.

40 Channing H. Cox, "Inaugural Address," January 5, 1921, in *Addresses and Messages to the General Court, Proclamations, Official Addresses, Correspondence, and Statements of His Excellency Governor Channing H. Cox* (n.p.: Commonwealth of Massachusetts, 1924), 1.

41 Cox, "Inaugural Address," 32.

42 "Sheppard Towner Bill Is Debated," *Christian Science Monitor*, February 21, 1922, 11. On the debate held at the lecture hall of the Boston Public Library, see "Sheppard Towner Law Is Discussed," *Christian Science Monitor*, February 11, 1922, 11.

43 "Women's Groups to Return to Capitol Soon," *Boston Globe*, March 27, 1922, 11; "Sheppard Towner Bill Is Debated."

44 Wilson, *Politics of Maternalism*, 48; Chepaitis, "The First Federal Social Welfare Measure," 73.

45 The senate would similarly endorse the plan; Senator Parkhurst's motion to reconsider failed, 4–21, though unfortunately no roll call was taken. *JS MA*, 1922, 379. "Sheppard Towner Act Effort Fails," *Christian Science Monitor*, March 11, 1922, 3.

46 *JH MA*, 1922, 382–383, 400–401.

47 J. Weston Allen, "Constitutional Law — Sheppard Towner Maternity and Infancy Act," *Official Opinions of the Attorney General of the Commonwealth of Massachusetts*, vol. 6: *1921–1922* (n.p.: Commonwealth of Massachusetts, n.d.), 492–507. Following citations are to the reprinting of that opinion within the *JH MA*, 1922.

48 Allen, "Constitutional Law," in *JH MA*, 1922, 873–874.

49 Allen, 874.

50 Allen, 874. Emphasis added.

51 Allen, 878.

52 Allen, 873.

53 Allen, 875–876.

54 Allen, 878. For a similar assessment of Hamilton's thought, see chapter 2, note 15.

55 Allen, 879.

56 Allen, 882.

57 Allen, 881

58 *JH MA*, 1922, 948–949; *JS MA*, 1922, 770–771. Michael Greve observes how striking it was for Massachusetts, as an institution, to resist this, since the economic and political logic arguably points to states receiving additional power from such issues. Michael Greve, *The Upside-Down Constitution* (Cambridge, MA: Harvard University Press, 2012), 247–248.

59 Wilson, *Politics of Maternalism*, 63; Stanley Lemons, "The Sheppard Towner Act: Progressivism in the 1920s," *Journal of American History* 55 (1969): 783–784. Chepaitis says Beck promised WJCC activist Cornelia Bryce, the wife of Pennsylvania governor Gifford Pinchot, that he would offer a vigorous defense.

Chepaitis, "First Federal Social Welfare Measure," 179. However, Congressman Beck would vigorously condemn efforts to resurrect the bill in 1929 and 1931. It may not have been declared unconstitutional by a court—ironically because of his efforts—but he added that did not stop legislators from blocking a bill they believed violated states' rights (286, 315). Hostility to Sheppard-Towner would certainly seem closer to the views expressed in his own constitutional treatise. See James M. Beck, *The Constitution of the United States* (New York: George H. Doran, 1928). On Beck's role defending laws he privately found unconstitutional (specifically Sheppard-Towner and the tax on child-labor goods), see Paul D. Moreno, *The American State from the Civil War to the New Deal* (New York: Cambridge University Press, 2013), 181, 187.

60 Chepaitis, "First Federal Social Welfare Measure," 184, 200. The ten states were Arizona, Arkansas, Colorado, Delaware, Indiana, Kentucky, Minnesota, Ohio, Pennsylvania, and Virginia. Pennsylvania filed a separate brief distinguishing the coercive power of the federal government blocked in the child-labor cases (*Hammer* and *Drexel*).

61 "Question of State Right Raised by Massachusetts in School Bill," *Reno Evening Gazette*, November 18, 1922, 5; Wickard v. Filburn, 317 U.S. 111 (1942); U.S. v. Lopez, 514 U.S. 549 (1995).

62 Cox, "Inaugural Address.".

63 *JH NH*, 1921, 604; *JS NH*, 1921, 93.

64 "Describes Aim of Sheppard-Towner," *Portsmouth Herald*, March 10, 1923, 6.

65 "House Kills Bill to Bar Maternity Aid," *PH*, April 11, 1923, 2; "Legislature to Adjourn Friday," *Portsmouth Herald*, May 2, 1923, 5; "Anti-Maternity Bill Dies in N.H. House," *Boston Globe*, April 11, 1923, 15.

66 *JH NH*, 1923, 599; *JS NH*, 1923, 270–271.

67 "House Would Tax Raw Material. . . . Sheppard Towner Bill Still an Issue Regardless of Opposition," *Portsmouth Herald*, March 31, 1923, 2.

68 Others believed the court's new conservative personnel were likely to strike the bill down, however. "Conference Called to Fight Wage Cut," *Wisconsin State Journal*, April 10, 1923, 5.

69 Duane Lockard, *New England State Politics* (Princeton, NJ: Princeton University Press, 1959), 47–65.

70 Daniel Beland, *Social Security: History and Politics from the New Deal to the Privatization Debate* (Lawrence: University Press of Kansas, 2005), 99–100.

71 "Some Fight and Others Welcome Maternity Act," *Bridgeport* (CT) *Telegram*, May 4, 1923, 11.

72 *JH VT*, 1925, 284–285. The vote was 195–44 in the house and a final voice vote in the senate, with 22–6 and 26–2 votes beforehand. *JS VT*, 1925, 147–149. The appropriation was a closer vote, however. *JH VT*, 1925, 453–454.

73 H.B. 878, in *JS CT*, 1923, 1210; *JH CT*, 1923, 1197.

74 Lemons, "The Sheppard Towner Act," 783.

75 Sean Beienburg, "The States-Rights, Anti-Klan Environmentalist Progressive: Constitutional and Political Thought of Maine's Governor Percival Baxter," pa-

per presented at the Annual Meeting of the New England Political Science Association, Portsmouth, New Hampshire, April 19–21, 2018.

76 "The Sheppard Towner Bill: Remarks of Franklin Payson Before the Governor and Council," June 26, 1922; and Letter from Henry L. Shattuck, June 27, 1922, folder 45, PBP. On *Hammer* and *Drexel*, see chapter 1, notes 54–55.

77 He did veto a state bounty on seagulls on the grounds that it put the state in conflict with the federal government's signing of the Migratory Bird Treaty. Maine Leg. Rec. 1377–1378 (1921).

78 John Stuart Mill, "*On Liberty*," in *J.S. Mill: On Liberty and Other Writings* (Cambridge: Cambridge University Press, 1989), 96–100.

79 Percival Baxter, "Inaugural Address," January 4, 1923, Maine Leg. R. 20–21 (1923).

80 Baxter, "Inaugural Address 1923," 35.

81 Maine Leg. Rec. 311–312 (1931).

82 For Baxter's firm insistence that his lands be kept out of federal hands, see Maine Leg. Rec. 75–76 (1939). Baxter was not alone in this; I found several other Maine state sovereignty protests regarding cooperating with the federal government on the topic of nature parks, including not only jurisdiction but the maintenance of roads and forests. See, for example, Maine Leg. Rec. 169–170, 235–238 (1933); and Maine Leg. Rec. 840–848 (1935).

83 For discussion of his angry tirades explaining the interruption of his giving pattern until he was assured of state control, see Beienburg, "The Constitutional and Political Thought of Maine's Governor Percival Baxter."

84 "Government Maternity Aid," *Kennebec* (ME) *Journal*, July 18, 1922. Emphasis added.

85 "Inaugural Address 1923," 35–36.

86 Maine Leg. Rec. 263 (1923).

87 Maine Leg. Rec. 265 (1923).

88 Maine Leg. Rec. 460–461, 279 (1923); "Woman Legislator Wins First Battle: Helps Carry Maternity Act in Maine House," *Boston Globe*, March 1, 1923, 9.

89 Maine Leg. Rec. 266 (1923).

90 Maine Leg. Rec. 267.

91 Maine Leg. Rec. 264–265.

92 Maine Leg. Rec. 267.

93 Maine Leg. Rec. 269.

94 "Southern States Lead in Taking Advantage of the Sheppard-Towner Bill," *Portsmouth Herald*, July 5, 1923, 7. See also "New England Slow to Accept Plan to Aid Mothers," *Bridgeport* (CT) *Telegram*, December 13, 1923, 8; Charles S. Groves, "Find Mothers Eager for Federal Advice," *Boston Globe*, June 24, 1923, 72.

95 Maine Leg. Rec. 271 (1923).

96 Maine Leg. Rec., 265–279.

97 *Annual Report to Congress of the Federal Board for Vocational Education*, vol. 5 (Washington, DC: Government Printing Office, 1921), 325–336, https://books

.google.com/books?id=UCwTAAAAIAAJ&printsec=frontcover&source=ghs _atb#v=onepage&q&f=false. Connecticut, Illinois, Kansas, Louisiana, Massachusetts, Rhode Island, and Vermont were the others refusing Sheppard-Towner.

98 Maine Leg. Rec. 459–460 (1923).

99 "Sheppard-Towner Veto Message," March 22, 1923, in Maine Leg. Rec. 638–639 (1923). Baxter did not veto the state's participation in the Industrial Rehabilitation Act. Maine Leg. Rec. 807, 841 [1921]).

100 Daniel Carpenter, *The Forging of Bureaucratic Autonomy: Reputations, Networks, and Policy Innovation in Executive Agencies, 1862–1928* (Princeton, NJ: Princeton University Press, 2001).

101 Kelley only succeeded in annoying the *Kennebec Journal*, the local paper that doubled as the legislative printer and was not pleased by her insinuation that anyone against federal control therefore condoned the death of babies. Florence Kelley, "Letter to the Editor"; and unsigned editorial response, "Is Maine So Poorly Off?," August 8, 1922, 6; Kelley, "Letter to the Editor"; and unsigned editorial, "That Sheppard Towner Bill," August 28, 1922, 6; Wilson, *Politics of Maternalism*, 58–59. Kelley would become a lightning rod in Maine's 1927 debates. For the comments of Dr. Anna Rude of the Children's Bureau, see "42 States Now Doing Sheppard-Towner Work," *Santa Fe New Mexican*, October 5, 1922, 6.

102 Maine Leg. Rec. 755 (1923). Pinkham would offer a few more words, grumbling that Baxter's inaugural address had offered the legislature the choice, which he had now overridden. Insinuating fickleness on top of treason, she alleged that "it is evident that something has happened since that time which has caused the governor to change his mind."

103 Maine Leg. Rec. 1001 (1925).

104 "Will Save Babies—Unconstitutional," *Boston Globe*, April 22, 1923, 67.

105 "New Friend of States Rights," *Goshen Daily Democrat*, August 7, 1922, 4; "Maine against Paternalism," *Indianapolis Star*, August 7, 1922, 6.

106 Both Baxter's note and Borah's response are in folder 45, PBP.

107 Massachusetts v. Mellon; Frothingham v. Mellon, 262 U.S. 447 (1923).

108 Miller, *Recollections*, 27. So important was this case's precedent, in fact, to the development of the New Deal that Barry Cushman sardonically includes it as part of his mock indictment of the Four Horsemen as a secret cabal for progressivism. Such cases, he cracks, proved that they were all "closet liberals. It appears that they struck a reactionary pose in celebrated cases in order to retain the good graces of the conservative sponsors to whom they owed their positions and whose social amenities they continued to enjoy." Barry Cushman, "Secret Lives of the Four Horsemen," *Virginia Law Review* 83 (1997): 562–565. A Sutherland biographer argues that "perhaps no other single decision in the Court's history has been fraught with such destructive implications for the idea of limited government." Joel F. Paschal, *Mr. Justice Sutherland: A Man against the State* (Princeton, NJ: Princeton University Press, 1951), 149. See also David Currie, "The Constitution in the Supreme Court: 1921–1930," *Duke Law Journal* (1985): 124. *Flast v. Cohen*, 392 U.S. 83 (1968), carved out a controversial exception for church-state is-

sues, but later cases have continued to suggest *Frothingham* remains controlling outside that narrow situation.

109 Chepaitis, "First Federal Social Welfare Measure," 272.

110 *Frothingham*, 485.

111 Maine Leg. Rec. 424–425, 700–703, 998–1011 (1925).

112 Maine Leg. Rec. 425.

113 Maine Leg. Rec. 701.

114 Maine Leg. Rec. 1006.

115 Maine Leg. Rec. 1001.

116 Maine Leg. Rec. 425, 703; Maine Leg. Rec. 1010–1011. The technical vote was to accept Fred Greenleaf's minority committee report (to reject the bill accepting Sheppard-Towner). Baxter's position actually did somewhat better among Democrats, as only five of the twenty-seven members of the Democratic opposition voted to accept the bill, compared to thirty-six Republicans voting to accept Sheppard-Towner and sixty-seven Republicans against it.

117 Maine Leg. Rec. 1033–1034 (1925).

118 Ralph Owen Brewster, "Inaugural Address," Maine Leg. Rec. 52–53 (1927).

119 Maine Leg. Rec. 637–638 (1927).

120 Maine Leg. Rec. 630–644. On the contemporary jurisprudence rejecting "class legislation" as beyond police powers, see Gillman, *Constitution Besieged*.

121 "Miss Gail Laughlin, A Suffrage Pioneer," *New York Times*, March 14, 1952, 23. The *New York Times* misstates the year of her entry into the legislature.

122 Maine Leg. Rec. 648–649 (1927).

123 Maine Leg. Rec. 650.

124 House roll call: Maine Leg. Rec. 651; senate voice vote, Maine Leg. Rec. 899.

125 See, e.g., "Repeal Home Building Bond Law in Senate," *Bismarck Tribune*, February 16, 1923, 1; "Funding Schools Debt Is Passed," *Sandusky* (OH) *Star Journal*, March 29, 1923, 13.

126 Moehling and Thomasson, "Political Economy of Saving Mothers."

127 Chepaitis, "The First Federal Social Welfare Measure," 222–229.

128 "Four Million Women Rally to Support of Bill to Aid Mothers," *Chicago Tribune*, October 22, 1926, 31.

129 Harvey, *Votes without Leverage*.

130 "Debate Federal Aid Proposed in Bills," *New York Times*, February 2, 1926, 13.

131 Chepaitis, "First Federal Social Welfare Measure," 250–270, 338–361. Even the AMA branches in rural areas turned against it. "Sheppard Towner Act Is Condemned," *Charleston* (WV) *Daily Mail*, May 25, 1926, 2.

132 Lemons argues the Woman Patriots were instrumental in reversing DAR, which had supported the bill in 1921 but firmly opposed it in 1926. Lemons, "The Sheppard Towner Act," 784–785; Wilson, *Politics of Maternalism*, 136–137.

133 "Federal Maternity and Hygiene," *New York Times*, January 18, 1927, 24, quoted in Chepaitis, "First Federal Social Welfare Measure," 245.

134 "Petticoats and Paternalism," *Los Angeles Times*, October 6, 1924, A4.

135 "Approaching the End of State Governments," *Chicago Tribune*, March 21, 1924, 8.

136 Chepaitis, "First Federal Social Welfare Measure," 250 270, 338–361.

137 Calvin Coolidge, *Foundations of the Republic* (Freeport, NY: Books for Libraries Press, 1926), reprinted in Thomas B. Silver, *Coolidge and the Historians* (Durham, NC: Carolina Academic Press, 1982), 27.

138 "Full Text of President Coolidge's Memorial Day Address at Arlington," *New York Times*, May 31, 1925, 2, quoted in Robert Post, "Federalism in the Taft Court Era: Can It Be Revived?" *Duke Law Journal* 51 (2002):1545. The Calvin Coolidge Presidential Foundation titles this speech "The Reign of Law," May 30, 1925, accessed July 9, 2023, https://coolidgefoundation.org/resources/the-reign -of-law/; "Curb Favored on Federal Aid," *Los Angeles Times*, December 29, 1924, 6; Chepaitis, "First Federal Social Welfare Measure," 216–217.

139 Coolidge, "Memorial Day Address at Arlington."

140 Skocpol, *Protecting Soldiers and Mothers*, 513–514; Chepaitis, "First Federal Social Welfare Measure," 24.

141 Chepaitis, 234.

142 Chepaitis, 223.

143 Chepaitis, 236, 275.

144 "'Rid Us of Reed,' Is Cry of Women in Missouri," *Baltimore Sun*, July 7, 1922, 1.

145 Chepaitis, "First Federal Social Welfare Measure," 275.

146 Chepaitis, 179.

147 These two are not listed as flipping in Chepaitis's list but did so. Borah and Moses were absent during part of the summer session and did not vote against the final bill, but they remained opponents and would be again during later renewal efforts. 69.2 Cong. Rec. 1113 (1927).

148 Chepaitis, "First Federal Social Welfare Measure," 275. Ransdall, also of Louisiana, contributed to the filibuster but does not appear in the list of opponents (236).

149 *JH MI*, 1927, 367; *JS MI*, 1927, 185. Michigan's Prohibition protests always avoided making them. For examples of state memorials endorsing federal grants, see Oklahoma's 1929 request for a federal Department of Education, or for various grants in 1931. *Acts OK*, 1929 (special session), 511–512; *Acts OK*, 1931, 386–387, 392–394.

150 Passage had been 32–1 and 66–15. *JH OK*, 1923, 1553; *JS OK*, 1923, 776. See, for example, H.C.R. 5, in *Acts OK*, 1929 (special session), 512, requesting more federal aid and a department of education; S.C.R. 1, *Acts OK*, 1931, 386, asking for farm relief aid.

151 Chepaitis, "First Federal Social Welfare Measure," 241–245.

152 Chepaitis, 290, 304, 326, 336.

153 Chepaitis, 293–304, 312–313.

154 Lemons, "The Sheppard Towner Act," 785–786.

155 Abbot, "The Federal Government in Relation to Maternity and Infancy," 99; Lemons, "The Sheppard Towner Act," 786.

156 Moehling and Thomasson, "Political Economy of Saving Mothers," 97–100.

157 Lemons, "The Sheppard Towner Act," 781.

158 Some opponents of Sheppard-Towner did as well. For example, the editorial board of one small Texas paper printed excerpts of Texas state commissioner of

agriculture George Terrell agreeing that Sheppard-Towner, Smith-Lever, and all the other grants needed to go. Both the commissioner and the paper feared that, in addition to displaying a lack of constitutional fidelity by assuming "authority . . . [never given] in the original constitution or by amendment," such loose interpretation would culminate in federal control over schools. "A Plea for the Constitution," *Llano* (TX) *News*, April 15, 1926, 6.

159 Among later commentators, Lemons, for example, noted twenty-two programs, including militia support, highway-building, and various agricultural grants, to cast aspersion on the veracity of Tenth Amendment claims. Lemons, "The Sheppard Towner Act," 783–784. Moehling and Thomasson smirk at Connecticut's acceptance of funds for an airplane squadron but not Sheppard-Towner; at best, they argue, skeptics used it as convenient cover to block bills opposed by legislators' pet interest groups and, at worst, sought spiteful revenge on suffragists:

> Connecticut's appropriations committee declined Sheppard-Towner money as a matter of principle, but then voted to accept federal aid for an airplane squadron. . . . The inconsistencies of these states' responses to other federal grant programs and their stated opposition to Sheppard-Towner suggest that "states' rights" may have been just a convenient excuse to vote against a program that was unpopular with politically influential groups. For example, suffragists were in favor of the bill, so anti-suffragists were opposed and organized early against it. (80–81)

David Greenberg's popular history of the Coolidge administration similarly ignores any effort to consider textual differences under the Constitution and charges Coolidge with hypocrisy, supporting grants-in-aid for road-building, for example, but demanding Sheppard-Towner be phased out. David Greenberg, *Calvin Coolidge* (New York: Times Books, 2006), 74–75.

160 Skocpol, *Protecting Soldiers and Mothers*, 495.

161 Chepaitis, "First Federal Social Welfare Measure," 180.

162 Wilson, *Politics of Maternalism*, 139.

163 Agriculture and transportation had longer pedigrees than vocational training under the Commerce Clause (see constitutional discussion of infrastructure in chapter 1, notes 26–28 and esp. note 29) though I did not find any legislators make this particular distinction.

164 Many state officials demanded various forms of aid but complained if any conditions were attached; state coercion arguments, whether constitutional or merely prudential, appeared to have wider support than a narrower Madisonian view of the taxing power, which would suggest the federal government was authorized to do neither. See, for example, H.B. 188 in North Dakota, in *JS ND*, 1925, 776; *JH ND*, 1925, 672; *Laws ND*, 1925, 309–310; Samuel Aaron Baker, "Inaugural Address," January 12, 1925, in *Messages and Proclamations of the Governors of the State of Missouri*, 268.

165 Moehling and Thomasson, "Political Economy," 83–84; Chepaitis, "First Federal Social Welfare Measure," 166–167.

166 Grace Abbot, "The Federal Government in Relation to Maternity and Infancy,"

Annals of the American Academy of Political and Social Science 151 (1930): 99; Lemons, "The Sheppard Towner Act," 786.

167 Moehling and Thomasson, "Political Economy of Saving Mothers," 93.
168 Chepaitis, "First Federal Social Welfare Measure," 229, 284.
169 Moehling and Thomasson, "Political Economy of Saving Mothers," 94.
170 "Minority Government Must Be Understood by Women," *Syracuse* (NY) *Herald*, November 4, 1924, 5.
171 Moehling and Thomasson, "Political Economy of Saving Mothers," 75–103; William E. Leuchtenberg, *The Perils of Prosperity, 1914–1932* (Chicago: University of Chicago Press, [1958] 1993), 161.
172 Illinois's rejection is an exception: it has been attributed to the powerful Illinois Medical Society, which had assailed the bill in Congress and was more active than the AMA. Chepaitis, "First Federal Social Welfare Measure," 168.
173 Moehling and Thomasson, "Political Economy of Saving Mothers," 92.
174 Chepaitis, "First Federal Social Welfare Measure," 340–341; Moehling and Thomason, "Political Economy of Saving Mothers," 82, 92.
175 Skocpol, *Protecting Soldiers and Mothers*, 509–510. Some of the newer works on the New Deal have attempted to argue that the relevant veto points shaping the legislation were not as animated by racial strategy as sometimes argued. See chapter 6, note 186.
176 Maine Leg. Rec. 701 (1925).
177 "South for Maternity Bill," *Washington Post*, December 19, 1922, 3.
178 Kimberly Johnson, *Governing the American State: Congress and the New Federalism, 1877–1929* (Princeton, NJ: Princeton University Press, 2007), 143. The only coverage of the bill that I could find in black newspapers made no acknowledgment of legal or constitutional issues. Like most white editors' coverage, the treatment was almost entirely policy based, simply saying that the bill was "an attempt to solve a situation which concerns very closely the Negro race," and observing without comment that forty-three states had participated so far. "Sheppard Towner Act and the Negro," *New York Amsterdam News*, March 31, 1926, 4.
179 Arguably, these big states could be said to be playing a long strategic game, but the point remains that they feared the alteration of precedents, not any immediate rational decisions.
180 Richard Bensel, *Sectionalism and American Political Development, 1880–1980* (Madison: University of Wisconsin Press, 1987).
181 See introduction, note 48.
182 See introduction, note 48.
183 The classic discussion of the status-quo bias of disorganized, nonpartisan politics is of course V. O. Key Jr. with Alexander Heard, *Southern Politics in State and Nation* (New York: Alfred A. Knopf, 1949).
184 See also the similar role of the Association Against the Prohibition Amendment (AAPA), an anti-Prohibition interest group that fulfilled a similar function and utilized similar tactics in keeping Prohibition a live issue at the states even though it had seemingly been resolved as a federal controversy. See *PCSR*.

Chapter 4. The Liberty of Contract: Federal Intervention in State Economic Policy

1 See John S. Goff, *George W. P. Hunt and his Arizona* (Pasadena: Socio Technical Publications, 1973), 206; Sean Beienburg, "Arizona: Born Angry," Constituting America, accessed May 10, 2023, https://constitutingamerica.org/arizona-born -angry-guest-essayist-sean-beienburg/.

2 David R. Berman, *George Hunt: Arizona's Crusading Seven Term Governor* (Tucson: University of Arizona Press, 2015), 9. Michael Cunniff, Hunt's floor leader in the Arizona legislature, was considered, along with Hunt, the leader of the very progressive state's progressive movement, but shared Hunt's conservative views on federalism. Sean Beienburg and Aaron Kushner, "Michael Cunniff: Conservative Progressivism, Federalism, and the Founding of Arizona," *American Political Thought* (forthcoming).

3 See, e.g., his nine-page letter to Calvin Coolidge, noting that Democrats, Republicans, and Coolidge alike all claimed to believe in states' rights. "Letter from George W. P. Hunt to President Calvin Coolidge," April 9, 1926, ASU Library PRISM. On Hunt's commitment to states' rights more broadly, see Berman, *George Hunt*, 9, 85, 171, 178, 221; and Goff, *George W. P. Hunt and his Arizona*, 244–245, 266–267.

4 Hunt to Oklahoma governor William Murray, November 6, 1931, quoted in Goff, *George W. P. Hunt*, 244. For arguments why this is the only legitimate method of constitutional change, see Keith E. Whittington, *Constitutional Interpretation: Textual Meaning, Original Intent, and Judicial Review* (Lawrence: University Press of Kansas, 1999); Randy Barnett, *Restoring the Lost Constitution: The Presumption of Liberty* (Princeton, NJ: Princeton University Press, 2004); Ilan Wurman, *A Debt against the Living: A Beginner's Guide to Originalism* (New York: Cambridge University Press, 2017); Sean Beienburg, *Prohibition, the Constitution, and States' Rights* (Chicago: University of Chicago Press, 2019), 83–84. For an account showing originalism's deep roots in American constitutionalism, see Johnathan O'Neill, *Originalism in Law and Politics: A Constitutional History* (Baltimore: Johns Hopkins University Press, 2007).

5 Hunt to Virginia governor John Pollard, no date, quoted in Goff, *George W. P. Hunt*, 245.

6 Quoted in William E. Forbath, *Law and the Shaping of the American Labor Movement* (Cambridge, MA: Harvard University Press, 1991), 80.

7 Proposition 104, Section 8: "No law shall be declared void by any court, because in the opinion of the court such law may be opposed to the general intent or spirit of this Constitution, or to public policy, but laws may be declared void only because of some express provision of this Constitution or necessary implication from such express provision."

8 Brutus, no. 11, January 31, 1788, *The Founders' Constitution*, University of Chicago Press, http://press-pubs.uchicago.edu/founders/documents/a3_2_1s19.html: "In their decisions they will not confine themselves to any fixed or established

rules, but will determine, according to what appears to them, the reason and spirit of the constitution."

9 Brutus 11 and 12.

10 Hunt to Murray, quoted in Goff, *George W. P. Hunt*, 244.

11 The Supreme Court confirmed the circuit decision in *Truax v. Raich*, 239 U.S. 33 (1915), with only Justice McReynolds in dissent (for jurisdictional reasons). Even he conceded "that the challenged act is invalid I think admits of no serious doubt." The Court's opinion officially invoked an equal protection violation but one in the service of *both* federal immigration law—that Arizona was infringing on foreign policy—and the ability to pursue a living, citing the formative liberty-of-contract cases *Allgeyer v. Louisiana*, 165 U.S. 578 (1897); and *Coppage v. Kansas*, 236 U.S. 1 (1915); both of discussed at length further in this chapter. On labor and racial exclusion, see Paul Frymer, *Black and Blue: African Americans, Labor Unions, and the Decline of the Democratic Party* (Princeton, NJ: Princeton University Press, 2007).

12 "Address to the Legislature," January 11, 1915, reprinted in *Arizona Legislative Journal*, 1915, 15.

13 "States Rights Is Hunt's Cry," *Los Angeles Times*, January 12, 1915, 4; "George W. P. Hunt's Position on State's Rights," *Arizona Labor Journal*, April 11, 1925, 1.

14 Berman, *George Hunt*, 84–85.

15 Only Justice Harlan (I) accepted incorporation of the Bill of Rights to the states via the Fourteenth Amendment in *Twining v. New Jersey*, 211 U.S. 78 (1908). *Chicago, Burlington, and Quincy Railroad Co. v. Chicago* (166 U.S. 226 [1897]) had implicitly required states to honor eminent domain protections (though the decision plausibly rested on procedural grounds), but it would be almost three decades from that case before the court would explicitly incorporate any of the enumerated protections of the Bill of Rights. Originalists today are in general agreement that the Fourteenth Amendment applies the Bill of Rights to the states. But whether the Fourteenth amendment's original meaning also protected such economic rights against state restriction, or largely left that sphere to state discretion, is widely contested. For the states' rights position accepting incorporation but largely rejecting "unenumerated" rights, see Kurt T. Lash, The *Fourteenth Amendment and the Privileges and Immunities of American Citizenship* (New York: Cambridge University Press, 2014). For the fundamental economic-rights position, see Randy E. Barnett and Evan Bernick, *The Original Meaning of the Fourteenth Amendment: Its Letter and Spirit* (Cambridge, MA: Harvard University Press, 2021). For an originalist treatment rejecting incorporation, see Ilan Wurman, *The Second Founding: An Introduction to the Fourteenth Amendment* (New York: Cambridge University Press, 2020).

16 In re Debs, 158 U.S. 564 (1895); Daniel R. Ernst, *Lawyers against Labor: From Individual Rights to Corporate Liberalism* (Urbana: University of Illinois Press, 1995), 76–77.

17 Forbath, *Law and the Shaping of the American Labor Movement*, 59–97, 158–166. The term appears to have been popularized, if not coined, by Altgeld in his

1895 address discussed later in this chapter. As will also be discussed, Norris-La Guardia also made yellow dog contracts unenforceable in federal court.

18 For a compilation of such works, see David N. Mayer, "The Myth of 'Laissez-Faire' Constitutionalism during the *Lochner* Era," *Hastings Constitutional Law Quarterly* 36 (2009): 217–222.

19 Richard White, *Railroaded: The Transcontinentals and the Making of Modern America* (New York: W. W. Norton, 2012).

20 At the national level, various court-curbing measures were floated but went nowhere due to the same fundamental faith in the Court. William G. Ross, *A Muted Fury: Populists, Progressives, and Labor Unions Confront the Courts, 1890–1937* (Princeton, NJ: Princeton University Press, 1994). As Stephen Engel has suggested in a modification of this argument, court-curbing measures, especially the more credible efforts, increasingly were the product of partisan efforts to correct and capture the Court for a particular constitutional vision rather than crush it entirely. Stephen Engel, *American Politicians Confront the Court: Opposition Politics and Changing Responses to Judicial Power* (Cambridge: Cambridge University Press, 2011). See also introduction, note 31.

21 For the text of the correspondence between Altgeld and Cleveland, see Harry Barnard, *Eagle Forgotten: The Life of John Peter Altgeld* (Indianapolis, IN: Bobbs Merrill, 1938), 291–310.

22 *JH IL*, 1895, 47–48.

23 Barnard, *Eagle Forgotten*, 216–234.

24 Barnard, 374–385; Waldo R. Browne, *Altgeld of Illinois: A Record of His Life and Work* (New York: B. W. Huebsch, 1924), 268–297.

25 See chapter 1.

26 Barnard, *Eagle Forgotten*, 385–387.

27 Printed in *The Counsellor: The New York Law School Law Journal* 5 (1895): 38.

28 Barnard, *Eagle Forgotten*, 328–329.

29 John Tanner, "Inaugural Address," January 11, 1897, in *JS IL*, 1897, 174–175.

30 However, as previous commentators have noted, Kansas Populists varied widely. Few were either reactionary agrarians or protosocialists; most instead fit within the broad contours of American thought. Within that broad range there was a left flank seeing railroads as simply one more case for a more active government and a right flank viewing the railroads as exceptional utilities (built with eminent domain and land-grant subsidies) within a broadly anti-monopolist, free-market, classical-liberal framework. Thomas Frank, "The Leviathan with Tentacles: Railroads in the Minds of Kansas Populists," *Western Historical Quarterly* 20 (1989): 37–54.

31 Lorenzo D. Lewelling, "Inaugural Address," January 17, 1893, in *JS KS*, 1893, 57–58.

32 Chicago, Milwaukee, and St. Paul Railway Company v. Minnesota, 134 U.S. 418 (1890).

33 *JH KS*, 1895, 46.

34 O. Gene Clanton, *A Common Humanity: Kansas Populism and the Battle for Justice and Equality, 1854–1903* (Manhattan, KS: Sunflower University Press, 2004), 130–138.

35 Nearly all house Populists reluctantly agreed to back this, although some insisted on still registering protest statements in the *Journal* next to their aye votes.

36 On the so-called Greenlee Bill (H.B. 119), see *JH KS*, 1893, 488–491, 964–974; Clanton, *Common Humanity*, 136. On the Dunsmore Railroad bill, see H.B. 281, in *JH KS*, 1893, 323. Republicans then dominated the 1894 elections — but not by enough to retake the state senate, leading to another stalemate and a further delayed commission law. Eventually, in 1898, Kansas legislators would create a "special commission court" that would perform many of the features of the commission, but the state supreme court overturned it. Clanton, *Common Humanity*, 201–215.

37 *JH KS*, 1895, 42.

38 US Congress, Senate, "Meaning of the Word 'Conspiracy,' etc.," Letter from Samuel Gompers, 57th Cong., 1st Sess., March 21, 1902, Document 266.

39 *JH KS*, 1895, 43.

40 *JH KS*, 1895, 43–44; on nullification, see chapter 1, note 20

41 "Farewell Address," January 4, 1895, in *JH CO*, 1895, 61–62.

42 On Bryan's commitment to dual federalist states' rights, see Gerard Magliocca, *The Tragedy of William Jennings Bryan: Constitutional Law and the Politics of Backlash* (New Haven, CT: Yale University Press, 2011); and *PCSR*, 60n37.

43 See chapter 1, esp. note 70.

44 Letter to Rev. J. H. Twichell, February 16, 1905, in Gary Bloomfield and Michael Richards, eds., *Mark Twain, his Words, Wit, and Wisdom* (New York: Rowman & Littlefield, 2017), 230–231.

45 See chapter 1, notes 68-72.

46 "Letter to John Crawford Anderson," December 30, 1907, in Elting E. Morison, ed., *Letters of Theodore Roosevelt*, vol. 5 (Cambridge, MA: Harvard University Press, 1952), 878.

47 Theodore Roosevelt, "Letter to Senator Elmer Burkett," September 27, 1907, in Morison, *Letters of Theodore Roosevelt*, vol. 5, 810.

48 Melvin Urofsky, "State Courts and Protective Legislation during the Progressive Era: A Reevaluation," *Journal of American History* 72 (1985): 63–91.

49 Allgeyer v. Louisiana, 165 U.S. 583, 589.

50 For example, Michael McConnell and Nathan Chapman have distinguished this nineteenth-century version of "substantive due process," which they argue is not about fundamental rights but is instead closer to a separation-of-powers claim excluding pretextual law from the legislative power, from twentieth-century in-vocations of the doctrine for fundamental individual rights, arguing the latter is both ahistorical and privileges judicial policy-making to assess what is and is not fundamental. See Nathan S. Chapman and Michael McConnell, "Due Process as Separation of Powers," *Yale Law Journal* 121 (2012): 1672–1807. Matthew J. Franck similarly argues this variant should be understood as a form of procedural

due process. Matthew J. Franck, "What Happened to the Due Process Clause in the *Dred Scott* Case? The Continuing Confusion over 'Substance' versus 'Process,'" *American Political Thought* 4 (2015): 120–148. Ilan Wurman extends this argument, suggesting that many of these cases were actually either questions about delegation to *municipal* governments or federal commerce clause or contract cases, not "fundamental rights" limits on states. Ilan Wurman, "The Origins of Substantive Due Process," *University of Chicago Law Review* 87 (2020): 815–881.

51 *Buchanan v. Warley*, 245 U.S. 60 (1917), striking a mandatory residential segregation scheme on property-rights claims, and *Truax v. Raich* (1915), the Arizona 80 percent law case discussed prior, similarly applied liberty-of-contract jurisprudence as a catchall to strike unusual state legislation in situations where the Equal Protection Clause, for example, would seem more naturally applicable.

52 Paul v. Virginia, 75 U.S. 168 (1869); Lucas A. Powe, *The Supreme Court and the American Elite, 1789–2008* (Cambridge, MA: Harvard University Press, 2009), 166.

53 *Allgeyer*, 583.

54 Powe, *Supreme Court and the American Elite*, 167. See, for example, *Northwestern National Life Insurance Co. v. Riggs*, 203 U.S. 243 (1906); and Nutting v. Massachusetts, 183 U.S. 55 (1902), which vindicated an 1894 Massachusetts law punishing out-of-state insurance companies for unlawfully engaging in unlicensed insurance sales

55 In his first major speech on the courts since returning to the political fray, Roosevelt attacked *Lochner*. Ross, *A Muted Fury*, 132; Keith Whittington, "Congress Before the Lochner Court," *Boston University Law Review* 85 (2005): 821–822, 839–841. Victoria Nourse argues that Roosevelt, as much as anybody, helped popularize *Lochner* as a bogeyman. Victoria Nourse, "A Tale of Two *Lochners*: The Untold History of Substantive Due Process and the Idea of Fundamental Rights," *California Law Review* 97 (2000): 751–800, esp. 775. Roosevelt had been angry about *Lochner* at the time it was decided, writing letters to both Justice William Day and to the author of an *Atlantic* article ("Some Equivocal Rights of Labor)" decrying the decision, which Roosevelt claimed he had been recommending to his friends. Theodore Roosevelt, "Letter to George Alger," March 10, 1906, in Morison, *Letters of Roosevelt*, vol. 5, 188; Theodore Roosevelt, "Letter to William Day," January 11, 1908, in Morison, *Letters of Roosevelt*, vol. 6, 903–904.

56 Howard Gillman, *The Constitution Besieged: The Rise and Demise of Lochner Era Police Powers Jurisprudence* (Durham, NC: Duke University Press, 1993); Powe, *Supreme Court and the American Elite*, 168.

57 Holden v. Hardy, 169 U.S. 366 (1898).

58 Paul Kens, *Judicial Power and Reform Politics: The Anatomy of* Lochner v. New York (Lawrence: University Press of Kansas, 1990), 117, 205; Barry Cushman, "Lost Fidelities," *William and Mary Law Review* 41 (1999): 101n24.

59 It also echoed themes he had raised in his *Plessy* dissent, as will be discussed in the conclusion.

60 *Lochner*, 73–74.

61 *Lochner*, 74.

62 Theodore Roosevelt, "Fifth Annual Message," December 5, 1905, Miller Center, accessed July 9, 2023, https://millercenter.org/the-presidency/presidential-speeches/december-5-1905-fifth-annual-message.

63 Ellis v. United States, 206 U.S. 246 (1907); Cushman, "Lost Fidelities."

64 "Address to Albany Women," January 20, 1921, in Oversize 1, *NMP*.

65 For passed, see, e.g., H.B. 155 (enacting maximum factory hours) in *JH MD*, 1906, 695; chapter 108 (setting maximum hours for those treating coal), *Laws MT*, 1907, 260–61; H.B. 336 (setting maximum hours for telegraph operators), in *JH TX*, 1907, 1432; and H.B. 364 (maximum hours for other railroad employees), in *JH TX*, 1907, 1060; H.B. 517 (maximum hours on railroads), in *Laws IN*, 1907, 215; A.B. 42 (maximum hours for cement mixers), in *Laws NV*, 1909, 48; A.B. 76 (maximum hours legislation for surface support staff at mines), in *Laws NV*, 1911, 373; S.B. 47/chapter 95 (expanding the professions covered by a maximum-hours initiative), in *Laws CO*, 1913, 3–5. For considered, see, e.g., S.B. 25 (maximum weekly hours, passes committee but dies on calendar), in *JS MO*, 1907, 715; S.B. 257 (maximum street railcar hours) passes senate, in *JS IL*, 1913, 1001.

66 Muller v. Oregon, 208 U.S. 412 (1908).

67 *JS OR*, 1911, 405; *JH OR*, 1911, 784, 788.

68 H.B. 38, in *JH OR*, 1913, 23; *JS OR*, 1913, 519–521, 677, 713–714.

69 Bunting v. Oregon, 243 U.S. 426 (1917).

70 Post New Deal–scholarship has shown that the federal courts were far more likely to uphold than block state legislation and, with a few exceptions like *Lochner v. New York*, were genuinely "hands-off" in letting states organize their economies, rediscovering a point made by contemporary legal commentators at the time. For such scholarship, see Melvin I. Urofsky, "Myth and Reality: The Supreme Court and Protective Legislation in the Progressive Era," *Journal of Supreme Court History* (1983): 53–72; Urofsky, "State Courts"; Michael J. Phillips, *The Lochner Court, Myth and Reality: Substantive Due Process from the 1890s to the 1930s* (Westport, CT: Praeger, 2000). See also this chapter, note 65. For contemporary accounts observing a mostly hands-off court, see Charles Warren, "The Progressiveness of the United States Supreme Court," *Columbia Law Review* 13 (1913): 294–313; Walter F. Dodd, "Social Legislation and the Courts," *Political Science Quarterly* 28 (1913): 1–17; Ray A. Brown, "Due Process of Law, Police Power, and the Supreme Court," *Harvard Law Review* (1927): 943–968; Ray A. Brown, "Police Power: Legislation for Health and Personal Safety," *Harvard Law Review* 42 (1929): 866–898. Even work predating the *Lochner* revisionists often conceded their basic point. For example, in arguing for an aggressive federal judiciary, Theda Skocpol cites Elizabeth Brandeis saying courts blocked and/or scared away protection legislation, but this actually is just a reference to *Lochner* nestled within a concession that state courts did most of the work in striking protective legislation. Theda Skocpol, *Protecting Soldiers and Mothers: Political Origins of Social Policy in the United States* (Cambridge, MA: Harvard University Press, 1992), 238.

71 Dodd, "Social Legislation and the Courts," 5.

72 In this case, writing the opinion upholding the legislation helped launch the presidential hopes of state judge Alton Parker, the conservative Cleveland ally who was the Democratic nominee in 1904. Ironically, the campaigning Parker himself explained that he thought the issue in the decision was "exceedingly close" and thus criticized Roosevelt's attack on the federal judiciary. Nourse, "Tale of Two Lochners," 780–781.

73 Walter F. Dodd, "Growth of Judicial Power," *Political Science Quarterly* 24 (1909): 193–207, 198—though outside of New York, state courts' reputation for activism was perhaps similarly overstated. See Urofsky, "State Courts and Protective Legislation."

74 Jean Yarbrough, *Theodore Roosevelt and the American Political Tradition* (Lawrence: University Press of Kansas, 2012), 212, 216, 224. This antipathy also extended to supporters of the decision: in a 1905 letter to William Day criticizing *Lochner*, Roosevelt explained he would not nominate a friend of even his close ally Elihu Root since Root's friend backed *Jacobs*. See "Letter to Day"; this chapter, note 55.

75 William E. Nelson, *The Legalist Reformation: Law, Politics, and Ideology in New York, 1920–1980* (Chapel Hill: University of North Carolina Press, 2001), 13–91.

76 For efforts to distill the principle of skepticism of class legislation from these cases (rather than attributing the overturning of police-powers laws to caprice or laissez-faire fanaticism), see Gillman, *Constitution Besieged*; Gary D. Rowe, "Lochner Revisionism Revisited," *Law and Social Inquiry* 24 (1999): 221–252.

77 David E. Bernstein, *Rehabilitating Lochner: Defending Individual Rights against Progressive Reform* (Chicago: University of Chicago Press, 2011), 14–20.

78 Adkins v. Children's Hospital, 261 U.S. 525 (1923), 564.

79 The disappearance of these arguments for a half century are in part due to a sharp shift in legal discourse largely inaugurated by Theodore Roosevelt and implemented by his cousin Franklin. Victoria Nourse argues that *Lochner* era legal elites generally acknowledged that police powers trump over liberty-of-contract "rights," as was noted by Charles Warren and Ray Brown, but their weaker bullhorns could not compete with skilled presidents who raised and exaggerated the salience of a strong notion of rights in their political quests against it. FDR's justices and allied academics like Corwin would continue to embrace this framing of strong rights even while choosing different ones to prefer. Nourse, "A Tale of Two *Lochners*," 751–800.

80 Barry Cushman, "Doctrinal Synergies and Liberal Dilemmas: The Case of the Yellow Dog Contract," *Supreme Court Review* (1992): 238–239; George I. Lovell, *Legislative Deferrals: Statutory Ambiguity, Judicial Power, and American Democracy* (Cambridge: Cambridge University Press, 2003), 76–80.

81 Lovell, *Legislative Deferrals*, 76–80; Felix Frankfurter and Nathan Greene, *The Labor Injunction* (Gloucester, MA: Peter Smith, [1930] 1963), 146.

82 For reviews of these early state statutes and cases, see Frankfurter and Greene, *The Labor Injunction*, 146; Joel I. Seidman, *The Yellow Dog Contract* (Baltimore, MD: Johns Hopkins University Press, 1932), 22; Wesley Davis, "Constitutional-

ity of the Yellow Dog Contract Statute," *St. John's Law Review* 9 (1935): 462; Donald MacDonald, "The Constitutionality of Wisconsin's Statute Invalidating 'Yellow Dog' Contracts," *Wisconsin Law Review* 6 (1931): 888; and Forbath, *Law and the Shaping of the American Labor Movement*, 200–201. For the text of model yellow-dog contracts, see Seidman, *Yellow Dog Contract*, 23. For examples of state courts citing federal cases to strike down anti-yellow-dog laws, see, People (of New York) v. Marcus (1905) (citing *Lochner*), or State (of Wisconsin) ex. Rel Zillmer v. Kreutzberg (1902) (citing *Allgeyer*).

83 Adair v. United States, 208 U.S. 161 (1908); Coppage v. Kansas, 236 U.S. 1 (1915).
84 See note 51 above.
85 William R. Brock, *Welfare, Democracy, and the New Deal* (Cambridge: Cambridge University Press, 1988), 10, 22–27.
86 Frank Lowden, "Inaugural Address," January 8, 1917, in *JH IL*, 1917, 65.
87 Frederick Dozier Gardner, "First Biennial Address," January 10, 1919, in *Messages and Proclamations of the Governors of the State of Missouri*, vol. 11 (Columbia: State Historical Society of Missouri), 307.
88 Karen Orren, *Belated Feudalism: Labor, the Law, and Liberal Development in the United States* (Cambridge: Cambridge University Press, 1992).
89 John Witt, *The Accidental Republic* (Cambridge, MA: Harvard University Press, 2004), 11.
90 New York Central Railroad Company v. White, 243 U.S. 188 (1917), 197–200. See also the similarly unanimous companion case—also authored by Pitney—*Hawkins v. Bleakly*, 243 U.S. 210 (1917), which gave states wide latitude in establishing a burden of proof against employers in liability law. Note that Pitney wrote *Coppage*, the state yellow-dog case rooted in liberty of contract.
91 *First Employers Liability Cases (Howard v. Illinois Central Railway Co*, 204 U.S. 263 [1908]); *Second Employers Liability Cases* (Mondou v. New York, New Haven, and Hartford Railroad Company, 223 U.S. 1 [1912]); Whittington, "Congress Before the *Lochner* Court," 838–841.
92 Nonetheless, there is, at the very least, a plausibility to the realistic critique that judicial lines seemed more than a bit arbitrary and result-oriented in shaping these federalism boundaries, as the Court's record on commerce clause cases suggests. Although individual justices remained more consistent, collectively the justices sustained prohibitions, among other things, against interstate transportation of lottery tickets (Champion v. Ames, 188 U.S. 321 [1903]) and stolen goods (Brooks v. U.S., 267 U.S. 432 [1925]), as well as women for prostitution and immoral purposes more generally (Hoke v. U.S., 227 U.S. 308 [1913]; Caminetti v. U.S., 242 U.S. 470 [1917]), but they blocked an almost identically drawn child-labor statute in *Hammer v. Dagenhart* (1918). Similarly, there is some tension, at the very least, between overturning an effectively prohibitory police power tax on child labor in *Drexel* (1922) but, over the dissent of four justices, not so striking a regulatory tax on narcotics through the Harrison Act (U.S. v Doremus, 249 U.S. 86 [1919]). Conservative critics of the Court's decision in *Gonzales v. Raich* have savagely criticized Antonin Scalia and Anthony Kennedy for a similar moral in-

flection that undermines the legitimacy of their professed federalism. However, just as George Sutherland and James McReynolds were largely consistent in the 1920s cases regardless of personal distaste for the nontraditional behavior, so were, generally speaking, the *Raich* dissenters. A. Christopher Bryant, "The Third Death of Federalism," *Cornell Journal of Law and Public Policy* 17 (2007): 101–160. For an example of the contemporary critique of the New Deal Court on these grounds, see Edward S. Corwin, *The Commerce Power versus States Rights: Back to the Constitution* (Princeton, NJ: Princeton University Press, 1936). For a collection of such critiques of *Hammer*, as well as an effort to see a coherence in it, see Logan E. Sawyer III, "Creating Hammer v. Dagenhart," *William and Mary Bill of Rights Journal* 21 (2012): 67–123.

93 *E. C. Knight Co.*, 11–13.

94 This will be discussed more in the next chapter.

95 Nourse, "Tale of Two Lochners," 770.

96 Melvin I. Urofsky and Paul Finkelman, *A March of Liberty: A Constitutional History of the United States*, vol. 2: *From 1877 to the Present* (New York: Oxford University Press, 2001), 570.

97 They point out, in particular, the federal child-labor cases as evidence for the similarity Urofsky and Finkelman, *A March of Liberty*, 549–551. See also Barry Cushman, "Regime Theory and Unenumerated Rights: A Cautionary Note," *University of Pennsylvania Journal of Constitutional Law* 9 (2006): 263–279, and chapter 1, note 55.

98 "Child Labor and the Courts," *New Republic*, July 26, 1922, quoted in Paul D. Moreno, *The American State from the Civil War to the New Deal* (New York: Cambridge University Press, 2013), 188. See, for example, the 1919 inaugural address from Colorado's governor who observed that states would now have to act to suppress the traffic in child-manufactured goods in the wake of the decision. *JS CO*, 1913, 46. See also this chapter, previous note.

Chapter 5. The Liberty of Contract II: State Resistance

1 Adkins v. Children's Hospital, 261 U.S. 525 (1923).

2 In other words, the case of yellow-dog contracts is a more complicated instance of progressive federalism but still fulfils its basic logic. The basic core of the era's progressive federalism is that the states should be able to and should actually employ their police powers expansively for the public good, with minimal intervention from the federal government (only cases of violating the Constitution's protections, etc.). To the extent state courts were invoking federal judicial doctrine, with cases such as *Allgeyer* and *Lochner* and then *Adair* and *Coppage*, it would still be a fairly classic case of states resisting federal policymaking, even if the implementation was being done by state institutions (since state courts are bound to follow the Constitution or, in this case, the federal courts' interpretation

of it). In the event state courts primarily cite state law to block progressive policy aims, a connection to states' rights would obviously be more tenuous.

3 Hitchman Coal Company v. Mitchell, 245 U.S. 229 (1917); Felix Frankfurter and Nathan Greene, *The Labor Injunction* (Gloucester, MA: Peter Smith, [1930] 1963), 148–149n64–66; David M. Kennedy, *Freedom from Fear* (New York: Oxford University Press, 1999), 26–27. See Sylvester Petro, "Injunctions and Labor Disputes: 1880–1932," *Wake Forest Law Review* (1978): 341–576, arguing that most labor injunctions issued were an appropriate response to specific acts of violence.

4 Edwin E. Witte, "'Yellow Dog' Contracts," *Wisconsin Law Review* 6 (1930): 30.

5 Barry Cushman, "Doctrinal Synergies and Liberal Dilemmas: The Case of the Yellow Dog Contract," *Supreme Court Review* (1992): 256–257. See also Robert Post, "Social and Economic Legislation and the Taft Court," chapter 5 of the Taft entry in the Holmes Devise (n.p.: n.d.), 110, manuscript on file with author. Taft also took a sympathetic view of labor in a subsequent case in which he distinguished rather than cited *Hitchman*. Peter Graham Fish, "*Red Jacket* Revisited: The Case that Unraveled John J. Parker's Supreme Court Appointment," *Law and History Review* 5 (1987): 87–88.

6 Charles Rowan, "The Yellow Dog Contract," *Marquette Law Review* 15 (1931): 111–114.

7 Witte, "Yellow Dog Contracts," 22.

8 Daniel Ernst, "The Yellow Dog Contract and Liberal Reform, 1917–1932," *Labor History* 30 (1989): 266–270; Clarence E. Bonnett, "The Yellow Dog Contract in Its Relation to Public Policy," *Tulane Law Review* (1933): 323.

9 *Adair*, 172.

10 *Adair*, 175.

11 See this chapter, note 8.

12 Quoted in Ernst, "The Yellow Dog Contract and Liberal Reform," 270. See also the AFL's testimony before Congress, citing Oliphant, Roscoe Pound, and other members of the legal academy distinguishing between unenforceability and criminal sanction, summarized in Bonnet, "The Yellow Dog Contract," 323. See also Donald MacDonald, "The Constitutionality of Wisconsin's Statute Invalidating 'Yellow Dog' Contracts," *Wisconsin Law Review* 6 (1931): 86–100, for a Wisconsinite rejecting efforts to distinguish the two types of laws, arguing that the Wisconsin law would hopefully urge the Court to reconsider its prior error.

13 Cornelius Cochrane, "Labor's Campaign against 'Yellow Dog' Contracts Makes Notable Gains," *American Labor Legislation Review* 17 (1927): 142–145. "Labor Wins as Contract Bill Passes Senate," *Cleveland Plain Dealer*, 4, 27, 1927, 1, 8; "Filibuster Fails to Halt J.P. Bill," *Cleveland Plain Dealer*, April 21, 1927, 3; "Donahey Vetoes Direct Tax Levy," *Cleveland Plain Dealer*, April 22, 1927, 4.

14 "Ohio Labor Backs Safety Campaign," *Cleveland Plain Dealer*, July 19, 1927, 13.

15 "Three States Plan to Outlaw Un-American Yellow Dog Contract," *Cedar Rapids Tribune*, April 1, 1927, 1; Cochrane, "Labor's Campaign," 145.

16 John Blaine, "Inaugural Address," January 11, 1925, in *JH WI*, 1925, 38. Blaine countered that "ordinary criminal processes are sufficient to protect life and property without resort to arbitrary power."

17 "'Yellow Dog Bill' Passed by Senate," *Appleton Post Crescent*, April 17, 1929, 1; "Weekly Legislative Review," *Oshkosh Daily Northwestern*, May 11, 1929, 22; "Badger Legislature Has Longest Session," *Capital Times*, December 31, 1929, 5.

18 "Kohler Signs 'Yellow Dog Contract Bill,'" *Appleton Post Crescent*, May 30, 1929, 13; "Kohler Acts on His Own Judgment, Led by No Group," *Oshkosh Daily Northwestern*, June 17, 1929, 5; "Wisconsin Governor Signs Drastic Labor Measure," *Washington Post*, May 31, 1929, 1; "Kohler's Acts Win Favor in Wisconsin," *New York Times*, June 9, 1929, E2. For more on Kohler, see Sean Beienburg, *Prohibition, the Constitution, and States' Rights* (Chicago: University of Chicago Press, 2019), 182–183.

19 "Senator Duncan Debunks Kohler Speech," *Capitol Times*, September 2, 1930, 16; "Padway Explodes Kohler Labor Record; Lauds Phil's Platform; Big Crowd at Program in City Park," *Capitol Times*, September 2, 1930, 1; "Labor Day Speaker Here Backs Reis: Kohler Hit in Address by Padway," *Wisconsin State Journal*, September 2, 1930, 1; Rowan, "The Yellow Dog Contract," 110; "Kohler Sees Need for Dry Law Change in Keynote Speech," *Wisconsin State Journal*, August 12, 1930, 4; "Kohler Defends Labor Record, Cites Gains in Legislation," *Wisconsin State Journal*, August 29, 1930, 12; "Kohler Hits Back at LaFolletteites," *New York Times*, September 7, 1930, E8.

20 "State Labor Code Awaits Governor's Pen for Approval," *Wisconsin State Journal*, June 23, 1931, 1.

21 "Rebels Drub Ohio House Leadership," *Cleveland Plain Dealer*, April 3, 1931, 1; "Assembly Faces Usual Mad Rush Before Quitting," *Piqua Daily Call*, April 10, 1931, 3; "Labor Wins Its Yellow Dog Bill," *Cleveland Plain Dealer*, 4, 11, 1931, 1 ; "Employers Will Take Yellow Dog Fight to White," *Coshocton Tribune*, April 20, 1931, 2; "Sunday Show Bill Signed by White; Yellow Dog Act Approved," *Cleveland Plain Dealer*, May 3, 1931, 3C.

22 Ambrose Doskow, "Statutes Outlawing Yellow Dog Contracts," *American Bar Association Journal* 17 (1931): 516–518; Bonnett, "Yellow Dog Contract," 320.

23 Bonnet, "Yellow Dog Contract," 323.

24 Davis, "Constitutionality of the Yellow Dog Statute," 464; "May Ask Supreme Court of Opinion on Labor Measures," *Springfield Republican*, May 9, 1931, 1; "'Yellow Dog' Bill Found Defective by Supreme Court," *Springfield Republican*, June 2, 1931, 1.

25 Frankfurter and Greene, *The Labor Injunction*, 65 (on Taft), 151–167 (on Roosevelt and the legislative history of the Clayton Act), and 145–147 (on court interpretation); P. F. Brissenden, "The Labor Injunction," *Political Science Quarterly* 48 (1933): 413–450, esp. 444–446; George I. Lovell, *Legislative Deferrals: Statutory Ambiguity, Judicial Power, and American Democracy* (Cambridge: Cambridge University Press, 2003), 99–161 (arguing that members of Congress intentionally wrote these features of the Clayton Act in a vague manner so as to

defer the issue to the courts, with Wilson's views on pages 116–117). Taft, though having expressed sympathy for anti-yellow-contract legislation and uneasy about labor injunctions, wrote for the Court in *Truax*, 257 U.S. 312 (1921). Taft's opinion recounted the evidentiary record to argue that the labor activists had gone beyond mere union organizing and on to libeling the proprietors and potentially threatening customers, and that the Arizona law, by providing aggressive civil and criminal immunity to labor activists for such illegal (but nonviolent) activity, crossed the line and violated both equal protection (by singling out employers for such treatment) and due process property protections (by subjecting them to a legal regime of extortion, in effect) (*Truax*, 326–34). Taft insisted the ruling was narrower than charged and did not threaten the anti-injunction Clayton Act (*Truax*, 340). Holmes, Pitney, Clarke, and Brandeis sharply disagreed, with Holmes and especially Brandeis writing angry dissents on the importance of allowing state experimentation of policy (*Truax*, 344 [Holmes]; *Truax*, 373–376 [Brandeis], quote from 376).

26 Brissenden, "The Labor Injunction,"413–450, esp. 444–446.
27 "We believe that injunctions in labor disputes have in some instances been abused and have given rise to a serious question for legislation." "Republican Party Platform of 1928," June 12, 1928, American Presidency Project, accessed May 11, 2023, https://www.presidency.ucsb.edu/documents/republican-party-platform -1928. The Democrats were more forceful: "No injunctions should be granted in labor disputes except upon proof of threatened irreparable injury and after notice and hearing and the injunction should be confined to those acts which do directly threaten irreparable injury." "1928 Democratic Party Platform," June 26, 1928, American Presidency Project, accessed May 11, 2023, https://www.presidency .ucsb.edu/documents/1928-democratic-party-platform.
28 Joel I. Seidman, *The Yellow Dog Contract* (Baltimore, MD: Johns Hopkins Press, 1932), 37; Fish, "*Red Jacket* Revisited"; International Union, United Mine Workers of America v. Red Jacket Consolidated Coal and Coke Company, 18 F.2d 839 (4th Cir. 1923); Kenneth W. Goings, *The NAACP Comes of Age: The Defeat of Judge John J. Parker* (Bloomington: Indiana University Press, 1990). Ironically, Parker's later moderate record rehabilitated his reputation and made him a serious contender for a subsequent seat Harry Truman filled with Harold Burton. See David A. Yalof, *Pursuit of Justices: Presidential Politics and the Selection of Supreme Court Nominees* (Chicago: University of Chicago Press, 2001), 23–24.
29 "Yellow Dog Bill Protects Labor in Five States," *Cedar Rapids Tribune*, October 16, 1931, 3; "Yellow Dogs Depart," *El Paso Herald Post*, May 11, 1931, 4.
30 Lovell, *Legislative Deferrals*, 169.
31 Edwin E. Witte, "The Federal Anti-Injunction Act," *Minnesota Law Review* (1932): 642–643, 655. Lovell argues that labor's influence and lobbying pressure were relatively ineffective in securing the bill, and the AFL's role was wildly exaggerated, noting the most relevant players were not affiliated with labor but were either scholars or the broad coalition of progressive and conservative policymakers, with the latter especially pivotal/credible, and a coalition clearly distinct

from the New Deal coalition. Lovell, *Legislative Deferrals*, 209–213. On the congressional debate on constitutional issues, see Lovell, 173–178.

32 Witte, "Federal Anti-Injunction Act," 642–643; Lovell, *Legislative Deferrals*, 169, see also 173–178.

33 Witte, "Federal Anti-Injunction Act," 658.

34 On the post-Norris-La Guardia state statutes, see Osmond K. Fraenkel, "Recent Statutes Affecting Labor Injunctions and 'Yellow Dog' Contracts," *Illinois Law Review* 30 (1936): 858–859; "Note: Constitutional Law: Injunctions, Labor Disputes, 1933 Anti-Injunction Legislation," *Minnesota Law Review* 18 (1934): 184; Brissenden, "The Labor Injunction," 447.

35 Just as the states were using their newly restored police powers to take action to suppress yellow-dog contracts, the federal government moved in, destroying yellow-dog contracts not merely in the narrower sphere of businesses moving goods across state lines (as with the old Erdman railroad law struck down in *Adair*) but, consistent with the newly expansive, almost plenary interpretation of federal commerce powers, in the American economy more generally. The 1935 Wagner Act strengthened the protections in Norris-La-Guardia and made some anti-labor practices (such as yellow-dog contracts) criminal and not merely unenforceable in federal court. Against concerns that such efforts violated the Court's due process jurisprudence, Senator Robert Wagner (D-NY) justified his bill on the grounds that the substantive due process public/private interest distinctions underpinning *Adair* and *Coppage* had already been reversed in cases such as *Nebbia v. New York* (291 U.S. 502) (1934). The Supreme Court's pre-1937 jurisprudence had, if not formally reversing the yellow-dog cases as Wagner indicated, implicitly undermined the liberty of contract framework; the justices formally acknowledged this overruling of *Coppage* and *Adair* in 1941: "The course of decisions in this Court since *Adair v. United States* and *Coppage v. Kansas* have completely sapped those cases of their authority." See Phelps-Dodge Corp. v. NLRB, 313 U.S. 177 (1941), 187; Cushman, "Yellow Dog Contracts," 280–281, 292. See this chapter, note 110.

36 Those states with commissions were Arkansas, California, Colorado, Kansas, Minnesota, North Dakota, Oregon, Texas, Washington, and Wisconsin, as well as the District of Columbia. *U.S. Bureau of Labor Statistics, Handbook of Labor Statistics: 1936 Edition* (Washington, DC: Government Printing Office, 1936), 479–482. No state had ever passed a minimum wage for men. *U.S. Bureau of Labor Statistics, Handbook of Labor Statistics: 1931 Edition* (Washington, DC: Government Printing Office, 1931), 447.

37 Stettler v. O'Hara, 243 U.S. 629.

38 Thomas Reed Powell, "The Judiciality of Minimum Wage Legislation," *Harvard Law Review* 37 (1924): 547. The decisions were unanimous in Oregon, Washington, and Minnesota. In Arkansas, the chief justice dissented from four colleagues, though another member of the majority concurred that it was likely unconstitutional but he would wait to strike it until the federal Supreme Court did. See also John William Desmond, "Constitutionality of Women's Minimum Wage Legis-

lation, with Emphasis on the Wisconsin Law" (BA thesis [advised by John Commons], University of Wisconsin, 1926), 13–21.

39 Vivien Hart, *Bound by Our Constitution: Women, Workers, and the Minimum Wage* (Princeton, NJ: Princeton University Press, 1994), 97. One of the attorneys arguing the case believed that Joseph Lamar had been writing an opinion overturning Oregon's minimum wage when he died. Upon his death, the justices decided to wait for his replacement to make the decisive ruling—only for the replacement to be Brandeis, whose views on minimum wage were of course well known—but who had to recuse himself. Rome G. Brown, "Oregon Minimum Wage Cases," *Minnesota Law Review* 1 (1917): 485. Brandeis would also have to sit out *Adkins*, since his daughter served on the DC wage commission, but this time it had no bearing on the case. Sar A. Levitan and Richard Belous, *More than Subsistence: Minimum Wages for the Working Poor* (Baltimore, MD: Johns Hopkins University Press, 1979), 35.

40 See Post, "Social and Economic Legislation and the Taft Court," 80–82, 114–116, for examples of writings both anticipating and reacting to the decision. As will be elaborated later, Post similarly argues a majority to uphold minimum wages existed until 1923.

41 *New York Post*, April 12, 1923, quoted in Desmond, "Constitutionality of Women's Minimum Wage Legislation,"49. Sutherland, however, was perfectly cognizant of this but viewed saddling a specific employer with societal obligations as illegitimate. *Adkins*, 557–558; Howard Gillman, *The Constitution Besieged: The Rise and Demise of Lochner Era Police Powers Jurisprudence* (Durham, NC: Duke University Press, 1993)196.

42 Coolidge called for an amendment to overturn *Dagenhart* and authorize Congress to regulate child labor as well as reinstitute a minimum wage for women everywhere the federal government wielded police-power jurisdiction (e.g., DC and federal territories). Calvin Coolidge, "First Annual Message," December 6, 1923, Miller Center, accessed May 11, 2023, https://millercenter.org/the-presidency/presidential-speeches/december-6-1923-first-annual-message. Coolidge's support for an amendment restoring minimum wages for women in the same breath as reducing child labor aggravated Alice Paul, who resented the comparison of women to children, while pleasing Bay State labor activists attempting to reinvigorate the state's minimum wages. "A New Coolidge for Congress," *Boston Globe*, December 7, 1923, 13; "The President's Message," *Atlanta Constitution*, December 7, 1923, 8; "Store Inspection Will Be Continued," *Christian Science Monitor*, December 18, 1923, 5. Moreover, when still a part of state politics, Coolidge had supported minimum wage laws, in addition to some of the other basic protective legislation like worker's compensation—linking a limited view of federal power with expansive state power and responsibilities. Robert Sobel, *Coolidge: An American Enigma* (Washington, DC: Regnery, 1998), 62–69; Donald R. McCoy, *Calvin Coolidge: The Quiet President* (New York: MacMillan, 1967), 46–49.

43 "Smith Favors Better Law for Women Labor," *New York Tribune*, November 2,

1919, 16; "Lauds Smith's Record," *New York Times*, August 25, 1918, 9; "Women Divided on 48 Hour Week Bill," *New York Times*, February 28, 1923, 6; "Albany Denies Four Year Term for Governor; Bloch Bill Is Defeated by Assembly Republicans; 48 Hour Week and Minimum Wage Measures Held Up," *New York Tribune*, March 19, 1925, 9; "Al Smith Banquet Attracts 500 Here," *Boston Globe*, April 20, 1928, 1. At the constitutional convention, Smith had, however, argued against a minimum wage for men on grounds that unions prevented such a need. Louis Zucarello, "The Political Thought of Alfred Smith" (PhD diss., Fordham University, 1970), 130; see chapter 3, note 24.

44 Zucarello, "The Political Thought of Alfred Smith," 138.

45 Ironically, progressive lawyer Albert Levitt told Alice Paul that the Court would be hostile to protective legislation until Taft left. Julie Novkov, *Constituting Workers, Protecting Women: Gender, Labor, and Law in the Progressive Era and New Deal Years* (Ann Arbor: University of Michigan Press, 2001), 120. Alexander Bickel argues that, as president, Taft had been concerned with correcting conservative excess on the Supreme Court while still appointing broadly conservative men. This would make sense if he thought the Court was mostly correct but had erred in *Lochner*, which would be perfectly consistent with his *Adkins* opinion. Alexander Bickel, "Mr. Taft Rehabilitates the Court," *Yale Law Journal* 79 (1969): 1–45. By the 1920s, Taft's concern with progressive legal movements, and particularly the realists' scorn for constitutional forms, made him much more cautious, indeed almost paranoid, in making sure to recommend conservative justices. Bickel, "Mr. Taft Rehabilitates the Court," 1–45. See chapter 6, note 25.

46 On the infrequency of Taft dissents, see Barry Cushman, "Inside the Taft Court: Lessons from the Docket Books," *Supreme Court Review* 2015 (2016): 345–410.

47 *Adkins*, 563–7.

48 Meyer v. Nebraska, 262 U.S. 390 (1923) (overturning a ban on teaching German to young students); Pierce v. Society of Sisters, 268 U.S. 510 (1925) (overturning a mandatory public education attendance law effectively banning private, especially parochial, school). It should be remembered, however, that the justices did not then wield *Adkins* as a cudgel overturning state protection laws en masse. For example, shortly after *Adkins*, the Court approved restrictions on women's overnight work, with Sutherland explaining that it was, unquestionably, a health measure and thus a legitimate exercise of police power. Radice v. New York, 264 U.S. 292 (1924); Novkov, *Constituting Workers*, 194–195.

49 Today these cases are often seen as more connected to First Amendment or privacy issues, as well as implicating important issues of state-building involving households and homes. The latter debates concerning the sanctity of the home and family versus the authority of the state were the same sorts of issues raised, for example, by some of the critics of Sheppard-Towner that *Meyer* and *Pierce* both drew from (and which have come up again, as will be discussed in the conclusion). At the time, however, *Meyer* and *Pierce* cited and invoked liberty-of-contract cases and reinforced the doctrine of the latter (as Hugo Black would object to later in Justice Douglas's decision to cite them in *Griswold v. Connecticut*

[1965]). As one scholar put it, "Despite their ringing declarations about human rights, *Meyer* and *Pierce* were both formally decided largely on the basis of property rights—the liberty of the schools to conduct a business, the right of private school teachers to follow their occupation, and the freedom of the schools and the parents to enter into contracts." William G. Ross, "The Contemporary Significance of *Meyer* and *Pierce* for Parental Rights Involving Education," *Akron Law Review* 34 (2001): 3–6. Regardless of the Court's doctrinal framing of these cases as liberty-of-contract (though the Court acknowledged these issues in contrasting America with the totalitarian child-rearing of Plato or, implicitly, other), they also served as a site of contestation over intrusion of a burgeoning governmental bureaucracy or government paternalism into homes, households, and domestic relations, such as compulsory schooling, as shown by Ken I. Kersch, *Constructing Civil Liberties* (New York: Cambridge University Press, 2004), 247–338, esp. 255–258, 265, 270–274.

50 Thomas Reed Powell, "The Supreme Court and State Police Power: VI," *Virginia Law Review* 18 (1932): 270–305, 305; and Thomas Reed Powell, "The Supreme Court and State Police Power: VII," *Virginia Law Review* 18 (1932): 379–414, 396–397. On the other side—arguing that a similar circumstance had spared minimum wages in *Stettler*—see also this chapter, note 39.

51 Cushman, "Inside the Taft Court," 381–383.

52 Murphy v. Sardell, 269 U.S. 530 (1925); Amicus Brief on behalf of Industrial Welfare Commission of California, *Murphy*, 30. Powell's findings in his 1932 piece, further contributing to perception of the arbitrariness of the decision uncovered in his earlier works, notably were published immediately before the major wave of resistance the following year, perhaps further motivating state pushback.

53 Donham v. West Nelson Manufacturing, 273 U.S. 65 (1927); Appellants Brief, *Donham*, 25–32.

54 Cushman, "Inside the Taft Court," 381–383.

55 In addition, legal uncertainty had contributed to several other states withdrawing minimum wage policies. Nebraska and Texas had repealed theirs in 1919 and 1921. Colorado never appropriated funds for its minimum wage boards. *Handbook of Labor Statistics 1931*, 447–448; and *Handbook of Labor Statistics 1936*, 481.

56 "Laws may be passed fixing and regulating the hours of labor, establishing a minimum wage, and providing for the comfort, health, safety and general welfare of all employees; and no other provision of the constitution shall impair or limit this power." Ohio Const. art. II, §34; Levitan and Belous, *More than Subsistence*, 34.

57 The decision did, however, prevent Massachusetts from *ordering* papers to print the decision, which rendered an already weak law even weaker. Novkov, *Constituting Workers*, 193. Massachusetts's commission did continue to operate until superseded by a more typical, binding wage commission in 1934. See "Boston Merchant Before Commission," *Springfield Republican*, October 21, 1931, 1.

58 "Borah Wants Minimum Wage Left to States," *New York Tribune*, April 11, 1923, 2. The article title is somewhat misleading; in the interview given, the careful

lawyer Borah explicitly says that he had not read the opinion so was not commenting on its legal merits but was merely expressing frustration with yet another divided decision and predicting what others would do, although he again noted his belief that constitutional rulings should require supermajority support from the justices. Nonetheless, considering Borah's combination of progressive belief in active government, and his decentralist views that saw him propose eliminating the Fourteenth Amendment due process clause altogether to put an end to federal judicial intervention in the states' police powers, the journalists were correct in imputing that position.

59 Hart, *Bound by Our Constitution*, 115–119, 131–137. Brandeis and Frankfurter both mused about getting rid of the due process clause and perhaps, for Brandeis at least, even the entire Fourteenth Amendment. David E. Bernstein, *Rehabilitating Lochner: Defending Individual Rights against Progressive Reform* (Chicago: University of Chicago Press, 2011), 92; Morton J. Horwitz, *Transformation of American Law, 1870–1960* (New York: Oxford University Press, 1992), 259; see also Brandeis's special concurrence in *Whitney v. California*, 274 U.S. 357 (1927), 373, objecting to any substantive rather than purely procedural component of the due process clause.

60 Hart, *Bound by Our Constitution*, 119.

61 Hart, 136.

62 "Seek State Wage Power: Senator Johnson Plans Amendment Affecting Women's Minimum Pay," *New York Times*, November 3, 1925, 4.

63 Florence Kelley, "Letter to Katharine Phillips Edson," December 12, 1925, in *Selected Letters of Florence Kelley, 1869–1931*, ed. Kathryn Kish Sklar and Beverly Wilson Palmer (Urbana-Champaign: University of Illinois Press, 2009), 373.

64 William Graebner, "Federalism in the Progressive Era: A Structural Interpretation of Reform," *Journal of American History* 64 (1977): 342. See, for example, the joint petition issued by the *Industrial Welfare Commissions of the Pacific Coast*, Fourth Biennial Report of the Industrial Welfare Commission of Oregon, 1921, 21, reprinted in Victor P. Morris, "Oregon's Experience with Minimum Wage Legislation" (PhD diss., Columbia University, 1930), 207–208.

65 On the relative success of Pacific wage policies, see "Minimum Wage Laws Declared of Little Avail," *Christian Science Monitor*, July 25, 1927, 3.

66 *Handbook of Labor Statistics 1931*, 448.

67 "Minimum Wage Law Violated," *Oregonian*, September 7, 1930, 19. Baffling observers, that year a state judge moved to block its minimum wage law, even after its state supreme court had twice upheld the law. "Minimum Wage Law Is Held Invalid by Tacoma's Court," *Seattle Daily Times*, October 30, 1930, 5.

68 Helen J. Knowles, "'Omak's Minimum Pay Law Joan d'Arc': Telling the Local Story of *West Coast Hotel v. Parrish* (1937)," *Journal of Supreme Court History* 37 (2012): 283–304; Helen J. Knowles, *Making Minimum Wage: Elsie Parrish versus the West Coast Hotel Company* (Norman: University of Oklahoma Press, 2021); Post, "Social and Economic Legislation and the Taft Court," 117n449.

69 Post, "Social," 117n449.

70 "Minimum Wage Law Hit—Labor Commissioner Says Oregon Statute Not Enforceable," *Oregonian*, July 29, 1927, 18.

71 Morris, "Oregon's Experience with Minimum Wage Laws," 221, 220–223.

72 "Tribute Paid M'Cusker: Support of Minimum Wage and Child Labor Laws Cited to Show Humanitarian Spirit," *Oregonian*, October 25, 1926, 7.

73 Morris, "Oregon's Experience with Minimum Wage Laws," 221, 220–223.

74 *Oregonian*, August 6, 1927, 3.

75 S.J.R. 19, in *JA CA*, 1923, 2235; *JS CA*, 1923, 1117; *Laws CA*, 1923, 1659. Another attempt, asking for an amendment allowing both minimum wage and maximum hours, died in committee in 1933 after Roosevelt had already come out in support of minimum wage laws. *JA CA*, 1933, 4637.

76 *JA CA*, 1933, 4637.

77 Roland M. Miller, "California's Reasonable Minimum Wage," *Sociology and Social Research* (1927), in Egbert Ray Nichols and Joseph H. Baccus, ed., *Minimum Wages and Maximum Hours* (New York: H. W. Wilson, 1936), 289; *Laws CA*, 1927, 438.

78 "Women's Wage Caution Issued," *Los Angeles Times*, October 23, 1925, A1; "Overturns Wage Law," *Los Angeles Times*, October 20, 1925, 1.

79 "Wage Law Suit to be Dropped," *Los Angeles Times*, January 5, 1925, 4; "Appeals to Justices in Test Action," *Los Angeles Times*, January 7, 1925, 4; "Heroine: Twenty Year Old Stenographer Outwits Big Lawyers," *Troy* (IL) *Call*, March 30, 1925, 5; John McGuire, "From the Courts to the State Legislatures: Social Justice Feminism, Labor Legislation, and the 1920s," *Labor History* 45 (2004): 236. Clifford Thies says California withdrew its minimum wage law in 1925 after *Gainer v. ABC Dohrman* (Clifford Thies, "The First Minimum Wage Laws," *Cato Review* 10 [1991]: 717), but newspapers report that the suit was withdrawn and, as explained in the following note, it seemed to be working well, at least through 1933.

80 "The Minimum Wage Law," *Los Angeles Times*, January 13, 1933, A4.

81 "Farewell Address," January 5, 1931, reprinted in *JS CA*, 1931, vol. 1, 77.

82 "Roosevelt Airs View on Wage Ruling," *Los Angeles Times*, June 6, 1936, 1.

83 "How Minimum Wage Affects Workers," *New York Times*, August 7, 1927, E19; "Women's Salaries Mounting," *Christian Science Monitor*, July 12, 1927, 6.

84 Mark Graber, "Almost Legal: Disobedience and Partial Nullification in American Constitutional Politics and Law," in *Nullification and Secession in Modern Constitutional Thought*, ed. Sanford Levinson (Lawrence: University Press of Kansas, 2016), 146.

85 H.B. 97, defunding the commission entirely, in *JH ND*, 1927, 527. North Dakota's commission provided data arguing its minimum wage commission proved effective even considering the lack of funding, but contemporary observers disagreed. "Mere Publicity Urged as Means of Enforcing Eight-Hour Law," *Bismarck Tribune*, December 18, 1928, 1. The head of the Workmen's Compensation Bureau, which oversaw minimum wages, decided to issue a penalty in 1932 to test the constitutionality of the state's minimum wage law, observing nearly identical laws

had been struck before. "Might Test State Law for Minimum Wages for Women," *Bismarck Tribune*, July 30, 1932, 3; "Fargo Interested in Minimum Wage," *Bismarck Tribune*, August 9, 1932, 3; *Handbook of Labor Statistics 1931*, 448.

86 "Editorial Comment," *Stevens Point Daily Journal*, August 20, 1924, 2.

87 Thus, for that editorial board, Coolidge and Davis were both wrong in downplaying court overreach, but La Follette's plan was even worse. "Face Facts Squarely," *Wisconsin State Journal*, October 4, 1924, 3.

88 "State Holds Wage Law Is Not General," *Manitowoc Herald News*, December 1, 1924, 16; Abraham Lincoln, "Speech on Dred Scott," June 26, 1857, in *Collected Works of Abraham Lincoln*, vol. 2., ed. Roy Basler (New Brunswick, NJ: Rutgers University Press, 1953), 399; and Abraham Lincoln, "First Inaugural Address," March 4, 1861, American Presidency Project, accessed May 11, 2023, https://www.presidency.ucsb.edu/documents/inaugural-address-34

89 "Badger Minimum Wage Act Held Illegal as Relating to Adult Women Workers," *La Crosse Tribune*, December 30, 1924, 1; "New Minimum Wage Law Is to Be Drawn," *Stevens Point Daily Journal*, January 2, 1925, 5.

90 Edwin Witte, Chief of Wisconsin Legislative Research Bureau, "Letter to Unknown Recipient," *WI LRB* (August 18, 1925), found in clippings, box "Minimum Wage," on file with author; Hart, *Bound by Our Constitution*, 140–141.

91 S.B. 378, *Laws WI*, 1925, 248. The state's policy evangelism could work both ways. A bitter Wisconsin industrialist visiting Oregon explained that citizens of that state should be wary of following the "Wisconsin Idea" since, the industrialist feared, it resulted in capital fleeing Wisconsin to surrounding areas that did not adopt the minimum wage and other policies. "Oregon Gains Reputation Questioned by Easterner: Forward Types of Legislation in Wage and Tax Matters Held Driving Industries Away from Wisconsin," *Oregonian*, November 21, 1932, 2.

92 Witte, "Letter to Unknown Recipient." A wire report interpreted the bill as "indicating a determination to meet the Court's opinion but at the same time get results" in the fact of "the generally disastrous effect among the states" after *Adkins*. "Years Gains in Labor Laws to Protect Health and Society," *Altoona Mirror*, September 4, 1925, 8.

93 Edwin E. Witte, Chief of Wisconsin Legislative Research Bureau, "Letter to Unknown Recipient," November 19, 1931, found in WI LRB clippings, box "Minimum Wage," on file with author.

94 Gillman, *Constitution Besieged*, 184.

95 "Roosevelt Lays Broken Pledges to Republicans," *New York Tribune*, April 4, 1929, 1.

96 Herbert Lehman, "Recommending Minimum Wage Legislation—Women and Children in Industry," February 27, 1933, in *Public Papers of Herbert H. Lehman, 1933* (Albany, NY: J. B. Lyon, 1934), 95–96 (also excerpted in *New York Times*, February 28, 1933, 12). Roosevelt proposed an advisory minimum wage commission in his 1931 address to the legislature. "Annual Message to the Legislature," January 7, 1931, in *Public Papers of Franklin D. Roosevelt, 48th Governor 1931* (Albany, NY: J. B. Lyon, 1937), 40.

97 "Minimum Wage Sought for Men," *New York Times*, March 23, 1933, 5; "Lehman Will Sign Minimum Wage Act," *New York Times*, April 14, 1923, 28; "Minimum Pay Bill Signed by Lehman," *New York Times*, May 2, 1933, 32; John Thomas McGuire, "A Catalyst for Reform: The Women's Joint Legislative Conference and Its Fight for Labor Legislation in New York State, 1918–1933" (PhD diss., SUNY Binghamton, 2001), 297–309; "Drafts Third Bill on Minimum Wage: Assemblyman Brownell Assets Democratic Plan Would Force Women Out of Jobs," *New York Times*, March 19, 1933, 8.

98 See previous note.

99 "New York State Backs Minimum Wage Measure," *New York Tribune*, February 19, 1923, 4; "Two Messages," *New York Times*, April 27, 1923, 16; "More Smith Bills Die in Assembly," *New York Times*, April 27, 1923, 2.

100 See Nichols and Baccus, *Minimum Wages and Maximum Hours*, 135–136 (emphasis added), for Smith's comments; other governors' critical responses are also included in the chapter.

101 Zucarello, "The Political Thought of Alfred Smith," 123–124. See also Alfred E. Smith, "Annual Message," January 24, 1924, in *Public Papers of Alfred E. Smith 1924* (Albany, NY: J. B. Lyon, 1924), 62–63. Ogden Mills, Smith's Republican opponent in 1926, also endorsed the commission in the campaign. "Mills Says Bad Milk Still Floods Queens; again Queries Smith," *New York Times*, October 16, 1926, 1. Albany Republicans had blocked it, however, to Smith's annoyance. "Smith Scores Legislature as Least Fruitful in Years; Lists Trivial Bills Passed," *New York Times*, March 24, 1928, 1; "Legislature Gets 48 HR Week Bill," *New York Times*, January 21, 1927, 5.

102 Zucarello, "The Political Thought of Al Smith," 225.

103 On Perkins's ambition to overcome *Adkins* and its progeny, see McGuire, "A Catalyst for Reform," 317–318.

104 Nichols and Baccus, *Minimum Wages and Maximum Hours*, 349–351; "Roosevelt Lauds Passage of Labor Bills in New York," *Christian Science Monitor*, April 17, 1933, 1; "President Seeks Minimum Pay Acts," *New York Times*, April 13, 1933, 1.

105 *Handbook of Labor Statistics 1936*, 482.

106 For more data on the composition of these 1933 and 1934 state legislatures and the respective governors, see Beienburg, "Progressivism and States' Rights," 44; Michael J. Dubin, *Party Affiliations in the State Legislatures, 1796–2006* (Jefferson, NC: McFarland, 2007).

   Unlike the almost totally one-party west, where factional differences within the Republican Party were the real divide, there was somewhat greater, but not total, ideological sorting in these states. As to the earlier holdouts for minimum wage, California, Oregon, Washington, and Wisconsin were all almost monolithically one-party Republican states, with ratios of 5:1, 10:1, and even 30:1 fairly constant throughout the twenties and early thirties. South Dakota was closer to parity with a ratio of 2:1 in favor of the GOP. North Dakota was also a one-party state but had a de-facto two-party system in which the Non-Partisan League and its affiliates served as a progressive caucus, and the Independent Voters Association served as an establishment/conservative wing. The North Dakota state party was about evenly divided between the two.

107 *JS NH*, 1933, 307; *JH NH*, 1933, 580; S.B. 415, in *JS CT*, 1933, 1870–1873; *JH CT*, 1933, 2020.

108 A.B. 681, in *JH OH*, 1933, 1008; *JS OH*, 1933, 725; A.B. 470, in *MA NJ*, 1933, 795.

109 Hart, *Bound by Our Constitution*, 141–143.

110 291 U.S. 502 (1934). For examples of contemporary commentary seeing *Nebbia* as overturning *Adkins*, see Cushman, "Lost Fidelities," 121n129. For the expanded version of this argument, which puts *Nebbia*, not the 1937 cases, as the key turning point in the New Deal Court's jurisprudence, see Barry Cushman, *Rethinking the New Deal Court: The Structure of a Constitutional Revolution* (New York: Oxford University Press, 1998).

111 Texas & N.O. R. Co v. Brotherhood of Railway & Steamship Clerks, 281 U.S. 548 (1930); Barry Cushman, "Inside the Constitutional Revolution of 1937," *Supreme Court Review* (2017): 367–409, 403–404.

112 Nelson, *The Legalist Reformation*, 68–70.

113 "Roosevelt Airs View on Wage Ruling," 1.

114 "Lehman Stresses Social Laws Passed Under the New Deal," *New York Herald Tribune*, June 27, 1936, 8; Herbert Lehman, "Annual Message," January 6, 1937, in *Public Papers of Herbert Lehman 1937* (Albany, NY: J. B Lyon, 1940), 21.

115 On Republicans' serious commitment to federalism, shared with and by nearly all major political figures between Reconstruction and the New Deal, see chapter 1, esp. notes 34–36.

116 "Roosevelt Airs View on Wage Ruling," 1; "Roosevelt Sees a No-Man's Land," *New York Times*, June 3, 1936, 1; "Hoover Favors Amendment on Pay-Fixing: Return to States' Rights Urged by Ex-President," *Washington Post*, June 7, 1936, M1; "Platform Battle Looms Over Hoover's Proposal," *Boston Globe*, June 8, 1936, 4.

117 Charles A. Beard, "Rendezvous with the Supreme Court," *New Republic*, September 2, 1936, 92. Lehman was also consulted. See also "The Texts of Governor Landon's Addresses at Madison Square Garden," *New York Times*, October 30, 1936, 16.

118 Cushman, "Inside the Constitutional Revolution of 1937," 377.

119 "70% of Voters Favor Constitutional Change," *Washington Post*, July 19, 1936, B1. See also Barry Cushman, "Mr. Dooley and Mr. Gallup: Public Opinion and Constitutional Change in the 1930s," *Buffalo Law Review* 50 (2002): 7–102.

120 "South for Federal Control," *Boston Globe*, July 19, 1936, B5.

121 Arthur M. Schlesinger Jr., *The Politics of Upheaval: The Age of Roosevelt*, vol. 3: 1935–1936 (New York: Houghton Mifflin, 1960), 489.

122 "An Unfortunate Decision," *Washington Post*, June 2, 1936, reprinted in Nichols and Baccus, *Minimum Wages and Maximum Hours*, 209–210.

123 Carter v. Carter Coal, 298 U.S. 238 (1936). See the collection of articles in Nichols and Baccus, *Minimum Wages and Maximum Hours*, e.g., 209–221.

124 "Ricochet," *Baltimore Sun*, June 8, 1936, 6.
125 *Christian Century*, June 17, 1936, 862, reprinted in Nichols and Baccus, *Minimum Wages and Maximum Hours*, 220–221.
126 74.2 Cong. Rec. 8886–8888 (June 3, 1986); for Costigan's original, see 74.1 Cong. Rec. 104 (January 4, 1935).
127 74.2 Cong. Rec. 9256–9257 (June 8, 1936).
128 Bruce Ackerman, *We the People: Transformations* (Cambridge, MA: Harvard University Press, 2000), 338–339.
129 Schlesinger, *Politics of Upheaval*, 288.
130 Novkov, *Constituting Workers*, 194–195; People v. Morehead, 270 N.Y. 237–239 (1936).
131 The district court contended that because the wages were fixed within and not across specific markets, the state was establishing a realm of value to negotiate while still preserving the market (e.g., not competing across industries with an artificially flat wage). Novkov, *Constituting Workers*, 195, 205.
132 "Supreme Court Will Review Women's Minimum Wage Act," *Boston Globe*, October 13, 1936, 32.
133 Novkov, *Constituting Workers*, 194; Parrish v. West Coast Hotel, 55 P.2D 1083, 1090 (1936).
134 Cushman's *Rethinking the New Deal Court* is the canonical and most thorough exposition of this point. See also James Patterson, *Congressional Conservatism and the New Deal* (Lexington: University of Kentucky Press, 1967),125; "Reed Flays Democrats' Platform," *Los Angeles Times*, June 28, 1936, 11.
135 Hart, *Bound by Our Constitution*, 146–147. For Roberts's memorandum outlining his summary of the cases, see Felix Frankfurter, "Mr. Justice Roberts," *University of Pennsylvania Law Review* 104 (1955): 311–317. See also Richard D. Friedman, "A Reaffirmation: The Authenticity of the Roberts Memorandum, or Felix the Non-Forger," *University of Pennsylvania Law Review* 142 (1993): 1985–1994; Schlesinger, *Politics of Upheaval*, 480.
136 *Tipaldo*, 60. Commentators seized on this language to recommend New York ask for an immediate rehearing, now calling for *Adkins* to be overruled, which the state's attorney general John Bennett began to do. Unsigned editorial, "Notes and Comment on New York Minimum Wage Decision," *US Law Review* 70 (1936): 295–311, reprinted in Nichols and Baccus, *Minimum Wages and Maximum Hours*, 160–174. Note also that the court took the first opportunity to hear *Parrish*, rather than simply remand it in light of *Tipaldo*, and commentators did expect Roberts to reverse his decision in a rehearing. "Hotel Lobbies Scornful of Al Smith and Mates," *Boston Globe*, June 22, 1936, 4.
137 *Tipaldo*, 619.
138 Cushman, "Inside the 'Constitutional Revolution' of 1937." If true, it seems plausible that Roberts, while eager to defend his own reputation, nonetheless refused to do so if it came at Hughes's expense.
139 Justice Hugo Black would reiterate, in joining or authoring later decisions like *Williamson v. Lee Optical*, 348 U.S. 483 (1955), and especially *Ferguson v.*

Skrupa, 372 U.S. 726 (1963), that the court had definitively left this realm of courts protecting unenumerated rights against the states' police powers: As he observed in the latter case: "The doctrine that prevailed in *Lochner*, *Adkins*, and like cases—that due process authorizes courts to hold laws unconstitutional when they believe the legislature has acted unwisely—has long since been discarded. We have returned to the original constitutional proposition that courts do not substitute their social and economic beliefs for the judgment of legislative bodies, who are elected to pass laws." That is part of why his dissent in *Griswold v. Connecticut*, 381 U.S. 479 (1965), 507, was so embittered and so biting: he accused his fellow justices, including William O. Douglas, who had been an ally in rejecting the court's *Adkins* progeny (and written *Williamson*), of turning their back on that decades-long project and substituting their own policy preferences under cover of rights not enumerated in the Constitution but apparently still demanded by it. (Black remained adamant, however, that courts enforce enumerated constitutional rights against the states per the privileges and immunities clause of the Fourteenth Amendment. For the development of this argument, see also chapter 4, note 15. Sounding like John Harlan (I), his old enemy Felix Frankfurter, or Louis Brandeis, Black charged these justices with weaponizing both "substantive due process" and, especially ironically considering its nonincorporation and its original purpose in protecting states' rights against federal overreach, the Ninth Amendment, against the states' proper police powers, now that those arguments could be marshaled on behalf of newer, more politically desirable ends.

Chapter 6. Popular Constitutionalism, the States, and the New Deal Revolution: The Fall of Progressive Federalism

1 S.J.R. 26, in *Laws WI*, 1921, 1170; A.J.R. 20, in *Laws WI*, 1935, 1224.
2 Wilson actually pressed for the nomination at the 1920 convention—which served to crowd out his political heir William McAdoo—but his supporters, fearing for his health, quietly scuttled his nomination. Wesley M. Bagby, "Woodrow Wilson, a Third Term, and the Solemn Referendum," *American Historical Review* 60 (1955): 567–575; Robert K. Murray, *The Harding Era: Warren G. Harding and His Administration* (Minneapolis: University of Minnesota Press, 1969), 81–92.
3 *JH NM*, 1921, 408.
4 Donald R. McCoy, *Calvin Coolidge: The Quiet President* (New York: MacMillan, 1967), 263.
5 On the struggle to control the direction of the Democratic Party during the 1920s, see Robert K. Murray, *The 103rd Ballot: Democrats and the Disaster in Madison Square Garden* (New York: Harper & Row, 1976); and Douglas B. Craig, *After Wilson: The Struggle for the Democratic Party, 1920–1934* (Chapel Hill: University of North Carolina Press, 1992). As all three presidential nominees during the decade suggest, the conservative branch managed to dominate the party's affairs until 1932.

6 Lucas A. Powe, *The Supreme Court and the American Elite, 1789–2008* (Cambridge, MA: Harvard University Press, 2009), 148–150.

7 Again, this is not to say the parties were not ferociously polarized on many policies—the tariff and protectionism, for example—but elites of both parties had a broadly common vision of the sphere of federal government power, even if ferociously combating the choices it should make within that sphere.

8 Craig, *After Wilson*, 19. In order to preserve his conservative wing's control of the Democratic Party, Cox joined the 1924 contest with the express purpose of blocking William McAdoo, Wilson's son-in-law and political heir of the progressive wing of the party (Craig, 52).

9 Harding also opposed nativist efforts to restrict parochial schools (that would become, for example, *Pierce v. Society of Sisters*), telling a pastor that he believed in the separation of church and state and thus felt religious schools could teach how they wanted. William G. Ross, *Forging New Freedoms: Nativism, Education, and the Constitution, 1917–1927* (Lincoln: University of Nebraska Press, 1994), 64. See also chapter 5, note 49. Harding biographer John Dean argues Harding was also quite progressive on race and suggests the potential for activism had he lived, but Dean's remains a minority position among scholars who hold Harding in low regard. John Dean, *Warren G. Harding* (New York: Times Books, 2004), 101, 125–126. For more on Harding's interest in civil rights enforcement, see Sean Beienburg, *Prohibition, the Constitution, and States' Rights* (Chicago: University of Chicago Press, 2019), 135–137, hereafter cited as *PCSR*.

10 Maxwell Bloomfield, *Peaceful Revolution: Constitutional Change and American Culture from Progressivism to the New Deal* (Cambridge, MA: Harvard University Press, 2001), 72.

11 Bloomfield, *Peaceful Revolution*, 72–77.

12 Bloomfield, 75.

13 W. E. B. Du Bois, *Black Reconstruction in America* (Oxford: Oxford University Press, [1935] 2007), 233–234, 279, 270, 275.

14 Coolidge would agree, however, that continued state failure arguably created a moral (if definitely not a legal) obligation for federal intervention. "Message to Short Session of 69th Congress," printed in Archibald E. Stevenson, *States' Rights and National Prohibition* (New York: Clark Boardman, 1927), 6–7.

15 "Radio Address on Colorado's Semicentennial," August 3, 1926, quoted in Stevenson, *States' Rights and National Prohibition*, 12–13. See also discussion of Coolidge's Memorial Address at Arlington in chapter 3.

16 *JH VT*, 1925, 188, 214; *JS VT*, 1925, 210.

17 S.J.M. 3, in *JH/S OR*, 1923, 30, 117; S.J.M. 2, in *JS WA*, 1923, 72.

18 *Laws AZ*, 1927, 437–4; *JS AR*, 1927, 106; *JH AR*, 1927, 154; *JH ID*, 1927, 627; *JS ID*, 1927, 327; *JS IN*, 1927, 714; *JS MD*, 1927, 1639–1640; *JS NV*, 1927, 47; *JA NV*, 1927, 20; *JH OR*, 1927, 396; *JS OR*, 1927, 128; *JS TX*, 1927, 72; *JH TX*, 1927, 35; *JS UT*, 1927, 264; *JH UT*, 1927, 129; *JH WV*, 1927, 116; *JS WV*, 1927, 13; *JS WY*, 1927, 332; *JH WY*, 1927, 228. Such resolutions failed in Illinois, Nebraska, North Carolina, Ohio, and Wisconsin. *JS IL*, 1927, 425; *JH IL*, 1927, 907;

JH NE, 1927, 654; *JH NC*, 1927, 744; *JS NC*, 1927, 107; *JH OH*, 1927, 183; *JH WI*, 1927. Kansas and Vermont deviated from the canned resolutions by passing protest resolutions without explicit federalism concerns (with Vermont instead explicitly invoking its native son Coolidge). A similar Michigan resolution offering policy objections failed. *JS KS*, 1927, 87; *JS MI*, 1927, 1018; *JS VT*, 1927, 39. Similar protests had appeared during the first use of the estate tax during World War I. See *JS VT*, 1917, 257.

19 Such pressure these resolutions held "is contrary to the theory of this government, unprecedented and offensive to the independence of the legislatures of the sovereign states." S.C.R. 3, in *JH OR*, 1927, 29. Connecticut and Florida used particularly strong states' rights language while fiercely anti-corporate Montana specifically modified its resolution to disavow states' rights and instead demanded Congress *keep* the estate tax as a matter of egalitarian justice. *JH FL*, 1927, 304; *JS FL*, 1927, 382; *Laws MT*, 1927, 598–99; *JS MT*, 1927, 268, 358; *JH MT*, 1927, 477.

20 S.J.R. 6, in *JS CO*, 1922, 70; H.J.R. 18, in *JH OH*, 1921, 291–292, 305; *Laws OK*, 1923, 495; *JH MN*, 1929, 75, 78; *JS MN*, 1929, 76; *JS MO*, 1923, 276.

21 *JH UT*, 1931, 30.

22 Bruce Ackerman, *We the People: Transformations* (Cambridge, MA: Harvard University Press, 2000), 355.

23 Paul D. Moreno, *The American State from the Civil War to the New Deal* (New York: Cambridge University Press, 2013), esp. 190; Walter F. Murphy, "In His Own Image: Mr. Chief Justice Taft and Supreme Court Appointments," *Supreme Court Review* (1961): 159–193.

24 Nathan Lewis Miller, *Recollections*, 1953, 29, in box 2, Nathan Lewis Miller Papers, Special Collections Research Center, Syracuse University Libraries, Syracuse, New York, hereafter cited as NLMP. See also Letter from W. H. Taft, May 19, 1922, in box 1, folder 1922/1–6, NLMP; Ira H. Carmen, "The President, Politics, and the Power of Appointment: Hoover's Nomination of Mr. Justice Cardozo," *Virginia Law Review* (1969): 618–620.

25 For the Bolsheviki quote, see Barry Cushman, *Rethinking the New Deal Court: The Structure of a Constitutional Revolution* (New York: Oxford University Press, 1998), 225; Artemus Ward and David J. Danelski: *The Chief Justice, Appointment and Influence* (Ann Arbor: University of Michigan Press, 2016), 74; James F. Simon, *FDR and Chief Justice Hughes* (New York: Simon & Schuster, 2012), 174–175. See also chapter 5, note 45. Then Attorney General Stone had received his nomination from his Amherst College friend Calvin Coolidge (who Stone wanted to see return to Washington in the Senate after his presidency) (McCoy, *Calvin Coolidge*, 395). The states' rights–committed Coolidge died before Stone delivered his New Deal opinions and likely would have viewed his friend's nomination with regret, as did Taft who recommended Stone to Coolidge (McCoy, 276). Stone's pre–New Deal views on federalism were quite mixed. During the 1924 election, he assailed La Follette's court reform schemes as leading to the end of the Tenth Amendment and the crucial core of federalism in the Constitution (since the US Supreme Court was the primary guarantor of it, rather than simply letting

Congress bootstrap its own power). Alpheus T. Mason, *Harlan Fiske Stone: Pillar of the Law* (New York: Viking Press, 1956), 177. Stone strongly supported the presidential campaign of his close friend Hoover on grounds Hoover would not lead to aggressive federal oversight of the economy and as a political conservative professed to be repulsed by much of the New Deal, even if he found it constitutional. Mason, *Harlan Fiske Stone*, 264, 305–306, 369–377. Thus, though he also claimed that the Fair Labor Standards Act "made me gag," he long plotted to write an opinion destroying dual federalism, which he would in *Darby* (554–556). See also Cushman, *Rethinking the New Deal Court*, 222–225. It should be noted, he also almost gleefully explained to the Roosevelt administration how the tax-and-spending power could be used to prop up Social Security (and grants-in-aid), which, perhaps more than anything, helped undermine decentralized federalism. Mason, *Harlan Fiske Stone*, 408; Josh Blackman, *Unprecedented: The Constitutional Challenge to Obamacare* (New York: Public Affairs, 2013), 97. A gap between Stone's political and constitutional views is potentially comprehensible enough; coherently integrating his various putative federalism ideas is more challenging.

26 Charles Evans Hughes, *The Supreme Court of the United States: Six Lectures* (New York: Columbia University Press, 1928), 95–96.

27 "Hughes Calls U.S. Lawyers to Defense of States' Rights" *New York Herald Tribune*, August 22, 1930, 1; "Hughes Champions Rights of States," *Boston Globe*, August 22, 1930, 1.

28 "Hughes Calls U.S. Lawyers to Defense of States' Rights."

29 Quoted in Robert Post, "Social and Economic Legislation and the Taft Court," Taft entry in the Holmes Devise (n.p: n.d.), chapter 5, 82, manuscript on file with author.

30 James T. Patterson, *The New Deal and the States: Federalism in Transition* (Princeton, NJ: Princeton University Press, 1969), 10–19, 91–92, 158, 197–200.

31 On Hoover's progressivism, see Moreno, *The American State from the Civil War to the New Deal*, 210–220, William Leuchtenberg, *Herbert Hoover* (New York: Times Books, 2009),45–49; and Post, "Social and Economic Legislation and the Taft Court," 24–26; (arguing Hoover saw himself as a mix of progressivism and conservatism). See also *PCSR*, 169, arguing Hoover's progressivism was deeply linked to a constitutional conservatism, akin to Al Smith (and unlike FDR). Hoover's increasing turn toward a more aggressively conservative politics in his post-presidency followed from his fear that Roosevelt was sweeping aside the constitutional order. See *PCSR*, 293n99.

32 "1932 Democratic Party Platform," American Presidency Project, accessed May 13, 2023, https://www.presidency.ucsb.edu/documents/1932-democratic-party-platform.

33 See chapter 1, note 32.

34 See this chapter, note 30. Michael Greve suggests that the New Deal does not illustrate that the states' collective demand for such policies was the cause of the New Deal but that the states would latch onto it; moreover, for those states that al-

ready provided various benefits, federalizing it served as a way to shift costs onto the federal government. This, he argues, helps explain why nonstates' rights progressives in Wisconsin would have embraced the plan even though, as McReynolds noted in his dissent in the Social Security cases, this required giving up control to the federal government. Michael Greve, *The Upside-Down Constitution* (Cambridge, MA: Harvard University Press, 2012), 252–253. Such an account also matches that of progressives who tolerated grants-in-aid as a stepping stone for federalization. See chapter 2, notes 20 and 21.

35 William R. Brock, *Welfare, Democracy, and the New Deal* (Cambridge: Cambridge University Press, 1988), 155–157.

36 In addition to his appearances in earlier chapters (e.g., with Sheppard-Towner and the liberty of contract), I have written about Al Smith, Roosevelt's other main challenger, and his commitment to federalism in *PCSR*. The brief summary is that Smith was very much like Ritchie and ended up as a leader of the Liberty League opposing his onetime protégé.

37 On the AAPA's transition into the Liberty League, see David Kyvig, *Repealing National Prohibition* (Chicago: University of Chicago Press, 1979), 183–202; *PCSR*, 228–232.

38 Craig, *After Wilson*; *PCSR*, 202, 217–220.

39 See discussion of George Hunt in chapter 4.

40 Franklin D. Roosevelt, "Constitution Day Proclamation," September 8, 1931, in *Public Papers of Franklin D. Roosevelt, 48th Governor* (Albany, NY: J. B. Lyons, 1931), 28, hereafter cited as *PPFDR*.

41 "Radio Address on States' Rights," March 2, 1930, reprinted in *The Public Papers and Addresses of Franklin D. Roosevelt*, vol. 1: *The Genesis of the New Deal, 1928–1932* (New York: MacMillan, 1941), 570, 572. See also Moreno, *The American State from the Civil War to the New Deal*, 221.

42 FDR, "Address before the Conference of Governors, New London," July 16, 1929, reprinted in *The Public Papers and Addresses of Franklin D. Roosevelt*, vol. 1, 367.

43 FDR, "Address before the Conference of Governors," 371.

44 FDR, 367.

45 FDR, 372. See also chapter 1.

46 "Roosevelt for 1932," *Atlanta Constitution*, November 7, 1930, 8; "Urges Roosevelt for 1932," *New York Times*, November 6, 1930, 3.

47 FDR, "Address before the Conference of Governors," 370.

48 Joseph B. Chepaitis, "Albert C. Ritchie in Power, 1920–1927," *Maryland Historical Magazine*, 1973, 397–400; Levin, "Albert C. Ritchie," 242–243.

49 Patterson, *New Deal and the States*, 19, quoting William Bruce, "Governor Albert C. Ritchie," *North American Review*, 1927; "Governors for Strict Dry Rule, 13 to 2: Ritchie and Cox Tell Harding Maryland and Massachusetts Oppose Enforcing Volstead Act," *New York Tribune*, December 19, 1922, 1; "Governors Accept Coolidge Program to Back Up Dry Law," *New York Times*, October 21, 1923, 1.

50 Albert C. Ritchie, "Ritchie and State Prohibition Enforcement," 3, quoted in Walsh, "Prohibition and Maryland," 294.
51 "Pinchot Charges Collapse of Dry Law Enforcing; Ritchie Urges States Rights," *Chicago Tribune*, April 27, 1924, 12; Joseph Chepaitis, "The First Federal Social Welfare Measure: The Sheppard-Towner Maternity and Infancy Act, 1918–1932" (PhD diss., Georgetown University, 1968), 271.
52 Levin, "Albert C. Ritchie," 172–174; Chepaitis, "Ritchie in Power," 390.
53 Albert C. Ritchie, "Back to States' Rights," *World's Work* 47 (March 1924): 525–529; Lynn Dumenil, "'The Insatiable Maw of Bureaucracy': Antistatism and Education Reform in the 1920s," *Journal of American History* 77 (1990): 519–520; Chepaitis, "Ritchie in Power," 383–404.
54 Craig, *After Wilson*, 278; Brock, *Welfare, Democracy, and the New Deal*, 155–157.
55 See "Gov. Ritchie Sees Curb on Freedom," *New York Times*, December 11, 1924, 28. On Miller, see chapter 3, note 10.
56 For the text of Ritchie's Jefferson Day dinner, see "Ritchie Cites States' Rights as Chief National Issue," *Baltimore Sun*, April 23, 1924, 7. Ritchie continued this theme even after the election, noting that the two parties did not disagree on federalism, but internal factions did, which Ritchie hoped would be replaced by differences between the parties. "Gov. Ritchie Sees Curb on Freedom."
57 On Van Buren's creation of the Democratic Party as a vehicle to consolidate what he saw as a proper Jeffersonian constitutional commitment to states' rights and strict construction, see chapter 1, note 43.
58 Chepaitis, "Ritchie in Power," 396, 401; *New York Times*, January 1, 1925, 3; Dorothy Brown, "The Election of 1934: The 'New Deal' in Maryland," *Maryland Historical Magazine*, 1973, 406.
59 Michael Thomas Walsh, "Wet and Dry in the 'Land of Pleasant Living': Baltimore, Maryland and the Policy of National Prohibition, 1913–1933" (PhD diss., University of Maryland, 2012), 410.
60 H.J.R. 11, in *JH MD*, 1931, 353.
61 *PCSR*, 219.
62 George I. Lovell, *Legislative Deferrals: Statutory Ambiguity, Judicial Power, and American Democracy* (Cambridge: Cambridge University Press, 2003),163; David Pietrusza, *1932* (New York: Lyons Press, 2016), 243, 252. Pietrusza argues that Roosevelt repented of the radical Commonwealth Club Address, which scared his inner circle, both with its economic radicalism and expansive federal vision, by giving the much more conservative address in Pittsburgh in October 1932 endorsing a message from Coolidge and Smith to reduce the scope of federal spending—one that Roosevelt looked on later, in office, as incompatible with how he actually ended up governing. Pietrusza, *1932*, 254–255, 294–295. On the sharp turn between Roosevelt's posturing and governing, see Moreno, *American State from the Civil War to the New Deal*, 221–223 (arguing a pre-president Roosevelt was ideologically incomprehensible/impossible to tell from Hoover);

Craig, *After Wilson*; *PCSR*, 202, 218, 231–233. On Hoover's ideology, see this chapter, note 31.

63 See note 37. FDR initially told the Liberty League he was for them and their efforts to maintain constitutional government 100 percent, telling his press secretary in their presence that he wanted a press release praising them when formally established; instead, on their debut, he slammed them as plutocrats. Kyvig, *Repealing National Prohibition*, 192. On Ritchie's rejection of the vice-presidential offer, see *PCSR*, 304n10

64 Barry Goldwater, *Conscience of a Conservative* (New York: McFadden Books, 1960), 25.

65 Arthur Krock, "In Washington," *New York Times*, July 18, 1935, 18, quoted in Lyle Denniston, "*Schecter Poultry v. U.S.* and *U.S. v. Butler*," in *The Public Debate over Controversial Supreme Court Decisions*, ed. Melvin Urofsky (Washington, DC: CQ Press, 2006), 139.

66 Quoted in William Leuchtenberg, *Franklin D. Roosevelt and the New Deal* (New York: Harper & Row, 1963), 340.

67 "Burying the Dead Horse," in *A Carnival of Buncombe*, ed. Malcolm Moos (Baltimore, MD: Johns Hopkins University Press, 1956), 314.

68 David E. Kyvig, "The Road Not Taken: FDR, the Supreme Court, and Constitutional Amendment," *Political Science Quarterly* 104 (1989): 463–481. Even Bruce Ackerman has conceded that amendments empowering expanded federal economic regulatory authority would likely have passed. Ackerman, *We the People*, 341–342.

69 Kyvig, "The Road Not Taken," 480; Arthur M. Schlesinger Jr., *The Politics of Upheaval: The Age of Roosevelt*, vol. 3: *1935–1936* (New York: Houghton Mifflin, 1960), 288–290, 448–453, 487–496; Jeff Shesol, *Supreme Power: Franklin Roosevelt vs. the Supreme Court* (New York: W. W. Norton, 2011), 150–157; Cushman, *Rethinking the New Deal Court*, 23.

70 Kyvig, "The Road Not Taken," 476.

71 See this chapter, notes 24 and 25.

72 Mason, *Harlan Fiske Stone*, 408; Blackman, *Unprecedented*, 97.

73 *PCSR*, 19–21 (Madison), and 229–232 (Liberty League).

74 Edwin Amenta, Elisabeth Clemens, Jefren Olsen, Sunitah Parikh, and Theda Skocpol, "The Political Origins of Unemployment Insurance in Five American States," *Studies in American Political Development* 2 (1987): 137–182, 155. For the earlier development of worker's compensation law, see chapter 4.

75 Roy Lubove, *The Struggle for Social Security, 1900–1935* (Pittsburgh, PA: University of Pittsburgh Press, [1968] 1986), 136.

76 David M. Kennedy, *Freedom from Fear* (New York: Oxford University Press, 1999), 224–227, 268.

77 Arthur Schlesinger Jr., *The Age of Roosevelt: The Coming of the New Deal* (New York: Houghlin Mifflin, 1958), 304 (emphasis added). Martha Derthick quotes a meeting of Roosevelt and his allies to suggest that Roosevelt, when initially confronted by a national plan drawn up by his advisors, still had some lingering

sympathy for federalism, particularly because the alternative was a stronger executive—which could be Huey Long. Thus, he initially demanded the plan be fundamentally federalist, not nationalist, believing it would be sufficiently cooperative. Martha Derthick, "Roosevelt as Madison: Social Security and American Federalism," in *Keeping the Compound Republic: Essays on Federalism* (Washington, DC: Brookings, 2001), 126.

78 Dora L. Costa, *The Evolution of Retirement: An American Economic History, 1880–1990* (Chicago: University of Chicago Press, [1998] 2008) 168–170.

79 Patterson, *New Deal and the States*, 10–19, 91–92, 158, 197–200.

80 Minton's speech was widely summarized as that, and it approximates his sentiment, but what he actually had said, though repeated differently in different speeches, was that "You can't walk up to a hungry man today and say, 'Here have a constitution.' You can't hand to the farmer who has been ground down into the soil a constitution and tell him to dig himself out! You can't hand to a man who has been turned out of his home with his wife and children a copy of the constitution to cover up with…" "Minton Emphasizes the Fact that Coming Campaign is a Clarion Call to Real Service," *Muncie* (IN) *Post-Democrat*, September 4, 1934 Even many of Minton's supporters found the remark appalling. Linda C. Gugin and James St. Clair, *Sherman Minton: New Deal Senator, Cold War Justice* (Indianapolis: Indiana Historical Society, 1997), 77, 215

81 "The Texts of Governor Landon's Addresses at Madison Square Garden," *New York Times*, October 30, 1936, 16; Ackerman, *We the People*, 307.

82 FDR, "Address at Madison Square Garden, New York City," October 31, 1936, American Presidency Project, accessed May 13, 2023, https://www.presidency .ucsb.edu/documents/address-madison-square-garden-new-york-city-1.

83 Amenta et al., "Political Origins of Unemployment Insurance," 145.

84 Ira Katznelson, *Fear Itself: The New Deal and the Origins of Our Time* (New York: Liveright, 2013) (showing that southerners provided core support for the New Deal provided racial protections were built in). See also Bruce Schulman; *From Cotton Belt to Sunbelt: Federal Policy, Economic Development, and the Transformation of the South, 1938–1980* (Durham, NC: Duke University Press, 1994); *Byron E. Shafer and Richard Johnston, The End of Southern Exceptionalism: Class, Race, and Partisan Change in the Postwar South* (Cambridge, MA: Harvard University Press, 2006).

85 *JS MO*, 1935, 353.

86 Lloyd Stark, "Biennial Address," January 11, 1937, in *Messages and Proclamations of the Governors of Missouri*, vol. 14 (Columbia: State Historical Society, 1949), 16–17.

87 Patterson, *The New Deal and the States*, 19.

88 "Biennial Address of Governor George Peery," January 8, 1936, Senate Document 1, in *JS VA*, 1936, 20–22.

89 *Laws KY*, 1934, 179.

90 *JS SC*, 1934, 798.

91 *JH SC*, 1934, 1146, 1462.

92 *JS SC*, 1934, 468. On old-age pensions, see *JH SC*, 1934, 916; *JS SC*, 1934, 986.
93 *JH SC*, 1937, 40–41.
94 *JH SC*, 1935, 31.
95 Olin Johnston, "Special Message on Social Security," February 16, 1937, in *JH SC*, 1937, 447–448.
96 *JH SC*, 1938, 45.
97 *JH SC*, 1939, 61, 1470.
98 *JS MS*, 1935 (special session), 15.
99 H.C.R. 3, chapter 348, in *Laws MS*, 1936, 618–619; U.S. v. Butler, 297 U.S. 1 (1936).
100 *JS GA*, 1935, 837.
101 *JS NC*, 1935, 20, 22.
102 *JS NC*, 1937, 37.
103 *JS NC*, 1937, 36–40.
104 *JS NC*, 1941, 24.
105 S.C.R. 35, in *JS TX*, 1935, 1026–1027.
106 *JH TX*, 1935, 861–865; *JS TX*, 1935, 1485.
107 H.B. 26, in *JH TX*, 1935 (2nd session), 56–58; *JS TX*, 1935 (2nd session), 265–267, 288–922.
108 *JS TX*, 1935 (2nd session), 266.
109 *JH TX*, 1935 (2nd session), 291.
110 Brock, *Welfare, Democracy, and the New Deal*, 155–157; Craig, *After Wilson*, 278.
111 Brown, "'New Deal' in Maryland," 414–421. For the connection between Prohibition and Ritchie's electoral strength, see Walsh, "Maryland and the Policy of National Prohibition," 285–290.
112 Harry Nice, "Inaugural Address," January 9, 1935, in *JH MD*, 1935, 119–120.
113 Nice, "Inaugural Address," 129–130.
114 S.B. 10, in *JH MD*, 1936 (special session), 368; *JH MD*, 442; *JH MD*, 1936 (2nd special session), 19–20. Nice did actually condemn the federal bill for being too stingy and proposed that the state be more generous and treat Roosevelt's program as a floor, not a ceiling, thus making his claims about good policy independent of compulsion more credible and consistent with a limited progressive federalism.
115 S.J.R. 170, in *JS FL*, 1935, 265; *JH FL*, 1935, 834; S.B. 606, in *JS FL*, 1935, 72; *JH FL*, 1935, 1061; H.C.R. 5 in 1937.
116 *JS WA*, 1935, 30.
117 *JS WA*, 1935, 156; House Bill 582. For the successor bill making further changes for compliance, see H.B. 481 in 1937.
118 H.J.M. 1, in *JH/S OR*, 1935, 88, 356.
119 H.J.M. 8, in *JH/S OR*, 1935, 89, 471.
120 A.J.R. 52, in *JS CA*, 1935, 1528; *JA CA*, 1935, 2333.
121 A.B. 7, in *JS CA*, 1935 (special session), 25 (a 27–7 vote).
122 *JS CO*, 1935, 60, 69.
123 H.J.M. 1 (pensions) and H.J.M. 4 (six-hour workday), in *Laws CO*, 1935, 1144, 1148; H.B. 2, in *JS CO*, 1936, 60.

124 H.B. 4, in *JH AZ*, 1937 (2nd special session), 302. The holdout was Yuma's William Wisener, who like the rest of the house was a Democrat. The third special session of 1937 did little but push through Social Security compliance bills.

125 See, e,g., his speech accepting the nomination, "Gov. Landon's Address," *New York Times*, July 24, 1936, 1; and his more extensive Milwaukee speech focusing on Social Security, "Landon Condemns the Security Law," *New York Times*, September 27, 1936, 1. The *Times* approved of Landon's Milwaukee speech but criticized it for omitting the constitutional difficulties with the program. "Landon on Social Security," *New York Times*, September 28, 1936, 18. See also Cushman, *Rethinking the New Deal Court*, 27–29.

126 "Landon's Speeches in Philadelphia and Baltimore Assailing Federal Spending," *New York Times*, October 27, 1936.

127 Alf Landon, "Inaugural Address," January 5, 1935, in *JH KS*, 1935, 13–14. On the politics behind the amendment, see the passage of S.C.R. 4 in the legislative journals of the 1936 special session.

128 Walter Huxman, "Inaugural Address," January 13, 1937, in *JH KS*, 1937, 12.

129 Patterson, *New Deal and the States*, 158.

130 Patterson, 91.

131 *JS CT*, 1936 (special session), 18.

132 Steward Machine v. Davis, 301 U.S. 548; Helvering v. Davis, 301 U.S. 619.

133 *JS CT*, 1937, 32.

134 H.B. 940, in *JS IL*, 1935, 963; *JH IL*, 1935, 1055; H.B. 1, in *JS IL*, 1936 (special session), 181.

135 Edwin Amenta, Elisabeth Clemens, Jefren Olsen, Sunitah Parikh, and Theda Skocpol, "The Political Origins of Unemployment Insurance in Five American States," *Studies in American Political Development* 2 (1987): 170.

136 Martin Davey, "Inaugural Address," in *JH OH*, 1935, 26–27; H.B. 558, in *JH OH*, 1935 (special session), 121–124; *JS OH*, 1935 (special session), 198–199. A few months later, Davey responded to an attack by Harry Hopkins, one of Roosevelt's chief aides, and swore out a warrant for Hopkins's arrest on criminal libel charges as well as attacking Hopkins for "dictatorial" management of the state's relief efforts, leading to the state house to come within a vote of requiring the attorney general to investigate further. *JH OH*, 1935, 437–443.

137 *PCSR*, 189; chapter 2, note 62. On assuming the governorship, James Curley, Boston mayor and Roosevelt's political maestro, still faced a Republican legislature. Curley resurrected the bipartisan commission-created unemployment law that had failed under Ely and, with a more unified Democratic Party, was able to peel a handful of Republicans to his side. Amanta et al., "Political Origins of Unemployment Insurance," 169–171.

138 Leveret Saltonstall, "Inaugural Address," January 5, 1939, in Leveret Saltonstall, *Messages, Proclamations, and Addresses of his Excellency, Governor Leverett Saltonstall* (Boston: Commonwealth of Massachusetts, 1945), 14–15.

139 "The True Temper of Massachusetts in the Bill of Rights," February 2, 1939, in Saltonstall, *Messages, Proclamations, and Addresses*, 27–28.

140 See chapter 4, note 15.

141 Leveret Saltonstall, "Second Inaugural Address," February 2, 1941, in *Messages, Proclamations, and Addresses*, 139.

142 Leveret Saltonstall, "The Crisis Is Here," January 22, 1941, in *Messages, Proclamations, and Addresses*, 163.

143 "Sentinels of the Republic Records," Williams College Archives and Special Collections, accessed May 27, 2023, https://archivesspace.williams.edu/repositories /2/resources/128.

144 Leveret Saltonstall, "Sesquicentennial and Commencement," October 24, 1943, in *Messages, Proclamations, and Addresses*, 290.

145 H.B. 1, in *JS/H VT*, 1935/1936 (special session).

146 Patterson, *New Deal and the States*, 141.

147 Maine Leg. Rec. Special Sess. 12–13, 24, 18–22 (1936).

148 Maine Leg. Rec. 36–42 (1936).

149 Burkett, Maine Leg. Rec. Special Sess. 17 (1936). For the debate, see 16–22. With a 24–4 vote on the senate, 22.

150 Maine Leg. Rec. Special Sess. 19 (1936).

151 Maine Leg. Rec. Special Sess. 19–20 (1936).

152 Maine Leg. Rec. 1037–39 (1937).

153 H.B. 564 established old-age pensions; vote totals: 41–8, in *JS IN*, 84; 80–13, *JH IN*, 5; H.B. 565 (unemployment insurance); vote totals: 66–25, in *JH IN*, 87–88; and *JS IN*, 565; H.B. 364 (technical implementation authorizing state officials to cooperate with federal issues) vote totals: 34–11; in *JS IN*, 24; and 74–14, *JH IN*, 89–90.

154 *JH IN*, 1936 (special session), 62.

155 *JH IN*, 1936 (special session), 58–59.

156 *JH IN*, 1936 (special session), 100–101.

157 *Steward Machine*, 620.

158 A J.R. 20 (entered as J.R. 95), in *Laws WI*, 1935, 1224. See also A J.R. 12/J.R. 44. Both passed the legislature without a vote.

159 S.J.R. 2, in *Laws WI*, 1939.

160 Carmichael v. Southern Coal and Coke Co, 301 U.S. 495 (1937).

161 See chapter 1, esp. note 20.

162 Gerard Magliocca, "Huey P. Long and the Guarantee Clause," *Tulane Law Review* 83 (2008): 1–43.

163 H.B. 26, in *Laws LA*, 1934, 71–72.

164 Richard K. White Jr., *Kingfish: The Reign of Huey Long* (New York: Random House, 2006), x.

165 White, *Kingfish*, 45.

166 T. Harry Williams, *Huey Long* (New York: Vintage, 1981), 813; 74.1 Cong. Rec. 6109–6113.

167 Williams, *Huey Long*, 833–835.

168 *JS LA*, 1935 (4th special session), 84; *JH LA*, 1935 (4th special session), 54, 59; Magliocca, "Huey P. Long and the Guarantee Clause," 34–35.

169 "Long Orders State to Jail Federal Aids Defying Rule," *Washington Post*, September 9, 1935, 1. The *New York Times* also raised the specter of the Civil War.
170 Williams, *Huey Long*, 860–862.
171 "Long Calls Legislature to Fight Roosevelt," *Boston Globe*, September 8, 1935, A2; "Long's Legislature Fights New Deal" *New York Times*, September 8, 1935, 1.
172 "Louisiana Solons Again Assemble," *Baltimore Sun*, September 8, 1935, 1; "Senator Long's Legislature in Special Session," *New York Herald Tribune*, September 8, 1935, 5; "Lawmakers Gather in Special Session," *Times-Picayune*, September 8, 1935, 1; Raymond Swing, "The Menace of Huey Long, II" *Nation*, January 16, 1935, 70.
173 H.B. 28, in *Laws LA*, 1935 (4th special session), 59–60.
174 H.B. 21, in *Laws LA*, 1935 (4th special session), 42–43.
175 H.C.R. 2/7, in *JH LA*, 1935 (15th special session), 35
176 H.B. 71 (state constitutional amendment implementing old-age pensions) and H.B. 72.
177 *JH LA*, 1940, 27–30.
178 Kevin J. McMahon, *Reconsidering Roosevelt on Race* (Chicago: University of Chicago Press, 2004). See also introduction, note 30.
179 Patterson, *Congressional Conservatism*, 198–200.
180 *Saturday Evening Post*, March 9, 1940, in Ackerman, *We the People*, 356.
181 *We the People*, vols. 1–3, esp. *Civil Right Revolution*.
182 For these normative critiques, see the conclusion's discussion of popular constitutionalism.
183 As Leuchtenberg has argued, the 1936 election was overdetermined in a way that made viewing it as a mandate for Roosevelt especially problematic: voters might have offered a valence vote on behalf of competence in fighting the Depression more effectively than Hoover; a repudiation of the bland Landon, support for patronage, or simply partisan loyalty, which, though not unlimited (as with the conservative Vice President Garner's lament that court-packing was where he would finally "cash in my chips, boys"), went a long way in securing loyalty. William Leuchtenberg, "When the People Spoke, What Did They Say? The Election of 1936 and the Ackerman Thesis," *Yale Law Journal* 108 (1999): 2077–2114; Barry Cushman, "Mr. Dooley and Mr. Gallup: Public Opinion and Constitutional Change in the 1930s," *Buffalo Law Review* 50 (2002): 7–102; Michael W. McConnell, "The Forgotten Constitutional Moment," *Constitutional Commentary* 11 (1994): 115–144 (arguing that Ackerman's metrics for constitutional moment elections would constitutionalize Jim Crow/prevent *Brown*). For political science work on the difficulty of discerning a programmatic meaning from elections, see Stanley Kelley Jr., *Interpreting Elections* (Princeton, NJ: Princeton University Press, 1983); and Robert Dahl, "Myth of the Presidential Mandate," in *Politicians and Party Politics*, ed. John Geer (Baltimore, MD: Johns Hopkins University Press, 1998), 239–258. See also Christopher H. Achen and Larry M. Bartels, *Democracy for Realists: Why Elections Do Not Produce Representative Government* (Princeton, NJ: Princeton University Press, 2016).

184 George Wolfskill, *The Revolt of the Conservatives: A History of the American Liberty League* (New York: Houghton Mifflin, 1962), 263.

185 Cushman, "Mr. Dooley."

186 See, e.g., Katznelson, *Fear Itself*; Ira Katznelson, *When Affirmative Action Was White: An Untold History of Racial Inequality in Twentieth-Century America* (New York: W. W. Norton, 2005); Joe Soss, Richard C. Fording, and Sanford F. Schram, "The Color of Devolution: Race, Federalism, and the Politics of Social Control," *American Journal of Political Science* 52 (2008): 536–553. Daniel Beland argues that much of Social Security's supposedly white supremacist construction was due more to administrative rather than racial calculations, adding that the exclusion of agricultural and domestic workers was universally supported but agrees that southern Democrats pressed for local administration for racial purposes. Daniel Beland, *Social Security: History and Politics from the New Deal to the Privatization Debate* (Lawrence: University Press of Kansas, 2005), 88–96.

187 Patterson, *New Deal and the States*, 91–92.

188 Patterson, 197.

189 Patterson, 197.

190 American federalism plausibly would have looked quite different, and remained far more decentralized, had the Supreme Court trimmed its excesses before pressure built up that would push it to so starkly flip the other way. For example, it could have unleashed the state police powers in *West Coast Hotel* without authorizing equivalent federal regulations in *Darby* and *Wickard* and/or grants-in-aid by embracing the Hamiltonian rather than traditional Madisonian tax power in *Steward Machine v. Davis*. Similarly, the Court could have reversed *Hammer v. Dagenhart* (to protect states from the economic policies of one another) without forging the almost limitless *Wickard* aggregation test. See discussion of *Hammer* in chapter 1.

191 Quoted in Schlesinger, *The Politics of Upheaval*, 280.

192 Cushman, *Rethinking the New Deal Court*, 223–224; Barry Cushman, "A Stream of Legal Consciousness: The Current of Commerce Doctrine from Swift to Jones and Laughlin," *Fordham Law Review* 61 (1992):102–160, 157–160, esp. 157.

193 Ackerman, *We the People: Transformations*, 315–316, 327, 338–342.

194 James R. Stoner: "Rational Compromise: Charles Evans Hughes as a Progressive Originalist," in *Towards an American Conservatism: Constitutional Conservatism in the Progressive Era*, ed. Joseph Postell and Johnathan O'Neill (New York: Palgrave Macmillan, 2013), 209–234.

195 James Patterson, *Congressional Conservatism and the New Deal* (Lexington: University of Kentucky Press, 1967), 99–110, 142.

196 Kimberly Johnson, *Governing the American State: Congress and the New Federalism, 1877–1929* (Princeton, NJ: Princeton University Press, 2007), 151–153.

197 On the 1936 election, see Craig, *After Wilson*, 275–305. On the 1938 primaries, see Susan Dunn, *Roosevelt's Purge: How FDR Fought to Change the Democratic Party* (Cambridge, MA: Harvard University Press, 2012); Patterson, *Congressio-*

nal Conservatism; Sidney Milkis, *The President and the Parties* (Oxford: Oxford University Press, 1993), 87–95.

198 See, e.g., H.J.R. 7, in *JH VT*, 1939, 68–70; H.J.R. 19, in *JS VT*, 1943, 72, 84; *JH VT*, 1943, 96, "Inaugural Address of William H. Wills," printed in *JS VT*, 1943, 211.

199 See the legislative debate over cooperating with national forests in Maine Leg. Rec. 840–848 (1935).

200 H.J.R. 37, in *Acts VA*, 1940, 947–948; S.J.R. 17, in *JH VA*, 1942, 344.

201 *JH MD*, 1939, 23–24.

202 *JS OH*, 1939, 1246–1251.

203 Dwight Griswold, "Inaugural Address," January 9, 1941, in *LJ NE*, 1941, 63.

204 S.C.R. 19, in *JS IN*, 1947, 492–494, 700 (31–10 vote). See also H.C.R. 2, in *JH IN*, 1947, for a companion bill.

205 Brokenburr (R) and Fleming (D) proposed S.C.R. 13–15, in *JS IN*, 1947, 215–217.

206 S.C.R. 54, in *Laws IN*, 1969, 1868.

207 Leveret Saltonstall, "Progress in Readjustment," January 10, 1944, in *Public Papers of Saltonstall*, 310–311.

208 *JH NH*, 1941, 28. Though, even Murphy had preferred interstate labor compacts to direct federal regulation (as the Fair Labor Standards Act would eventually institute). *JH NH*, 1937, 64. Murphy's inaugural address (January 5, 1939) had called for harmonizing state wage and hours laws for intrastate activity to match federal standards set for interstate commerce.

209 On the centrality of federalism to the American Revolution, see chapter 1.

210 *JH NH*, 1941, 47–48.

211 For an analysis of the iconography of the Roosevelt administration, see Wolfgang Schivelbusch, *Three New Deals: Reflections on Roosevelt's America, Mussolini's Italy, and Hitler's Germany, 1933–39* (New York: Picador, 2006).

Conclusion: Progressive Federalism's End . . . and Beginning?

1 "Address to the Governors' Conference," June 24, 1957, in *Public Papers of the Presidents of the United States: Dwight D. Eisenhower 1957*, 490–495. See also David A. Nichols, *A Matter of Justice: Eisenhower and the Beginning of the Civil Rights Revolution* (New York: Simon & Schuster, 2007), 153–154. While often derided by conservatives as a me-tooer little different than the Democrats, Eisenhower privately shared their views in despising the New Deal (other than its defense of labor unions, which he favored); unlike them, however, he recognized an attack on it was politically suicidal at the time. Douglas Harris, "Dwight Eisenhower and the New Deal: The Politics of Preemption," *Presidential Studies Quarterly* 27 (1997): 333–342.

2 See preceding chapter.

3 Frederick Rudolph, "The American Liberty League, 1934–1940," *American His-*

torical Review 56 (1950): 20–23, and introduction 1, notes 31 and 32 and chapter 1, esp. notes 34–36.

4   William H. Riker, *Federalism: Origin, Operation, Significance* (New York: Little Brown, 1964), 155, but more generally 139–155. For a typical popular example, see David Greenberg, "What Reagan Meant by States' Rights," Slate, November 20, 2007, http://www.slate.com/articles/news_and_politics/history_lesson/2007 /11/dogwhistling_dixie.html.

5   Lucas A. Powe, *The Warren Court and American Politics* (Cambridge, MA: Harvard University Press, 2000), 494–495.

6   Bradley D. Hays, *States in American Constitutionalism: Interpretation, Authority, and Politics* (New York: Routledge, 2019), 73–74.

7   Robert Schapiro, *Polyphonic Federalism: Toward the Protection of Fundamental Rights* (Chicago: University of Chicago Press, 2009), 46, 45–50.

8   Phillip Klinkner with Rogers Smith, *The Unsteady March* (Chicago: University of Chicago Press, 1999), 328–329. See also Rogers M. Smith, *Civic Ideals: Conflicting Visions of Citizenship in U.S. History* (New Haven, CT: Yale University Press, 1997), 277–285, 296–312, 332–335 (arguing that the republican tradition's states' rights constitutionalism joined with the ascriptive tradition of racism, as well as some free-labor manifestations of liberalism, to trump the liberal egalitarianism promised with Reconstruction); Lisa Miller, "Invisible Black Victims: How American Federalism Perpetuates Racial Inequality in Criminal Justice," *Law and Society Review* 44 (2010): 805–842; also chapter 6, note 186. Federalism had countervailing tendencies as well, dating back to the invocation of states' rights to justify antislavery liberty laws. For one, states passed their own public accommodations laws both before and after the overturned 1875 federal statute. Sean Beienburg and Ben Johnson, "Black Popular Constitutionalism and Federalism after the *Civil Rights Cases*" *Arizona Law Review* 65 (forthcoming). See also Marcia G. Synnott, "Federalism Vindicated: University Desegregation in South Carolina and Alabama, 1962–1963," *Journal of Policy History* 1 (1989): 292–318. See also this chapter, note 86.

9   Pauline Maier, *Ratification: The People Debate the Constitution, 1787–1788* (New York: Simon & Schuster, 2010), 467; Martha Derthick, *Keeping the Compound Republic: Essays on Federalism* (Washington, DC: Brookings, 2001), 4.

10   Herman V. Ames, *State Documents on Federal Relations* (Philadelphia: University of Pennsylvania Press, 1906), 91.

11   See Beienburg and Johnson, "Black Popular Constitutionalism and Federalism after the *Civil Rights Cases*," and Sean Beienburg, "The Fifteenth Amendment: How Republicans Tried to Reconcile Black Rights and States Rights, and How State Legislatures Debated it via the Blair and Lodge Bills" (n.p.: n.d.), manuscript on file with author.

12   Sean Beienburg, *Prohibition, the Constitution, and States' Rights* (Chicago: University of Chicago Press, 2019), chapter 2, hereafter cited as *PCSR*.

13   Michael Klarman, *From Jim Crow to Civil Rights: The Supreme Court and the Struggle for Racial Equality* (New York: Oxford University Press, 2004), 68.

14 For accounts discussing the late nineteenth-century Lost Cause creation and rec-reation of a South devoted to federalism rather than slavery, see Gary W. Galla-gher and Alan T. Nolan, eds., *The Myth of the Lost Cause and Civil War History* (Bloomington: Indiana University Press, 2000); and Paul Herron, *Framing the Solid South: The State Constitutional Conventions of Secession, Reconstruction, and Redemption, 1860–1902* (Lawrence: University Press of Kansas, 2017). For contemporary primary-source treatments showing that slavery, not federalism, animated secession, see Charles B. Dew, *Apostles of Disunion: Southern Seces-sion Commissioners and the Causes of the Civil War* (Charlottesville: Univer-sity of Virginia Press, 2002); and James W. Loewen and Edward Sebesta, ed., *The Confederate and Neo-Confederate Reader: The Great Truth About the Lost Cause* (Jackson: University of Mississippi Press, 2011). For the nineteenth-century northern interest in decentralized states' rights federalism, see chapter 1, esp. notes 34–36, and *PCSR*, chapter 2.
15 See introduction, note 30.
16 S. J. Lawrence W. Moore, "Federalism, Racism, and Yahooism," *Loyola Law Re-view* 29 (1983): 946. Moore speculates that left-leaning antipathy toward feder-alism results from what he dubs "yahooism," a cosmopolitan scorn for insular, local, homogeneous, and provincial communities and beliefs distinct from the na-tional elite (947).
17 Heather K. Gerken, "A New Progressive Federalism," *Democracy: A Journal of Ideas*, 2012, http://www.democracyjournal.org/24/a-new-progressive-federalism .php?page=all.
18 Gerken. "New Progressive Federalism"; Heather K. Gerken, "Foreword: Feder-alism All the Way Down," *Harvard Law Review* 124 (2010): 4. Moore offered an explicitly Rawlsian defense of federalism on similar participatory grounds. Moore, "Federalism, Racism, and Yahooism," 948–950. Ilya Somin, favorably commenting on Gerken's proposals, adds that "foot voting" (relocating to more sympathetic locations) would help strengthen the case by adding even more power to electoral participation. Ilya Somin, "Taking Dissenting by Deciding All the Way Down," *Tulsa Law Review* 48 (2013): 523–534.
19 On the effort to resurrect interest in federalism on the Left, see Gerken, "A New Progressive Federalism"; and Gerken, "A New Progressive Federalism"; Gary Gerstle, "Federalism in America: Beyond the Tea Partiers," *Dissent* (Fall 2010): 29–36. For a cooperative, rather than national-limiting, federalism, Robert A. Schapiro, "Not Old or Borrowed: The Truly New Blue Federalism," *Harvard Law and Policy Review* 3 (2009): 33–57; Richard B. Freeman and Joel Rogers, "The Promise of Progressive Federalism," in *Remaking America: Democracy and Public Policy in an Age of Inequality*, ed. Joe Soss, Jacob Hacker, and Suzanne Mettler (New York: Russell Sage Foundation, 2010); Erwin Chemerinsky, *En-hancing Government: Federalism for the 21st Century* (Stanford, CA: Stanford University Press, 2008).
20 It is hard to understate the discrediting of federalism that massive resistance had for progressives, especially in the wake of it already being severely weakened

by New Deal political reconstruction. I am agnostic on the corollary question of whether the New Deal or massive resistance did more to ultimately sever ties between states' rights constitutionalism and progressivism. Whether one considers turning the leading states' rights party into an antistates' rights party and changing the nation's jurisprudence to match or making the rhetoric itself toxic, is more significant, is an interesting question and worthy of further research but beyond the scope of this inquiry.

21 Similarly, as Brad Hays notes, slavery defeated or distorted other institutions such as judicial review. Hays, *States in American Constitutionalism*, 7.

22 On the racially biased construction of the welfare state, see chapter 6, note 186.

23 "The Roberts Court and Federalism," *New York University Journal of Law and Liberty* 4 (2009): 366–367.

24 William Brennan Jr., "The Bill of Rights and the States: The Revival of State Constitutions as Guardians of Individual Rights," *NYU Law Review* 61 (1986): 535. For a similar, contemporary exhortation to turn to state constitutions as sites of egalitarianism, see Sanford Levinson, *Framed: America's 51 Constitutions and the Crisis of Government* (New York: Oxford University Press, 2012). See also introduction, note 8.

25 United States v. Windsor, 570 U.S. 744 (2013); Ernest A. Young, "Exit, Voice and Loyalty as Federalism Strategies: Lessons from the Same-Sex Marriage Debate," *University of Colorado Law Review* 85 (2014): 1134–1153; Schapiro, "The Truly New Blue Federalism," 43–45.

26 See chapter 1, note 44.

27 Nolan McCarty, Keith Poole, and Howard Rosenthal, *Polarized America* (Cambridge, MA: MIT Press, 2006), 27–32.

28 Barry Cushman, "Regime Theory and Unenumerated Rights: A Cautionary Note," *University of Pennsylvania Journal of Constitutional Law* 9 (2006): 263–279.

29 That core ideological sympathy to federalism thus meant that the doctrine can be and has been easily and opportunistically invoked, especially in cases where it is more rhetorically appealing than the substantive policy ground. Obviously, northeastern states' rights, like southern invocations for white supremacy, had an often-instrumental purpose, as the business-connected legal community no doubt feared both redistribution to the less-developed parts of the country or Prohibition's seeming approval of the national government's suppression of property rights. It is hard to attribute the constitutional interest of the members of the National Association of Manufacturers to vindicating federalism for its own sake, but they worked with and through groups like the Sentinels or lawyers, like Elihu Root, who provided material support for constitutional principles and guaranteeing the best cases possible through adversarial law. Similarly, invoking federalism in opposition to Sheppard-Towner offered a more appealing rhetorical gloss in warding off the prospect of redistributive appeals from the West and South. But, as with civil liberties, the invocation of an otherwise valid constitutional principle by unpopular or unsympathetic plaintiffs should not be sufficient grounds to dis-

credit it. On the insufficiency of motivated reasoning to discredit constitutional-ism, see Keith E. Whittington, "Extrajudicial Constitutional Interpretation: Three Objections and Responses," *North Carolina Law Review* 80 (2002):774–852, esp. 821–822, 841–844.

30 See introduction, notes 7 and 47 (on extrajudicial constitutionalism) and notes 44–46 (on popular constitutionalism).

31 Larry Kramer, *The People Themselves* (New York: Oxford University Press, 2005), 228–229. Ironically, by focusing almost exclusively on the federal level, his own history reinforces the very trend he seeks to undo.

32 See, e.g., Larry Alexander and Lawrence B. Solum, "Popular? Constitutionalism? The People Themselves: Popular Constitutionalism and Judicial Review," *Harvard Law Review* 118 (2005): 1594–1640; Lucas A. Powe Jr., "Are 'the People' Missing in Action (and Should Anyone Care)? The People Themselves: Popular Constitutionalism and Judicial Review," *Texas Law Review* 83 (2005): 855–896; McConnell, "The Forgotten Constitutional Moment." Some of these critics of popular constitutionalism are themselves advocates of extrajudicial constitutionalism but fear the former does not take seriously *constitutionalism*. See, e.g., George Thomas, *The Madisonian Constitution* (Baltimore, MD: Johns Hopkins University Press, 2008), 13–15, 158, 237; Keith E. Whittington, *Political Foundations of Judicial Supremacy* (Princeton, NJ: Princeton University Press, 2007), 48; *PCSR*, 234–238. For a recent piece attempting to take these critiques seriously by situating a legitimate popular constitutionalism within institutions and within *law* (specifically state constitutions), see G. Alan Tarr, "Popular Constitutional-ism in State and Nation," *Ohio State Law Journal* 77 (2016): 237–280.

33 The weaker versions of these theories, usually but not always classed as extraju-dicial constitutionalism, merely reject the idea that judges should be the exclusive interpreters and enforcers of the Constitution. Instead, they hold that elected of-ficials should also enforce the Constitution as additional or redundant checks en-suring fidelity to its text and as required by their oaths (on oaths, see introduction, note 47). In other words, these theories are agnostic about the proper way to in-terpret the Constitution, holding only that the task, however it should be imple-mented (originalist, aspirationalist, etc.), belongs to more than judges.

However, stronger forms of these theories, not just Kramer's but most notably Bruce Ackerman's "constitutional moments" framework outlined in his *We the People* trilogy, are less about *who* implements the Constitution than *how* it should be interpreted. Such normative theories hold that popular action and the regular electoral processes can faithfully remake the proper, binding meaning of the Con-stitution and thus are closer to a constitutional methodology explaining *how* the Constitution should be interpreted today.

If anything, the constitutional theorizing of the state political actors discussed in this book does not resemble the ultrademocratic populism feared by popular constitutionalism's critics. Rather, it looks more like the constitutionally conser-vative originalism loathed by many advocates of the stronger forms of popular constitutionalism. To put it more bluntly, George Hunt, Al Smith, and the like would agree, against the popular constitutionalists, that Article V is the only legitimate method of constitutional change (see chapter 4, note 4).

Incorporating state constitutional interpretation as a source of constitutional meaning would thus resist the implicit consolidation of accounts such as Bruce Ackerman's *We the People*. Ackerman's constitutional history builds an explicitly nationalist story of a series of refounding "constitutional moments" (Reconstruction, the New Deal, and perhaps the civil rights revolution), all of which culminate in the declaration that Article V is obsolete because we are "a nation-centered people stuck with a state-centered system of formal revision." See Ackerman, *We the People: Civil Rights Revolution* (Cambridge: Harvard University Press, 2014, 28). At the very least, the account in this book argues that the "middle republic" period between his first and second refounding American moments was arguably much more state-oriented than he understands it to be.

34 See this chapter, notes 17–19.

35 Danny Vinik, "Inside the New Battle Against Google," Politico, September 17, 2017, https://www.politico.com/agenda/story/2017/09/17/open-markets-google-antitrust-barry-lynn-000523.

36 Sanford Levinson, "The 21st Century Rediscovery of Nullification and Secession in American Political Rhetoric," in *Nullification and Secession in Modern Constitutional Thought*, ed. Sanford Levinson (Lawrence: University Press of Kansas, 2016); Sean Beienburg, "States Rights' Gone Wrong? Secession, Nullification, and Reverse-Nullification in Contemporary America," *Tulsa Law Review* 52 (2018): 191–204. For discussion of the Court's flimsy treatment of secession, see also *PCSR*, 23, and 261–262, notes 25 and 27. For the Second Vermont Republic, see "Vermont Declaration of Independence," Second Vermont Republic, April 22, 2019, https://vermontrepublic.org/vermont-declaration-of-independence/.

37 For example, an opportunistic federalism obviously could use more aggressive Tenth Amendment challenges to argue the federal government is exceeding its enumerated powers, should conservatives push through, say, morals legislation, but such a federalism would almost inevitably collapse into and more closely resemble the third type.

38 Malcom M. Feeley and Edward Rubin, *Federalism; Political identity and Tragic Compromise* (Ann Arbor: University of Michigan Press, 2008), 22.

39 Alexander Hertel-Fernendez, *State Capture: How Conservative Activists, Big Business, and Wealth Donors Reshaped the American States—and the Nation* (New York: Oxford University Press, 2019).

40 Hertel-Fernandez, *State Capture*; Lydia Bean, "Progressive Elites Only Remember that States Exist When They're Out of Power in DC. That's a Problem," Vox, April 3, 2019, https://www.vox.com/polyarchy/2019/4/3/18294140/state-politics-legislatures-democrats.

41 Michael Doonan, "Opportunistic Federalism and a Liberal Resurgence," American Prospect, December 14, 2017, https://prospect.org/article/opportunistic-federalism-and-liberal-resurgence.

42 On polarization more generally, see Nolan McCarty, *Polarization: What Every-
    one Needs to Know* (New York: Oxford University Press, 2019). On negative
    polarization, see Shanto Iyengar and Masha Krupenkin, "The Strengthening of
    Partisan Affect," *Political Psychology* 39 (2018): 201–218. On federalism as a
    solution, see Jenna Bednar, "Polarization, Diversity, and Democratic Robust-
    ness," *Proceedings of the National Academy of Sciences* 118, no. 50 (2021).

43 The piece's unfortunately inflammatory title, "It's Time for a Bluexit," hinted at
    separatism and was derided as such, but instead the piece effectively proposes
    something akin to what many of the progressives in this book sought: no grants-
    in-aid and instead state-taxed and funded welfare states. Kevin Baker, "It's Time
    for a Bluexit," *New Republic*, March 9, 2017, https://newrepublic.com/article
    /140948/bluexit-blue-states-exit-trump-red-america.

44 Jacob M. Grumbach, "From Backwaters to Major Policymakers: Policy Polar-
    ization in the States, 1970–2014," *Perspectives on Politics* 16 (2018): 416–435;
    Daniel J. Hopkins, *The Increasingly United States* (Chicago: University of Chi-
    cago Press, 2018); Charles Kesler, "The New War between the States," Clare-
    mont Review of Books, 2023, https://claremontreviewofbooks.com/the-new-war
    -between-the-states/.

45 See introduction, note 31, and chapter 6 more generally.

46 See, e.g., Gerken "A New Progressive Federalism"; and Gerken, "Federalism All
    the Way Down."

47 See introduction, note 19.

48 Ironically, subsequent originalist scholarship has offered a plausible and indeed com-
    pelling case that, while the federal government's domain of activity was to be lim-
    ited, the procedural protections of noncommandeering were not present until shortly
    after the Constitution went into effect—almost, but not quite, the Founding under-
    standing. See Wesley J. Campbell, "Commandeering and Constitutional Change,"
    Yale Law Journal 122 (2013): 1104–1181. The noncommandeering understand-
    ing appeared a few years later in the mid-1790s, anchored the US Supreme
    Court's *Prigg v. Pennsylvania* case in 1842, and became well-settled as the ef-
    fectively consensus position and presumptive rule by the time of Prohibition.
    See *PCSR*.

49 Skeptics of federalism like Feeley, Rubin, and Barber, however, criticize noncom-
    mandeering for setting significant limits on federal power, even if it is merely lim-
    iting one means, rather than any end, of the federal government

50 "Government of the United States," *National Gazette*, February 4, 1792, https://
    founders.archives.gov/documents/Madison/01-14-02-0190.

51 Charles C. W. Cooke, a libertarian-leaning and Trump-skeptical writer at the con-
    servative *National Review*, was happily eyeing a progressive discovery of doc-
    trines like federalism and the separation of powers as a means of constraining
    Donald Trump. "Post Election, Progressives Are Embracing Conservative Tradi-
    tions," *Los Angeles Times*, December 31, 2016, https://www.latimes.com/opinion
    /op-ed/la-oe-cooke-left-embraces-conservatism-20161213-story.html.

52 David French, "Of Course America's Too Big to Govern," *National Review On-*

line, May 18, 2018, https://www.nationalreview.com/2018/05/america-too-big
-to-govern-needs-federalism/.

53 *PCSR*.

54 Sean Beienburg and Nicholas Jacobs, "An Introduction to Federalism and the
Arizona Constitution," Arizona State University Center for Political Thought
and Leadership, accessed May 8, 2023, https://cptl.asu.edu/az-constitution
-introduction.

55 Sean Beienburg "Prohibition and Federalism: Lessons for Today," *National Review Online*, December 13, 2019, https://www.nationalreview.com/2019/12
/prohibition-lessons-in-federalism/.

56 See, e.g., on plutocracy, Sotirios A. Barber, *The Fallacies of States' Rights* (Cam-
bridge, MA: Harvard University Press, 2013), 208–209; Hertel-Fernendez, *State
Capture*. On hypocrisy, see Feeley and Rubin, *Federalism*, 107–117; and Barber,
Fallacies of States' Rights, 145–147.

57 Indeed, the fact Americans insist on this baseline of rights is part of Feeley and
Rubin's case for arguing America should be thought of merely as a single community. Feely and Rubin, *Federalism*, 115–116. For the argument recognizing both
the idea of a federal floor of rights and differences in America's political communities, see Jeffrey Sutton, *51 Imperfect Solutions: States and the Making of American Constitutional Law* (New York: Oxford University Press, 2018).

58 Barber, *Fallacies*, 22, 101–118; Feeley and Rubin, *Federalism*, 24, 84–86. For an
example of what they are criticizing, see Michael Greve, *The Upside-Down Constitution* (Cambridge, MA: Harvard University Press, 2012.)

59 As John Grove has observed, Barber's critique of federalism is actually as much
against such libertarians and free-marketers as against constitutional federalism,
even "states rights federalism." John G. Grove, Review of *Fallacies of States'
Rights*, *American Political Thought* 2 (2015): 348.

60 Barber, *Fallacies*; Feeley and Rubin, *Federalism*.

61 For just recent treatments of progressives so decrying the Constitution, see Ryan
D. Doerfler and Samuel Moyn, "The Constitution Is Broken and Should Not
be Reclaimed," *New York Times*, August 19, 2022, https://www.nytimes.com
/2022/08/19/opinion/liberals-constitution.html; Ositwa Nawvenu, "The Constitution Is the Crisis," *New Republic*, October 19, 2020, https://newrepublic.com
/article/159823/constitution-crisis-supreme-court; Sanford Levinson, "The Constitution Is the Crisis," *Atlantic*, October 1, 2019, https://www.theatlantic.com/ideas
/archive/2019/10/the-constitution-is-the-crisis/598435/; Megan Day and Baskhar
Sunkara, "Think the Constitution Will Save Us? Think Again," *New York Times*,
August 9, 2018, https://www.nytimes.com/2018/08/09/opinion/constitution-
founders-democracy-trump.html; Ryan Cooper, "The Case Against the Constitution," *Week*, February 1, 2017, http://theweek.com/articles/677164 /case
-against-american-constitution; Matthew Yglesias, "American Democracy Is
Doomed," Vox, March 2, 2015, https://www.vox.com/2015/3/2/8120063 /ameri
can-democracy-doomed. This does not include all the critiques of federalism as
obsolete, either, which is a cottage industry in and of itself.

62 Ruy Teixeira, the coauthor of the influential book *The Emerging Democratic Majority* that best laid out this view, has argued that subsequent political developments and coalitional realignments, particularly working-class and Hispanic defections to the GOP, suggest much less cause for confidence from the Left. Ruy Teixeira, "The Democrats' Hispanic Voter Problem," Liberal Patriot, November 9, 2021, https://theliberalpatriot.substack.com/p/the-democrats-hispanic -voter-problem-dfc. For an early observation of this asymmetry of federalism only constraining conservatives, see Antonin Scalia, "The Two Faces of Federalism," *Harvard Journal of Law and Public Policy* 6 (1982): 20.

63 Ed Kilgore, "The Rights Blue States May Lose if the GOP Returns to Power," *New York Magazine*, January 1, 2022, https://nymag.com/intelligencer/article /rights-blue-states-may-lose-gop-returns-power.html.

64 Jeremiah Poff, "House Republicans Propose Bill Encouraging History of Communism in High Schools," *Washington Examiner*, December 2, 2021, https:// www.washingtonexaminer.com/policy/education/house-republicans-propose -requiring-history-of-communism-in-high-schools.

65 Barber, *Fallacies of States' Rights*, 155–156, Feeley and Rubin, *Federalism*, 140–143.

66 They noted the lawyers challenging the federal bill did not invoke the argument that it exceeded the enumerated power of the commerce clause, so the two justices declined to rule against the bill on those federalism grounds but invited future consideration of the issue. See Gonzales v. Carhart, 550 U.S. 124 (2007). See Jordan Goldberg, "The Commerce Clause and Federal Abortion Law: Why Progressives Might Be Tempted to Embrace Federalism," *Fordham Law Review* 75 (2006): 301.

67 See Beienburg and Johnson, "Black Popular Constitutionalism and Federalism after the *Civil Rights Cases*."

68 On George, see Michael New, "Abortion and the 14th Amendment," *National Review*, September 6, 2011, https://www.nationalreview.com/corner/abortion -and-14th-amendment-michael-j-new/. It is worth noting that George defends this exception within a general sympathy for and admiration of constitutional federalism and its implementation via the Ninth and Tenth Amendments but believes the Fourteenth Amendment is more relevant here. See Robert P. George, "Ruling to Serve," First Things, April 2013, https://www.firstthings.com/article/2013/04 /ruling-to-serve.

69 US Supreme Court, *Brief of Amici Curiae, Scholars of Jurisprudence John M Finnis and Robert P. George* (Washington, DC: Legal Printers, 2021), https:// www.supremecourt.gov/DocketPDF/19/19–1392/185196/20210729093557582 _210169a%20Amicus%20Brief%20for%20efiling%207%2029%2021.pdf.

70 *Dobbs*, opinion of the Court, slip opinion 29, 38, Kavanaugh, concurring slip opinion 3–4. Since it was dealing with a question of whether an individual right existed or not, the *Dobbs* opinion did not address whether Congress had or lacked the power to regulate it in the states. The various opinions allude to action by Congress, but it is unclear whether this is simply in the realm of, say, federal health benefits, federal districts and territories, and the like, or whether it would

uphold a regulation of abortion in the states of the kind Scalia and Thomas implicitly rejected.

71 Graham had done this before, but it had new salience in light of *Dobbs*. Whether this was a serious bill, or mere position-taking, especially counter-messaging to a contemporaneous Democratic proposal of a federal bill that would set nationwide abortion rights and prohibit states from regulating abortion, was debated but is ultimately irrelevant. Igor Bobic, "Republicans Introduce Bill to Ban Abortion after 15 Weeks," Huffington Post, September 13, 2022, https://news.yahoo.com /republicans-introduce-bill-ban-abortion-165837981.html; Amy Wang and Eugene Scott, "House Passes Bill to Codify Abortion Rights," *Washington Post*, July 15, 2022, https://www.washingtonpost.com/politics/2022/07/15/house-abortion -roe-v-wade/.

72 See, e.g., Ken I. Kersch, *Conservatives and the Constitution: Imagining Constitutional Restoration in the Heyday of American Liberalism* (Cambridge: Cambridge University Press, 2019); Joseph Lowndes, *From the New Deal to the New Right: Race and the Southern Origins of Modern Conservatism* (New Haven, CT: Yale University Press, 2008).

73 "Congress Should Work to End Infanticide in America," *National Review*, 2022, https://www.nationalreview.com/2022/09/congress-should-work-to-end-infanti cide-in-america/; Andrew C. McCarthy, "Dissent from NR's Editorial Favoring Federal Abortion Ban," *National Review*, September 14, 2022, https:// www.nationalreview.com/corner/dissent-from-nrs-editorial-favoring-federal -abortion-ban/; Charles C. W. Cooke, "Another Dissent from NR's Editorial Favoring Federal Abortion Ban," *National Review*, September 15, 2022, https:// www.nationalreview.com/corner/another-dissent-from-nrs-editorial-favoring -federal-abortion-ban/; Philip Klein, "In Favor of Abortion Federalism," *National Review*, September 15, 2022, https://www.nationalreview.com/corner/in -favor-of-abortion-federalism/. See also Ramesh Ponnuru, "Republicans Must Act on a Late Term Abortion Ban," *National Review* August 25, 2022, https:// www.nationalreview.com/magazine/2022/09/12/republicans-must-act-on -a-late-term-abortion-ban/; Ramesh Ponnuru, "Yes, It's Constitutional for Congress to Pass Abortion Laws," *National Review*, January 23, 2015, https://www .nationalreview.com/2015/01/yes-its-constitutional-congress-pass-abortion-laws -ramesh-ponnuru. For the pre-*Dobbs* debate between Edward Whelan (adopting Scalia's position) and John Finnis and Joshua Craddock (adopting the view the Fourteenth Amendment restricts abortion), see Joshua Craddock, "John Finnis Is Right," First Things, March 2021, https://www.firstthings.com/web-exclusives /2021/03/john-finnis-is-right; and Joshua Craddock, "Protecting Prenatal Persons: Does the Fourteenth Amendment Prohibit Abortion?" *Harvard Journal of Law and Public Policy* 40 (2017): 539–571.

74 See this chapter, note 71.

75 Fulton v. Philadelphia, 593 U.S. ____2020; Employment Division of Oregon v. Smith, 494 U.S. 872 (1990); City of Boerne v. Flores, 521 U.S. 507 (1997). Mid-twentieth-century progressives had other views—the expansive version of

the free exercise clause was developed by progressives, most notably by the Warren Court in *Sherbert v. Verner*, 374 U.S. 398 (1963) (over the protest of the
conservative John Harlan II, joined only by *Roe* dissenter Byron White). This expansive understanding was reiterated in the progressive justices' dissent in the
Smith case, most famously leading to Chuck Schumer and Ted Kennedy working to pass the federal RFRA while decrying Scalia—who had merely adopted the
minimalist states' rights position of Harlan, as *Smith's* author.

76 They may be correct, as may be George and his allies on abortion, insofar as even
states' rights federalists concede state sovereignty is bounded by the Constitution's text; the point is that any possible progressive success will require a states'
rights argument.

77 See, e.g., Michael McConnell, "The Origins and Historical Understanding of Free
Exercise of Religion," *Harvard Law Review* 103 (1990): 1409–1517 (arguing
that the original understanding of the free clause provides some exemption from
otherwise neutral laws). For the claim that it did not, see Phillip Hamburger, "A
Constitutional Right to Religious Exemptions: A Historical Perspective," *George
Washington Law Review* 60 (1992): 915; Vincent Phillip Munoz, *Religious Liberty
and the American Founding: Natural Rights and the Original Meanings of the First
Amendment Religion Clauses* (Chicago: University of Chicago Press, 2022).

78 Adrian Vermeule, *Common-Good Constitutionalism* (Hoboken, NJ: Wiley, 2022);
Adrian Vermeule, "Beyond Originalism," *Atlantic*, March 31, 2020, https://
www.theatlantic.com/ideas/archive/2020/03/common-good-constitutionalism
/609037/. For a conservative critique of Vermeule's ideas partly on grounds it
has contempt for federalism, see James Stoner, "A Constitution for the Common Good?" Law & Liberty, August 1, 2022, https://lawliberty.org/forum
/a-constitution-for-the-common-good/. On some social conservatives' more recent turn from constitutional proceduralism, see Kersch, *Conservatives and the
Constitution*, esp. chapters 5–6, and for complications to that theory (arguing that
there has been greater consistency of and commitment to constitutional procedure among *originalist* conservatives, at least, if not for nonoriginalist conservatives like Vermeule), see Sean Beienburg, "Originalists Were Always for (Some)
Judicial Engagement," Law & Liberty, January 22, 2020, https://lawliberty.org
/originalists-were-always-for-some-judicial-engagement/.

79 Edmund Burke Foundation, "National Conservatism: A Statement of Principles,"
American Conservative, June 15, 2022, https://www.theamericanconservative
.com/national-conservatism-a-statement-of-principles/. Samuel Gregg notes that
the recognition seems a grudging "concession to experimentation and freedom
at the level of states rather than characterized as one of America's fundamental
contributions to Western constitutional thought." Samuel Gregg, "The Poverty of
National Conservatism," National Interest, July 18, 2022, https://nationalinterest
.org/feature/poverty-national-conservativism-203647. This is, perhaps, a result of
disagreement among the national conservatives, especially between those coming
primarily from the American constitutional tradition who thus view federalism as
a key part of a distinctive American national tradition and those more invested in

more unitary polities such as the United Kingdom or Israel. While Yoram Hazony, the chairman of the Edmund Burke Foundation and arguably its preeminent intellectual, was signatory on that nod to federalism, his other work tends to either ignore or dismiss federalism. See Yoram Hazony, "Conservative Democracy," First Things, January 2019, https://www.firstthings.com/article/2019/01/conservative -democracy (ignoring federalism); Yoram Hazony, *The Virtues of Nationalism* (New York: Basic Books, 2018) (dismissing federalism); or Yoram Hazony, *Conservatism: A Rediscovery* (Washington, DC: Regnery 2022) (repeatedly hailing the more centralizing figures in American politics, such as Alexander Hamilton).

80 This is why, for example, conservatives sometimes look fondly back on the populists, versus the (conventionally understood) progressives such as Wilson and the Roosevelts, whom conservatives regard with contempt. See introduction, note 37.

81 For example, with the federal "partial-birth" abortion ban in 2003, discussed in this chapter, note 66.

82 See this chapter, note 61.

83 Kersch, *Conservatives and the Constitution*, vii.

84 Although Baker (see this chapter, note 43) offers an argument for returning tax-and-spending welfare policies to the states, the provision of welfare or entitlement spending is an issue where those on the left would presumably be less likely to accept a 1920s model of progressive federalism due to fear of race-to-the-bottom effects. One partial solution offered by other progressives—such as Hugo Black and even the explicitly anti-state nationalists like Earl Warren—was to defend residence requirements as a way to partially offset the demand side of welfare provisions: states would have the political incentive to provide generously for their own people by ensuring a magnet effect would not be created, though that position was rejected by the other progressives on the Supreme Court. Shapiro v. Thompson, 394 U.S. 618 (1969). On Warren's nationalist contempt for states, see Powe, *Warren Court and American Politics*, 494–495. As a practical matter, however, it is hard to see even a much more strictly federalist conservative coalition return to the pre-Roosevelt, Madisonian understanding of the spending power, although there have been recent calls for it. Philip Hamburger, *Purchasing Submission* (Cambridge, MA: Harvard University Press, 2021). Aggressive block-granting of federally collected taxes, rather than, say, Baker's proposal to reduce federal taxes and raise state taxes to relocate welfare and entitlement there, seems more feasible.

85 This was upheld 5–4 in *Wilson v. New*, 243 U.S. 332 (1917).

86 For example, Frederick Douglass argued that such a consequence of federalism offered opportunities for blacks fleeing to the North during Jim Crow; this was also President Grant's theory in working with Douglass, then a diplomatic envoy, to procure annexation of the Dominican Republic and add pressure to southern whites to improve their treatment of blacks. Paul Frymer, *Building an American Empire: The Era of Territorial and Political Expansion* (Princeton, NJ: Princeton University Press, 2017), 212–218; Ilya Somin, "Foot Voting, Political Ig-

norance, and Constitutional Design," *Social Philosophy and Policy* 28 (2010): 202–227.

87 See chapter 1, notes 54–56.

88 See esp. chapter 1, notes 54–56.

89 See chapter 3, note 10.

90 Randy Barnett, *Restoring the Lost Constitution: The Presumption of Liberty* (Princeton, NJ: Princeton University Press, 2004), 277–322; John O. McGinnis and Michael Rappaport, "Where Have All the Amendments Gone," Law & Liberty, January 11, 2021, https://lawliberty.org/forum/where-have-all-the -amendments-gone/; *Convention of States: A Handbook for Legislators and Citizens*, 3rd ed. (n.p.: COSAction, 2014), 4, 8.

91 U.S. v. Lopez, 514 U.S. 549 (1995).

92 James M. McGoldrick Jr., "The Dormant Commerce Clause: The Origin Story and the 'Considerable Uncertainties,' 1824 to 1945," *Creighton Law Review* 52 (2019): 243–292.

93 Hugo Black assailed it in 1945 in the *Southern Pacific v. Arizona* case (325 U.S. 761 [1945]), while more recently Clarence Thomas and Antonin Scalia criticized it on both federalism and separation-of-powers grounds in *United Haulers v. Oneida-Herkimer Solid Waste Management Authority* (550 U.S. 330 [2007]). See more recently Comptroller of Treasury v. Wynn, 575 U.S. __ (2015) (Justice Thomas dissenting, joined by Scalia). See also National Pork Producers Council v. Ross, 598 U.S. __ (2023) (declining to vindicate a Dormant Commerce Clause challenge to a California animal welfare law); and introduction, notes 1 and 2. Justice Brandeis criticized the Court's use of the doctrine in blocking a Pennsylvania law requiring a license to sell certain kinds of steamship tickets, and a decade later he similarly rejected a dormant commerce clause challenge on grounds that agriculture remained a state issue. DiSanto v. Pennsylvania, 273 U.S. 38 (1927); Chassaniol v. City of Greenwood, 291 U.S. 584 (1934).

94 In 2019, the Trump administration moved against California's efforts to impose fuel standards. Although this effort was revoked by the Biden administration and the specifics of this particular case are not a true dormant commerce clause situation—since the relevant federal statute explicitly establishes federal preemption, albeit with a waiver for California—commentators have noted it nonetheless implicates many of the same issues and foreshadows repeated conflicts. Tyler Runsten, "Climate Change Regulation, Preemption, and the Dormant Commerce Clause," *Hastings Law Journal* 72 (2021): 1313–1346.

95 James Madison, "Vices of the Political System of the United States," Founders Online, April 1787, https://founders.archives.gov/documents/Madison/01-09-02 -0187. See also this chapter, note 50.

96 Beienburg, "Originalists Were Always for (Some) Judicial Engagement."

97 Timbs v. Indiana, 586 U.S. __ (2019).

98 See chapter 4, note 15.

99 Michael Rappaport, "Originalism and the Colorblind Constitution," *Notre Dame*

Law Review 89 (2013): 72–132. On the other hand, see Cass R. Sunstein, "Race and Affirmative Action," in *Radicals in Robes* (New York: Basic Books, 2005), 131–151; and Jeb Rubenfeld, "Affirmative Action," *Yale Law Journal* (1997): 427–472 (arguing originalists must uphold affirmative action to be consistent).

100 See chapter 5, note 59.

101 Sean Beienburg, "After Dobbs," Law & Liberty, December 6, 2021, https://lawliberty.org/after-dobbs/.

102 Beienburg, "After Dobbs." Sandra Day O'Connor's special concurrence, even as it rejected substantive due process like the dissents, argued *Lawrence* should have been an equal protection case.

103 Washington v. Glucksberg, 521 U.S. 702 (1997). As associate justice and as part of his defense of the states' police powers, Rehnquist had long objected to substantive due process, beginning with his early years on the Court (as one sees in *Roe*). Despite being the most conservative member of the Court, Rehnquist had been the sole dissenter, for example, in holding that commercial speech wasn't really speech, as understood under the First Amendment, and charging the justices with imposing free-market views on the states, just as in the *Lochner* era. Virginia State Board of Pharmacy v. Virginia Citizens Consumer Council, 425 U.S. 748 (1976), 781. *Glucksberg* followed an earlier effort by Justice Scalia to all but kill off substantive due process. Michael H. v. Gerald D., 491 U.S. 110 (1989).

104 Poe v. Ullman, 367 U.S. 497 (1961), 553 (which Harlan cited in *Griswold* in lieu of explaining his reasoning at length). Note that this passage was approvingly quoted by Arthur Goldberg's concurrence, joined by both Chief Justice Warren and Justice Brennan. *Griswold*, 498. Brennan would, however, reverse himself and go where Harlan almost certainly would not have, in applying *Griswold* to unmarried persons in Eisenstadt v. Baird, 405 U.S. 438 (1972), decided after Harlan left the Court.

105 Michael Toth, "Parental Authority Gets a Boost from *Dobbs*," *Wall Street Journal*, July 27, 2022, https://www.wsj.com/articles/parental-authority-gets-a-boost-from-dobbs-justice-alito-glucksberg-unenumerated-rights-history-tradition-education-meyer-pierce-11658941498?mod=djemalertNEWS. See also chapter 5, note 49.

106 See the concurring opinion of now Fifth Circuit judge, then Texas Supreme Court justice Don Willett, joined by two other justices, in *Patel v. Dept of Licensing and Regulation*, 58 Texas, Supreme Court 1298 (2015), https://www.txcourts.gov/media/1008502/120657c1.pdf.

107 Troxel v. Granville, 530 U.S. 57, 91 (2000). Scalia argued *Meyer*, *Pierce*, and the like were wrongly reasoned, and while he would "not overrule those earlier cases . . . neither would [he] extend the theory upon which they rested to this new context." On Black's critique, see chapter 5, note 139.

108 Harlan's *Civil Rights Cases* dissent (109 U.S. 3, 57–73), finding state action in a specific but prominent set of private businesses (inns, restaurants, transportation, and other historic public accommodations or common carriers) that had been treated as agents of the state dating back to English common law, would similarly

find an enumerated power allowing Title II of the Civil Rights Act of 1964 under the Fourteenth Amendment, even if one were to reject the New Deal expansion of the commerce clause in *Darby* and especially *Wickard*. See also Beienburg and Johnson, "Black Popular Constitutionalism and Federalism After the Civil Rights Cases." On incorporation, see Twining v. New Jersey, 211 U.S. 124–126 (1908). "I do not understand that the courts have anything to do with the policy or expediency of legislation. A statute may be valid, and yet, upon grounds of public policy, may well be characterized as unreasonable." Plessy v. Ferguson, 163 U.S. 537 (1896), 558. See also chapter 1 for further discussion of Harlan's views.

109 For his treatment of the interstate commerce power, see Brian L Frye, Josh Blackman, and Michael McCloskey, eds., "Justice John Marshall Harlan: Lectures on Constitutional Law, 1897–98," *George Washington Law Review Arguendo* 81 (2013): 117–132.

110 Harlan used the phrase several times in his law lectures (Frye, Blackman, and McCloskey, "Lectures," 72, 117).

111 Frye, Blackman, and McCloskey, "Lectures," 34. He discussed the importance of decentralized federalism and its limits often in that series. See, e.g., Frye, Blackman, and McCloskey, 42, 45, 47–49, 72, 99, 114, 117–132, 337–338.

112 See, e.g., in both *Coppage* and as alternate grounds in *Adair*.

113 See this chapter, note 50.

114 James M. Glaser, Jeffrey M. Berry, and Deborah J. Schildkraut, "Ideology and Support for Federalism in Theory—and in Practice," *Publius: The Journal of Federalism* (2023), pjad003, https://doi.org/10.1093/publius/pjad003; John Dinan and Jac. C. Heckelman, "Stability and Contingency in Federalism Preferences," *Public Administration Review* 80 (2020): 234–243. Hunter Rendleman and Jon Rogowski find an underlying ideological support for conservatives and federalism but that, at least in May 2020, partisanship was a poorer predictor. Hunter Rendleman and Jon C. Rogowski, "Americans' Attitudes toward Federalism," *Political Behavior* (2022), https://doi.org/10.1007/s11109-022-09820-3. This perhaps indicates the turn from federalism many suspected would be a consequence of a Republican realignment under Trump further discussed later. Experimental work by Nicholas Jacobs finds that conservatives are notably more common to retrospectively explain constitutional authorization or lack thereof mattered to their thought process, but he finds weaker evidence of an "intuitive federalism" among American voters. Nicholas Jacobs, "An Experimental Test of How Americans Think about Federalism," *Publius* 47 (2017): 572–598, 586; Nicholas Jacobs, "Federalism, Polarization, and Policy Responsibility during COVID-19: Experimental and Observational Evidence from the United States," *Publius: The Journal of Federalism* 51 (2021): 693–719.

115 *PCSR*, 1–3, 241–249.

116 Andrew Coulson, "The Constitution Left Behind," Reason, December 13, 2007, https://reason.org/reason-roundtable/the-constitution-left-behind/.

117 This, of course, depends on how one defines the right, or why one is in it. Those whose connection with conservatism is primarily social or who are on the eco-

nomically libertarian right may find national uniformity more tempting than those from the constitutionalist right more interested in the process and procedure. See, for example, Chris Pope, "Degenerate Federalism," *National Review*, May 28, 2018, 29–32—calling for aggressive patrolling of states by the federal government and the recognition states are often anti-free market—as the progressive federalists hoped it would be at times.

118 For discussion of the conflation of the unconstitutionality of the individual mandate on federalism and individual-rights grounds, see James H. Read, "Constitutionalizing the Dispute: Federalism in Hyper-Partisan Times," *Publius* 46 (2016): 337–365.

119 " "Republican Presidential Candidates Debate in Ames, Iowa," American Presidency Project, August 11, 2011, https://www.presidency.ucsb.edu/documents/republican-presidential-candidates-debate-ames-iowa; "GOP Presidential Forum," Transcripts, September 5, 2011, http://transcripts.cnn.com/TRANSCRIPTS/1109/05/se.01.html. Perry presumably would have also defended Romney's constitutional theory had he been in attendance at either of those debates rather than sidelined due to surgery complications. See the introduction's discussion of *Fed Up!* Previewing some social conservatives' turn against constitutional proceduralism, former senator Rick Santorum criticized use of the Tenth Amendment as an obstacle to social conservative objectives. Robert Hendin, "10th Amendment Up for Debate within the Republican Presidential Field," CBS, August 12, 2011, http://www.cbsnews.com/news/10th-amendment-up-for-debate-within-the-republican-presidential-field/.

120 One could add, as well, the occasional flirtations with nullification—in which states insist on the unilateral authority to block federal activity. For a discussion of this deployment in recent politics, see introduction, note 26.

121 Andrew Busch, *The Constitution on the Campaign Trail: The Surprising Political Career of America's Founding Document* (Lanham, MD: Rowman & Littlefield, 2007), 48. For an earlier, even more pessimistic framing, see also Phillip Kurland, "Impotence of Reticence," *Duke Law Journal* 4 (1968): 634–635. Kurland bemoans the citizenry's turn from means to ends (that is, solely with the specific policy consequences independent of whatever constitutional machinery is necessary to achieve them).

122 Even several of the other contenders—Jeb Bush, Marco Rubio, and Carly Fiorina—nodded to federalism or robustly cited the Tenth Amendment, especially but not exclusively in the context of marijuana. See, for example, *PCSR*, 241.

INDEX

Abbott, Grace, 44, 98
Ableman v. Booth, 2
abortion law, 5, 215–216, 226, 228,
  317n70, 318n71, 318n73, 319n76. *See
  also Roe v. Wade*
Ackerman, Bruce, 188–189, 191, 193, 195,
  302n68, 313n33
Adair v. United States, 125, 129, 132, 134,
  152, 227
Adams, Henry, 74, 85
Adams, John, 18
Adamson Act, 122, 220
Adkins v. Children's Hospital, 128, 130,
  136–147, 150–153, 192, 229, 288n48
Affordable Care Act, 1, 3, 5, 13, 68, 215
Agricultural Adjustment Act, 173
Aiken, George, 180
Alabama, 56, 170
alcohol. *See* Prohibition
Alien and Sedition Acts, 20, 25
Allen, Harmon, 86
Allen, Katharine, 89
Allen, Weston, 77–81, 83, 89
Allgeyer v. Louisiana, 119–120, 125
Altgeld, John Peter, 109, 112–114, 116–
  118, 190, 275n17
American Federation of Labor (AFL),
  134–135, 283n12, 285n31
American Legislative Exchange Council,
  209
American Medical Association (AMA),
  47–48, 65, 92, 98, 100–101
American political development (APD), 11
Americans for Prosperity, 209
antidiscrimination law, 4
Arizona, 60–61, 105–108, 133–134, 136,
  177, 275n11, 278n51
Arizona Constitutional Convention, 107
Arkansas, 56, 286n38
Article I, Section 8, 23, 78, 86, 94. *See
  also* Tenth Amendment
Article I, Section 10, 23, 200, 212

Article IV, Section 4, 79, 184
Article V, 56, 79, 140, 167–168, 188,
  191–192, 313n33
Articles of Confederation, 17, 41
Association against the Prohibition
  Amendment (AAPA), 162, 166–168,
  204, 273n184
Association of Land Grant Colleges, 80
Autobiography (Roosevelt), 118

Babcock, William, 183
Bachman, Michelle, 229
Bailey v. Drexel Furniture, 83–84, 128,
  248n55, 281n92
Baker, Kevin, 209, 320n84
Barber, Sotirios, 212–213, 315n49
Barkley, Alben, 148
Barrett, Amy Coney, 216
Bass, Robert, 81
Bateman, David, 236n30
Baxter, Percival, 63, 67, 82–90, 99, 190,
  204, 206, 268n82
Baxter State Park, 83
Bayard, Thomas, 93–95
Beck, James, 80, 95, 135, 158, 266n59
Beland, Daniel, 308n186
Berman, David, 108
Bernstein, David, 124
Bickel, Alexander, 288n45
Biggs, Robert, 53–54
Bill of Rights, 17–18, 23, 25, 179, 201,
  219, 227; incorporation of, 108, 223–
  224, 275n15
Bingham, Hiram, 95
Black, Hugo, 223–224, 226, 295n139,
  320n84
Black Reconstruction (Du Bois), 158
Blackwood, Ira, 172
Blaine, John, 2, 36, 63, 133
Blair Bill, 199
Blease, Cole, 95
Blood, Robert, 195

Bloomfield, Maxwell, 157
Borah, William, 13, 43–44, 47, 61, 88, 94,
  139, 150, 160, 271n147, 289n58
Brandeis, Elizabeth, 279n70
Brandeis, Louis, 4, 8, 31–34, 134, 136,
  139, 143, 149, 190–191, 220, 223–224
Bratton, Sam, 57
Brennan, William, 203–204
Brewster, Owen, 89–90
Breyer, Stephen, 80, 216, 220
Broughton, Joseph Melville Jr., 173
Broussard, Edwin, 43, 94
Brown, Jerry, 4
Brown, Ray, 280n79
Brownell, Herbert, 145
Brown v. Board of Education of Topeka,
  199, 224
Bruce, William Cabbell, 95
Brutus, 107
Bryan, William Jennings, 113–114, 117
Buck, Douglass, 146–147
Bunting v. Oregon, 122, 124, 136–138
Burger, Warren, 204
Burkett, Elmer, 118
Busch, Andrew, 230, 238n45
Bush, George W., 228
Butler, Pierce, 126, 138, 151, 183–184
Byrd, Harry, 52, 95, 171–172, 189, 194

Calhoun, John C., 1, 8–9, 20–21, 35, 103,
  112, 143. *See also* nullification
California, 61, 133, 135, 140–143, 153,
  176–177, 293n106, 321n94
campaign finance reform, 5
*Carmichael v. Southern Coal and Coke
  Co.*, 184
Catholic Church, 48–49, 76, 92, 100–101,
  252n5
Cermak, Anton, 178
Chamberlain-Kahn Act, 42, 49
Chapman, Nathan, 277n50
Chepaitis, Joseph, 45
Child Labor Amendment, 249n66
Children's Bureau, 39–40, 45, 78–79,
  86–89, 98, 255n53
citizen engagement, 3, 10, 20
Civil Rights Act, 24, 322n108

Civil Rights Cases, 199, 227, 240n54,
  322n108
class legislation, 69–70, 90–91, 120, 125,
  131–132, 145, 157
Clay, Henry, 22–23, 43, 244n25
Clayton Act, 33, 134, 284n25
Cleveland, Grover, 24, 54, 112–113, 117
coercive federalism, 14–15, 210, 234n11
Colorado, 117, 133, 159, 177
Commerce Clause, 21, 24, 80, 162, 166,
  168, 216, 219–223, 317n66. *See also*
  Dormant Commerce Clause; interstate
  commerce
common-good constitutionalism, 216–217
Commons, John, 132, 144
compact theory, 8–9, 84, 112, 118
competitive federalism, 212
Comstock, William, 146
conflict expansion, 11–12
Connecticut, 66, 77, 82, 86, 96, 98, 100,
  147, 177–178, 272n159, 298n19
Conner, Martin, 173
consolidation, 22–23
Constitutional Convention, 17–19, 222
*Constitutional Government in the United
  States* (Wilson), 32
Constitutional Liberty League, 179
constitutional moments theory, 188
constitutional theory, 9–11, 21, 206–230,
  310n8, 311n20, 312n29, 313n33,
  323n114
Constitution of the United States. *See*
  oath, constitutional; Reconstruction;
  separation of powers; state constitutions;
  textualism; *specific amendments*;
  specific articles
Cooke, Charles C. W., 215
Cooley, Thomas, 114
Coolidge, Calvin: and labor, 137, 152, 179,
  287n42; opposition to, 106, 272n159;
  and Sheppard-Towner, 68, 75–76, 87,
  90, 93–97, 99, 104; and state authority,
  9, 157–158, 190, 229
Coolidge, Louis, 49
cooperative federalism, 7, 14–15, 36–42,
  168, 173
Coppage v. Kansas, 125, 129, 132, 134

Trump, Donald, 4–5, 210–211, 230,
315n50, 321n94, 323n114
Tucker, Henry St. George, 89
Turner, Edward, 132–133
Tushnet, Mark, 11
Twain, Mark, 118
Tydings, Millard, 55, 96, 258nn85–86
Tyler, John, 24

Underwood Tariff, 33
unemployment, 178, 183
United Mine Workers of America
(UMWA), 130
United States v. E. C. Knight, 27, 127, 227
Upton, Harriet Taylor, 43
Urofsky, Melvin, 127
U.S. v. Butler, 173, 184
U.S. v. Darby Lumber Co, 191, 247n54
U.S. v. Lopez, 80, 216, 220–221
Utah, 61, 136, 139, 147, 159

vaccinations, 25, 214–215, 227
Van Buren, Martin, 25
Van Devanter, Willis, 126–127
Vermeule, Adrian, 216–217
Vermont, 18, 66, 82, 86, 96, 158, 180–181,
194, 297n18. *See also* Second Vermont
Republic
Virginia, 51–53, 172, 194
Virginia Plan, 17
Virginia Resolution (1798), 20, 103, 156

*Wabash, St. Louis and Pacific Railway Co.
v. Illinois*, 232n2
Wadsworth, James, 43–44, 55, 93–94
Wadsworth-Garrett Amendment, 55–56,
140, 175
Wagner, Robert, 286n35
Wagner Act, 286n35
Waite, Davis Hanson, 117
Wald, Albert, 145–146
Wallace, George, 186
Walsh, David, 94–96
Warren, Charles, 280n79
Warren, Earl, 198, 222, 318n75, 320n84
Warren, Francis, 43, 94
Washington, 60, 96, 140–141, 143, 150,
152–153, 286n38, 293n106

Washington, George, 17, 23
Washington v. Glucksberg, 225–226,
322n103
Watson, Thomas, 43, 56, 94
Webb-Kenyon Act, 27
Webster, Daniel, 22–23
Weeks, Harold, 84–85
Weeks Act, 42
welfare, 12–13, 41, 53, 69–70, 79–80,
98–99, 103, 125, 156, 202–203, 320n84.
See also New Deal; pensions; Sheppard-
Towner Act; Social Security; Spending
Power
Wessels, John H., 58
the West, 60–62, 67, 91, 140, 176, 205. *See
also specific states*
West Coast Hotel v. Parrish, 141,
150–152, 191
West Virginia, 56
We the People (Ackerman), 188, 313n33
Wheeler, Burton, 167, 192
Whelan, Ed, 215
Whigs, 21–23
White, George, 133
White, William Allen, 100
Whitney v. California, 224
Whittington, Keith, 8–9
Wickard v. Filburn, 80, 188, 190–191, 194,
221
Wilkie, Wendell, 188
Williamson v. Lee Optical, 295n139
Wilson, James, 17, 134, 241n6
Wilson, Woodrow, 2, 8, 31–34, 42, 127,
156–157, 159, 200, 202
Winant, John, 81–82, 147
Winslow, Samuel, 43, 46
Wisconsin, 1–2, 62–63, 66, 125, 131–135,
139, 143–144, 147, 153–157, 183–184,
293n106
Witte, Edwin, 131–132, 134–135, 144, 169
Witte, John, 169
Woman Patriots, 48–50, 88, 90–93,
100–101
women: and activism, 44–50, 52–53, 60–
61, 77, 92–94, 100–101, 145, 256n54;
and minimum wage, 122, 136–139,
142–147, 287n42; and sexism, 87–88.
See also League of Women Voters;

women (*cont.*)
   National Council of Catholic Women;
   National Woman's Party; Nineteenth
   Amendment; suffrage
Women's Constitutional League of
   Maryland, 52–53
Women's Joint Congressional Committee
   (WJCC), 46–47, 49–50, 52, 55, 57, 85,
   92, 97, 101
Women's Municipal League of New York, 72

Wood, George, 82
worker's compensation, 75, 126–127
Wurman, Ilan, 277n50
Wynehamer v. New York, 123
Wyoming, 60

Yates, Robert, 18
yellow-dog contracts, 111, 124–125, 127–
   135, 147, 152, 282n2, 286n35
Young, C. C., 142

Printed in the USA
CPSIA information can be obtained
at www.ICGtesting.com
CBHW030931110524
8405CB00007B/75/J

9 780700 636198